GOULD & LINCOLN,

PUBLISHERS AND BOOKSELLERS,

59 WASHINGTON STREET, BOSTON.

CHARLES D. GOULD. JOSHUA LINCOLN.

G. & L. would call attention to their extensive list of publications, embracing valuable works in THEOLOGY, SCIENCE, LITERATURE AND ART, TEXT BOOKS FOR SCHOOLS AND COLLEGES and MISCELLANEOUS, etc., in large variety, the productions of some of the ablest writers, and most scientific men of the age, among which will be found those of Chambers, Hugh Miller, Agassiz, Gould, Guyot, Marcou, Bayne, Rogers, Dr. Harris, Dr. Wayland, Dr. Williams, Dr. Ripley, Dr. Kitto, Dr. Krummacher, Dr. Tweedie, Dr. Choules, Dr. Sprague, Newcomb, Banvard, "Walter Aimwell," Bungener, Miall, Archdeacon Hare, and others of like standing and popularity; and to this list they are constantly adding. Among their late publications are the following, viz.:—

Knowledge is Power. The Productive Forces of Modern Society, and the Results of Labor, Capital, and Skill. By KNIGHT. Illustrated. Am. Edi. Revised, with additions. By D. A. WELLS. 12mo. Cloth, $1.25.

Emphatically a book for the people, containing an immense amount of important information, which everybody ought to possess.

Annual of Scientific Discovery in Science and Art, exhibiting the most important Discoveries and Improvements in Mechanics, Useful Arts, Natural Philosophy, Chemistry, Astronomy, Meteorology, Zoology, Botany, Mineralogy, Geology, Geography, Antiquities, &c. Edited by D. A. WELLS, A. M. With a Portrait of Prof. Wyman. 12mo. Cloth, $1.25.

VOLUMES OF THE SAME WORK for 1850, 1851, 1852, 1853, 1854, 1855, 1856. With Portraits. $1.25 per volume.

Chambers' Cyclopædia OF ENGLISH LITERATURE. The choicest productions of English Authors, from the earliest to the present time. Connected by a Biographical History. 2 octavo vols. of 700 pages each. 300 elegant Illustrations. Cloth, $5.

Open where you will, you will find matter for profit and delight. The selections are gems.—"*A whole English Library fused into one Cheap Book!*"

Chambers' Miscellany. With Illustrations. Ten vols. Cloth, $7.50.

Chambers' Home Book. A Choice Selection of Interesting and Instructive Reading, for the Old and Young. 6 vols. 16mo. Cloth, $3.

Cyclopædia of Anecdotes. A Choice Selection of Anecdotes of the various forms of Literature and the Arts, and of the most celebrated Literary Characters and Artists By KAZLITT ARVINE, A.M. With Illustrations. 725 pages, octavo. Cloth, $3.

The choicest collection of anecdotes ever published. It contains 3040 anecdotes, 350 fine illustrations, and such is the wonderful variety, that it will be found an almost inexhaustible fund of interest for every class of readers.

Works by Hugh Miller:

- Testimony of the Rocks.
- Footprints of the Creator.
- Old Red Sandstone.
- My First Impressions of England and its People.
- My Schools and Schoolmates.

Life of James Montgomery. Abridged from the recent London seven vol. ed. By Mrs. H. C. KNIGHT, author of "Lady Huntington and her Friends." Illustrated. 12mo. Cloth, $1.25.

Essays; in Biography and Criticism. By PETER BAYNE, author of the "Christian Life." 12mo. Cloth, $1.25.

Text Books:

- WAYLAND'S *Moral Science and Political Economy.* The same, *abridged.*
- BLAKE'S *Philosophy and Astronomy.*
- BAILEY'S *Young Ladies' Class-Book.*
- DILLAWAY'S *Roman Antiquities.*
- PALEY'S *Theology.*
- AGASSIZ' and GOULD'S *Zoölogy.*
- LOOMIS' *Geology.*
- HAVEN'S *Mental Philosophy.*
- GUYOT'S *Earth and Man,* and *Mural Maps.*
- BARTON'S *Grammar,* and *Exercises in Composition.*

Thesaurus OF ENGLISH WORDS AND PHRASES. So classified as to facilitate the expression of ideas, and to assist in literary composition. By PETER MARK ROGET. Revised and Edited, with a List of Foreign Words defined in English, by BARNAS SEARS, D. D., Pres. of Brown Univ. 12mo. Cloth, $1.50.

Facilitates a writer in seizing upon just the right word for his purpose.

Visits to European Celebrities. By W. B. SPRAGUE, D. D. 12mo. Cl., $1.00.

A series of graphic and life-like Personal Sketches of the most Distinguished Men and Women of Europe.

Cruise of the North Star. The Excursion made to England, Russia, Denmark, France, Spain, Italy, Malta, Turkey, Madeira, etc. By Rev. J. O. CHOULES, D. D. Illustrations, etc. 12mo. Cloth, gilt, $1.50.

The Natural History OF THE HUMAN SPECIES: Its Typical Forms and Primeval Distribution. By CHAS. HAMILTON SMITH. With an Introduction containing an abstract of the views of writers of repute. By SAMUEL KNEELAND, Jr., M. D. With Illustrations. 12mo. Cloth, $1.25.

The Camel: His Organization, Habits and Uses, considered with reference to his introduction into the United States. By GEORGE P. MARSH, late U. S. Minister at Constantinople. 12mo. Cloth, 63 cts.

This book treats of a subject of great interest, especially at the present time. It furnishes the only complete and reliable account of the Camel in the language.

VALUABLE WORKS.

Diary and Correspondence of the late Amos Lawrence. Edited by his son, Wm. R. Lawrence, M. D. Octavo, cloth, $1.25; also, royal 12mo. ed., cl., $1.00.

Kitto's Popular Cyclopædia of Biblical Literature. 500 illustrations. One vol., octavo. 812 pages. Cloth, $3.

Intended for ministers, theological students, parents, Sabbath-school teachers, and the great body of the religious public.

Analytical Concordance of the Holy Scriptures; or, The Bible presented under Classified Heads or Topics. By John Eadie, D. D. Octavo, 836 pp. $3.

Dr. Williams' Works.
Lectures on the Lord's Prayer — Religious Progress — Miscellanies.

☞ Dr. Williams is a profound scholar and a brilliant writer. — *New York Evangelist.*

Modern Atheism. Considered under its forms of Pantheism, Materialism, Secularism, Development and Natural Laws. By James Buchanan, D. D., LL. D. 12mo. Cloth, $1.25.

The Hallig: or the Sheepfold in the Waters. A Tale of Humble Life on the Coast of Schleswig. From the German, by Mrs. George P. Marsh. 12mo. Cl., $1.

The Suffering Saviour. By Dr. Krummacher. 12mo. Cloth, $1.25.

Heaven. By James Wm. Kimball. 12mo.

Christian's Daily Treasury. Religious Exercise for every Day in the Year. By Rev. E. Temple. 12mo. Cloth, $1.

Wayland's Sermons. Delivered in the Chapel of Brown Univ. 12mo. Cl., $1.00.

Entertaining and Instructive Works for the Young. Elegantly illustrated. 16mo. Cloth, gilt backs.

The American Statesman. Life and Character of Daniel Webster. — *Young Americans Abroad;* or Vacation in Europe. — *The Island Home;* or the Young Cast-aways. — *Pleasant Pages for Young People.* — *The Guiding Star.* — *The Poor Boy and Merchant Prince.*

The Aimwell Stories. Resembling and quite equal to the "Rollo Stories." — *Christian Register.* By Walter Aimwell. *Oscar;* or the Boy who had his own way. — *Clinton;* or Boy-Life in the Country. — *Ella;* or Turning over a New Leaf. — *Whistler;* or The Manly Boy. — *Marcus;* or the Boy Tamer.

Works by Rev. Harvey Newcomb. *How to be a Lady.* — *How to be a Man.* — *Anecdotes for Boys.* — *Anecdotes for Girls.*

Banvard's Series of American Histories. *Plymouth and the Pilgrims.* — *Romance of American History.* — *Novelties of the New World, and Tragic Scenes in the History of Maryland and the old French War.*

God Revealed in Nature and in Christ. By Rev. James B. Walker Author of "The Philosophy of the Plan of Salvation." 12mo. Cloth, $1.

Philosophy of the Plan of Salvation. New enlarged edition. 12mo. Cloth, 75 c.

Christian Life; Social and Individual. By Peter Bayne. 12mo. Cloth, $1.25.

All agree in pronouncing it one of the most admirable works of the age.

Yahveh Christ; or the Memorial Name. By Alex. MacWhorter. With an Introductory Letter, by Nath'l W. Taylor, D. D., in Yale Theol. Sem. 16mo. Cloth, 60 c.

The Signet Ring, and its Heavenly Motto. From the German. 16mo. Cl., 31 c.

The Marriage Ring; or How to Make Home Happy. 18mo. Cloth, gilt, 75 c.

Mothers of the Wise and Good. By Jabez Burns, D. D. 16mo, Cloth, 75 c.

☞ A sketch of the mothers of many of the most eminent men of the world.

My Mother; or Recollections of Maternal Influence. 12mo. Cloth, 75c.

The Excellent Woman, with an Introduction, by Rev. W. B. Sprague, D. D. Splendid Illustrations. 12mo. Cloth, $1.

The Progress of Baptist Principles in the Last Hundred Years. By T. F. Curtis, Prof. of Theology in the Lewisburg University. 12mo. Cloth, $1.25.

Dr. Harris' Works.
The Great Teacher. — The Great Commission. — The Pre-Adamite Earth. — Man Primeval. — Patriarchy. — Posthumous Works, 4 volumes.

The Better Land; or The Believer's Journey and Future Home. By Rev. A. C. Thompson. 12mo. Cloth, 85 c.

Kitto's History of Palestine, from the Patriarchal Age to the Present Time. With 200 Illustrations. 12mo. Cloth, $1.25.

An admirable work for the Family, the Sabbath and week-day School Library.

The Priest and the Huguenot; or, Persecution in the Age of Louis XV. From the French of L. F. Bungener. Two vols., 12mo. Cloth, $2.25.

This is not only a work of thrilling interest, but is a masterly Protestant production.

The Psalmist. A Collection of Hymns for the Use of Baptist Churches. By Baron Stow and S. F. Smith. With a Supplement, containing an Additional Selection of Hymns, by Richard Fuller, D. D., and J. B. Jeter, D. D. Published in various sizes, and styles of binding.

This is unquestionably the best collection of Hymns in the English language.

☞ In addition to works published by themselves, they keep an extensive assortment of works in all departments of trade, which they supply at publishers' prices. ☞ They particularly invite the attention of Booksellers, Travelling Agents, Teachers, School Committees, Librarians, Clergymen, and professional men generally (to whom a liberal discount is uniformly made), to their extensive stock. ☞ To persons wishing copies of Text-books, for examination, they will be forwarded, per mail or otherwise, on the reception of *one half* the price of the work desired. ☞ Orders from any part of the country attended to with faithfulness and dispatch.

Painted by Wm Bonnar, RSA. Engd by A.H. Ritchie.

Yours very truly
Hugh Miller

Gould & Lincoln, Boston.

FIRST IMPRESSIONS

OF

ENGLAND AND ITS PEOPLE.

BY

HUGH MILLER,

AUTHOR OF THE "FOOT-PRINTS OF THE CREATOR,"
THE "OLD RED SANDSTONE," ETC.

"Do you not think a man may be the wiser — I had almost said the better — for going a hundred or two of miles?" — GRAY'S LETTERS.

BOSTON:
GOULD AND LINCOLN,
59 WASHINGTON STREET.
NEW YORK: SHELDON AND COMPANY.
CINCINNATI: GEO. S. BLANCHARD.
1860.

Stereotyped by
HOBART & ROBBINS;
NEW ENGLAND TYPE AND STEREOTYPE FOUNDERY,
BOSTON.

Printed by Geo. C. Rand & Co No. 3 Cornhill.

TO THE READER.

TIMES have changed since our earlier British Novelists, when they sought to make the incidents lie thick in their fictions, gave them the form of a journey, and sent their heroes a travelling over England. The one-half of "Tom Jones," two-thirds of "Joseph Andrews," not a few of the most amusing chapters in "Roderick Random" and "Launcelot Greaves," and the whole of "Humphrey Clinker," are thrown into this form. They are works of English travels; and the adventures with which they are enlivened arise by the wayside.

It would be rather a difficult matter, in these later times, to make a novel out of an English tour. The country, measured by days' journeys, has grown nine-tenths smaller than it was in the times of Fielding and Smollett. The law has become too strong for Captain Macheath the highwayman, and the public too knowing for Mr Jenkinson the swindler. The journeyer by moonlight, who accidentally loses his road, stumbles on no "Hermit of the Hill," wrapped up in a grotesque dress of skins; but merely encounters, instead, some suspicious gamekeeper, taking his night-rounds in behalf of the Squire's pheasants. When mill-dams give way during the rains, honest Mat Brambles do not discover, in consequence their affinity to devoted Humphrey Clinkers: there is merely a half-hour's stoppage of the train, barren of incident, save that the male passengers get out to smoke, while the ladies sit still. And as for the frequent tragedy of railway collision accidents, it has but little of the classic about it, and is more appropriately recorded in newspaper columns, struck off for the passing day, than in pages of higher pretensions, written for to-morrow. England has become a greatly less fertile field of adventure than when, according to the *Angliæ Metropolis* for 1690, the "weekly wagon of Richard Hamersly the carrier" formed the sole conveyance, for passengers who did not ride horses of their own, between *Brumegham* and the capital.

But though the age of personal adventure has to a certainty gone by, the age which has succeeded is scarcely less fertile in incident on a larger scale, and of a greatly more remarkable character. It would seem as if the same change which has abridged the area of the country had given condensation to its history. We are not only travelling, but also, as a people, living fast; and see revolutions which were formerly the slow work of ages matured in a few brief seasons. Opinion, during the last twenty years, has accomplished, though in a reverse order, the cycle of the two previous centuries. From the Reformation to the Revolution, the *ecclesiastical* reigned paramount in men's minds: from the Revolution to the breaking out of the first American war, — a quiet time in the main, — governments managed their business much through the medium of individual influence, little personal interests carried the day, and monarchs and ministers bulked large in the forefront of the passing events: from the first American war till the rise of Napoleon, the hot political delirium raged wide among the masses, and even statesmen of the old school learned to recognize the people as a power. Now, such, in effect, has been the cycle of the last twenty years. The reign of George the Fourth was also that of personal and party influence. With the accession of William the political fever again broke out, and swept the country in a greatly more alterative and irresistible form than at first. And now, here, in the times of Victoria, are we scarce less decidedly enveloped in the still thickening ecclesiastical element than our ancestors of the sixteenth century. If there be less of personal adventure in the England of the present day than in that of Queen Anne and the two first Georges, there is, as if to make amends, greatly more of incident in the history of the masses. It has been remarked by some students of the Apocalypse, that the course of the predicted events at first moves slowly, as, one after one, six of the seven seals are opened; that, on the opening of the seventh seal, the progress is so considerably quickened that the seventh period proves as fertile in events, — represented by the sounding of the seven trumpets, — as the foregoing six taken together; and that, on the sounding of the seventh trumpet, so great is the further acceleration, that there is an amount of incident condensed in this seventh part of the seventh period, equal, as in the former case, to that of all the previous six parts in one.

There are three cycles, it has been said, in the scheme, — cycle within cycle ; the second comprised within a seventh portion of the first, and the third within a seventh portion of the second. Be this as it may, we may at least see something that exceedingly resembles it in that actual economy of change and revolution manifested in English history for the last two centuries. It would seem as if events, in their downward course, had come under the influence of that law of gravitation through which falling bodies increase in speed, as they descend, according to the squares of the distances.

Though there may be little to encounter in such a state of society, there must, of necessity, be a good deal to observe : the traveller may have few incidents to relate, and yet many appearances to describe. He finds himself in the circumstances of the mariner who sits listlessly in the calm and sunshine of a northern summer and watches the ever-changing aspect of some magnificent iceberg, as its sun-gilt pinnacles sharpen and attenuate, and its deep fissures widen and extend, and the incessant rush of the emancipated waters is heard to reëcho from amid the green light of the dim twilight caverns within. Society in England, in the present day, exists, like the thawing iceberg, in a transition state, and presents its consequent shiftings of aspect and changes of feature ; and such is the peculiar degree of sensitiveness at which the government of the country has arrived, — partly, it would seem, from the fluctuating nature of the extended basis of representation on which it now rests — that, like some nervous valetudinarian, open to every influ ence of climate and the weather, there is scarce a change that can come over opinion, or affect the people in even their purely physical concerns, which does not more or less fully index itself in the statute-book. The autumn of 1845, in which I travelled over England, was ungenial and lowering, and I saw wheaten fields deeply tinged with brown, — an effect of the soaking rains, — and large tracts of diseased potatoes. A season equally bad, however, twenty years ago would have failed to influence the politics of the country. Its frequent storms might have desolated the fruits of the earth, but they would have made no impression on the Statutes at Large. But the storms of 1845 proved greatly more influential. They were included in the cycle of rapid change, and annihilated at once the Protectionist policy and party of the empire. And amid the fermenting components of English society there may be detected elements of revolution in their first causes, destined, apparently, to exercise an influence on public affairs at least not less considerable than the rains and tempests of the Autumn of Forty-Five. The growing Tractarianism of the National Church threatens to work greater changes than the bad potatoes; and the semi-infidel liberalism of the country, fast passing into an aggressive power, than the damaged corn.

The reader will find in the following pages, as from these remarks he may be led to anticipate, scarce any personal anecdote or adventure: they here and there record a brief dialogue by the way-side, or in some humble lodging-house, and here and there a solitary stroll through a wood, or a thoughtful lounge in a quarry; but there is considerably more of eye and ear in them, — of things seen and heard, — than of aught else. They index, however, not much of what he might be led equally to expect, — those diagnostic symptoms impressed on the face of society, that indicate the extensive changes, secular and ecclesiastical, which seem so peculiarly characteristic of the time. The journey of which they form a record was undertaken purely for purposes of relaxation, in that state of indifferent health, and consequent languor, which an over-strain of the mental faculties usually induces, and in which, like the sick animal that secludes itself from the herd, man prefers walking apart from his kind, to seeking them out in the bustle and turmoil of active life, there to note peculiarities of aspect or character, like an adventurous artist taking sketches amid the heat of a battle. They will, however, lead the reader who accompanies me in my rambles considerably out of the usual route of the tourist, into sequestered corners, associated with the rich literature of England, or amid rocks and caverns, in which the geologist finds curious trace of the history of the country as it existed during the long cycles of the bygone creations. I trust I need scarce apologize to the general reader for my frequent transitions from the actual state of things to those extinct states which obtained in what is now England, during the geologic periods. The art, so peculiar to the present age, of deciphering the ancient hieroglyphics sculptured on the rocks of our country, is gradually extending from the few to the many: it will be comparatively a common accomplishment half a generation hence; and when the hard names of the science shall have become familiar enough no longer to obscure its poetry, it will be found that what I have attempted to do will be done, proportionally to their measure of ability, by travellers generally. In hazarding the prediction, I build on the fact, that it is according to the intellectual nature of man to delight in the metaphor and the simile, — in pictures of the past and dreams of the future, — in short, in whatever introduces amid one set of figures palpable to the senses another visible but to the imagination, and thus blends the ideal with the actual, like some fanciful allegorist, sculptor, or painter, who mixes up with his groups of real personages qualities and dispositions embodied in human form, — angelic virtues with wings growing out of their shoulders, and brutal vices furnished with tails and claws. And it is impossible, such being the mental constitution of the species, to see the events of other creations legibly engraved all around, as with an iron pen, on the face of nature, without letting the mind loose to expatiate on those historic periods to which the record so graphically refers. The geologist in our own country feels himself in exactly the circumstances of the traveller who journeys amid the deserts of Sinai, and sees the front of almost every precipice roughened with antique inscriptions of which he has just discovered the key, — inscriptions that transport him from the silence and solitude of the present, to a darkly remote past, when the loneliness of the wilderness was cheered by the white glitter of unnumbered tents, and the breeze, as it murmured by, went laden with the cheerful hum of a great people.

It may be judged, I am afraid that to some of the localities I devoted too much and to some too little time, in proportion to the degree of interest which attached to them. The Leasowes detained me considerably longer than Stratford-on-Avon ; and I oftener refer to Shenstone than to Shakspeare. It will, I trust, be found, however, that I was influenced in such cases by no suspicious sympathy with the little and the mediocre ; and that, if I preferred at times the less fertile to the richer and better field, it has been simply, not because I failed to estimate their comparative values, but because I found a positive though scanty harvest awaiting me on the one, and on the other the originally luxuriant swathe cut down and carried away, and but a vacant breadth of stubble left to the belated gleaner. Besides, it is not in his character as a merely tasteful versifier, but as a master in the art of developing the beauties of landscape, that I have had occasion to refer to Shenstone. He is introduced to the reader as the *author* of the Leasowes, — a work which cost him more thought and labor than all his other compositions put together, and which the general reader, who has to prosecute his travels by the fire-side, can study but at second hand, — as it now exists in sketches such as mine, or as it existed, at the death of its author, in the more elaborate description of Dodsley. It is thus not to a minor poet that I have devoted a chapter or two, but to a fine rural poem, some two or three hundred acres in extent, that cannot be printed, and that exists nowhere in duplicate.

It does matter considerably in some things that a man's cradle should have been rocked to the north of the Tweed ; and as I have been at less pains to suppress in my writings the peculiarities of the

Scot and the Presbyterian than is perhaps common with my country-folk and brother Churchmen, the Englishman will detect much in these pages to remind him that mine was rocked to the north of the Tweed very decidedly. I trust, however, that if he deem me in the main a not ill-natured companion, he may feel inclined to make as large allowances for the peculiar prejudices of my training as he sees me making on most occasions for the peculiar prejudices of his; that he may forgive me my partialities to my own poor country, if they do not greatly warp my judgment nor swallow up my love for my kind; that he may tolerate my Presbyterianism, if he find it rendering a reason for its preferences, and not very bigoted in its dislikes; and, in short, that we may part friends, not enemies, if he can conclude, without over-straining his charity, that I have communicated fairly, and in no invidious spirit, my First Impressions of England and its People.

CONTENTS.

CHAPTER I.

CHAPTER II.

CHAPTER III.

CHAPTER IV.

CHAPTER V.

CHAPTER VI.

CHAPTER VII.

CHAPTER VIII.

CHAPTER IX.

CHAPTER X.

CHAPTER XI.

CHAPTER XII.

CHAPTER XIII.

CHAPTER XIV.

CHAPTER XV.

CHAPTER XVI.

CHAPTER XVII.

CHAPTER XVIII.

CHAPTER XIX.

CHAPTER XX.

FIRST IMPRESSIONS

OF

ENGLAND AND ITS PEOPLE.

CHAPTER I.

Led to convert an intended Voyage to Orkney into a Journey to England. — Objects of the Journey. — Carter Fell. — The Border Line. — Well for England it should have been so doggedly maintained by the weaker Country. — Otterburn. — The Mountain Limestone in England, what it is not in Scotland, a true *Mountain* Limestone. — Scenery changes as we enter the Coal Measures. — Wretched Weather. — Newcastle. — Methodists. — Controversy on the Atonement. — The Popular Mind in Scotland mainly developed by its Theology. — Newcastle Museum; rich in its Geology and its Antiquities; both branches of one subject. — *Geologic* History of the Roman Invasion. — Durham Cathedral. — The Monuments of Nature greatly more enduring than those of Man. — *Cyathophyllum Fungites.* — The Spotted Tubers, and what they indicated. — The Destiny of a Nation involved in the Growth of a minute Fungus.

I HAD purposed visiting the Orkneys, and spending my few weeks of autumn leisure in exploring the Old Red Sandstone of these islands along the noble coast sections opened up by the sea. My vacations during the five previous seasons had been devoted to an examination of the fossiliferous deposits of Scotland. I had already in some degree acquainted myself with the Palæozoic and Secondary formations of the northern half of the kingdom and the Hebrides. One vacation more would have acquainted me with those of Orkney also, and completed my survey of Scotland to the north of the Grampians; and would have reckoned at least half my self-imposed task at an end. When laboring professionally, however, during the previous winter and spring, I had, I am afraid, sometimes failed to remember, what the old chivalric knights used never to forget, that "man is but of mould;" and I had, in consequence, subjected the "mould" to a heavier pressure than, from its yielding nature, it is suited to bear. And now that play-time had once more come round, I found I had scarce health and strength enough left me to carry me in quest of more. I could no longer undertake, as formerly, long journeys a-foot in a wild country, nor scramble, with sure step, and head that never failed, along the faces of tall precipices washed by the sea. And so, for the time at least, I had to give up all thought of visiting Orkney.

"I will cross the Border," I said, "and get into England. I know the humbler Scotch better than most men, — I have at least enjoyed better opportunities of knowing them; but the humbler English I know only from hearsay. I will go and live among them for a few weeks, somewhere in the midland districts. I shall lodge in humble cottages, wear a humble dress, and see what is to be seen by humble men only, — society without its mask. I shall explore, too, for myself, the formations wanting in the geologic scale of Scotland, — the Silurian, the Chalk, and the Tertiary; and so, should there be future years in store for me, I shall be enabled to resume my survey of our Scottish deposits with a more practised eye than at present, and with more extended knowledge." August was dragging on to its close through a moist and cloudy atmosphere; every day had its shower, and some days half a dozen but I hoped for clearer skies and fairer weather in the south and so, taking my seat at Edinburgh on the top of the New castle coach, I crossed Carter Fell a little after mid-day, and found myself, for the first time, in England. The sun on the Scottish side looked down clear and kindly on languid fields surcharged with moisture, that exhibited greener and yet greener tints as we ascended from the lowland districts to the uplands; while on the southern side, though all was fair in the foreground, a thick sullen cloud hung low over the distant prospect, resembling the smoke of some vast city.

And this was the famous Border-line, made good by the weaker against the stronger nation, — at how vast an amount of blood and suffering! — for more than a thousand years. It wore to-day, in the quiet sunshine, a look of recluse tranquillity, that seemed wholly unconscious of the past. A tumbling sea of dark-green hills, delicately checkered with light and shadow, swelled upwards on either side towards the line of boundary, like the billows of opposing tide-ways, that rise over the general level where the currents meet; and passing on and away from wave-top to wave-top, like the cork baulk of a fisherman's net afloat on the swell, ran the separating line. But all was still and motionless, as in the upper reaches of the Baltic, when the winter frost has set in. We passed, on the Scottish side, a group of stalwart shepherds, — solid, grave-featured men, who certainly did not look as if they loved fighting for its own sake; and on the English side, drove by a few stout, ruddy hinds, engaged in driving carts, who seemed just as little quarrelsome as their Scottish neighbors. War must be intrinsically mischievous. It must be something very bad, let us personify it as proudly as we may, that could have set on these useful, peaceable people, — cast in so nearly the same mould, speaking the same tongue, possessed of the same common nature, lovable, doubtless, in some points, from the development of the same genial affections, — to knock one another on the head simply because the one half of them had first seen the light on the one side of the hill, and the other half on the other side. And yet, such was the state of things which obtained in this wild district for many hundred years. It seems, however, especially well for England, since the quarrel began at all, that it should have been so doggedly maintained by the weaker people, — so well maintained that the border hamlet, round which they struggled, in the days of the first Edward, as a piece of doubtful property, is a piece of doubtful property still, and has, in royal proclamation and act of Parliament, its own separate clause assigned to it, as the "town called Berwick-upon-Tweed." It is quite enough for the English, as shown by the political history of modern times, that they conquered Ireland; had they conquered Scotland also, they would have been ruined utterly. "One such victory more, and they would have been undone." Men have long suspected the trade of the hero to be a bad one; but it is only now they are fairly beginning to learn, that of all great losses and misfortunes, his master achievement — the *taking* of a nation — is the greatest and most incurably calamitous.

The line of boundary forms the water-shed in this part of the island: the streams on the Scottish side trot away northwards toward the valley of the Tweed; while on the English side they pursue a southerly course, and are included in the drainage of the Tyne. The stream which runs along the bare, open valley on which we had now entered, forms one of the larger tributaries of the latter river. But everything seemed as Scottish as ever, — the people, the dwelling-houses, the country. I could scarce realize the fact, that the little gray parish-church, with the square tower, which we had just passed, was a church in which the curate read the Prayer-book every Sunday, and that I had left behind me the Scottish law, under which I had been living all life-long till now, on the top of the hill. I had proof, however, at our first English stage, that such was actually the case. "Is all right?" asked the coachman, of a ta l, lanky Northumbrian, who had busied himself in changing the horses. "Yez, all roit," was the reply; "roit as the Church of England." I was, it was evident, on Presbyterian ground no longer.

We passed, as the country began to open, a spot marked by two of the crossed swords of our more elaborate maps: they lie thick on both sides the Border, to indicate where the old battle-fields were stricken; and the crossed swords of this especial locality are celebrated in chronicle and song. A rude, straggling village runs for some one or two hundred yards along both sides of the road. On the left there is a group of tall trees, elevated on a ridge, which they conceal; and a bare, undulating, somewhat wild country, spreads around. All is quiet and solitary; and no scathe on the landscape corresponds with the crossed swords on the map. There were a few children at play, as we passed, in front of one of the cottages, and two old men sauntering along the road. And such now is Otterburn, — a name I had never associated before, save with the two noble ditties of Chevy Chase, the magnificent narrative of Froissart, and the common subject of both ballads and narrative, however various their descriptions of it, — that one stern night's slaughter, four hundred years ago,

"When the dead Douglas won the field."

It was well for the poor victors they had a Froissart to celebrate them. For though it was the Scotch who gained the battle, it was the English who had the writing of the songs; and had not the victors found so impartial a chronicler in the generous Frenchman, the two songs, each a model in its own department, would have proved greatly an overmatch for them in the end.

The wilder tracts of Northumberland are composed of the Millstone Grit and Mountain Limestone; and never before had I seen this latter deposit developed in a style that so bears out the appropriateness of its name. It is in Northumberland, what it is rarely or never in Scotland, a true *Mountain* Limestone, that rises into tall hills, and sinks into deep valleys, and spreads laterally over a vast extent of area. The ocean of the Carboniferous era in England must have been greatly more persistent and extended than the ocean whose deposits form the base of the Coal Measures in the sister country: it appears to have lain further from the contemporary land, and to have been much less the subject of alternate upheavals and depressions. We were several hours in driving over the formation. As we entered upon the true Coal Measures, the face of the country at once altered: the wild, open, undulating surface sunk into a plain, laid out, far as the eye could reach, into fields closely reticulated with hedge-rows; the farm-houses and gentlemen's seats thickened as we advanced; and England assumed its proper character. With a change of scenery, however, we experienced a change of weather. We had entered into the cloud that seemed so threatening in the distance from the top of Carter Fell; and a thick, soaking rain, without wind, accompanied by a lazy fog that lay scattered along the fields and woods in detached wreaths of gray, saddened the landscape. As we drove on, we could see the dense smoke of the pit-engines forming a new feature in the prospect; the tall chimneys of Newcastle, that seemed so many soot-black obelisks, half lost in the turbid atmosphere, came next in view; and then, just as the evening was falling wet and cheerless, we entered the town, through muddy streets, and along ranges of melancholy-looking houses, dropping from all their eaves, and darkened by the continuous rain of weeks. I was directed by the coachman to by far the most splendid temperance coffee-house I had ever seen; but it seemed too fine a lodging-house for harboring the more characteristic English, and I had not crossed the Border to see cosmopolites; and so, turning away from the door, I succeeded in finding for myself a humbler, but still very respectable house, in a different part of the town.

There were several guests in the public room: some two or three smart commercial gentlemen from the midland trading towns; two young Sheffield mechanics, evidently of the respectable class, who earn high wages and take care of them; and a farmer or two from the country. In the course of the evening we had a good deal of conversation, and some controversy. The mechanics were Methodists, who had availed themselves of a few days' leisure to see the north country, but more especially, as I afterwards learned, to be present at a discussion on controverted points of theology, which was to take place in Newcastle on the following evening, between a prodigiously clever preacher of the *New Connection*, very unsound in his creed, of whom I had never heard before, and a more orthodox preacher of the same body, profound in his theology, of whom I had heard just as little. From the peculiar emphasis placed by the two lads on the word *orthodox*, I inferred that neither of them deemed orthodoxy so intellectual a thing as the want of it; and I ultimately discovered that they were partisans of the clever preacher. One of the two seemed anxious to provoke a controversy on his favorite points; but the commercial men, who appeared rather amused to hear so much about religion, avoided all definite statement; and the men from the country said nothing. A person in black entered the room, — not a preacher apparently, but, had I met him in Scotland, I would have set him down for at least an elder; and the young mechanics were gratified.

The man in black was, I found, a Calvinist,—not, however, of the most profound type; the Methodists were wild nondescripts in their theology, more Socinian than aught else, and yet not consistently Socinian neither. A Scottish religious controversy of the present time regards the *nature* and *extent* of the atonement; the two Wesleyans challenged, I found, the very *existence* of the doctrine. There was really no such thing as an atonement, they said; the atonement was a mere *orthodox* view taken by the *Old Connection.* The Calvinist referred to the ordinary evidences to prove it something more; and so the controversy went on, with some share of perverted ingenuity on the one side, and a considerable acquaintance with Scripture doctrine on the other. A tall, respectable-looking man, with the freshness of a country life palpable about him, had come in shortly after the commencement of the discussion, and took evidently some interest in it. He turned from speaker to speaker, and seemed employed in weighing the statements on both sides. At length he struck in, taking part against the Calvinist. "Can it really be held," he said, "that the all-powerful God—the Being who has no limits to his power—could not forgive sin without an atonement? That would be limiting his illimitable power with a vengeance!" The remark would scarcely have arrested a theologic controversy on the same nice point in Scotland,—certainly not among the class of peasant controversialists so unwisely satirized by Burns, nor yet among the class who, in our own times, have taken so deep an interest in the Church question; but the English Calvinist seemed unfurnished with a reply.

I was curious to see how the metaphysics of our Scotch Calvinism would tell on such an audience; and took up the subject much in the way it might be taken up in some country church-yard, ere the congregation had fully gathered, by some of the "grave-livers" of the parish, or as it might be discussed in the more northern localities of the kingdom, at some evening meeting of "the men." I attempted showing, step by step, that God did not give to himself his own nature, nor any part of it; that it exists *as it is*, as independently of *his* will as our human nature exists *as it is* independently of ours; that his moral nature, like his nature in general, is underived, unalterable, eternal; and that it is this underived moral nature of the Godhead which forms the absolute law of his conduct in all his dealings with his moral agents. "You are, I daresay, right," said the countryman; "but how does all this bear on the doctrine of the atonement?"

"Very directly on your remark respecting it," I replied. "It shows us that the will and power of God, in dealing with the sins of his accountable creature, man, cannot, if we may so speak, be arbitrary, unregulated power and will, but must spring, of necessity, out of his underived moral nature. If it be according to this moral nature, which constitutes the governing law of Deity, — the law which *controls* Deity, — that without the 'shedding of blood there can be no remission,' then blood must be shed, or remission cannot be obtained; atonement for sin there must be. If, on the contrary, there *can* be remission without the shedding of blood, we may be infallibly certain the unnecessary blood will not be demanded, nor the superfluous atonement required. To believe otherwise would be to believe that God deals with his moral agent, man, on principles that do not spring out of his own moral nature, but are mere arbitrary results of an unregulated will." — "But are you not leaving the question, after all, just where you found it?" asked the countryman. — "Not quite," I replied: "of

God's moral nature, or the conduct which springs out of it, we can but know what God has been pleased to tell us: the fact of the atonement can be determined but by revelation; and I believe, with the gentleman opposite, that revelation determines it very conclusively. But if fact it be, then must we hold that it is a fact which springs directly out of that underived moral nature of God which constitutes the governing law of his power and will; and that, his nature being what it is, the antagonist fact of remission without atonement is in reality an impossibility. Your appeal in the question lay to the *omnipotence* of God; it is something to know that in that direction there can lie *no* appeal. Mark how strongly your own great poet brings out this truth. In his statement of the doctrine of the atonement, — a simple digest of the Scriptural statement, — all is made to hinge on the important fact, that God having once willed the salvation of men, an atonement became as essentially necessary to Him, in order that the moral nature which He did not give himself might not be violated, as to the lapsed race, who might recognize in it their sole hope of restoration and recovery. Man, says the poet,

'To expiate his treason hath nought left,
But to destruction, sacred and devote,
He, with his whole posterity, must die:
Die he, or justice must; unless for him
Some other, able, and as willing, pay
The rigid satisfaction, death for death.'"

The countryman was silent. "You Scotch are a strange people," said one of the commercial gentlemen. "When I was in Scotland two years ago, I could hear of scarce anything among you but your Church question. What good does all your theology do you?" — "Independently altogether of religious considerations," I replied, "it has done for our people what all your Societies for the Diffusion of Useful Knowledge, and all your Penny and Saturday Magazines, will never do for yours; it has awakened their intellects, and taught them how to think. The development of the popular mind in Scotland is a result of its theology."

The morning rose quite as gloomily as the evening had fallen: the mist cloud still rested lazily over the town; the rain dashed incessantly from the eaves, and streamed along the pavement. It was miserable weather for an invalid in quest of health; but I had just to make the best I could of the circumstances, by scraping acquaintance with the guests in the travellers' room, and beating with them over all manner of topics, until mid-day, when I sallied out, under cover of an umbrella, to see the town museum. I found it well suited to repay the trouble of a visit; and such is the liberality of the Newcastle people, that it cost me no more. It is superior, both in the extent and arrangement of its geologic department, to any of our Scotch collections with which I am acquainted; and its Anglo-Roman antiquities, from the proximity of the place to the wall of Hadrian, are greatly more numerous than in any other museum I ever saw, — filling, of themselves, an entire gallery. As I passed, in the geologic apartment, from the older Silurian to the newer Tertiary, and then on from the newer Tertiary to the votive tablets, sacrificial altars, and sepulchral memorials of the Anglo-Roman gallery, I could not help regarding them as all belonging to one department. The antiquities piece on in natural sequence to the geology; and it seems but rational to indulge in the same sort of reasonings regarding them. They are the fossils of an extinct order of things, newer than the Tertiary, — of an extinct race, — of an extinct religion, — of a state of society and a class of enterprises which the world saw once, but which it will never see again. And with but little assistance from the direct testimony of history, one has to grope one's way along this comparatively modern formation, guided chiefly, as in the more ancient deposits, by the clue of circumstantial evidence. In at least its leading features, however, the story embodied is remarkably clear. First, we have evidence that in those remote times when the northern half of the island had just become a home of men, the land was forest-covered, like the woody regions of North America, and that its inhabitants were rude savages, unacquainted with the metals, but possessed of a few curious arts which an after age forgot, — not devoid of a religion which at least indicated the immortality of the soul, — and much given to war. The extensive morass, in which huge trunks lie thick and frequent, — the stone battle-axe, — the flint arrow-head, — the Druidic circle, — the vitrified fort, — the Picts' house, — the canoe hollowed out of a single log, — are all fossils of this early period. Then come the memorials of an after formation. This wild country is invaded by a much more civilized race than the one by which it is inhabited; we find distinct marks of their lines of march, — of the forests which they cut down, — of the encampments in which they intrenched themselves, — of the battle-fields in which they were met in fight by the natives. And they, too, had their religion. More than half the remains which testify to their progress consist of sacrificial altars, and votive tablets dedicated to the gods. The narrative goes on: another class of remains show us that a portion of the country was conquered by the civilized race. We find the remains of tesselated pavements, baths, public roads, the foundations of houses and temples, accumulations of broken pottery, and hoards of coin. Then comes another important clause in the story; we ascertain that the civilized people failed to conquer the whole of the northern country; and that, in order to preser e what they *had* conquered, they were content to construct, at an immense expense of labor, a long chain of forts, connected by a strong wall flanked with towers. Had it been easier to conquer the rest of the country than to build the wall, the wall would not have been built. We learn further, however, that the laboriously-built wall served its purpose but for a time: the wild people beyond at length broke over it; and the civilized invader, wearied out by their persevering assaults, which, though repelled to-day, had again to be repelled to-morrow, at length left their country to them entire, and retreating beyond its furthest limits, built for his protection a second wall. Such is the history of this bygone series of occurrences, as written, if one may so speak, in the various fossils of the formation. The antiquities of a museum should always piece on to its geologic collection.*

* Some of the operations of the Romans in Scotland have, like the catastrophes of the old geologic periods, left permanent marks on the face of the country. It is a curious fact, that not a few of our southern Scottish mosses owe their origin to the Roman invasion. Of their lower tiers of trees, — those which constituted the nucleus of the peaty formation, — many have been found still bearing the marks of the Roman hatchet, — a thin-edged tool, somewhat like that of the American woodsman, but still narrower. In some instances the axe-head, sorely wasted, has been detected still sticking in the buried stump, which is generally found to have been cut several feet over the soil, just where the tool might be plied with most effect; and in many, Roman utensils and coins have been discovered, where they had been hastily laid down by the soldiery among the tangled brushwood, and forthwith covered up and lost. Rennie, in his "Essay on Peat Moss," furnishes an interesting list of these curiosities, that tell so significant a story. "In Ponsil Moss, near Glasgow," he says, "a leather bag, containing about two hundred silver coins of Rome, was found; in Dundaff Moor, a number of similar coins were found about forty years ago; in Annan Moss, near the Roman Causeway, an ornament of pure gold was discovered; a Roman camp-kettle was found, eight feet deep, under a moss, on the estate of Ochtertyre; in Flanders Moss a similar utensil was found; a Roman jug was found in Locker Moss, Dum

The weather was still wretchedly bad; but I got upon the Great Southern Railway, and passed on to Durham, expecting to see, in the city of a bishop, a quiet English town of the true ancient type. And so I would have done, as the close-piled tenements of antique brick-work, with their secluded old-fashioned courts and tall fantastic gables, testified in detail, had the circumstances been more favorable; but the mist-cloud hung low, and I could see little else than dropping eaves, darkened walls, and streaming pavements. The river which sweeps past the town was big in flood. I crossed along the bridge; saw beyond, a half-drowned country, rich in fields and woods, and varied by the reaches of the stream; and caught between me and the sky, when the fog rose, the outline of the town on its bold ridge, with its stately cathedral elevated highest, as first in place, and its grotesque piles of brick ranging adown the slope in picturesque groups, continuous yet distinct. I next visited the cathedral. The gloomy day was darkening into still gloomier evening, and I found the huge pile standing up amid the descending torrents in its ancient grave-yard, like some mass of fretted rock-work enveloped in the play of a fountain. The great door lay open, but I could see little else within than the ranges of antique columns, curiously moulded,

friesshire; a pot and decanter, of Roman copper, was found in a moss in Kirkmichael parish in the same county; and two vessels, of Roman bronze, in the Moss of Glanderhill, in Strathaven." And thus the list runs on. It is not difficult to conceive how, in the circumstances, mosses came to be formed. The felled wood was left to rot on the surface; small streams were choked up in the levels; pools formed in the hollows; the soil beneath, shut up from the light and the air, became unfitted to produce its former vegetation: but a new order of plants, — the thick water-mosses, — began to spring up; one generation budded and decayed over the ruins of another; and what had been an overturned forest, became, in the course of years, a deep morass, — an unsightly but permanent monument of the formidable invader.

and of girth enormous, that separate the aisles from the nave; and half lost in the blackness, they served to remind me this evening of the shadowy, gigantic colonnades of Martin. Their Saxon strength wore, amid the vagueness of the gloom, an air of Babylonish magnificence.

The rain was dashing amid the tombstones outside. One antique slab of blue limestone beside the pathway had been fretted many centuries ago into the rude semblance of a human figure; but the compact mass, unfaithful to its charge, had resigned all save the general outline; the face was worn smooth, and only a few nearly obliterated ridges remained, to indicate the foldings of the robe. It served to show, in a manner sufficiently striking, how much more indelibly nature inscribes her monuments of the dead than art. The limestone slab had existed as a churchyard monument for perhaps a thousand years; but the story which it had been sculptured to tell had been long since told for the last time; and whether it had marked out the burial-place of priest or of layman, or what he had been or done, no one could now determine. But the story of an immensely earlier sepulture, — earlier, mayhap, by thrice as many twelvemonths as the thousand years contained days, — it continued to tell most distinctly. It told that when it had existed as a calcareous mud deep in the carboniferous ocean, a species of curious zoophyte, long afterwards termed *Cyathophyllum fungites*, were living and dying by myriads; and it now exhibited on its surface several dozens of them, cut open at every possible angle, and presenting every variety of section, as if to show what sort of creatures they had been. The glossy wet served as a varnish; and I could see that not only had those larger plates of the skeletons that radiate outwards from the centre been preserved, but even the microscopic reticulations of the cross partitioning. Never was there ancient inscription held in such faithful keeping by the founder's bronze or the sculptor's marble; and never was there epitaph of human composition so scrupulously just to the real character of the dead.

I found three guests in the coffee-house in which I lodged,—a farmer and his two sons: the farmer still in vigorous middle life; the sons robust and tall; all of them fine specimens of the ruddy, well-built, square-shouldered Englishman. They had been travelling by the railway, and were now on their return to their farm, which lay little more than two hours' walk away; but so bad was the evening, that they had deemed it advisable to take beds for the night in Durham. They had evidently a stake in the state of the weather; and as the rain ever and anon pattered against the panes, as if on the eve of breaking them, some one or other of the three would rise to the window, and look moodily out into the storm. "God help us!" I heard the old farmer ejaculate, as the rising wind shook the casement; "we shall have no harvest at all." They had had rain, I learned, in this locality, with but partial intermissions, for the greater part of six weeks, and the crops lay rotting on the ground. In the potatoes served at table I marked a peculiar appearance: they were freckled over by minute circular spots, that bore a ferruginous tinge, somewhat resembling the specks on iron-shot sandstone, and they ate as if but partially boiled. I asked the farmer whether the affection was a common one in that part of the country. "Not at all," was the reply: "we never saw it before; but it threatens this year to destroy our potatoes. The half of mine it has spoiled already, and it spreads among them every day." It does not seem natural to the species to associate mighty consequences with phenomena that wear a very humble aspect. The teachings of experience are essentially necessary to show us that the seeds of great events may be little things in themselves; and so I could not see how important a part these minute iron-tinted specks — the work of a microscopic fungus — were to enact in British history. The old soothsayers professed to read the destinies of the future in very unlikely pages, — in the meteoric appearances of the heavens, and in the stars, — in the flight and chirping of birds, — in the entrails of animals, — in many other strange characters besides; and in the remoter districts of my own country I have seen a half-sportive superstition employed in deciphering characters quite as unlikely as those of the old augurs, — in the burning of a brace of hazel-nuts, — in the pulling of a few oaten stalks, — in the grounds of a tea-cup, — above all, in the Hallowe'en egg, in which, in a different sense from that embodied in the allegory of Cowley,

> "The curious eye,
> Through the firm shell and the thick white may spy
> Years to come a-forming lie,
> Close in their sacred secundine asleep."

But who could have ever thought of divining over the spotted tubers? or who so shrewd as to have seen in the grouping of their iron-shot specks Lord John Russell's renunciation of the fixed duty, — the conversion to free-trade principles of Sir Robert Peel and his Conservative ministry, — the breaking up into sections of the old Protectionist party, — and, in the remote distance, the abolition in Scotland of the law of entail, and in England the ultimate abandonment, mayhap, of the depressing tenant-at-will system? If one could have read them aright, never did the flight of bird or the embowelment of beast indicate so wonderful a story as these same iron-shot tubers.

CHAPTER II

Weather still miserably bad; suited to betray the frequent Poverty of English Landscape. — Gloomy Prospects of the Agriculturist. — Corn-Law League. — York; a true Sacerdotal City. — Cathedral; noble Exterior; Interior not less impressive; Congreve's sublime Description. — Unpardonable Solecism. — Procession. — Dean Cockburn; Crusade against the Geologists. — Cathedral Service unworthy of the Cathedral. — Walk on the City Ramparts. — Flat Fertility of the surrounding Country. — The more interesting Passages in the History of York supplied by the *Makers*. — Robinson Crusoe. — Jeanie Deans. — Trial of Eugene Aram. — Aram's real Character widely different from that drawn by the Novelist.

Rain, rain! — another morning in England, and still no improvement in the weather. The air, if there was any change at all, felt rather more chill and bleak than on the previous evening; and the shower, in its paroxysms, seemed to beat still heavier on the panes. I was in no mood to lay myself up in a dull inn, like Washington Irving's stout gentleman, and so took the train for York, in the hope of getting from under the cloud somewhere on its southern side, ere I at least reached the British Channel. Never surely was the north of England seen more thoroughly in dishabille. The dark woods and thick-set hedgerows looked blue and dim through the haze, like the mimic woodlands of a half-finished drawing in gray chalk; and, instead of cheering, added but to the gloom of the landscape. They seemed to act the part of mere sponges, that first condensed and then retained the moisture,—that became soaked in the shower, and then, when it had passed, continued dispensing their droppings on the rotting sward beneath, until another shower came. The character of the weather was of a kind suited to betray the frequent poverty of English landscape. When the sky is clear and the sun bright, even the smallest and tamest patches of country have their charms: there is beauty in even a hollow willow pollard fluttering its silvery leaves over its patch of meadow-sedges against the deep blue of the heavens; but in the dull haze and homogeneous light, that was but light and shadow muddled into a neutral tint of gray, one could not now and then avoid remarking that the entire prospect consisted of but one field and two hedgerows.

As we advanced, appearances did not improve. The wheaten fields exhibited, for their usual golden tint slightly umbered, an ominous tinge of earthy brown; the sullen rivers had risen high over the meadows; and rotting hay-ricks stood up like islands amid the water. At one place in the line the train had to drag its weary length in foam and spray, up to the wheel-axles, through the overflowings of a neighboring canal. The sudden shower came ever and anon beating against the carriage windows, obscuring yet more the gloomy landscape without; and the passengers were fain to shut close every opening, and to draw their great-coats and wrappers tightly around them, as if they had been journeying, not in the month of August, scarcely a fortnight after the close of the dog-days, but at Christmas. I heard among the passengers a few semi-political remarks, suggested by the darkening prospects of the agriculturist. The Anti-Corn-Law League, with all its formidable equipments, had lain for years, as if becalmed in its voyage, a water-logged hulk, that failed to press on towards its port of destination. One good harvest after another had, as sailors say, taken the wind out of its sails; and now here evidently was there a strong gale arising full in its poop. It was palpably on the eve of making great way in its course; and the few political remarks which I heard bore reference to the fact. But they elicited no general sympathy. The scowling heavens, the blackening earth, the swollen rivers, the ever-returning shower-blast, with its sharp-ringing patter, were things that had nought of the gayety of political triumph in them; and the more solid English, however favorable to free trade, could not deem it a cause of gratulation that for so many weeks "the sun, and the light, and the stars, had been darkened, and the clouds returned after the rain." The general feeling seemed not inadequately expressed by a staid elderly farmer, with whom I afterwards travelled from York to Manchester. "I am sure," he said, looking out into the rain, which was beating at the time with great violence, — "I am sure I wish the League no harm; but Heaven help *us* and the country, if there is to be no harvest! The League will have a dear triumph, if God destroy the fruits of the earth."

Old sacerdotal York, with its august cathedral, its twenty-three churches in which Divine service is still performed, its numerous ecclesiastical ruins besides, — monasteries, abbeys, hospitals and chapels, — at once struck me as different from anything I had ever seen before. St. Andrews, one of the two ancient archiepiscopal towns of Scotland, may have somewhat resembled it on a small scale in the days of old Cardinal Beaton; but the peculiar character of the Scottish Reformation rendered it impossible that the country should possess any such ecclesiastical city ever after. Modern improvement has here and there introduced more of its commonplace barbarisms into the busier and the genteeler streets than the antiquary would have bargained for; it has been rubbing off the venerable rust, somewhat in the style adopted by the serving-maid, who scoured the old Roman buckler with sand and water till it shone: but York is essentially an ancient city still. One may still walk round it on the ramparts erected in the times of Edward the First, and tell all their towers, bars, and barbacans; and in threading one's way along antique lanes, flanked by domiciles of mingled oak and old brick-work, that belly over like the sides of ships, and were tenanted in the days of the later Henrys, one stumbles unexpectedly on rectories that have their names recorded in Doomsday Book, and churches that were built before the Conquest. My first walk through the city terminated, as a matter of course, at the cathedral, so famous for its architectural magnificence and grandeur. It is a noble pile, — one of the sublimest things wrought by human hands which the island contains. As it rose gray and tall before me in the thickening twilight, — for another day had passed, and another evening was falling, — I was conscious of a more awe-struck and expansive feeling than any mere work of art had ever awakened in me before. The impression more resembled what I have sometimes experienced on some solitary ocean shore, o'erhung by dizzy precipices, and lashed high by the foaming surf; or beneath the craggy brow of some vast mountain, that overlooks, amid the mute sublimities of nature, some far-spread uninhabited wilderness of forest and moor. I realized better than ever before the justice of the eulogium of Thomson on the art of the architect, and recognized it as in reality

> "The art where most magnificent appears
> The little builder man."

It was too late to gain admission to the edifice, and far too late to witness the daily service; and I was desirous to see not only the stately temple itself, but the worship performed in it. I spent, however, an hour in wandering round it, — in marking the effect on buttress and pinnacle, turret and arch, of the still deepening shadows, and in catching the general outline between me and the sky. The night had set fairly in long ere I reached my lodging-house. York races had just begun; and, bad as the weather was, there was so considerable an influx of strangers into the town, that there were few beds in the inns unoccupied, and I had to content myself with the share of a bed-room in which there were two. My co-partner in the room came in late and went away early; and all I know of him, or shall perhaps ever know, is, that after having first ascertained, not very correctly, as it proved, that I was asleep, he prayed long and earnestly; that, as I afterwards learned from the landlord, he was a Wesleyan Methodist, who had come from the country, *not* to attend the races, for he was not one of the race-frequenting sort of people, but on some business; and that he was much respected in his neighborhood for the excellence of his character.

Next morning I attended service in the cathedral; and being, I found, half an hour too early, spent the interval not unpleasantly in pacing the aisles and nave, and studying the stories so doubtfully recorded on the old painted glass. As I stood at the western door, and saw the noble stone roof stretching away more than thirty yards overhead, in a long vista of five hundred feet, to the great eastern window, I again experienced the feeling of the previous evening. Never before had I seen so noble a cover. The ornate complexities of the groined vaulting, — the giant columns, with their foliage-bound capitals, sweeping away in magnificent perspective, — the colored light that streamed through more than a hundred huge windows, and but faintly illumined the vast area, after all, — the deep withdrawing aisles, with their streets of tombs, — the great tower, under which a ship of the line might hoist top and top-gallant mast, and find ample room overhead for the play

o. her vane, -- the felt combination of great age and massive durability, that made the passing hour in the history of the edifice but a mere half-way point between the centuries of the past and the centuries of the future, — all conspired to render the interior of York Minster one of the most impressive objects I had ever seen. Johnson singles out Congreve's description of a similar pile as one of the finest in the whole range of English poetry. It is at least description without exaggeration, in reference to buildings such as this cathedral.

> "*Almeria.* It was a fancied noise; for all is hushed.
> *Leonora.* It bore the accent of a human voice.
> *Almeria.* It was thy fear, or else some transient wind
> Whistling through hollows of this vaulted aisle.
> We 'll listen —
> *Leonora.* Hark!
> *Almeria.* No, all is hushed and still as death : 't is dreadful.
> How reverend is the face of this tall pile,
> Whose ancient pillars rear their marble heads,
> To bear aloft its arched and ponderous roof,
> By its own weight made steadfast and immovable, —
> Looking tranquillity! It strikes an awe
> And terror on the aching sight: the tombs
> And monumental caves of death look cold,
> And shoot a chillness to the trembling heart.
> Give me thy hand, and let me hear thy voice;
> Nay, quickly speak to me, and let me hear
> Thy voice: my own affrights me with its echoes."

But though I felt the poetry of the edifice, so little had my Presbyterian education led me to associate the not unelevated impulses of the feeling with the devotional spirit, that, certainly without intending any disrespect to either the national religion or one of the noblest ecclesiastical buildings of England, I had failed to uncover my head, and was quite unaware of the gross solecism I was committing, until two of the officials, who had just ranged themselves in front of the organ-screen, to usher the dean and choristers into the choir, started forward, one from each side of the door, and, with no little gesticulatory emphasis, ordered me to take off my hat. "Off hat, sir! off hat!" angrily exclaimed the one. "Take off your *hat*, sir!" said the other, in a steady, energetic, determined tone, still less resistible. The peccant beaver at once sunk by my side, and I apologized. "Ah, a Scotchman!" ejaculated the keener official of the two, his cheek meanwhile losing some of the hastily-summoned red; "I thought as much." The officials had scarcely resumed their places beside the screen, when Dean and Sub-dean, the Canons Residentiary and the Archdeacon, the Prebendaries and the Vicars Choral, entered the building in their robes, and, with step slow and stately, disappeared through the richly-fretted entrance of the choir. A purple curtain fell over the opening behind them, as the last figure in the procession passed in; while a few lay saunterers, who had come to be edified by the great organ, found access by another door, which opened into one of the aisles.

The presiding churchman, on the occasion, was Dean Cockburn, — a tall, portly old man, fresh-complexioned and silvery-haired, and better fitted than most men to enact the part of an imposing figure in a piece of impressive ceremony. I looked at the dean with some little interest; he had been twice before the public during the previous five years, — once as a dealer in church offices, for which grave offence he had been deprived by his ecclesiastical superior, the archbishop, but reponed by the queen, — and once as a redoubtable asserter of what he deemed Bible cosmogony, against the facts of the geologists. The old blood-boltered barons who lived in the times of the Crusades used to make all square with Heaven, when particularly aggrieved in their consciences, by slaying a few scores of infidels a-piece ; — the dean had fallen, it would seem, in these latter days, on a similar mode of doing penance, and expiated the crime of making canons residentiary for a consideration, by demolishing a whole conclave of geologists.

The cathedral service seemed rather a poor thing, on the whole. The coldly-read or fantastically-chanted prayers, commonplace by the twice-a-day repetition of centuries, — the mechanical responses, — the correct inanity of the choristers, who had not even the life of music in them, — the total want of lay attendance, for the loungers who had come in by the side-door went off *en masse* when the organ had performed its introductory part, and the prayers began, — the ranges of empty seats, which, huge as is the building which contains them, would scarce accommodate an average-sized Free Church congregation, — all conspired to show that the cathedral service of the English Church does not represent a living devotion, but a devotion that perished centuries ago. It is a petrifaction, — a fossil, — existing, it is true, in a fine state of keeping, but still an exanimate stone. Many ages must have elapsed since it was the living devotion I had witnessed on the previous evening in the double-bedded room, — if, indeed, it was ever so living a devotion, or aught, at best, save a mere painted image. Not even as a piece of ceremonial is it in keeping with the august edifice in which it is performed. The great organ does its part admirably, and is indisputably a noble machine; its thirty-two feet double-wood diapason pipe, cut into lengths, would make coffins for three Goliahs of Gath, brass armor and all: but the merely human part of the performance is redolent of none of the poetry which plays around the ancient walls, or streams through the old painted glass. It reminded me of the story told by the eastern traveller, who, in exploring a magnificent temple, passed through superb porticoes and noble halls, to find a monkey enthroned in a little dark sanctum, as the god of the whole.

I had a long and very agreeable walk along the city ramparts. White watery clouds still hung in the sky; but the day was decidedly fine, and dank fields and glistening hedgerows steamed merrily in the bright warm sunshine. York, like all the greater towns of England, if we except the capital and some two or three others, stands on the New Red Sandstone; and the broad extent of level fertility which it commands is, to a Scotch eye, very striking. There is no extensive prospect in even the south of Scotland that does not include its wide ranges of waste, and its deep mountain sides, never furrowed by the plough; while in our more northern districts, one sees from every hill-top which commands the coast a landscape colored somewhat like a russet shawl with a flowered border; — there is a mere selvage of green cultivation on the edge of the land, and all within is brown heath and shaggy forest. In England, on the contrary, one often travels, stage after stage, through an unvarying expanse of flat fields laid out on the level formations, which, undisturbed by trappean or metamorphic rocks, stretch away at low angles for hundreds of miles together, forming blank tablets, on which man may write his works in whatever characters he pleases. Doubtless such a disposition of things adds greatly to the wealth and power of a country; — the population of Yorkshire, at the last census, equalled that of Scotland in 1801. But I soon began to weary of an infinity of green enclosures, that lay spread out in undistinguishable sameness, like a net, on the flat face of the landscape, and to long for the wild free moors and bold natural features of my own poor country. One likes to know the place of one's birth by other than artificial marks: by some hoary mountain, severe yet kindly in its aspect, that one has learned to love as a friend; by some long withdrawing arm of the sea, sublimely guarded, where it opens to the ocean, by its magnificent portals of rock; by some wild range of precipitous coast, that rears high its ivy-bound pinnacles, and where the green wave ever rises and falls along dim resounding caverns; by some lonely glen, with its old pine forests hanging dark on the slopes, and its deep-brown river roaring over linn and shallow in its headlong course to the sea. Who could fight for a country without features,— that one would scarce be sure of finding out on one's return from the battle, without the assistance of the mile-stones?

As I looked on either hand from the ancient ramparts, now down along the antique lanes and streets of the town, now over the broad level fields beyond, I was amused to think how entirely all my more vivid associations with York — town and country — had been derived from works of fiction. True, it was curious enough to remember, as a historical fact, that Christianity had been preached here to the pagan Saxons in the earlier years of the Heptarchy, by missionaries from Iona. And there are not a few other picturesque incidents, that, frosted over with the romance of history, glimmer with a sort of phosphoric radiance in the records of the place, — from the times when King Edwyn of the Northumbrians demolished the heathen temple that stood where the cathedral now stands, and erected in its room the wooden oratory in which he was baptized, down to the times when little crooked Leslie broke over the city walls at the head of his Covenanters, and held them against the monarch, in the name of the king. But the historical facts have vastly less of the vividness of truth about them than the *facts* of the *makers*. It was in this city of York that the famous Robinson Crusoe was born; and here, in this city of York, did Jeanie Deans rest her for a day, on her London journey, with her hospitable countrywoman, Mrs. Bickerton of the Seven Stars; and it was in the country beyond, down in the West Riding, that Gurth and Wamba held high colloquy together, among the glades of the old oak forest; and that Cedric the Saxon entertained, in his low-browed hall of Rotherwood, the Templar Brian de Bois-Guilbert and Prior Aymer of Jorvaulx.

I visited the old castle, now a prison, and the town museum, and found the geological department of the latter at once very extensive and exquisitely arranged; but the fact, announced in the catalogue, that it had been laid out under the eye of Phillips, while it left me much to admire in the order exhibited, removed at least all cause of wonder I concluded the day — the first very agreeable one I had spent in England — by a stroll along the banks of the Ouse, through a colonnade of magnificent beeches. The sun was hastening to its setting, and the red light fell, with picturesque effect, on the white sails of a handsome brig, that came speeding up the river, through double rows of tall trees, before a light wind from the east. On my return to my lodging-house, through one of the obscure lanes of the city, I picked up, at a book-stall, what I deemed no small curiosity, — the original "Trial of Eugene Aram," well known in English literature as the hero of one of Bulwer's most popular novels, and one of Hood's most finished poems, and for as wonderful a thing as either, his own remarkable defence. I had never before seen so full an account of the evidence on which he was condemned, nor of the closing scene in his singular history; nor was I aware there existed such competent data for forming an adequate estimate of his character, which, by the way, seems to have been not at all the character drawn by Bulwer. Knaresborough, the scene of Aram's crime, may be seen from the bat tlements of York Minster. In York Castle he was imprisoned, and wrote his Defence and his Autobiography; at York Assizes he was tried and convicted; and on York gallows he was hung. The city is as intimately associated with the closing scenes in his history, as with the passing visit of Jeanie Deans, or the birth of Robinson Crusoe. But there is this important difference in the cases, that the one story has found a place in literature from the strangely romantic cast of its facts, and the others from the intensely truthful air of their fictions.

Eugene Aram seems not to have been the high heroic character conceived by the novelist, — not a hero of tragedy at all, nor a hero of any kind, but simply a poor egotistical *litterateur*, with a fine intellect set in a very inferior nature. He represents the extreme type of unfortunately a numerous class, — the men of vigorous talent, in some instances of fine genius, who, though they can think much and highly of themselves, seem wholly unable to appreciate their true place and work, or the real dignity of their standing, and so are continually getting into false, unworthy positions, — in some instances falling into little meannesses, in others into contemptible crimes. I am afraid it is all too evident that even the sage Bacon belonged to this class; and there can be little doubt that, though greatly less a criminal, the elegant and vigorous poet who described him as

"The greatest, wisest, meanest of mankind,"

belonged to it also. The phosphoric light of genius, that throws so radiant a gloom athwart the obscurities of nature, has in some cases been carried by a frivolous insect, in some by a creeping worm: there are brilliant intellects of the fire-fly and of the glow-worm class; and poor Eugene Aram was one of them. In his character, as embodied in the evidence on which he was convicted and condemned, we see merely that of a felon of the baser sort: a man who associated with low companions; married a low wife; entered into low sharping schemes with a poor dishonest creature, whom, early in his career he used to accompany at nights in stealing flower-roots, — for they possessed in common a taste for gardening, — and whom he afterwards barbarously murdered, to possess himself of a few miserable pounds, — the proceeds of a piece of disreputable swindling, to which he had prompted him. Viewed, however, in another phase, we find that this low felon possessed one of those vigorous intellectual natures that, month after month, and year after year, steadily progress in acquirement, as the forest-tree swells in bulk of trunk and amplitude of bough; till, at length, with scarce any educational advantages, there was no learned language which he had not mastered, and scarce a classic author which he had not read. And, finally, when the learned felon came to make his defence, all Britain was astonished by a piece of pleading that, for the elegance of the composition and the vigor of the thought, would have done no discredit to the most accomplished writers of the day. The defence of Eugene Aram, if given to the public among the defences, and under the name, of Thomas Lord Erskine, so celebrated for this species of composition, would certainly not be deemed unworthy of the collection or its author. There can be no question that the Aram of Bulwer is a well-drawn character, and rich in the picturesque of tragic effect; but the exhibition is neither so melancholy nor so instructive as that of the Eugene Aram who was executed at York for murder in the autumn of 1759, and his body afterwards hung in chains at "the place called St. Robert's Cave, near Knaresborough."

CHAPTER III.

Quit York for Manchester. — A Character. — Quaker Lady. — Peculiar Feature in the Husbandry of the Cloth District. — Leeds. — Simplicity manifested in the Geologic Framework of English Scenery. — The Denuding Agencies almost invariably the sole Architects of the Landscape. — Manchester; characteristic Peculiarities; the Irwell; Collegiate Church; light and elegant Proportions of the Building; its grotesque Sculptures; these indicative of the Scepticism of the Age in which they were produced. — St. Bartholomew's Day. — Sermon on Saints' Day. — Timothy's Grandmother. — The Puseyite a High Churchman become earnest. — Passengers of a Sunday Evening Train. — Sabbath Amusements not very conducive to Happiness. — The Economic Value of the Sabbath ill understood by the Utilitarian. — Testimony of History on the point.

On the following morning I quitted York for Manchester, taking Leeds in my way. I had seen two of the ecclesiastical cities of *Old* England, and I was now desirous to visit two of the great trading towns of the modern country, so famous for supplying with its manufactures half the economic wants of the world.

At the first stage from York, we were joined by a young-lady passenger, of forty or thereabouts, evidently a character. She was very gaudily dressed, and very tightly laced, and had a bloom of red in her cheeks that seemed to have been just a little assisted by art, and a bloom of red in her nose that seemed not to have been assisted by art at all. Alarmingly frank and portentously talkative, she at once threw herself for protection and guidance on "the gentlemen." She had to get down at one of the intermediate stages, she said; but were she to be so unlucky as to pass it, she would not know what to do, — she would be at her wit's end; but she trusted she would not be permitted to pass it: she threw herself upon the generosity of the gentlemen, — she always did, indeed; and she trusted the generous gentlemen would inform her, when she came to her stage, that it was time for her to get out. I had rarely seen, except in old play-books, written when our dramatists of the French school were drawing ladies'-maids of the time of Charles the Second, a character of the kind quite so stage-like in its aspect; and in a quiet way was enjoying the exhibition. And the passenger who sat fronting me in the carriage — an elderly lady of the Society of Friends — was, I found, enjoying it quite as much and as quietly as myself. A countenance of much transparency, that had been once very pretty, exhibited at every droll turn in the dialogue the appropriate expression. Remarking to a gentleman beside me that good names were surely rather a scant commodity in England, seeing they had not a few towns and rivers, which, like many of the American ones, seemed to exist in duplicate and triplicate, — they had three Newcastles, and four Stratfords, and at least two river Ouses, — I asked him how I could travel most directly by railway to Cowper's Ouse. He did not know, he said; he had never heard of a river Ouse except the Yorkshire one, which I had just seen. The Quaker lady supplied me with the information I wanted, by pointing out the best route to Olney and the circumstance led to a conversation which only terminated at our arrival at Leeds. I found her possessed, like many of the Society of Friends, whom Howitt so well describes, of literary taste, conversational ability, and extensive information; and we expatiated together over a wide range. We discussed English poets and poetry; compared notes regarding our critical formulas and canons, and found them wonderfully alike; beat over the Scottish Church question, and some dozen or so other questions besides; and at parting, she invited me to visit her at her house in Bedfordshire, within half a day's journey of Olney. She was at present residing with a friend, she said; but she would be at home in less than a fortnight; and there was much in her neighborhood which, she was sure, it would give me pleasure to see. I was unable ultimately to avail myself of her kindness; but in the hope that these chapters may yet meet her eye, I must be permitted to reiterate my sincere thanks for her frank and hospitable invitation. The frankness struck me at the time as characteristically English; while the hospitality associated well with all I had previously known of the Society of Friends.

I marked, in passing on to Leeds, a new feature in the husbandry of the district, — whole fields of teazles, in flower at the time, waving gray in the breeze. They indicated that I was approaching the great centre of the cloth-trade in England. The larger heads of this plant, bristling over with their numerous minute hooks, are employed as a kind of brushes or combs for raising the nap of the finer broadcloths; and it seems a curious enough circumstance that, in this mechanical age, so famous for the ingenuity and niceness of its machines, no effort of the mechanician has as yet enabled him to supersede, or even to rival, this delicate machine of nature's making. I failed to acquaint myself very intimately with Leeds: the rain had again returned, after a brief interval of somewhat less that two days; and I saw, under cover of my old friend the umbrella, but the outsides of the two famous cloth-halls of the place, where there are more woollen stuffs bought and sold than in any other dozen buildings in the world; and its long uphill-street of shops, with phlegmatic Queen Anne looking grimly adown the slope, from her niche of dingy sandstone. On the following morning, which was wet and stormy as ever, I took the railway train for Manchester, which I reached a little after mid-day.

In passing through Northumberland, I had quitted the hilly district when I quitted the Mountain Limestone and Millstone Grit; and now, in travelling on to Manchester, I had, I found, again got into a mountainous, semi-pastoral country. There were deep green valleys, traversed by lively tumbling streams, that opened on either hand among the hills; and the course of the railway train was, for a time, one of great vicissitude, — now elevated high on an embankment, now burrowing deep in a tunnel. It is, the traveller finds, the same Millstone Grit and Mountain Limestone which form the hilly regions of Northumberland, that give here their hills and valleys to Lancashire and the West Riding of Yorkshire; and that, passing on to Derby, in the general south-western range of the English formations, compose the Peak, so famous for its many caves and chasms, with all the picturesque groups of eminences that surround it. There are few things which so strike the Scotch geologist who visits England for the first time, as the simplicity with which he finds he can resolve the varying landscape into its geologic elements. The case is different in Scotland, where he has to deal, in almost every locality, with both the denuding and the Plutonic agents, and where, as in the neighborhood of Edinburgh, many independent centres of internal action, grouped closely together, connect the composition of single prospects with numerous and very varied catastrophes. But in most English landscapes one has to deal with the denuding agents alone. In passing along an open sea-coast, on which strata of the Secondary or Palæozoic formations have been laid bare, one finds that the degree of prominence exhibited by the bars and ridges of rock exposed to the waves corresponds always with their degree of tenacity and hardness. A bed of soft shale or clay we find represented by a hollow trough; the surf has worn it down till it can no longer be seen, and a strip of smooth gravel rests over it; a stratum of sandstone, of the average solidity, rises above the hollow like a mole, for the waves have failed to wear the sandstone down; while a band of limestone or chert we find rising still higher, because still better suited, from its great tenacity, to resist the attrition of the denuding agents. And such, on a great scale, is the principle of what one may term the geologic framework of English landscape. The softer formations of the country we find represented, like the shale-beds on the shore, by wide flat valleys or extensive plains; the harder, by chains of hills of greater or lesser altitude, according to the degree of solidity possessed by the composing material. A few insulated districts of country, such as part of North Wales, Westmoreland, and Cornwall, where the Plutonic agencies have been active, we find coming under the more complex law of Scottish landscape; but in all the rest, — save where here and there a minute trappean patch imparts its inequalities to the surface, as in the Dudley coal-field, — soft or hard, solid or incoherent, determines the question of high or low, bold or tame. Here, for instance, is a common map of England, on which the eminences are marked, but not the geologic formations. These, however, we may almost trace by the chains of hills, or from the want of them. This hilly region, for instance, which extends from the northern borders of Northumberland to Derby, represents the Millstone Grit and Mountain Limestone, — solid deposits of indurated sandstone and crystalline lime, that stand up amid the landscape like the harder strata on the wave-worn sea-coast. On both sides of this mountainous tract there are level plains of vast extent, that begin to form on the one side near Newcastle, and at Lancaster on the other, and which, uniting at Wirksworth, sweep on to the Bristol Channel in the diagonal line of the English formations. These level plains represent the yielding, semi-coherent New Red Sandstone of England. The denuding agents have worn it down in the way we find the soft shale-beds worn down on the sea-shore. On the west we see it flanked by the Old Red Sandstone and Silurian systems of Wales and western England, — formations solid enough to form a hilly country; and on the east, by a long hilly line, that, with little interruption, traverses the island diagonally from Whitby on the Yorkshire coast, to Lyme Regis on the English Channel. This elevated line traverses longitudinally the Oolitic formation, and owes its existence to those coralline reefs and firm calcareous sandstones of the system that are so extensively used by the architect. Another series of hilly ridges, somewhat more complicated in their windings, represent the Upper and Lower Chalk; while the softer Weald, Gault, Greensand, and Tertiary deposits, we find existing as level plains or wide shallow valleys. In most of our geologic maps the hill-ranges are not indicated; but in a country such as England, where these are so palpably a joint result of the geologic formations and the denuding agencies, the omission is surely a defect.

Manchester I found as true a representative of the great manufacturing town of modern England, as York of the old English ecclesiastical city. One receives one's first intimation of its existence from the lurid gloom of the atmosphere that overhangs it. There is a murky blot in one section of the sky, however clear the weather, which broadens and heightens as we approach, until at length it seems spread over half the firmament. And now the innumerable chimneys come in view, tall and dim in the dun haze, each bearing atop its own troubled pennon of darkness. And now we enter the suburbs, and pass through mediocre streets of brick, that seem as if they had been built wholesale by contract within the last half-dozen years. These humble houses are the homes of the operative manufacturers. The old walls of York, built in the reign of Edward the First, still enclose the city; — the antique suit of armor made for it six hundred years ago, though the fit be somewhat of the tightest, buckles round it still. Manchester, on the other hand, has been doubling its population every half-century for the last hundred and fifty years; and the cord of cotton twist that would have girdled it at the beginning of the great revolutionary war, would do little more than half-girdle it now. The field of Peterloo, on which the yeomanry slashed down the cotton-workers assembled to hear Henry Hunt, — poor lank-jawed men, who would doubtless have manifested less interest in the nonsense of the orator, had they been less hungry at the time, — has been covered with brick for the last ten years.

As we advance, the town presents a new feature. We see whole streets of warehouses, — dead, dingy, gigantic buildings, barred out from the light; and, save where here and there a huge wagon stands, lading or unlading under the mid-air crane, the thoroughfares, and especially the numerous *cul de sacs*, have a solitary, half-deserted air. But the city clocks have just struck one, — the dinner hour of the laboring English; and in one brief minute two-thirds of the population of the place have turned out into the streets. The rush of the human tide is tremendous, — headlong and arrowy as that of a Highland river in flood, or as that of a water-spout just broken amid the hills, and at once hurrying adown a hundred different ravines. But the outburst is short as fierce: we have stepped aside into some door-way, or out towards the centre of some public square, to be beyond the wind of such commotion; and in a few minutes all is over, and the streets even more quiet and solitary than before. There is an air of much magnificence about the public buildings devoted to trade; and the larger shops wear the solid aspect of long-established business. But nothing seems more characteristic of the great manufacturing city, though disagreeably so, than the river Irwell, which runs through the place, dividing it into a lesser and larger town, that, though they bear different names, are essentially one. The hapless river — a pretty enough stream a few miles higher up, with trees overhanging its banks, and fringes of green sedge set thick along its edges — loses caste as it gets among the mills and the print-works. There are myriads of dirty things given it to wash, and whole wagon-loads of poisons from dye-houses and bleach-yards thrown into it to carry away; steam-boilers discharge into it their seething contents, and drains and sewers their fetid impurities; till at length it rolls on, — here between tall dingy walls, there under precipices of red sandstone, — considerably less a river than a flood of liquid manure, in which all life dies, whether animal or vegetable, and which resembles nothing in nature, except perhaps the stream thrown out in eruption by some mud volcano. In passing along where the river sweeps by the old Collegiate Church, I met a party of town-police dragging a female culprit — delirious, dirty, and in drink — to the police-office; and I bethought me of the well-known comparison of Cowper, beginning,

> "Sweet stream, that winds through yonder glade,
> Apt emblem of a virtuous maid," —

of the maudlin woman not virtuous, — and of the Irwell. According to one of the poets contemporary with him of Olney, slightly altered,

"In spite of fair Zelinda's charms,
And all her bards express,
Poor Lyce made as true a stream,
And I but flattered less."

I spent in Manchester my first English Sabbath; and as I had crossed the border, not to see countrymen, nor to hear such sermons as I might hear every Sunday at home, I went direct to the Collegiate Church. This building — a fine specimen of the florid Gothic — dates somewhere about the time when the Council of Constance was deposing Pope John for his enormous crimes, and burning John Huss and Jerome of Prague for their wholesome opinions; and when, though Popery had become miserably worn out as a code of belief, the revived religion of the New Testament could find no rest for the sole of its foot amid a wide weltering flood of practical infidelity and epicurism in the Church, and gross superstition and ignorance among the laity. And the architecture and numerous sculptures of the pile bear meet testimony to the character of the time. They approve themselves the productions of an age in which the priest, engaged in his round of rite and ceremony, could intimate knowingly to a brother priest, without over-much exciting lay suspicion, that he knew his profession to be but a joke. Some of the old Cartularies curiously indicate this state of matters. "The Cartulary of Moray," says an ingenious writer in the *North British Review*, "contains the *Constitutiones Lyncolnienses*, inserted as proper rules for the priests of that northern province, from which we learn that they were to enter the place of worship, not with insolent looks, but decently and in order; and were to be guilty of no laughing, or of attempting the perpetration of any base jokes (*turpi risu aut jocu*), and at the same time to conduct their whisperings in an under tone. A full stomach, however, is not the best provocative to lively attention; and it is therefore far from wonderful that the fathers dozed. Ingenuity provided a remedy even for this; and the curious visiter will find in the niches of the ruined walls of the ecclesiastical edifices of other days oscillating seats, which turn upon a pivot, and require the utmost care of the sitter to keep steady. The poor monk who would dare to indulge in one short nap would by this most cruel contrivance be thrown forward upon the stone-floor of the edifice, to the great danger of his neck, and be covered at the same time with the 'base laughter and joking' of his brethren."

Externally the Collegiate Church is sorely wasted and much blackened; and, save at some little distance, its light and elegant proportions fail to tell. The sooty atmosphere of the place has imparted to it its own dingy hue; while the soft New Red Sandstone of which it is built has resigned all the nicer tracery intrusted to its keeping to the slow wear of the four centuries which have elapsed since the erection of the edifice. But in the interior all is fresh and sharp as when the field of Bosworth was stricken. What first impresses as unusual is the blaze of light which fills the place. For the expected dim solemnity of an old ecclesiastical edifice, one finds the full glare of a modern assembly-room; the day-light streams in through numerous windows, mullioned with slim shafts of stone curiously intertwisted atop, and plays amid tall slender columns, arches of graceful sweep, and singularly elegant groinings, that shoot out their clusters of stony branches, light and graceful as the expanding boughs of some lime or poplar grove. The air of the place is gay, not solemn; nor are the subjects of its numerous sculptures of a kind suited to deepen the impression. Not a few of the carvings which decorate every patch of wall are of the most ludicrous character.

Rows of grotesque heads look down into the nave from the spandrels: some twist their features to the one side of the face, some to the other; some wink hard, as if exceedingly in joke; some troll out their tongue; some give expression to a lugubrious mirth, others to a ludicrous sorrow. In the choir, — of course, a still holier part of the edifice than the nave, — the sculptor seems to have let his imagination altogether run riot. In one compartment there sits, with a birch over his shoulder, an old fox, stern of aspect as Goldsmith's schoolmaster, engaged in teaching two cubs to read. In another, a respectable-looking boar, elevated on his hind legs, is playing on the bag-pipe, while his hopeful family, four young pigs, are dancing to his music behind their trough. In yet another, there is a hare, contemplating with evident satisfaction a boiling pot, which contains a dog in a fair way of becoming tender. But in yet another the priestly designer seems to have lost sight of prudence and decorum altogether: the chief figure in the piece is a monkey administering extreme unction to a dying man, while a party of other monkeys are plundering the poor sufferer of his effects, and gobbling up his provisions. A Scotch Highlander's faith in the fairies is much less a reality now than it has been; but few Scotch Highlanders would venture to take such liberties with their neighbors the "good people," as the old ecclesiastics of Manchester took with the services of their religion.

It is rather difficult for a stranger in such a place to follow with strict attention the lesson of the day. To the sermon, however, which was preached in a surplice, I found it comparatively easy to listen. The Sabbath — a red-letter one — was the twice famous St. Bartholomew's day, associated in the history of Protestantism with the barbarous massacre of the French Huguenots, and in the history of Puritanism with the

6*

ejection of the English non-conforming ministers after the Restoration; and the sermon was a labored defence of saints' days in general, and of the claims of St. Bartholomew's day in particular. There was not a very great deal known of St. Bartholomew, said the clergyman; but this much at least we all know, — he was a good man, — an exceedingly good man: it would be well for us to be all like him; and it was evidently our duty to be trying to be as like him as we could. As for saints' days, there could be no doubt about them: they were very admirable things; they had large standing in tradition, as might be seen from ecclesiastical history, and the writings of the later fathers; and large standing, too, in the Church of England, — a fact which no one acquainted with "our excellent Prayer-Book" could in the least question; nay, it would seem as if they had even some standing in Scripture itself. Did not St. Paul remind Timothy of the faith that had dwelt in Lois and Eunice, his grandmother and mother? and had we not therefore a good Scriptural argument for keeping saints' days, seeing that Timothy must have respected the saint his grandmother? I looked round me to see how the congregation was taking all this, but the congregation bore the tranquil air of people quite used to such sermons. There were a good many elderly gentlemen who had dropped asleep, and a good many more who seemed speculating in cotton; but the general aspect was one of heavy, inattentive decency: there was, in short, no class of countenances within the building that bore the appropriate expression, save the stone countenances on the wall.

My fellow-guests in the coffee-house in which I lodged were, an English Independent, a man of some intelligence, — and a young Scotchman, a member of the Relief body. They had been hearing they told me, an excellent discourse, in which the preacher had made impressive allusion to the historic associations of the day; in especial, to the time

> "When good Coligny's hoary hair was dabbled all in blood."

I greatly tickled them, by giving them, in turn, a simple outline, without note or comment, of the sermon I had been hearing. The clergyman from whom it emanated, maugre his use of the surplice in the pulpit, and his zeal for saints' days, was, I was informed, not properly a Puseyite, but rather one of the class of stiff High Churchmen, that germinate into Puseyites when their creed becomes vital within them. For the thorough High Churchman bears, it would appear, the same sort of resemblance to the energetic Puseyite, that a dried bulb in the florist's drawer does to a bulb of the same species in his flower-garden, when swollen with the vegetative juices, and rich in leaf and flower. It is not always the most important matters that take the strongest hold of the mind. The sermon and the ludicrous carvings, linked as closely together, by a trick of the associative faculty, as Cruikshank's designs in Oliver Twist with the letter-press of Dickens, continued to haunt me throughout the evening.

I lodged within a stone-cast of the terminus of the Great Manchester and Birmingham Railway. I could hear the roaring of the trains along the line, from morning till near mid-day, and during the whole afternoon; and, just as the evening was setting in, I sauntered down to the gate by which a return train was discharging its hundreds of passengers, fresh from the Sabbath amusements of the country, that I might see how they looked. There did not seem much of enjoyment about the wearied and somewhat draggled groups: they wore, on the contrary, rather an unhappy physiognomy, as if they had missed spending the day quite to their minds, and were now returning sad and disappointed, to the round of toil, from which it ought to have proved a sweet interval of relief. A congregation just dismissed from hearing a vigorous evening discourse would have borne, to a certainty, a more cheerful air. There was not much actual drunkenness among the crowd, — thanks to the preference which the Englishman gives to his ale over ardent spirits, — not a tithe of what I would have witnessed, on a similar occasion, in my own country. A few there were, however, evidently muddled; and I saw one positive scene. A young man considerably in liquor had quarrelled with his mistress, and, threatening to throw himself into the Irwell, off he had bolted in the direction of the river. There was a shriek of agony from the young woman, and a cry of "stop him, stop him," to which a tall, bulky Englishman, of the true John Bull type, had coolly responded, by thrusting forth his foot as he passed, and tripping him at full length on the pavement; and for a few minutes all was hubbub and confusion. With, however, this exception, the aspect of the numerous passengers had a sort of animal decency about it, which one might in vain look for among the Sunday travellers on a Scotch railway. Sunday seems greatly less connected with the fourth commandment in the humble English mind than in that of Scotland, and so a less disreputable portion of the people go abroad. There is a considerable difference, too, between masses of men simply ignorant of religion, and masses of men broken loose from it; and the Sabbath-contemning Scotch belong to the latter category. With the humble Englishman trained up to no regular habit of church-going, Sabbath is pudding-day, and clean-shirt-day, and a day for lolling on the grass opposite the sun, and, if there be a river or canal hard by, for trying how the gudgeons bite, or, if in the neighborhood of a railway, for taking a short trip to some country inn, famous for its cakes and ale; but to the humble Scot become English in his Sabbath views, the day is, in most cases, a time of sheer recklessness and dissipation. There is much truth in the shrewd remark of Sir Walter Scott, that the Scotch, once metamorphosed into Englishmen, make very mischievous Englishmen indeed.

Among the existing varieties of the genus philanthropist, — benevolent men bent on bettering the condition of the masses, — there is a variety who would fain send out our working people to the country on Sabbaths, to become happy and innocent in smelling primroses, and stringing daisies on grass stalks. An excellent scheme theirs, if they but knew it, for sinking a people into ignorance and brutality, — for filling a country with gloomy workhouses, and the workhouses with unhappy paupers. 'T is pity rather that the institution of the Sabbath, in its economic bearings, should not be better understood by the utilitarian. The problem which it furnishes is not particularly difficult, if one could be but made to understand, as a first step in the process, that it is really worth solving. The mere animal, that has to pass six days of the week in hard labor, benefits greatly by a seventh day of mere animal rest and enjoyment: the repose according to its nature proves of signal use to it, just because *it is* repose according to its nature. But man is not a mere animal: what is best for the ox and the ass is not best for him; and in order to degrade him into a poor unintellectual slave, over whom tyranny, in its caprice, may trample rough-shod, it is but necessary to tie him down, animal-like, during his six working days, to hard, engrossing labor, and to convert the seventh into a day of frivolous, unthinking relaxation. History speaks with much emphasis on the point. The old despotic Stuarts were tolerable adepts in the art of king-craft, and knew well what they were doing when they backed with their authority the Book of Sports. The merry, unthinking serfs, who, early in the reign of Charles the First, danced on Sabbaths round the Maypole, were afterwards the ready tools of despotism, and fought that England might be enslaved. The Ironsides, who, in the cause of civil and religious freedom, bore them down, were staunch Sabbatarians.

In no history, however, is the value of the Sabbath more strikingly illustrated than in that of the Scotch people during the seventeenth and the larger portion of the eighteenth centuries. Religion and the Sabbath were their sole instructors, and this in times so little favorable to the cultivation of mind, so darkened by persecution and stained with blood, that, in at least the earlier of these centuries, we derive our knowledge of the character and amount of the popular intelligence mainly from the death-testimonies of our humbler martyrs, here and there corroborated by the incidental evidence of writers such as Burnet.* In these noble addresses from prison and scaffold, — the composition of men drafted by oppression almost at random from out the general mass, — we see how vigorously our Presbyterian people had learned to think, and how well to give their thinking expression. In the quieter times which followed the Revolution, the Scottish peasantry existed as at once the most provident and intellectual in Europe; and a moral and

* Burnet, afterwards the celebrated Whig Bishop, was one of six divines sent out by Archbishop Leighton, in 1670, to argue the Scotch people into Episcopacy. But the mission was by no means successful. "The people of the country," says Burnet, "came generally to hear us, though not in great crowds. We were indeed amazed to see a poor commonalty so capable to argue upon points of government, and on the bounds to be set to the power of princes in matters of religion. Upon all these topics they had texts of Scripture at hand, and were ready with their answers to anything that was said to them. This measure of knowledge was spread even among the meanest of them, — their cottagers and their servants." (Memoirs, vol. i. p. 431.)

instructed people pressed outwards beyond the narrow bounds of their country, and rose into offices of trust and importance in all the nations of the world. There were no Societies for the Diffusion of Useful Knowledge in those days. But the Sabbath was kept holy: it was a day from which every dissipating frivolity was excluded by a stern sense of duty. The popular mind, with weight imparted to it by its religious earnestness, and direction by the pulpit addresses of the day, expatiated on matters of grave import, of which the tendency was to concentrate and strengthen, not scatter and weaken, the faculties; and the secular cogitations of the week came to bear, in consequence, a Sabbath-day stamp of depth and solidity. The one day in the seven struck the tone for the other six. Our modern apostles of popular instruction rear up no such men among the masses as were developed under the Sabbatarian system in Scotland. Their aptest pupils prove but the loquacious *gabbers* of their respective workshops, — shallow superficialists, that bear on the surface of their minds a thin diffusion of ill-remembered facts and crude theories; and rarely indeed do we see them rising in the scale of society: they become Socialists by hundreds, and Chartists by thousands, and get no higher. The disseminator of mere useful knowledge takes aim at the popular ignorance; but his inept and unscientific gunnery does not include in its calculations the parabolic curve of man's spiritual nature; and so, aiming direct at the mark, he aims too low, and the charge falls short.

CHAPTER IV.

Quit Manchester for Wolverhampton. — Scenery of the New Red Sandstone; apparent Repetition of Pattern. — The frequent Marshes of England; curiously represented in the National Literature; Influence on the National Superstitions. — Wolverhampton. — Peculiar Aspect of the Dudley Coal-field; striking Passage in its History. — The Rise of Birmingham into a great Manufacturing Town an Effect of the Development of its Mineral Treasures. — Upper Ludlow Deposit; Aymestry Limestone; both Deposits of peculiar Interest to the Scotch Geologist. — The *Lingula Lewisii* and *Terebratula Wilsoni.* — General Resemblance of the Silurian Fossils to those of the Mountain Limestone. — First-born of the Vertebrata yet known. — Order of Creation. — The Wren's Nest. — Fossils of the Wenlock Limestone; in a State of beautiful Keeping. — Anecdote. — *Asaphus Caudatus;* common, it would seem, to both the Silurian and Carboniferous Rocks. — Limestone Miners. — Noble Gallery excavated in the Hill.

I QUITTED Manchester by the morning train, and travelled through a flat New Red Sandstone district, on the Birmingham Railway, for about eighty miles. One finds quite the sort of country here for travelling over by steam. If one misses seeing a bit of landscape, as the carriages hurry through, and the objects in the foreground look dim and indistinct, and all in motion, as if seen through water, it is sure to be repeated in the course of a few miles, and again and again repeated. I was reminded, as we hurried along, and the flat country opened and spread out on either side, of webs of carpet stuff nailed down to pieces of boarding, and presenting, at regular distances, returns of the same rich pattern. Red detached houses stand up amid the green fields; little bits of brick villages lie grouped beside cross roads; irregular patches of wood occupy nooks and corners; lines of poplars rise tall and taper amid straggling cottages; and then, having once passed houses, villages, and woods, we seem as if we had to pass them again and again; the red detached houses return, the bits of villages, the woody nooks and corners, the lines of taper poplars amid the cottages; and thus the repetitions of the pattern run on and on.

In a country so level as England there must be many a swampy hollow furnished with no outlet to its waters. The bogs and marshes of the midland and southern counties formed of old the natural strongholds, in which the people, in times of extremity, sheltered from the invader. Alfred's main refuge, when all others failed him, was a bog of Somersetshire. When passing this morning along frequent fields of osiers and wide-spread marshes, bristling with thickets of bulrushes and reeds, I was led to think of what had never before occurred to me, — the considerable amount of imagery and description which the poets of England have transferred from scenery of this character into the national literature. There is in English verse much whispering of osiers beside silent streams, and much waving of sedges over quiet waters. Shakspeare has his exquisite pictures of slow-gliding currents,

> "Making sweet music with the enamelled stones,
> And giving gentle kisses to each sedge
> They overtake in their lone pilgrimage."

And Milton, too, of water-nymphs

> "Sitting by rushy fringed bank,
> Where grows the willow and the osier dank;
>
> "Under the glassy, cool, translucent wave,
> In twisted braids of lilies knitting
> The loose train of their amber-dropping hair;

7

or of "sighing sent," by the "parting genius,"

> "From haunted spring and dale,
> Edged with poplar pale."

We find occasional glimpses of the same dank scenery in Collins, Cowper, and Crabbe; and very frequent ones, in our own times, in the graphic descriptions of Alfred Tennyson and Thomas Hood.

> "One willow o'er the river wept,
> And shook the wave as the wind did sigh;
> Above in the wind sported the swallow,
> Chasing itself at its own wild will;
> And far through the marish green, and still,
> The tangled water-courses slept,
> Shot over with purple, and green, and yellow."

Not less striking is at least one of the pictures drawn by Hood:—

> "The coot was swimming in the reedy pool,
> Beside the water-hen, so soon affrighted;
> And in the weedy moat, the heron, fond
> Of solitude, alighted;
> The moping heron, motionless and stiff,
> That on a stone as silently and stilly
> Stood, an apparent sentinel, as if
> To guard the water-lily."

The watery flats of the country have had also their influence on the popular superstitions. The delusive tapers that spring up a-nights from stagnant bogs and fens must have been of frequent appearance in the more marshy districts of England; and we accordingly find, that of all the national goblins the goblin of the wandering night-fire, whether recognized as Jack-of-the-Lantern or Will-of-the-Wisp, was one of the best known.

"She was pinched and pulled, she said,
And he by friar's lantern led."

Or, as the exquisite poet who produced this couplet more elaborately describes the apparition in his "Paradise Lost,"

"A wandering fire,
Compact of unctuous vapor, which the night
Kindles through agitation to a flame,
Which oft, they say, some evil spirit attends,
Hovering and blazing with delusive light,
Leading the amazed night-wanderer from his way
Through bogs and mires, and oft through pond or pool,
There swallowed up and lost, from succor far."

Scarce inferior to even the description of Milton is that of Collins: —

"Ah, homely swains! your homeward steps ne'er lose;
Let not dank Will mislead you on the heath:
Dancing in mirky night, o'er fen and lake,
He glows, to draw you downward to your death,
In his bewitched, low, marshy willow-brake.
What though, far off from some dark dell espied,
His glimmering mazes cheer the excursive sight?
Yet turn, ye wanderers, turn your steps aside,
Nor trust the guidance of that faithless light;
For watchful, lurking, 'mid the unrustling reed,
At these mirk hours, the wily monster lies,
And listens oft to hear the passing steed,
And frequent round him rolls his sullen eyes,
If chance his savage wrath may some weak wretch surprise."

One soon wearies of the monotony of railway travelling, — of hurrying through a country, stage after stage, without incident or advantage; and so I felt quite glad enough, when the train stopped at Wolverhampton, to find myself once more at freedom and afoot. There will be an end, surely, to all works of travels when the railway system of the world shall be completed. I passed direct through Wolverhampton, — a large but rather uninteresting assemblage of red-brick houses, copped with red-tile roofs, slippered with red-tile floors, and neither in its component parts nor in its grouping differing in any perceptible degree from several scores of the other assemblages of red-brick houses that form the busier market-towns of England. The town has been built in the neighborhood of the Dudley coal-basin, on an incoherent lower deposit of New Red Sandstone, unfitted for the purposes of the stone-mason, but peculiarly well suited, in some of its superficial argillaceous beds, for those of the brick-maker. Hence the prevailing color and character of the place ; and such, in kind, are the circumstances that impart to the great majority of English towns so very different an aspect from that borne by our Scottish ones. They are the towns of a brick and tile manufacturing country, rich in coal and clay, but singularly poor in sandstone quarries.

I took the Dudley road, and left the scattered suburbs of the town but a few hundred yards behind me, when the altered appearance of the country gave evidence that I had quitted the New Red Sandstone, and had entered on the Coal Measures. On the right, scarce a gun-shot from the way-side, there stretched away a rich though comparatively thinly-inhabited country, — green, undulated, lined thickly, lengthwise and athwart, with luxuriant hedge-rows, sparsely sprinkled with farm-houses, and over-canopied this morning by a clear blue sky; while on the left, far as the eye could penetrate through a mud-colored atmosphere of smoke and culm, there spread out a barren uneven wilderness of slag and shale, the debris of lime-kilns and smelting works, and of coal and ironstone pits; and amid the dun haze there stood up what seemed a continuous city of fire-belching furnaces and smoke-vomiting chimneys, blent with numerous groups of little dingy buildings, the dwellings of iron-smelters and miners. Wherever the New Red Sandstone extends, the country wears a sleek unbroken skin of green; wherever the Coal Measures spread away, lake-like, from the lower edges of this formation, all is verdureless, broken, and gray. The coloring of the two formations could be scarcely better defined in a geological map than here on the face of the landscape. There is no such utter ruin of the surface in our mining districts in Scotland. The rubbish of the subterranean workings is scarce at all suffered to encroach, save in widely-scattered hillocks, on the arable superficies; and these hillocks the indefatigable agriculturist is ever levelling and carrying away, to make way for the plough; whereas, so entirely has the farmer been beaten from off the field here, and so thickly do the heaps cumber the surface, that one might almost imagine the land had been seized in the remote past by some mortal sickness, and, after vomiting out its bowels, had lain stone-dead ever since. The laboring inhabitants of this desert — a rude, improvident, Cyclopean race, indifferent to all save the mineral treasures of the soil — are rather graphically designated in the neighboring districts, where I found them exceedingly cheaply rated, as "the lie-wasters." Some six or eight centuries ago, the Dudley coal-field existed as a wild forest, in which a few semi-barbarous iron-smelters and charcoal-burners carried on their solitary labors; and which was remarkable chiefly for a seam of coal thirty feet in thickness, which, like some of the coal-seams of the United States, cropped out at the surface, and was wrought among the trees in the open air. A small colony of workers in iron of various kinds settled in the neighborhood, and their congregated forges and cottage-dwellings formed a little noisy hamlet amid the woodlands. The miner explored, to greater and still greater depths, the mineral treasures of the coal-field, the ever-resounding, ever-smoking village added house to house and forge to forge, as the fuel and the ironstone heaps accumulated; till at length the three thick bands of dark ore, and the ten-yard coal-seam of the basin, though restricted to a space greatly less in area than some of our Scottish lakes, produced, out of the few congregated huts, the busy town of Birmingham, with its two hundred and twenty thousand inhabitants. And as the rise of the place has been connected with the development of the mineral treasures of its small but exceedingly rich coal-field, their exhaustion, unless there open up to it new fields of industry, must induce its decline. There is a day coming, though a still distant one, when the miner shall have done with this wilderness of debris and chimneys, just as the charcoal-burner had done with it when the woodlands were exhausted ages ago, or as the farmer had done with it at a considerably later period; and when it shall exist as an uninhabited desert, full of gloomy pitfalls, half-hidden by a stunted vegetation, and studded with unseemly ruins of brick; and the neighboring city, like a beggared spendthrift, that, after having run through his patrimony, continues to reside in the house of his ancestors, shall have, in all probability, to shut up many an apartment, and leave many a forsaken range of offices and outhouses to sink into decay.

The road began to ascend from the low platform of the coal-field, along the shoulder of a green hill that rises some six or seven hundred feet over the level of the sea, — no inconsiderable elevation in this part of the kingdom. There were no longer heaps of dark-colored debris on either hand; and I saw for the first time in England, where there had been a cutting into the acclivity, to lower the angle of the ascent, a section of rock much resembling our Scotch grauwacke of the southern counties. Unlike our Scotch grauwacke, however, I found that almost every fragment of the mass contained its fossil, — some ill-preserved terebratula or leptæna, or some sorely weathered coralline: but all was doubtful and obscure; and I looked round me, though in vain, for some band of lime compact enough to exhibit in its sharp-edged casts the characteristic peculiarities of the group. A spruce wagoner, in a blue frock much roughened with needle-work, came whistling down the hill beside his team, and I inquired of him whether there were limestone quarries in the neighborhood. "Yez, yez, lots of lime just afore thee," said the wagoner; "can't miss the way, if thou lookest to the hill-side." I went on for a few hundred yards, and found an extensive quarry existing as a somewhat dreary-looking dell, deeply scooped out of the acclivity on the left, with heaps of broken grass-grown debris on the one side of the excavation, and on the other a precipitous front of gray lichened rock, against which there leaned a line of open kilns and a ruinous hut.

The quarriers were engaged in playing mattock and lever on an open front in the upper part of the dell, which, both from its deserted appearance and the magnitude of its weather-stained workings, appeared to be much less extensively wrought than at some former period. I felt a peculiar interest in examining the numerous fossils of the deposit, — such an interest as that experienced by the over-curious Calender in the Arabian Nights, when first introduced into the hall of the winged horse, from which, though free to roam over all the rest of the palace, with its hundred gates and its golden doors, he had been long sedulously excluded. I had now entered, for the first time, into a chamber of the grand fossiliferous museum, — the great stone-record edifice of our island, — of which I had not thought the less frequently from the circumstance that I was better acquainted with the chamber that lies directly over head, if I may so speak, with but a thin floor between, than with any other in the erection. I had been laboring for years in the Lower Old Red Sandstone, and had acquainted myself with its winged and plate-covered, its enamelled and tubercle-roughened ichthyolites; but there is no getting down in Scotland into the cellarage of the edifice: it is as thoroughly a mystery to the mere Scotch geologist as the cellarage of Todgers' in Martin Chuzzlewit, of which a stranger kept the key, was to the inmates of that respectable tavern. Here, however, I had got fairly into the cellar at last. The frontage of fossiliferous grauwacke-looking rock, by the way-side, which I had just examined, is known, thanks to Sir Roderick Murchison, to belong to the Upper Ludlow deposit, — the Silurian base on which the Old Red Sandstone rests; and I had now got a story further down, and was among the Aymestry Limestones.

The first fossil I picked up greatly resembled in size and form a pistol-bullet. It proved to be one of the most characteristic shells of the formation, — the *Terebratula Wilsoni.* Nor was the second I found — the *Lingula Lewisii*, a bivalve formed like the blade of a wooden shovel — less characteristic. The Lingula still exists in some two or three species in the distant Moluccas. There was but one of these known in the times of Cuvier, the *Lingula anatina;* and so unlike was it deemed by the naturalist to any of its contemporary mollusca, that of the single species he formed not only a distinct genus, but also an independent class. The existing, like the fossil shell, resembles the blade of a wooden shovel; but the shovel has also a handle, and in this mainly consists its dissimilarity to any other bivalve: a cylindrical cartilaginous stem or foot-stalk elevates it some three or four inches over the rocky base to which it is attached, just as the handle of a shovel, stuck half a foot into the earth, at the part where the hand grasps it, would elevate the blade over the surface, or as the stem of a tulip elevates the flower over the soil. A community of Lingulæ must resemble, in their deep-sea haunts, a group of Lilliputian shovels, reversed by the laborers to indicate their work completed, or a bed of half-folded tulips, raised on stiff, dingy stems, and exhibiting flattened petals of delicate green. I am not aware that any trace of the cartilaginous foot-stalk has been yet detected in fossil Lingulæ; — like those of this quarry, they are mere shovel-blades divested of the handles: but in all that survives of them, or could be expected to survive, — the calcareous portion, — they are identical in type with the living mollusc of the Moluccas. What most strikes in the globe-shaped terebratula, their contemporary, is the singularly antique character of the ventral margin: it seems moulded in the extreme of an ancient fashion, long since gone out. Instead of running continuously round in one plane, like the margins of our existing cockle, venus, or mactra, so as to form, when the valves are shut, a rectilinear line of division, it presents in the centre a huge dovetail, so that the lower valve exhibits in its middle front a square gateway, which we see occupied, when the mouth is closed, by a portcullis-like projection, dependent from the margin of the upper valve. Margins of this antique form characterize some of the terebratulæ of even the Chalk, and the spirifers of the Carboniferous Limestone; but in none of the comparatively modern shells is the square portcullis-shaped indentation so strongly indicated as in the *Terebratula Wilsoni.* I picked up several other fossils in the quarry: the *Orthis orbicularis* and *Orthis lunata;* the *Atrypa affinis;* several ill-preserved portions of orthoceratite, belonging chiefly, so far as their state of keeping enabled me to decide, to the *Orthoceras bullatum;* a small, imperfectly conical coral, that more resembled the *Stromatopora concentrica* of the Wenlock rocks, than any of the other Silurian corals figured by Murchison; and a few minute sprigs of the *Favosites polymorpha.* The concretionary character of the limestone of the deposit has militated against the preservation of the larger organisms which it encloses. Of the smaller shells, many are in a beautiful state of keeping: like some of the comparatively modern shells of the Oolite, they still retain unaltered the silvery lustre of the nacre, and present outlines as sharp and well defined, with every delicate angle unworn, and every minute stria undefaced, as if inhabited but yesterday by the living molluscs; whereas most of the bulkier fossils, from the broken and detached nature of the rock, — a nodular limestone embedded in strata of shale, — exist as mere fragments. What perhaps first strikes the eye is the deep-sea character of the deposit, and its general resemblance to the Mountain Limestone. Nature, though she dropped between the times of the Silurian and Carboniferous oceans many of her genera, and, with but a few marked exceptions, all her species,* seems to have scarce at all altered the general types after which the productions of both oceans were moulded.

I could find in this quarry of the Aymestry Limestone no trace of aught higher than the Cephalopoda, — none of those plates, scales, spines, or teeth, indicative of the vertebrate animals, which so abound in the Lower Old Red Sandstones of Scotland. And yet the vertebrata seem to have existed at the

* "Upwards of eight hundred extinct species of animals have been described as belonging to the earliest or Protozoic and Silurian period; and of these, only about one hundred are found also in the overlying Devonian series; while but fifteen are common to the whole Palæozoic period, and not one extends beyond it." (*Ansted*, 1844.)

time. The famous bone-bed of the Upper Silurian system, with its well-marked ichthyolitic remains, occurs in the Upper Ludlow Rock, — the deposit immediately over head. We find it shelved high, if I may so speak, in the first story of the system, reckoning from the roof downwards; the calcareous deposit in which this hill-side quarry has been hollowed forms a second story; the Lower Ludlow Rock a third; and in yet a fourth, the Wenlock Limestone: just one remove over the Lower Silurians, — for the Wenlock Shale constitutes the base story of the upper division, — there have been found the remains of a fish, or rather minute portions of the remains of a fish, the most ancient yet known to the geologist. "Take the Lower Silurians all over the globe," says Sir Roderick Murchison, in a note to the writer of these chapters, which bears date no further back than last July, "and they have never yet offered the trace of a fish." It is to be regretted that the ichthyolite of the Wenlock Limestone — the first-born of the vertebrata whose birth and death seem entered in the geologic register — has not been made the subject of a careful memoir, illustrated by a good engraving. One is naturally desirous to know all that can be known regarding the first entrance in the drama of existence of a new class in creation, and to have the place and date which the entry bears in the record fairly established. The evidence, however, though not yet made patent to the geological brotherhood, seems to be solid. It has at least satisfied a writer in the *Edinburgh Review* of last year, generally recognized as one of the master-geologists of the age. "We have seen," says Mr. Sedgwick, the understood author of the article, "characteristic portions of a fish derived from the shales alternating with the Wenlock Limestone. This ichthyolite, to speak in the technical language of Agassiz, undoubtedly belongs to the Cestraciont family, of the Placoid order. —

proving to demonstration that the oldest known fossil fish belongs to the highest type of that division of the vertebrata.'

A strange *debut* this, and of deep interest to the student of nature. The veil of mystery must forever rest over the *act* of creation; but it is something to know of its *order*, — to know that, as exhibited in the great geologic register, graven, like the decalogue of old, on tables of stone, there is an analogy maintained, that indicates identity of *style* with the order specified in the Mosaic record as that observed by the Creator in producing the scene of things to which we ourselves belong. In both records, — the sculptured and the written, — periods of creative energy are indicated as alternating with periods of rest, — *days* in which the Creator labored, with *nights* in which He ceased from his labors, again to resume them in the morning. According to both records, higher and lower existences were called into being successively, not simultaneously; — according to both, after each interval of repose, the succeeding period of activity witnessed loftier and yet loftier efforts of production; — according to both, though in the earlier stages there was incompleteness in the scale of existence, there was yet no imperfection in the individual existences of which the scale was composed; — at the termination of the first, as of the last day of creation, all in its kind was *good*. Ere any of the higher natures existed,

> " God saw that all was good,
> When even and morn recorded the third day."

I quitted the quarry in the hill-side, and walked on through the village of Sedgley, towards a second and much more striking hill, well known to geologists and lovers of the picturesque as the "Wren's Nest." A third hill, that of Dudley, beautifully wooded and capped by its fine old castle, lies direct in the same line; so that the three hills taken together form a chain of eminences, which run diagonally, for some four or five miles, into the middle of the coal-basin; and which, rising high from the surrounding level, resemble steep-sided islets in an Alpine lake. It is a somewhat curious circumstance, that while the enclosing shores of the basin are formed of the Lower New Red Sandstone, and the basin itself of the Upper and Lower Coal Measures, these three islets are all Silurian; the first,—that of Sedgley,—which I had just quitted, presenting in succession the Upper Ludlow Rock and Aymestry Limestone, with some of the inferior deposits on which these rest; and the second and third the Wenlock Shale and Wenlock Limestone. The "Wren's Nest," as I approached it this day along green lanes and over quiet fields, fringed with trees, presented the appearance of some bold sea-promontory, crowned atop with stunted wood, and flanked by a tall, pale-gray precipice, continuous as a rampart for a full half-mile. But, to borrow from one of Byron's descriptions,

> "There is no sea to lave its base,
> But a most living landscape, and the wave
> Of woods and corn-fields, and the abodes of men
> Scattered at intervals, and wreathing smoke
> Rising from rustic roofs."

Such is the profile of the hill on both sides. Seen in front, it presents the appearance of a truncated dome; while atop we find it occupied by an elliptical, crater-like hollow, that has been grooved deep, by the hand of Nature, along the flat summit, so as to form a huge nest, into which the gigantic roc of eastern story might drop a hundred such eggs as the one familiar to the students of the great voyager Sinbad. And hence the name of the eminence. John Bull, making merry, in one of his humorous moods, with its imposing greatness, has termed it the " *Wren's* Nest." I came up to its gray lines of sloping precipice, and found them so thickly charged with their sepulchral tablets and pictorial epitaphs, that, like the walls of some Egyptian street of tombs, almost every square yard bears its own lengthened inscription. These sloping precipices, situated as they now are in central England, once formed a deep-sea bottom, far out of reach of land, whose green recesses were whitened by innumerable corals and corallines, amid which ancient shells, that loved the profounder depths, terebratula, leptæna, and spirifer, lay anchored; while innumerable trilobites crept sluggishly above zoophyte and mollusc, on the thickly-inhabited platform; and the orthoceras and the bellerophon floated along the surface high over head. A strange story, surely, but not more strange than true: in at least the leading details there is no possibility of mistaking the purport of the inscriptions.

The outer front of precipice we find composed of carbonate of lime, alternating with thin layers of a fine-grained aluminous shale, which yields to the weather, betraying, in every more exposed portion of the rock, the organic character of the lime-stone. Wherever the impalpable shale has been washed away, we find the stone as sharply sculptured beneath as a Chinese snuff-box; with this difference, however, that the figures are more nicely relieved, and grouped much more thickly together. We ascertain that every component particle of the roughened ground on which they lie, even the most minute, is organic. It is composed of portions of the most diminutive zoophytes,— retipora, or festinella, or the microscopic joints of thread-like crinoideal tentacula; while the bolder figures that stand up in high relief over it are delicately sculptured shells of antique type and proportions, crustacea of the trilobite family, corals massive or branched, graceful gorgonia, and the stems and pelvic bulbs of crinoidea. The impalpable shales of the hill seem to have been deposited from above, — the soil of aluminous shores carried far by the sea, and thrown down in the calm on beds of zoophytes and shells; whereas the lime appears to have been elaborated, not deposited: it grew upon the spot slowly and imperceptibly as age succeeded age, — a secretion of animal life.

After passing slowly around the hill, here striking off a shell, there disinterring a trilobite, — here admiring some huge mass of chain-coral, that, even when in its recent state, I could not have raised from the ground, — there examining, with the assistance of the lens, the minute meshes of some net-like festinella, scarce half a nail's breadth in area, — I sat me down in the sunshine in the opening of a deserted quarry, hollowed in the dome-like front of the hill, amid shells and corallines that had been separated from the shaly matrix by the disintegrating influences of the weather. The organisms lay as thickly around me as recent shells and corals on a tropical beach. The labors of Murchison had brought me acquainted with their forms, and with the uncouth names given them in this late age of the world, so many long *creations* after they had been dead and buried, and locked up in rock; but they were new to me in their actually existing state as fossils; and the buoyant delight with which I squatted among them, glass in hand, to examine and select, made me smile a moment after, when I bethought me that my little boy Bill could have shown scarce greater eagerness, when set down, for the first time, in his third summer, amid the shells and pebbles of the sea-shore. But I daresay most of my readers, if transported for a time to the ocean shores of Mars or of Venus, would manifest some such eagerness in ascertaining the types in which, in these remote planets, the Creator exhibits life. And here, strewed thickly around me, were the shells and corals of the Silurian ocean,— an ocean quite as dissimilar in its productions to that of the present day, as the oceans of either Mars or Venus. It takes a great deal to slacken the zeal of some pursuits. have been told by a relative, now deceased,— a man strongly imbued with a taste for natural history, who fought under Abercromby in Egypt,— that though the work was rather warm on the day he first leaped ashore on that celebrated land, and the beach somewhat cumbered by the slain, he could not avoid casting a glance at the white shells which mingled with the sand at his feet, to see whether they greatly differed from those of his own country; and that one curious shell, which now holds an honored place in my small collection, he found time to transfer, amid the sharp whizzing of the bullets, to his waistcoat pocket.

I filled a small box with minute shells and corals,— terebratulæ of some six or eight distinct species, a few leptænæ and orthes, a singularly beautiful astrea, figured by Murchison as *Astrea ananas*, or the pine-apple astrea, several varieties of cyathophyllum, and some two or three species of porites and limaria. To some of the corals I found thin mat-like zoophytes of the character of flustræ attached; to others, what seemed small serpulæ. Out of one mass of shale I disinterred the head of a stone lily,— the *Cyathocrinites pyriformis*,— beautifully preserved; in a second mass I found the fully-expanded pelvis and arms of a different genus,— the *Actinocrinites moniliformis*,— but it fell to pieces ere I could extricate it. I was more successful in detaching entire a fine specimen of what I find figured by Murchison, though with a doubtful note of interrogation attached, as a gorgonia or sea-fan. I found much pleasure, too, in acquainting myself, though the specimens were not particularly fine, with disjointed portions of trilobites, — now a head turned up, — now the caudle portion of the shell, exhibiting the inner side and abdominal rim, — now a few detached joints. In some of the specimens, — invariably headless ones, — the body seems scarce larger than that of a common house-fly. Here, as amid the upper deposits at Sedgley, I was struck with the general resemblance of the formation to the Carboniferous Limestone: not a few of the shells are at least generically similar; there is the same abundance of crinoideæ and festinellæ; and in some localities nearly the same profusion of the large and the minuter corals. And though trilobites are comparatively rare in the Mountain Limestone of Britain, I have found in that of Dryden, in the neighborhood of Edinburgh, the body of at least one trilobite, which I could not distinguish from a species of frequent occurrence in the Wenlock Limestone, — the *Asaphus Caudatus*. I may remind the reader, in corroboration of the fact, that Buckland, in his "Bridgewater Treatise," figures two decapitated specimens of this trilobite, one of which was furnished by the Carboniferous Limestone of Northumberland, and the other by the Transition Limestone near Leominster. There obtains, however, one striking difference between the more ancient and more modern deposits: I have rarely explored richly fossiliferous beds of the Mountain Limestone, without now and then finding the scales of a fish, and now and then the impression of some land-plant washed from the shore; but in the Silurian hills of the Dudley coal-field, no trace of the vertebrata has yet been found, and no vegetable product of the land.

The sun had got far down in the west ere I quitted the deserted quarry, and took my way towards the distant town, not over, but through the hill, by a long gloomy corridor. I had been aware all day, that though apparently much alone, I had yet near neighbors: there had been an irregular succession of dull, half-smothered sounds, from the bowels of the earth; and at times, when in contact with the naked rock, I could feel, as the subterranean thunder pealed through the abyss, the solid mass trembling beneath me. The phenomena were those described by Wordsworth, as eliciting, in a scene of deep solitude, the mingled astonishment and terror of Peter Bell,—

"When, to confound his spiteful mirth,
A murmur pent within the earth,
In the dead earth, beneath the road,
Sudden arose! It swept along,
A muffled noise, a rumbling sound:
'Twas by a troop of miners made,
Plying with gunpowder their trade,
Some twenty fathoms under ground."

I was scarce prepared, however, for excavations of such imposing extent as the one into which I found the vaulted corridor open. It forms a long gallery, extending for hundreds of yards on either hand, with an overhanging precipice bare to the hill-top leaning perilously over on the one side, and a range of supporting buttresses cut out of the living rock, and perforated with lofty archways, planting at measured distances their strong feet, on the other. Through the openings between the buttresses,—long since divested, by a shaggy vegetation, of every stiff angularity borrowed from the tool of the miner,—the red light of evening was streaming, in well-defined patches, on the gray rock and broken floor. Each huge buttress threw its broad bar of shadow in the same direction; and thus the gallery, through its entire extent, was barred, zebra-like, with alternate belts of sun-light and gloom,—the "ebon and ivory" of Sir Walter's famed description. The rawness of artificial excavation has long since disappeared under the slow incrustations of myriads of lichens and mosses,—for the quarrier seems to have had done with the place for centuries; and if I could have but got rid of the recollection that it had been scooped out by handfuls for a far different purpose than that of making a grotto, I would have deemed it one of the finest caverns I ever saw. Immediately beside where the vaulted corridor enters the gallery, there is a wide dark chasm in the floor, furnished with a rusty chain-ladder, that gives perilous access to the lower workings of the hill. There was not light enough this evening to show half-way down; but far below, in the darkness, I could see the fiery glimmer of a torch reflected on a sheet of pitch-black water; and I afterwards learned that a branch of the Dudley and Birmingham Canal, invisible for a full mile, has been carried thus far into the bowels of the hill. I crossed over the nest-like valley scooped in the summit of the eminence, — a picturesque, solitary spot, occupied by a corn-field, and feathered all around on the edges with wood; and then crossing a second deep excavation, which, like the gallery described, is solely the work of the miner, I struck over a range of green fields, pleasantly grouped in the hollow between the Wren's-Nest-hill and the Castle-hill of Dudley, and reached the town just as the sun was setting. The valleys which interpose between the three Silurian islets of the Dudley basin are also Silurian; and as they have been hollowed by the denuding agencies out of useless beds of shale and mudstone, the miner has had no motive to bore into their sides and bottom, or to cumber the surface, as in the surrounding coal-field, with the ruins of the interior; and so the valleys, with their three lovely hills, form an oasis in the waste.

CHAPTER V.

Dudley significant Marks of the Mining Town. — Kindly Scotch Landlady. — Temperance Coffee-house. — Little Samuel the Teetotaller. — Curious Incident. — Anecdote. — The Resuscitated Spinet. — Forbearance of Little Samuel. — Dudley Museum; singularly rich in Silurian Fossils. — *Megalichthys Hibberti.* — Fossils from Mount Lebanon; very modern compared with those of the Hill of Dudley. — Geology peculiarly fitted to revolutionize one's Ideas of Modern and Ancient. — Fossils of extreme Antiquity furnished by a Canadian Township that had no name twenty years ago. — Fossils from the Old Egyptian Desert found to be comparatively of Yesterday. — Dudley Castle and Castle-hill. — Cromwell's Mission. — Castle finds a faithful Chronicler in an old Serving-maid. — Her Narrative. — Caves and Fossils of the Castle-hill. — Extensive Excavations. — Superiority of the Natural to the Artificial Cavern. — Fossils of the Scottish Grauwacke. — Analogy between the Female Lobster and the Trilobite.

The town of Dudley has been built half on the Silurian deposit, half on the coal-field, and is flanked on the one side by pleasant fields, traversed by quiet green lanes, and on the other by ruinous coal-workings and heaps of rubbish. But as the townspeople are not "lie-wasters," we find, in at least the neighborhood of the houses, the rubbish heaps intersected with innumerable rude fences, and covered by a rank vegetation. The mechanics of the place have cultivated without levelling them, so that for acres together they present the phenomenon of a cockling sea of gardens, — a rural Bay of Biscay agitated by the ground-swell, — with rows of cabbages and beds of carrots riding on the tops of huge waves, and gooseberry and currant bushes sheltering in deep troughs and hollows. I marked, as I passed through the streets, several significant traits of the mining town: one of the signboards, bearing the figure of a brawny half-naked man, armed with a short pick, and coiled up like an Andre Ferrara broadsword in a peck basket, indicates the inn of the "Jolly Miner;" the hardware shops exhibit in their windows rows of Davy's safety lamps, and vast piles of mining tools; and the footways show their sprinkling of rugged-looking men, attired in short jackets and trousers of undyed plaiding, sorely besmutted by the soil of an underground occupation. In some instances, the lamp still sticking in the cap, and the dazzled expression of countenance, as if the eye had not yet accommodated itself to the light, indicate the close proximity of the subterranean workings. I dropped into a respectable-looking tavern to order a chop and a glass of ale, and mark, meanwhile, whether it was such a place as I might convert into a home for a few days with any reasonable prospect of comfort. But I found it by much too favorite a resort of the miners, and that, whether they agreed or disputed, they were a noisy generation over their ale. The landlady, a kindly, portly dame, considerably turned of fifty, was a Scotchwoman, a native of Airdrie, who had long ago married an Englishman in her own country, and had now been settled in Dudley for more than thirty years. My northern accent seemed to bespeak her favor; and taking it for granted that I had come into England in quest of employment, but had not yet been successful in procuring any, she began to speak comfort to my dejection, by assuring me that *our* country folk in that part of the world were much respected, and rose always, if they had but character, into places of trust. I had borne with me, on my homely suit of russet, palpable marks of my labors at Sedgley and the Wren's Nest, and looked, I daresay, rather geological than genteel. Character and scholarship, said the landlady, drawing her inference, were just everything in that neighborhood. Most of the Scotch people who came the way, however poor, had both; and so, while the Irish always remained drudges, and were regarded with great jealousy by the laboring English, the Scotch became overseers and book-keepers, sometimes even partners in lucrative works, and were usually well liked and looked up to. I could fain have taken up my abode at the friendly Scotchwoman's; but the miners in a neighboring apartment were becoming every moment more noisy; and when they began to strike the table with their fists till the glasses danced and rung, I got up, and, taking leave of my countrywoman, sallied into the street.

After sauntering about the town for half an hour, I found in one of the lanes a small temperance coffee-house, with an air of quiet sobriety about it that at once recommended it to my favor. Finding that most of the customers of the place went into the kitchen to luxuriate over their coffee in front of the fire, I too went into the kitchen, and took my seat on a long wooden settle, with tall upright back and arms, that stretched along the side of the apartment, on the clean red tiles. The English are by much a franker people than the Scotch, — less curious to know who the stranger may be who addresses them, and more ready to tell what they themselves are, and what they are doing and thinking; and I soon found I could get as much conversation as I wished. The landlady's youngest son, a smart little fellow in his ninth year, was, I discovered, a stern teetotaller. He had been shortly before at a temperance meeting, and had been set up to make a speech, in which he had acquitted himself to the admiration of all. He had been a teetotaller for about nine years, he said, and his father was a teetotaller too, and his mother, and brother and sisters, were all teetotallers; and he knew men, he added, who, before taking the pledge, had worn ragged clothes, and shoes without soles, who, on becoming teetotallers, had improved into gentlemen. He was now engaged in making a second speech, which was, however, like a good many other second speeches produced in such circumstances, very much an echo of the first; and every one who dropped in this evening, whether to visit the landlady and her daughters, or to drink coffee, was sure to question little Samuel regarding the progress of his speech. To some of the querists Samuel replied with great deference and respect; to some with no deference or respect at all. Condition or appearance seemed to exert as little influence over the mind of the magnanimous speech-maker as over that of the eccentric clergyman in Mr. Fitzadam's *World*, who paid to robust health the honor so usually paid to rank and title, and looked down as contemptuously on a broken constitution as most other people do on dilapidated means. But Samuel had quite a different standard of excellence from that of the eccentric clergyman. He had, I found, no respect save for pledged teetotalism; and no words to bestow on drinkers of strong drink, however moderate in their potations. All mankind consisted, with Samuel, of but two classes, — drunkards and teetotallers. Two young ladies, daughters of the supervisor of the district, came in, and asked him how he was getting on with his speech; but Samuel deigned them no reply. "You were rude to the young ladies, Samuel," said his mother when they had quitted the room; "why did you not give them an answer to their question?" — "They drink," replied the laconic Samuel. — "Drink!" exclaimed his mother, — "Drink! — the young ladies!" — "Yes, drink," reiterated Samuel; "they have not taken the pledge."

I found a curious incident which had just occurred in the neighborhood forming the main topic of conversation, — exactly such a story as Crabbe would have chosen for the basis of a descriptive poem. A leaden pipe had been stolen a few even ings before from one of the town churches: it was a long ponderous piece of metal; and the thieves, instead of carrying, had dragged it along, leaving behind them, as they went, a significant trail on grass and gravel, which had been traced on the morrow by the sexton to the house of an elderly couple, in what, for their condition, were deemed snug circumstances, and who for full thirty years had borne a fair character in the place. There lived with them two grown-up sons, and they also bore fair characters. A brief search, however, revealed part of the missing lead; a still further search laid open a vast mine of purloined movables of every description. Every tile in the back court, every square yard in the garden, every board in the house-floor, covered its stolen article; — kitchen utensils and fire-irons, smiths' and miners' tools, sets of weights from the market-place, pieces of hardware goods from the shops, garden railings, sewerage grates, house-spouts, — all sorts of things useful and useless to the purloiners, — some of them missed but yesterday, some of them abstracted years before, — were found heaped up together, in this strange jay's nest. Two-thirds of the people of Dudley had gone out to mark the progress of discovery; and as the police furrowed the garden, or trenched up the floor, there were few among the numerous spectators who were not able to detect in the mass some piece of their own property. I saw the seventh cart-load brought this evening to the police-office; and every fresh visiter to the coffee-house carried with him the intelligence of further discoveries. The unhappy old man, who had become so sudden a bankrupt in reputation when no one had doubted his solvency, and the two sons whom he had trained so ill, had been sent off to Gloucester jail the evening before, to abide their trial at the ensuing assizes. I was reminded, by the incident, of an occurrence which took place some time in the last age in a rural district in the far north. A parish smith had lived and died with an unsuspected character, and the population of half the country-side gathered to his funeral. There had been, however, a vast deal of petty pilfering in his time. Plough and harrow irons were continually disappearing from the fields and steadings of the farmers, his nearer neighbors; not a piece of hem-mounting or trace-chain, not a cart-axle or wheel-rim, was secure; but no one had ever thought of implicating the smith. Directly opposite his door there stood a wall of loose, uncemented stones, against which a party of the farmers who had come to the burial were leaning, until the corpse should be brought out. The coffin was already in the passage; the farmers were raising their shoulders from the wall, to take their places beside it; in ten minutes more the smith would have been put under the ground with a fair character; when, lo! the frail masonry behind suddenly gave way; the clank of metal was heard to mingle with the dull rumble of the stones; and there, amid the rubbish, palpable as the coffin on the opposite side of the road, lay, in a scattered heap, the stolen implements so mysteriously abstracted from the farmers. The awe-struck men must have buried the poor smith with feelings which bore reference to both worlds, and which a poet such as Wordsworth would perhaps know how to describe.

My landlady's eldest son, a lad of nineteen, indulged a strong predilection for music, which, shortly prior to the date of my visit, had received some encouragement, in his appointment as organist in one of the town churches. At a considerable expense of patient ingenuity, he had fitted up an old spinet, until it awoke into life, in these latter days of Collards and Broadwoods, the identical instrument it had been a century before. He had succeeded, too, in acquiring no imperfect mastery over it; and so, by a series of chances all very much out of the reach of calculation, I, who till now had never seen but dead spinets, — rickety things of chopped wainscot, lying in waste garrets from the days of the grandmothers and great-grandmothers of genteel families, — was enabled to cultivate acquaintance with the capabilities of a resuscitated spinet, vocal and all alive. It gave me the idea, when at its best, of a box full of Jew's harps, all twanging away at the full extent of their compass, and to the best of their ability. The spirit of the musician, however, made such amends for the defects of his instrument, that his evening performances, carried on when his labors for the day had closed, were exceedingly popular in the neighborhood: the rude miner paused under the windows to listen; and groups of visiters, mostly young girls, came dropping in every night to enjoy the nice fresh melodies brought out of the old musty spinet. Lovers of the fine arts draw naturally together; and one of the most frequent guests of the coffee-house was an intelligent country artist, with whom I had scraped acquaintance, and had some amusing conversation. With little Samuel the speech-maker I succeeded in forming a friendship of the superlative type; though, strange to relate, it must be to this day a profound mystery to Samuel whether his *fidus Achates* the Scotchman be a drinker of strong drink or a teetotaller. Alas for even teetotalised human nature, when placed in trying circumstances! Samuel and I had a good many cups of coffee together, and several glasses of *Sampson*, — a palatable Dudley beverage, compounded of eggs, milk, and spicery; and as on these occasions a few well-directed coppers enabled him to drive hard bargains with his mother for his share of the tipple, he was content to convert in my behalf the all-important question of the pledge into a moot-point of no particular concernment. I unfortunately left Dudley ere he had an opportunity presented him of delivering his second speech. But he entertained, he assured me, no fears for the result. It was well known in the place, he said, that he was to speak at the first temperance meeting; there were large expectations formed, so the audience could not be other than very numerous and attentive; and he was quite satisfied he had something worth while to give them. My friend Samuel bore a good deal of healthy precocity about him. It would be, of course, consummately absurd to found aught on a single instance; but it has been so often remarked that English children of the lively type develop into cleverness earlier than the Scotch, that the observation has, in all likelihood, some foundation in reality. I find, too, from the experiments of Professor Forbes, of Edinburgh, that the English lad in his sixteenth, seventeenth, and eighteenth years, possesses more bodily strength than the Scot of the same years and standing, and that it is not until their nineteenth year that the young men of both countries meet on a footing of equality. And it seems not irrational to infer, that the earlier development of body in the case of the embryo Englishman should be accompanied by a corresponding development of mind also, — that his school exercises should be better than those of the contemporary Scot, and his amateur verses rather more charged with meaning, and more smoothly rounded.

Dudley has its Geological Museum, — small, but very valuable in some departments, and well arranged generally. Its Silurian organisms are by far the finest I ever saw. No sum of money would enable the fossil collector to complete such a set. It contains original specimens of the trilobite family, of which, in other museums, even the British, one finds but the casts. Nor can anything be more beautiful than its groups of delicately relieved crinoidea of all the different Silurian genera, — some of them in scarce less perfect keeping than when they spread out their many-jointed arms in quest of prey amid the ancient seas. It contains, however, none of the vertebral remains furnished by the celebrated bone-bed of the Upper Ludlow rocks, nor any of the ichthyolitic fragments found still lower down; though, of course, one misses them all the more from the completeness of the collection in contemporary organisms; and its group of Old Red Sandstone fossils serves but to contrast the organic poverty of this system in its development in England, with the vast fossil riches which it exhibits in our northern division of the island. The neighboring coal-field I found well represented by a series of plants and ichthyolites; and I had much pleasure in examining, among the latter, one of the best preserved specimens of *Megalichthys* yet found, — a specimen disinterred some years ago from out an ironstone bed near Walsall, known to the miners as the "gubbin iron." The head is in a remarkably fine state of keeping: the strong enamelled plates, resembling pieces of japanned mail, occupy their original places; they close round the snout as if tightly riveted down, and lie nicely inlaid in patterns of great regularity on the broad forehead; the surface of each is finely punctulated, as if by an exceedingly minute needle; most of them bear, amid the smaller markings, eyelet-like indentations of larger size, ranged in lines, as if they had been half-perforated for ornament by a tin-worker's punch; and the *tout ensemble* is that of the head of some formidable reptile encased in armor of proof: though, from the brightly burnished surface of the plates, the armature resembles rather that of some of the more brilliant insects, than that common to fishes or reptiles. The occipital covering of the crocodile is perhaps more than equally strong, but it lacks the glossy japan, and the tilt-yard cast, if I may so speak, of the many-jointed headpiece of the *Megalichthys*. The occipital plates descend no lower than the nape, where they join on to thickly-set ranges of glittering quadrangular scales of considerable size and great thickness, that gradually diminish, and become more angular as they approach the tail. The fins are unluckily not indicated in the specimen. In all fossil fish, of at least the Secondary and Palæozoic formations, the coloring depends on the character of the deposits in which they have lain entombed. I have seen scales and plates of the *Megalichthys*, in some instances of a sienna yellow, in some of a warm chestnut brown; but the finer specimens are invariably of a glossy black. The Dudley *Megalichthys*, and a *Megalichthys* in the possession of Dr. John Fleming, which, though greatly less entire, is valuable, from exhibiting the vertebral column of the animal, are both knights in black armor.*

* This ancient fish was at one time confounded with its contemporary, the *Holoptychius Hibberti*. A jaw of the latter animal, with its slim ichthyolite teeth bristling around its huge reptile tusks, may be seen figured as that of *Megalichthys*, in the singularly interesting Memoir of Dr. Hibbert on the Limestone of Burdie House, and we find single teeth similarly misassigned in some other geological works of credit. But no two ichthyolites in the geologic scale in reality less resemble each other than these two fish of the Coal Measures. The *Megalichthys*, from head to tail, was splendent with polished enamel; the *Holoptychius* was, on the contrary, a dull-coated fish. The *Megalichthys* rarely exceeded four feet in length, and commonly fell short of three; the *Holoptychius* was one of the most gigantic of the ganoids: some individuals, judging from the fragments, must, like the great basking shark of the northern seas, have exceeded thirty feet in length. The scales of the *Megalichthys* are smooth, quadrangular, and of great thickness, but rarely exceed an inch, or three quarters of an inch, across; those of the *Holoptychius* are thin, nearly circular in form, thickly ridged on the upper surface, and vary from an inch to more than five inches in diameter. The head of the *Megalichthys* was covered, as has been shown, with brightly-japanned plates; that of the *Holoptychius*, with plates thickly fretted on the surface, like pieces of shagreen, only the tubercles are more confluent, and

Among the donations to the Dudley Museum, illustrative of the geology of foreign parts, I saw an interesting group of finely-preserved fossil fish from Mount Lebanon, — a very ancient mountain, in its relation to human history, compared with the Castle-hill of Dudley (which, however, begins to loom darkly through the haze of the monkish annalists as early as the year 700, when Dud the Saxon built a stronghold on its summit), but an exceedingly recent hill in its relation to the geologic eras. The geologist, in estimating the respective ages of the two eminences, places the hill with the modern history immensely in advance of the hill with the ancient one. The fish dug out of the sides of Lebanon, some five or six thousand feet over the level of the sea, are all fish of the modern type, with horny scales and bony skeletons; and they cannot belong

lie ranged in irregular ridges. It may be mentioned in the passing, that the *Holoptychius* of the Coal Measures, if there be value in the distinguishing characteristics of Owen, — and great value there certainly is, — was not even generically related to the *Holoptychius* of the Old Red Sandstone. The reptile teeth of the Old Red *Holoptychius* are of *bone*, marked by the true dendrodic character of the genus, and so thickly cancellated towards the base, as to resemble, in the cross section, pieces of open lacework. The reptile teeth of the *Holoptychius Hibberti*, on the contrary, are of *ivory*, presenting towards the point, where the surface is smooth and unfurrowed, the common tubular, radiating character of that substance, and exhibiting towards the base, where the Gothic-like rodding is displayed, a strange intricacy of pattern, that becomes more involved as we cut lower down, till what in the middle section resembles the plaiting of a ruff seen in profile, is found to resemble, immediately over the line where the base rests on the jaw, the labyrinthine complexity of a Runic knot. The scales of the creatures, too, are very dissimilar in their microscopic structure, though both possess in common ridged surfaces, — the only point of resemblance from which their generic identity has been inferred. Even the internal structure of their occipital plates is wholly different. So far as is yet known, the Coal Measures contain no *Holoptychius* akin to the dendrodic genus of that name so abundant in the Old Red Sandstone.

to a remoter period, Agassiz tells us, than the times of the Chalk. Fish were an ancient well-established order in these comparatively recent days of the Cretaceous system; whereas their old Placoid predecessors, contemporary with the *crustacea brachipoda* of the Hill of Dudley, seem but to have just started into being at the earlier time, as the first-born of their race, and must have been regarded as mere upstart novelties among the old plebeian crustaceans and molluscs they had come to govern. The trilobites of Dudley are some four or five creations deeper in the bygone eternity, if I may so speak, than the *cycloids* and *ctenoids* of Lebanon. I was a good deal struck, shortly before leaving home, by this curious transposition of idea which Geology in such cases is suited to accomplish. I found waiting my inspection, one morning in the house-lobby, a box and basket, both filled with fossils. Those in the basket, which had been kindly sent me by Dr. John Wilson, of Bombay, consisted of ichthyolites and shells from the Holy Land, and fossil wood from the old Egyptian desert; while those in the box, which had been obligingly transmitted me by Dr. James Wilson, of Upper Canada, — a gentleman who, amid the wild backwoods, with none to assist and few to sympathize, has cultivated a close acquaintance with science for its own sake, — had been collected in the modern township of Pakenham, not far from the banks of the Ottawa. The fossil wood of the old desert — unequivocally dicotyledonous, of the oak or mahogany structure — could not, I found, be older than the Tertiary period; the fish and shells of Palestine, like those of the Dudley Museum, belong apparently to the times of the Chalk; but the organisms of the modern township, that had no name twenty years ago, boasted an incomparably higher antiquity: they consisted of corals, crustacea, and cephalopoda, from the Lower Silurians.

No one who visits Dudley should omit seeing its castle and castle-hill. The castle, a fine old ruin of the true English type, with moat, court and keep, dungeon and treble gateway, chapel, guard-room and hall, resembles in extent rather a ruinous village than a single building; while the hill on which it stands forms, we find, a picturesquely wooded eminence, seamed with rough, bosky ravines, and bored deep with gloomy chasms, that were excavated centuries ago as limestone quarries. But their lime has been long since exhausted, and the miner now plies his labors unseen, though not unheard, deep amid the bowels of the mountain. The visiter may hear, in recesses the most recluse and solitary, the frequent rumble of his subterraneous thunder, and see the aspen trembling in the calm, under the influence of the earthquake-like tremor communicated to it from beneath.

The old keep, by much the strongest and most ancient portion of the building, rises on the highest part of the eminence, and commands the town below, part of which lies grouped around the hill-foot, almost within pistol-shot of the walls. In the olden time, this fortress occupied the centre of an extensive woodland district, and was known as the "Castle of the Woods." It had some rather high-handed masters in its day, — among the rest, the stern Leofric, husband of the Lady Godiva, so celebrated in chronicle and song for her ride through Coventry. Even as late as the close of the reign of Elizabeth, a lord of Dudley, at feud with a neighboring proprietor, ancestor of the well-known Lord Lyttleton, issued from the triple gateway, "having," says a local historian of the time, "one hundred and forty persons with him, weaponed, some with bows and sheffes of arrows, some with forest-bills and staves, and came to Mr. Lyttleton's lands at Prestwood and Ashwood; and out of Ashwood he took three hundred and forty-one sheep, and caused some of his company drive them towards Dudley; and therewith not satisfied, he entered also into the enclosed grounds at Prestwood, and there, with great violence, chased fourteen kyne, one bull, and eight fat oxen, and brought them to Dudley Castle, and kept them within the walls of the castle; and part of the said cattle and sheep he did kill and eat, and part he sent to Coventry, guarded by sixty men strongly armed with bows and arrows, calyvers, and forest-bills, there to be sold." Somewhat rough doings these, and rather of a Scotch than an English type: they remind one of a Highland *creach* of the days of Rob Roy. England, however, had a boy born to it twenty years after the event, who put an effectual stop to all such acts of lordly aggression for the future; and the keep of Dudley Castle shows how. Two of its rock-like towers, with their connecting curtain, remain scarce less entire than in the days of Dud or of Leofric; but the other two have disappeared, all save their foundations, and there have been thirty-two-pound shot dug out from among the ruins, that in some sort apologize for their absence. The iron hand of Cromwell fell heavy on the Castle of the Woods, — a hand, of which it may be said, as Barbour says of the gauntleted hand of the Bruce, that

> "Where it strook with even stroke,
> Nothing mocht against it stand;"

and sheep and cattle have been tolerably safe in the neighborhood ever since. It was a breezy, sunshiny day on which I climbed the hill to the old keep, along a steep paved roadway o'ershaded by wood. In the court behind, — a level space some two or three acres in extent, flanked on the one side by the castle buildings, and on the other by a gray battlemented wall, — I found a company of the embodied pensioners going through their exercises, in their uniforms of red and blue. Most of them — old, gray-headed veterans, with medals dangling at their breasts, and considerably stiffened by years — seemed to perform their work with the leisurely air of men quite aware that it was not of the greatest possible importance. The broken ruins lay around them, rough with the scars of conflict and conflagration; and the old time-worn fortress harmonized well with the old time-worn soldiery.

It must be a dull imagination that a scene so imposing as that presented by the old castle does not set in motion: its gloomy vaults and vast halls, — its huge kitchen and roomy chapel, — its deep fosse and tall rampart, — its strong portcullised gateway and battered keep, — are all suggestive of the past, — of many a picturesque group of human creatures, impressed, like the building in which they fed and fought, worshipped and made merry, with the character of a bygone age. The deserted apartments, as one saunters through them, become crowded with life; the gray, cold, evanished centuries assume warmth and color. In Dudley, however, the imagination receives more help in its restorations than in most other ruins in a state of equal dilapidation. The building owes much to a garrulous serving-maid, that followed her mistress, about a hundred and twenty years ago, to one of its high festivals, — a vast deal more, at least, than to all the great lords and ladies that ever shared in its hospitality. The grandmother of that Mrs. Sherwood of whom, I daresay, most of my readers retain some recollection since their good-boy or good-girl days, as a pleasing writer for the young, was a ladies' maid, some time early in the last century, in a family of distinction that used to visit at the castle; and the authoress has embodied in her writings one of her grandmother's descriptions of its vanished glories, as communicated to her by the old woman many years after. I must give, by way of specimen, a few characteristic snatches of her story, — a story which will scarce fail to recall to the learned in romance the picturesque narratives of Mrs. Ratcliffe's garrulous housekeepers, or the lengthened anecdotes of the communicative Annette.

"I was delighted," says the old serving-maid, "when it was told me that I was to accompany my lady and a friend of hers to the castle, in order that I might be at hand to wait on them next morning; for they were to stay at the castle all night. So we set out in the coach, the two ladies being seated in front, and myself with my back to the horses; and it was quite dark when we arrived at the foot of the castle-hill, for it was the dead of winter, and the snow lay on the ground. However, there were lamps fixed upon the trees, all along the private road up to the castle; and there were lights upon the towers, which shone as beacons far and near; for it was a great day at the castle. The horses, though we had four, had hard work to drag us up the snowy path. However, we got up in time; and, passing under the gateway, we found ourselves in the court-yard. But oh, how different did it then show to what it does now, being littered with splendid equipages, and sounding with the rattling of wheels and the voices of coachmen and grooms calling to each other, and blazing with lights from almost every window! and the sound of merry voices, and of harps and viols, issued from every doorway. At length, having drawn up to the steps of the portico, my ladies were handed out by a young gentleman wearing an embroidered waistcoat with deep pockets, and a bag-wig and sword; and I was driven to another door, where I was helped out by a footboy, who showed me the way to the housekeeper's room." The serving-maid then goes on to describe the interior. She saw on the dark wainscoting hard, stiff paintings, in faded colors, of antiquely-dressed dames, and knights in armor; but the housemaid, she said, could tell her nothing of their history. Some of the rooms were hung with tapestry; some with tarnished paper that looked like cut velvet. The housekeeper was an old, bustling dame, "with a huge bunch of keys hanging to her girdle by a strong chain of steel." "There was not a window which was sashed, but all were casemented in stone frames, many of the panes being of colored glass; and there was scarce one chamber on the same level with another, but there was a step to go up or a step to go down to each: the chimney-pieces of carved wood or stone were so high, that I could hardly reach to the mantel-shelves when standing on tiptoe; and instead of grates, such as we have now, there were mostly *dogs* upon the hearths. The chairs were of such a size, that two of the present sort would stand in the room of one; and the doors, though very thick and substantial, were each an inch or two from the floor, so that the wind whistled all along the passages, rattling and shaking the casements, and often making a sort of wild and mournful melody."

The great hall which constituted the grand centre of the festivities of this evening now forms one of the most dilapidated portions of the ruin. The front walls have fallen so low that we can barely trace their foundations, and a rank vegetation waves over the floor. I think it is Macculloch who says, that full one-half the ancient strongholds of our Scotch Highlands thrown together into a heap would be found scarce equal in the aggregate to a single English castle of the more magnificent type; and certainly enough remains of the great hall here, broken as it is, to illustrate, and in some degree corroborate the remark, disparaging to the Highlands as it may seem. We can still ascertain that this single room measured seventy-five feet in length by fifty-six feet in breadth, — a space considerably more than equal in area to most of our north-country fortalices. It was remarkable at one time for containing, says Dr. Plott, an oak table, composed of a single plank, three feet in breadth, that extended from end to end of the apartment. The great hall must have presented a gay scene when seen by the grandmother of Mrs. Sherwood. "Three doors opened into it from the gallery above. At one of these," says the garrulous old woman, "all the servant-maids were standing, and I took my place among them. I can hardly tell how to describe this hall to you, unless by saying that the roof was arched or groined, not unlike that of some ancient church which you may have seen. and it had large and lofty windows, painted and carved in the fashion called Gothic. It was illuminated with many candles, in sconces of brass hanging from the ceiling; and every corner of it, wide as it was, was bright as the day. There was a gallery at the further end of it, filled with musicians; and the first and foremost among them was an old harper from Wales, who used, in those days, to travel the country with his harp on his back, ever presenting himself at the doors of the houses where feasts and merry-makings might be expected. The dresses of the time were very splendid; the ladies shone with glossy silks and jewels, and the gentlemen with embroidery and gold and silver lace; and I have still before me the figures of that gay and distinguished company, for it consisted of the noble of the land, with their families. It may be fancy; but I do not think I ever in these days see faces so fair as some of those which shone that night in the old castle-hall." Such were some of the reminiscences of the ancient serving-maid. A few years after the merry-making which she records, the castle was deserted by the inmates for a more modern building; and in 1750 it was reduced by fire to a blackened group of skeleton walls. A gang of coiners were suspected at the time of harboring among its concealments; and the conflagration is said to have been the work of an incendiary connected with the gang. An unfinished stanza, spelt amiss, and carved rudely on one of the soft sandstone lintels, used to be pointed out as the work of the felon; but, though distinctly legible till within the last few years, it can now be pointed out no longer: —

> "Water went round it, to garde it from the Fooe.
> The fire shall burn it ———"

Can the reader complete the couplet? If not, he may be perhaps apt to suspect the man who first filled up the gap with sense and rhyme as the original author, and, of course, the incendiary. But though every boy and girl in Dudley has learned to add the missing portion, no one seems to know who the individual was who supplied it first.

> "Water went round it, to garde it from the Fooe:
> The fire shall burn it, *and lay its towers low.*"

Some of the dells and caverns of the castle-hill I found exceedingly picturesque. Its limestone is extensively employed in the smelting furnaces as a flux. Every ton of clay ironstone must be mixed up with half a ton of lime, to facilitate the separation of the metal from the argillaceous dross; and so, from the earliest beginnings of the iron-trade, the work of excavation has been going on in the Hill of Dudley. The first smelter who dug up a barrowful of ironstone to make a sword must have come to the hill for half a barrowful of lime, to mix up with the brown mass, ere he committed it to the fire. And so some of the caverns are very vast, and, for caverns of man's making, very old; and some of the open dells, deserted by the quarrier for centuries, bear amid their precipices trees of large size, and have long since lost every mark of the tool. The recesses of the hill, like those of the Wren's Nest, are threaded by a subterranean canal, which, in passing under the excavation of an ancient quarry, opens to the light; and so in a thickly-wooded walk, profoundly solitary, when one is least thinking of the possibility of such a thing, one comes full upon a wide and very deep chasm overhung by trees, the bottom of which is occupied by a dark basin, crowded with boats. We may mark the boatmen emerging from out the darkness by one cavern, and reëntering it by another. They see the sun, and the sky, and the green trees, far above, but nothing within reach save rough rocks and muddy water; and if they do not think, as they pass, of human life, bounded by the darkness of the two eternities, with no lack of the gloomy and the turbid in closest contact, but with what the heart most desires hung too high for the hand to grasp, it is not because there are no such analogies furnished by the brief passage through, but merely because they have failed to discover them.

A little further on there may be found a grand though somewhat sombre cavern, which, had it come direct from the hand of nature, I would have perhaps deemed one of the most remarkable I ever explored. We enter a long narrow dell, wooded atop, like all the others, with an overhanging precipice rising tall on the one side, and the strata sloping off on the other in a continuous plane, like the face of a rampart. Nor is this sloping wall devoid of its characteristic sculpturings. We find it fretted with shells and corals, and well-marked heads and joints of the *Calymene Blumenbachii*, so abundant an organism in these rocks as to be familiarly known as the Dudley trilobite. I scarce know on what principle it should have occurred; but certainly never before, even when considerably less familiar with the wonders of Geology, was I so impressed by the appearance of marine fossils in an inland district, as among these wooded solitudes. Perhaps the peculiarity of their setting, if I may so speak, by heightening the contrast between their present circumstances and their original habitat, gave increased effect to their appeals to the imagination. The green ocean depths in which they must have lived and died associate strangely in the mind with the forest retreats, a full hundred miles from the sea-shore, in which their remains now lie deposited. Taken with their accompaniments, they serve to remind one of that style of artificial grotto-work in which corals and shells are made to mingle with flowers and mosses. The massy cyathophyllum sticks out of the sides of gray lichened rocks, enclasped by sprigs of ivy, or overhung by twigs of thorn and hazel; deep-sea terebratulæ project in bold relief from amid patches of the delicate wood sorel; here a macerated oak-leaf, with all its skeleton fibres open as a net, lies glued by the damps beside some still more delicately reticulated festinella; there a tuft of graceful harebells projects over some prostrate orthoceratite; yonder there peeps out from amid a drapery of green liver-wort, like a heraldic helmet from the mantling, the armed head of some mailed trilobite: the deep-sea productions of the most ancient of creations lie grouped, as with an eye to artistic effect, amid the floral productions of our own times. At the further end of this retired dell, so full of interest to the geologist, we see, where the rock closes, two dark openings separated by a rude limestone column. One of these forms a sort of window to the cavern within, so exceedingly lofty in the sill as to be inaccessible to the explorer; through the other we descend along a damp, mouldy path, and reach the twilight bank of a canal, which stretches away into the darkness between two gloomy walls of rock of vast height, connected half-way up, — as flooring-beams connect the walls of a skeleton building, — by a range of what seems rafters of rock. The cavern had once an upper story, — a working separated from the working below by a thin sloping floor; and these stone rafters are remains of the floor, left as a sort of reclining buttresses, to support the walls. They form one of the most picturesque features of the cavern, straddling overhead from side to side, and receding in the more than twilight gloom of the place, each succeeding rafter dimmer and more dim, in proportion to its distance from the two openings till the last becomes so indistinctly visible, that if but a cloud pass over the sun, it disappears. A rustic bridge leads across the canal; but we can see only the one end of it, — the other is lost in the blackness; the walls and floor are green with mould; the dark water seems a sullen river of pitch: we may occasionally mark the surface dimpled by the track of a newt, or a toad puffing itself up, as if it fed on vapor, on the damp earthy edge; but other inhabitants the cavern has none. I bethought me of the wild description of Kirke White: —

> "And as she entered the cavern wide,
>   The moonbeam gleamed pale,
> And she saw a snake on the craggy rock, —
>   It clung by its slimy tail.
> Her foot it slipped, and she stood aghast,
>   For she trod on a bloated toad."

Solitary as the place usually is, it presented a singularly animated appearance six years ago, when it was visited by the members of the British Association, and converted by Sir Roderick Murchison into a geological lecture-room. He discoursed of rocks and fossils in the bowels of the hill, with the ponderous strata piled high on every side, like courses of Cyclopean masonry, and the stony forms of the dead existing by millions around him.

But, after al , there are no caverns like those of nature's making: they speak to the imagination in a bolder and freer style than any mere excavation of the quarrier, however huge ; and we find, in consequence, that they have almost always engaged tradition in their behalf. There hangs about them some old legend of spectral shapes seen flitting across the twilight vestibule; or of ancient bearded men, not of this world, standing, porter-like, beside the door; or of somnolent giants reposing moodily in the interior; or of over-bold explorers, who wandered so deep into their recesses that they never again returned to the light of day. I bethought me, when in Sir Roderick's lecture-room, of one of the favorite haunts of my boyhood, — a solitary cave, ever resounding to the dash of the billows, — and felt its superiority. Hollowed of old by the waves of an unfrequented shore, just above the reach of the existing tide-line, — its gray roof bristling with stalactites, its gray floor knobbed with stalagmite, — full of all manner of fantastic dependencies from the top and sides, — with here little dark openings branching off into the living rock, and there unfinished columns standing out from it, roughened with fretted irregularities, and beaded with dew, — with a dim twilight resting even at noonday within its further recesses, and steeped in an atmosphere of unbreathing silence, rarely broken save by the dash of the wave or the shriek of the sea-fowl, — it is at all times a place where the poetry of deep seclusion may be felt, — the true hermit-feeling, in which self is absorbed and forgotten amid the silent sublimities of nature. The unfrequent visiter scares the seal from the mid-tide rock in the opening, or encounters the startled otter in its headlong retreat to the sea. But it seemed redolent, when I last saw it, of a still higher poetry. Night had well-nigh fallen, though the nearly vanquished daylight still struggled with the darkness. The moon at full rose slowly over the sea,

"'All pale and dim, as if from rest
The ghost of the late buried sun
Had crept into the skies.'"

The level beam fell along a lonely coast, on brown precipice and gray pebbly shore, here throwing into darker shade some wooded recess, there soliciting into prominence some tall cliff whitened by the cormorant. The dark-browed precipice, in which the cavern is hollowed, stood out in doubtful relief; while the cavern itself — bristling gray with icicles, that showed like the tags of a dead dress — seemed tenanted, in the exaggerative gloom, with all manner of suggestive shapes. Here a sheeted uncertainty sat beside the wall, or looked out from one of the darker openings upon the sea; there a broken skeleton seemed grovelling upon the floor. There was a wild luxury in calling to mind, as one gazed from the melancholy interior on the pale wake of the moon, that for miles on either hand there was not a human dwelling, save the deserted hut of a fisherman who perished in a storm. The reader may perhaps remember, that in exactly such a scene does the poet Collins find a home for his sublime personification of Fear.

"Say, wilt thou shroud in haunted cell,
Or in some hollowed seat,
'Gainst which the big waves beat,
With shuddering, meek, submitted thought,
Hear drowning seamen's cries in tempests brought?"

I spent the greater part of a week among the fossiliferous deposits of Dudley, and succeeded in procuring a tolerably fair set of fossils, and in cultivating a tolerably competent acquaintance with the appearances which they exhibit in their various states of keeping. It is an important matter to educate the eye. Should there be days of health and the exploration of the Scottish Grauwacke in store for me, I may find my brief sojourn among the English Silurians of some little advantage. Fossils in our ancient southern deposits are exceedingly rare; and there is, in consequence, a lack of data by which to ascertain the age of the formations in which they occur, and which they fail sufficiently to mark. The tablets are devoid of inscriptions, save that we here and there find a half-effaced character, or the outline of some sorely worn hieroglyphic. And yet, had the few fossils hitherto discovered been preserved and brought together, their joint testimony might be found to amount to something. The Graptolites of Peebles-shire and Galloway are tolerably well known as identical with English species, — the *Graptolithus Ludensis* and *Graptolithus foliaceus*, — which possess, however, a wide range in the more ancient rocks, passing downwards from beds of the Upper Silurian, to deposits that lie deep in what was once termed the Cambrian series. In Peebles-shire, at Wrae-hill, says Mr. Nicol, shells have been detected in a Grauwacke limestone, now unluckily no longer accessible. It is stated by Mr. Maclaren, in his elaborate and singularly satisfactory Treatise on the Geology of Fife and the Lothians, that he succeeded in disinterring two organisms, — a small orthoceratite, and what seemed to be a confused accumulation of the shattered fragments of minute trilobites, — from out of one of the Grauwacke patches which occur among the Pentlands. I have been informed by the late Mr. William Laidlaw, the trusted friend of Sir Walter Scott, that he once disinterred a large bivalve from amid the Grauwackes of Selkirkshire. The apparent remains of broken terebratulæ have been found in various localities in the Grauwacke of Galloway, and atrypæ and tentaculites in a rather equivocal deposit at Girvan, deemed Silurian. Were the various scattered fragments of the fossiliferous record to be brought carefully together, they might be found sufficiently complete to give one at least a few definite ideas regarding the times which preceded in Scotland the age of the *Coccosteus* and *Pterichthys*.

There wons a barber in Dudley, who holds a sort of fossil agency between the quarrier and the public, of whom I purchased several fine trilobites, — one of them, at least, in the most perfect state of keeping I have yet seen: the living creature could not have been more complete in every plate and joint of the head and back; but, as in all the other specimens of trilobite known to the geologist, it presents no trace of the abdominal portion. I procured another specimen rolled up in the peculiar ball-form so often figured, with the tail in contact with the head. It seems not unworthy of remark, that the female lobster, when her spawn is ripening in an external patch on her abdomen, affects for its protection the same rolled form. Her dorsal plates curve round from the joint at the carpace, till the tail-flap rests on her breast; and the multitudinous dark-colored eggs, which, having no hard shell of their own to protect them, would be otherwise exposed to every hungry marauder of the deep, are thus covered up by the strong mail with which the animal is herself protected. When we take the fact into account, that in no specimen of trilobite, however well preserved, do we find abdominal plates, and that the ball-like form is so exceedingly common, may we not infer that this ancient crustacean was shelled on but the back and head, and that it coiled itself round, to protect a defenceless abdomen, in the manner the female lobster coils itself round to protect its defenceless spawn? In yet another specimen which I purchased from the barber there is an eye of the *Asaphus Caudatus*, which presents, in a state of tolerable keeping, its numerous rows of facets. So far as is yet known, the eye which first saw the light on this ancient earth of ours gave access to it through four hundred and fifty distinct spherical lenses. The barber had been in the way of selling Dudley fossils, he told me, for a good many years; and his father had been in the way of selling them for a good many more; but neither he nor his father had ever seen among them any portion of an ichthyolite. The crustaceans, with their many-jointed plates and many-windowed eyes, are, so far as is yet known, the highest organisms of the deposit.

CHAPTER VI.

Stourbridge. — Effect of Plutonic Convulsion on the surrounding Scenery. — Hagley; Description in the "Seasons." — Geology the true Anatomy of Landscape. — Geologic Sketch of Hagley. — The Road to the Races. — The old Stone-cutter. — Thomson's Hollow. — His visits to Hagley. — Shenstone's Urn. — Peculiarities of Taste founded often on a Substratum of Personal Character. — Illustration. — Rousseau. — Pope's Haunt. — Lyttelton's high Admiration of the Genius of Pope. — Description. — Singularly extensive and beautiful Landscape; drawn by Thomson. — Reflection. — Amazing Multiplicity of the Prospect illustrative of a Peculiarity in the Descriptions of the "Seasons." — Addison's Canon on Landscape; corroborated by Shenstone.

I LEFT Dudley by the morning coach for Stourbridge, and arrived, all unwittingly, during the bustle of its season of periodic license, — the yearly races. Stourbridge is merely a smaller Wolverhampton, — built on the same lower deposit of the New Red Sandstone, of the same sort of red brick, and roofed and floored with the same sort of red tiles. The surrounding country is, however, more pleasingly varied by hill and valley. Plutonic convulsion from beneath has given to the flat incoherent formation a diversity of surface not its own; and we see it tempested into waves, over the unseen trappean masses, like ocean over the back of some huge sea-monster. In passing on to the south and west, one finds bolder and still bolder inequalities of surface; the hills rise higher, and are more richly wooded, until at length, little more than three miles from Stourbridge, in a locality where the disturbing rock has broken through, and forms a chain of picturesque trap eminences, there may be seen some of at once the finest and most celebrated scenery in England. Certainly for no scenery either at home or abroad, has the Muse done more. Who, acquainted with the poetry of the last century, has not heard of Hagley, the "British Tempe," so pleasingly sung by Thomson in his "Seasons," and so intimately associated, in the verse of Pope, Shenstone, and Hammond, with the Lord Lyttelton of English literature? It was to walk over Hagley that I had now turned aside half-a-day's journey out of my purposed route. Rather more from accident than choice, there were no poets with whom I had formed so early an acquaintance as with the English poets who flourished in the times of Queen Anne and the first two Georges. I had come to be scarce less familiar with Hagley and the Leasowes, in consequence, than Reuben Butler, when engaged in mismanaging his grandmother's farm, with the agriculture of the "Georgics;" and here was my first opportunity, after the years of half a lifetime had come and gone, of comparing the realities as they now exist, with the early conceptions I had formed of them. My ideas of Hagley had been derived chiefly from Thomson, with whose descriptions, though now considerably less before the reading public than they have been, most of my readers must be in some degree acquainted.

"The love of Nature works,
And warms the bosom; till at last, sublimed
To rapture and enthusiastic heat,
We feel the present Deity, and taste
The joy of God to see a happy world!
These are the sacred feelings of thy heart,
O Lyttelton, the friend! Thy passions thus
And meditations vary, as at large,
Courting the Muse, through Hagley Park thou strayest,
The British Tempe! There along the dale,
With woods o'erhung, and shagged with mossy rocks,
Where on each hand the gushing waters play,

And down the rough cascade white dashing fall,
Or gleam in lengthened vista through the trees,
You silent steal, or sit beneath the shade
Of solemn oaks that tuft the swelling mounts,
Thrown graceful round by Nature's careless hand,
And pensive listen to the various voice
Of rural peace, — the herds, the flocks, the birds,
The hollow whispering breeze, the plaint of rills,
That, purling down amid the twisted roots
Which creep around, their dewy murmurs shake
On the soothed ear."

In all the various descriptions of Hagley and the Leasowes which I have yet seen, however elaborate and well-written, I have found such a want of leading outlines, that I could never form a distinct conception of either place as a whole. The writer — whether a Thomson or a Dodsley — introduced me to shaded walks and open lawns, swelling eminences and sequestered hollows, wooded recesses with their monumental urns, and green hill-tops with their crowning obelisks; but, though the details were picturesquely given, I have always missed distinct lines of circumvallation to separate and characterize from the surrounding country the definite locality in which they were included. A minute anatomical acquaintance with the bones and muscles is deemed essential to the painter who grapples with the difficulties of the human figure. Perhaps, when the geological vocabulary shall have become better incorporated than at present with the language of our common literature, a similar acquaintance with the stony science will be found scarce less necessary to the writer who describes natural scenery. Geology forms the true anatomy — the genuine osteology — of landscape; and a correct representation of the geologica skeleton of a locality will be yet regarded, I doubt not, as the true mode of imparting adequate ideas of its characteristic outlines. The osteology of Hagley, if I may so speak, is easily definable. On the southern shore of the Dudley coal-basin, and about two miles from its edge, there rises in the New Red Sandstone a range of trap hills about seven miles in length, known as the Clent Hills, which vary in height from six to eight hundred feet over the level of the sea. They lie parallel, in their general direction, to the Silurian range, already described as rising, like a chain of islands, amid the coal; but, though parallel, they are, like the sides of the parallel ruler of the geometrician when fully stretched, not opposite; the southernmost hill of the Silurian range lying scarce so far to the south as the northernmost hill of the trap range. The New Red Sandstone, out of which the latter arises, forms a rich, slightly undulating country, reticulated by many a green lane and luxuriant hedge-row; the hills themselves are deeply scoped by hollow dells, furrowed by shaggy ravines, and roughened by confluent eminences; and on the south-western slopes of one of the finest and most variegated of the range, half on the comparatively level red sandstone, half on the steep-sided billowy trap, lie the grounds of Hagley. Let the Edinburgh reader imagine such a trap hill as that which rises on the north-east between Arthur's Seat and the sea, tripled or quadrupled in its extent of base, hollowed by dells and ravines of considerable depth, covered by a soil capable of sustaining the noblest trees, mottled over with votive urns, temples, and obelisks, and traversed by many a winding walk, skilfully designed to lay open every beauty of the place, and he will have no very inadequate idea of the British Tempe sung by Thomson. We find its loveliness compounded of two simple geologic elements, — that abrupt and variegated picturesqueness for which the trap rocks are so famous, and which may be seen so strikingly illustrated in the neighborhood of Edinburgh; and that soft-lined and level beauty, — an exquisite component in landscape when it does not stand too much alone, — so characteristic, in many localities, of the Lower New Red Sandstone formation.

I was fortunate in a clear, pleasant day, in which a dappled sky over head threw an agreeable mottling of light and shadow on the green earth below. The road to Hagley was also that to the races, and so there were many passengers. There were carts and wagons rumbling forward, crowded with eager ruddy faces of the round Saxon type; and gigs and carriages in which the faces seemed somewhat less eager, and were certainly less ruddy and round. There were numerous parties, too, hurrying afoot: mechanics from the nearer towns, with pale unsunned complexions, that reminded one of the colorless vegetation which springs up in vaults and cellars; stout, jovial ploughmen, redolent, in look and form, of the open sky and the fresh air; bevies of young girls in gypsy bonnets, full of an exuberant merriment, that flowed out in laughter as they went; and bands of brown Irish reapers, thrown out of their calculations by the backward harvest, with their idle hooks slung on their shoulders, and fluttering in rags in a country in which one saw no rags but their own. And then there came, in long procession, the boys of a free-school, headed by their masters; and then the girls of another free-school, with their mistresses by their side; but the boys and girls were bound, I was told, not for the races, but for a pleasant recess among the Clent Hills, famous for its great abundance of nuts and blackberries, in which they were permitted to spend once a-year, during the season of general license, a compensatory holiday. To the right of the road, for mile beyond mile, field succeeds field, each sheltered by its own rows of trees, stuck into broad wasteful hedges, and which, as they seem crowded together in the distance, gave to the remote landscape the character of a forest.

On the left, the ground rises picturesque and high, and richly wooded, forming the first beginnings of the Clent Hills; and I could already see before me, where the sky and the hill met, the tufted vegetation and pointed obelisk of Hagley.

I baited at Hagley village to take a glass of cider, which the warmth of the day and the dustiness of the road rendered exceedingly grateful; and entered into conversation with an old gray-headed man, of massive frame and venerable countenance, who was engaged by the wayside in sawing into slabs a large block of New Red Sandstone. The process, though I had hewn, as I told him, a great many stones in Scotland, was new to me; and so I had not a few questions to ask regarding it, which he answered with patient civility. The block on which he was operating measured about six feet in length by four in breadth, and was from eighteen to twenty inches in thickness; and he was cutting it by three draughts, parallel to its largest plane, into four slabs. Each draught, he said, would employ him about four days; and the formation of the slabs, each containing a superficies of about twenty-four feet, at least a fortnight. He purposed fashioning them into four tombstones. Nearly half his time was occupied, he reckoned, in sawing, — rather hard work for an old man; and his general employment consisted chiefly in fashioning the soft red sandstone into door-pieces, and window-soles, and lintels, which, in the better brick-houses in this locality, are usually of stone, tastefully carved. His saw was the common toothless saw of the marble-cutter, fixed in a heavy wooden frame, and suspended by a rope from a projecting beam; and the process of working consisted simply in swinging it in the line of the draught. I would have no difficulty, he informed me, in getting admission to the Lyttelton grounds: I had but to walk up to the gardener's lodge, and secure the services of one of the under gardeners; and, under his surveillance, I might wander over the place as long as I pleased. At one time, he said, people might enter the park when they willed, without guide or guard; but the public, left to its own discretion, had behaved remarkably ill: it had thrown down the urns, and chipped the obelisks, and scrabbled worse than nonsense on the columns and the trees; and so it had to be set under a keeper, to insure better behavior.

I succeeded in securing the guidance of one of the gardeners; and passing with him through part of the garden, and a small but well-kept greenhouse, we emerged into the park, and began to ascend the hill by a narrow inartificial path, that winds, in alternate sunshine and shadow, as the trees approach or recede, through the rich moss of the lawn. Half way up the ascent, where the hill-side is indented by a deep, irregularly semi-circular depression, open and grassy in the bottom and sides, but thickly garnished along the rim with noble trees, there is a semi-octagonal temple, dedicated to the genius of Thomson, — "a sublime poet," says the inscription, "and a good man," who greatly loved, when living, this hollow retreat I looked with no little interest on the scenery that had satisfied so great a master of landscape; and thought, though it might be but fancy, that I succeeded in detecting the secret of his admiration; and that the specialties of his taste in the case rested, as they not unfrequently do in such cases, on a substratum of personal character. The green hill spreads out its mossy arms around, like the arms of a well-padded easy-chair of enormous proportions, imparting, from the complete seclusion and shelter which it affords, luxurious ideas of personal security and ease; while the open front permits the eye to expatiate on an expansive and lovely landscape. We see the ground immediately in front occupied by an uneven sea of tree-tops, chiefly oaks of noble size, that rise, at various levels, on the lower slopes of the park. The clear sunshine imparted to them this day exquisite variegations of fleecy light and shadow. They formed a billowy ocean of green, that seemed as if wrought in floss silk. Far beyond — for the nearer fields of the level country are hidden by the oaks — lies a blue labyrinth of hedge-rows, stuck over with trees, and so crowded together in the distance, that they present, as has already been said, a forest-like appearance; while, still further beyond, there stretches along the horizon a continuous purple screen, composed of the distant highlands of Cambria.

Such is the landscape which Thomson loved. And here he used to saunter, the laziest and best-natured of mortal men, with an imagination full of many-colored conceptions, by far the larger part of them never to be realized, and a quiet eye, that took in without effort, and stamped on the memory, every meteoric effect of a changeful climate, which threw its tints of gloom or of gladness over the diversified prospect. The images sunk into the quiescent mind as the silent shower sinks into the crannies and fissures of the soil, to come gushing out, at some future day, in those springs of poetry which so sparkle in the "Seasons," or that glide in such quiet yet lustrous beauty through that most finished of English poems, the "Castle of Indolence." Never before or since was there a man of genius wrought out of such mild and sluggish elements as the bard of the "Seasons." A listless man was James Thomson; kindly-hearted; much loved by all his friends; little given to think of himself; who "loathed much to write, ne cared to repeat."* And to Hagley he used to come, as Shenstone tells us, in "a

* The stanza in the "Castle of Indolence," "by another hand," which portrays so happily the character of Thomson, was written by Lyttelton; and there are perhaps more of those felicities of phrase which sink into

hired chaise, drawn by two horses ranged lengthwise," to lie abed till long past mid-day, because he had "nae motive" to rise; and to browse in the gardens on the sunny side of the peaches, with his hands stuck in his pockets. He was hourly expected at Hagley on one of his many visits, when the intelligence came, instead, of his death. With all his amazing inertness, he must have been a lovable man, — an essentially different sort of person from either of his two poetical Scotch acquaintances, Mallet or Armstrong. Quin wept for him no feigned tears on the boards of the theatre; poor Collins, a person of warm and genial affections, had gone to live beside him at Richmond, but on his death quitted the place forever; even Shenstone, whose nature it was to think much and often of himself, felt life grow darker at his departure, and, true to his hobby, commemorated him in an urn, on the principle on which the late Lord Buchan was so solicitous to bury Sir Walter Scott. "He was to have been at Hagley this week," we find Shenstone saying, in a letter dated from the Leasowes, in which he records his death, "and then I should probably have seen him here. As it is, I will erect an urn in Virgil's Grove to his memory. I was really as much shocked to hear of his death as if I had known and loved him for a number of years,

the memory of a people, in the nine lines of which it consists, than in any single poem of ten times the length his Lordship ever produced.

"A bard here dwelt, more fat than bard beseems,
Who, void of envy, guile, and lust of gain,
On virtue still, and nature's pleasing themes,
Poured forth his unpremeditated strain;
The world forsaking with a calm disdain,
Here laughed he careless in his easy seat;
Here quaffed, encircled with the joyous train, —
Oft moralizing sage: his ditty sweet
He loathed much to write, ne cared to repeat."

God knows, I lean on a very few friends, and if they drop me, I become a wretched misanthrope."

Passing upwards from Thomson's hollow, we reach a second and more secluded depression in the hill-side, associated with the memory of Shenstone; and see at the head of a solitary ravine a white pedestal, bearing an urn. The trees droop their branches so thickly around it, that, when the eye first detects it in the shade, it seems a retreating figure, wrapped up in a winding-sheet. The inscription is eulogistic of the poet's character and genius. "In his verses," it tells us, with a quiet elegance, in which we at once recognize the hand of Lyttelton, "were all the natural graces, and in his manners all the amiable simplicity of pastoral poetry, with the sweet tenderness of the elegiac." This secluded ravine seems scarce less characteristic of the author of the "Ode to Rural Elegance," and the "Pastoral Ballad," than the opener hollow below, of the poet of the "Seasons." There is no great expansion of view, of which, indeed, Shenstone was no admirer. "Prospects," he says, in his "Canons on Landscape," "should never take in the blue hills so remotely that they be not distinguishable from clouds; yet this mere extent is what the vulgar value." Thomson, however, though not quite one of the vulgar, valued it too. As seen from his chosen recess, the blue of the distant hills seems melting into the blue of the sky; or, as he himself better describes the dim outline,

> "The Cambrian mountains, like far clouds,
> That skirt the blue horizon, dusky rise."

It is curious enough to find two men, both remarkable for their nice sense of the beautiful in natural scenery, at issue on so important a point; but the diversity of their tastes indicates, one may venture to surmise, not only the opposite character of their genius, but of their dispositions also. Shenstone was naturally an egotist, and, like Rousseau, scarce ever contemplated a landscape without some tacit reference to the space occupied in it by himself. "An air of greatness," remarks the infirm philosopher of Geneva, "has always something melancholy in it: it leads us to consider the wretchedness of those who affect it. In the midst of extended grass-plats and fine walks, the little individual does not grow greater; a tree of twenty feet high will shelter him as well as one of sixty; he never occupies a space of more than three feet; and in the midst of his immense possessions, is lost like a poor worm." Alas! it was but a poor worm, ever brooding over its own mean dimensions, — ever thinking of the little entity self, and jealous, in its egotism, of even the greatness of nature, — that could have moralized in a strain so unwholesome. Thomson, the least egotistic of all poets, had no such jealousy in his composition. Instead of feeling himself lost in any save vignette landscapes, it was his delight, wholly forgetful of self and its minute measurements, to make landscapes even larger than the life, — to become all eye, — and, by adding one long reach of the vision to another, to take in a kingdom at a glance. There are few things finer in English poetry than the description in which, on this principle, he lays all Scotland at once upon the canvas.

"Here a while the Muse,
High hovering o'er the broad cerulean scene,
Sees Caledonia in romantic view;
Her airy mountains, from the waving main
Invested with a keen diffusive sky,
Breathing the soul acute; her forests huge,
Incult, robust, and tall, by Nature's hand
Planted of old; her azure lakes between,
Poured out extensive, and her watery wealth
Full; winding deep and green her fertile vales;
With many a cool translucent brimming flood

> Washed lovely, from the Tweed (pure parent stream,
> Whose pastoral banks first heard my Doric reed,
> With sylvan Jed, thy tributary brook),
> To where the north's inflated tempest foams
> O'er Orca's or Betubium's highest peak."

Shenstone's recess, true to his character, excludes, as I have said, the distant landscape. It is, however, an exceedingly pleasing, though somewhat gloomy spot, shut up on every side by the encircling hills, — here feathered with wood, there projecting its soft undulating line of green against the blue sky; while, occupying the bottom of the hollow, there is a small sheltered lake, with a row of delicate lines, that dip their pendent branches in the water.

Yet a little further on, we descend into an opener and more varied inflection in the hilly region of Hagley, which is said to have been as favorite a haunt of Pope as the two others of Thomson and Shenstone, and in which an elaborately-carved urn and pedestal records Lyttelton's estimate of his powers as a writer, and his aims as a moralist: "the sweetest and most elegant," says the inscription, "of English poets; the severest chastiser of vice, and the most persuasive teacher of wisdom." Lyttelton and Pope seem to have formed mutually high esti mates of each other's powers and character. In the "Satires," we find three several compliments paid to the "young Lyttelton,"

> "Still true to virtue, and as warm as true."

And when, in the House of Commons, one of Sir Robert Walpole's supporters accused the rising statesman of being the facile associate of an "unjust and licentious lampooner," — for, as Sir Robert's administration was corrupt and the satirist severe, such was Pope's character in the estimate of the ministerial majority, — he rose indignantly to say, "that he deemed it an honor to be received into the familiarity of so great a poet." But the titled paid a still higher, though perhaps undesigned compliment, to the untitled author, by making his own poetry the very echo of his. Among the English literati of the last century, there is no other writer of equal general ability, so decidedly, I had almost said so servilely, of the school of Pope as Lyttelton. The little crooked man, during the last thirteen years of his life, was a frequent visiter at Hagley; and it is still a tradition in the neighborhood, that in the hollow in which his urn has been erected he particularly delighted. He forgot Cibber, *Sporus*, and Lord *Fanny;* flung up with much glee his poor shapeless legs, thickened by three pairs of stockings apiece, and far from thick, after all; and called the place his "own ground." It certainly does no discredit to the taste that originated the gorgeous though somewhat indistinct descriptions of "Windsor Forest." There are noble oaks on every side, — some in their vigorous middle-age, invested with that "rough grandeur of bark, and wide protection of bough," which Shenstone so admired, — some far gone in years, mossy and time-shattered, with white skeleton branches atop, and fantastic scraggy roots projecting, snakelike, from the broken ground below. An irregular open space in front permits the eye to range over a prospect beautiful though not extensive; a small clump of trees rises so near the urn, that, when the breeze blows, the slim branch-tips lash it as if in sport; while a clear and copious spring comes bubbling out at its base.

I passed somewhat hurriedly through glens and glades, — over rising knolls and wooded slopes, — saw statues and obelisks, temples and hermitages, — and lingered a while, ere I again descended to the lawn, on the top of an eminence which commands one of the richest prospects I had yet seen. The landscape from this point, — by far too fine to have escaped the eye of Thomson, — is described in the "Seasons;" and the hill which overlooks it represented as terminating one of the walks of Lyttelton and his lady, — that Lucy Lady Lyttleton whose early death formed, but a few years after, the subject of the monody so well known and so much admired in the days of our great-grandmothers: —

> "The beauteous bride,
> To whose fair memory flowed the tenderest tear
> That ever trembled o'er the female bier."

It is not in every nobleman's park one can have the opportunity of comparing such a picture as that in the "Seasons" with such an original. I quote, with the description, the preliminary lines, so vividly suggestive of the short-lived happiness of Lyttelton: —

> "Perhaps thy loved Lucinda shares thy walk,
> With soul to thine attuned. Then Nature all
> Wears to the lover's eye a look of love;
> And all the tumult of a guilty world,
> Tossed by the generous passions, sinks away;
> The tender heart is animated peace;
> And, as it pours its copious treasures forth
> In various converse, softening every theme,
> You, frequent pausing, turn, and from her eyes, —
> Where meekened sense, and amiable grace,
> And lively sweetness dwell, — enraptured drink
> That nameless spirit of ethereal joy, —
> Unutterable happiness! — which love
> Alone bestows, and on a favored few.
> Meantime you gain the height from whose fair brow
> The bursting prospect spreads immense around,
> And, snatched o'er hill and dale, and wood and lawn,
> And verdant field, and darkening heath between,
> And villages embosomed soft in trees,
> And spiry towns by surging columns marked

Of household smoke, your eye excursive roams,
Wide stretching from the *Hall*, in whose kind haunt
The *Hospitable Genius* lingers still,
To where the broken landscape, by degrees
Ascending, roughens into rigid hills,
O'er which the Cambrian mountains, like far clouds
That skirt the blue horizon, dusky rise."

As I called up the passage on the spot where, as a yet unformed conception, it had first arisen in the mind of the writer, I felt the full force of the contrast presented by the two pictures which it exhibits, — the picture of a high but evanescent human happiness, whose sun had set in the grave nearly a century ago; and the picture of the enduring landscape, unaltered in a single feature since Lyttelton and his lady had last gazed on it from the hill-top. "Alas!" exclaimed the contemplative Mirza, "man is but a shadow, and life a dream." A natural enough reflection, surely, — greatly more so, I am afraid, than the solace sought by the poet Beattie under its depressing influence, in a resembling evanescence and instability in all nature and in all history.

"Art, empire, earth itself, to change are doomed:
Earthquakes have raised to heaven the humble vale,
And gulfs the mountain's mighty mass entombed,
And where the Atlantic rolls, wide continents have bloomed."

All very true, — none the less so, certainly, from the circumstance of its being truth in advance of the age in which the poet wrote; but it is equally and still more emphatically true, that the instability of a mountain or continent is a thing to be contrasted, not compared, with the instability of the light clouds that, when the winds are up, float over it, and fling athwart the landscape their breadth of fitful shadow. And, alas! what is human life? "even a vapor, that appeareth for a little time, and then vanisheth away." There need be no lack of mementoes to remind one, as I was this day reminded by the passage in Thomson, what a transitory shadow man is, compared with the old earth which he inhabits, and how fleeting his pleasures, contrasted with the stable features of the scenes amid which, for a few brief seasons, he enjoys them.

The landscape from the hill-top could not have been seen to greater advantage, had I waited for months to pick out their best day. The far Welsh mountains, though lessened in the distance to a mere azure ripple, that but barely roughened the line of the horizon, were as distinctly defined in the clear atmosphere as the green luxuriant leafage in the foreground, which harmonized so exquisitely with their blue. The line extended from far beyond the Shropshire Wrekin on the right, to far beyond the Worcestershire Malverns on the left. Immediately at the foot of the eminence stands the mansion-house of Hagley, — the "*Hall*," where the "hospitable genius lingers still;" — a large, solid-looking, but somewhat sombre edifice, built of the New Red Sandstone on which it rests, and which too much reminds one, from its peculiar tint, of the prevailing red brick of the district. There was a gay party of cricket-players on the lawn. In front, Lord Lyttelton, a fine-looking young man, stripped of coat and waistcoat, with his bright white shirt puffed out at his waistband, was sending the ball far beyond bound, amid an eager party, consisting chiefly, as the gardener informed me, of tenants and tenants' sons; and the cheering sounds of shout and laughter came merrily up the hill. Beyond the house rises a noble screen of wood, composed of some of the tallest and finest trees in England. Here and there the picturesque cottages of the neighboring village peep through; and then, on and away to the far horizon, there spreads out a close-wrought net-work of fenced fields, that, as it recedes from the eye, seems to close its meshes, as if drawn awry by the hand, till at length the openings can be no longer seen, and the hedge-rows lie piled on each other in one bosky mass. The geologic framework of the scene is various, and each distinct portion bears its own marked characteristics. In the foreground we have the undulating trap, so suited to remind one, by the picturesque abruptnesses of its outlines, of those somewhat fantastic backgrounds one sees in the old prints which illustrate, in our early English translations, the pastorals of Virgil and Theocritus. Next succeeds an extended plane of the richly-cultivated New Red Sandstone, which, occupying fully two-thirds of the entire landscape, forms the whole of what a painter would term its middle ground, and a little more. There rises over this plane, in the distance, a ridgy acclivity, much fretted by inequalities, composed of an Old Red Sandstone formation, coherent enough to have resisted those denuding agencies by which the softer deposits have been worn down; while the distant sea of blue hills, that seems as if toppling over it, has been scooped out of the Silurian formations, Upper and Lower, and demonstrates, in its commanding altitude and bold wavy outline, the still greater solidity of the materials which compose it.

The entire prospect, — one of the finest in England, and eminently characteristic of what is best in English scenery, — enabled me to understand what I had used to deem a peculiarity, — in some measure a defect, — in the landscapes of the poet Thomson. It must have often struck the Scotch reader, that in dealing with very extended prospects, he rather enumerates than describes. His pictures are often mere catalogues, in which single words stand for classes of objects, and in which the entire poetry seems to consist in an overmastering sense of vast extent, occupied by amazing multiplicity. I cannot better illustrate my meaning than by his introductory description to the "Panegyric on Great Britain": —

> "Heavens! what a goodly prospect spreads around,
> Of hills, and dales, and woods, and lawns, and spires,
> And glittering towns, and gilded streams, till all
> The stretching landscape into smoke decays!"

Now, the prospect from the hill at Hagley furnished me with the true explanation of this enumerative style. Measured along the horizon, it must, on the lowest estimate, be at least fifty miles in longitudinal extent; measured laterally, from the spectator forwards, at least twenty. Some of the Welsh mountains which it includes are nearly thrice that distance; but then they are mere remote peaks, and the area at their bases not included in the prospect. The real area, however, must rather exceed than fall short of a thousand square miles; the fields into which it is laid out are small, scarcely averaging a square furlong in superficies; so that each square mile must contain about forty, and the entire landscape, — for all is fertility, — about forty thousand. With these there are commixed innumerable cottages, manor-houses, villages, towns. Here the surface is dimpled by unreckoned hollows; there fretted by uncounted mounds; all is amazing, overpowering multiplicity, — a multiplicity which neither the pen nor the pencil can adequately express; and so description, in even the hands of a master, sinks into mere enumeration. The picture becomes a catalogue; and all that genius can accomplish in the circumstances is just to do with its catalogue what Homer did with his, — dip it in poetry. I found, however, that the innumerable details of the prospect, and its want of strong leading features, served to dissipate and distract the mind, and to associate with the vast whole an idea of littleness, somewhat in the way that the minute hieroglyphics on an Egyptian obelisk serve to divert attention from the greatness of the general mass, or the nice integrity of its proportions; and I would have perhaps attributed the feeling to my Scotch training, had I not remembered that Addison, whose early prejudices must have been of an opposite cast, represents it as thoroughly natural. Our ideas of the great in nature he describes as derived from vastly-extended, not richly-occupied, prospects. "Such," he says, "are the prospects of an open champaign country, a vast uncultivated desert of huge heaps of mountains, high rocks, and precipices, or a wide expanse of water. . . . Such extensive and undetermined prospects," he adds, "are as pleasing to the fancy as the speculations of eternity or infinitude are to the understanding." Shenstone, too, is almost equally decided on the point; and certainly no writer has better claims to be heard on questions of this kind than the *author* of the Leasowes. "Grandeur and beauty," he remarks, "are so very opposite, that you often diminish the one as you increase the other. Large, unvariegated, simple objects have always the best pretensions to sublimity: a large mountain, whose sides are unvaried by art, is grander than one with infinite variety. Suppose it checkered with different-colored clumps of wood, scars of rock, chalk-quarries, villages, and farm-houses, — you will perhaps have a more beautiful scene, but much less grand, than it was before. The hedge-row apple-trees in Herefordshire afford a lovely scenery at the time they are in blossom; but the prospect would be really grander did it consist of simple foliage. For the same reason, a large oak or beech in autumn is grander than the same in spring. The sprightly green is then obfuscated '

CHAPTER VII.

Hagley Parish Church. — The Sepulchral Marbles of the Lytteltons. — Epitaph on the Lady Lucy. — The Phrenological Doctrine of Hereditary Transmission; unsupported by History, save in a way in which History can be made to support anything. — Thomas Lord Lyttelton; his Moral Character a strange Contrast to that of his Father. — The Elder Lyttelton; his Death-bed. — Aberrations of the Younger Lord. — Strange Ghost Story; Curious Modes of accounting for it. — Return to Stourbridge. — Late Drive. — Hales Owen.

The parish church of Hagley, an antique Gothic building of small size, much hidden in wood, lies at the foot of the hill, within a few hundred yards of the mansion-house. It was erected in the remote past, long ere the surrounding pleasure-grounds had any existence; but it has now come to be as thoroughly enclosed in them as the urns and obelisks of the rising ground above, and forms as picturesque an object as any urn or obelisk among them all. There is, however, a vast difference between jest and earnest; and the *bona fide* tomb-stones of the building inscribed with names of the dead, and its dark walls and pointed roof reared with direct reference to a life to which the present is but the brief vestibule, do not quite harmonize with temples of Theseus and the Muses, or political columns erected in honor of forgotten Princes of Wales, who quarrelled with their fathers, and were cherished, in consequence, by the Opposition. As I came upon it unawares, and saw it emerge from its dense thicket of trees, I felt as if, at an Egyptian feast, I had unwittingly brushed off the veil from the admonitory skeleton. The door lay open, — a few workmen were engaged in paving a portion of the floor, and repairing some breaches in the vault; and as I entered, one of their number was employed in shovelling, some five or six feet under the pavement, among the dust of the Lytteltons. The trees outside render the place exceedingly gloomy. "At Hagley," the too celebrated Thomas Lord Lyttelton is made to say, in the posthumous volume of Letters which bears his name, "there is a temple of Theseus, commonly called by the gardener the temple of Perseus, which stares you in the face wherever you go; while the temple of God, commonly called by the gardener the parish church, is so industriously hid by trees from without, that the pious matron can hardly read her Prayer-book within."* A brown twilight still lingers in the place: the lettered marbles along the walls glisten cold and sad in the gloom, as if invested by the dun Cimmerian atmosphere described by the old poet as brooding over the land of the dead, —

> "the dusky coasts
> Peopled by shoals of visionary ghosts."

One straggling ray of sunshine, colored by the stained glass of a narrow window, and dimmed yet more by the motty dust-reek raised by the workmen, fell on a small oblong tablet, the plainest and least considerable in the building, and, by lighting up its inscription of five short lines, gave to it, by one of those

* This volume, though it contains a good many authentic anecdotes of the younger Lyttelton, is not genuine. It was written, shortly after his Lordship's death, when the public curiosity regarding him was much excited, by a person of resembling character, — *Duke* Combe, a man who, after dissipating in early life a large fortune, lived precariously for many years as a clever but rather unscrupulous author of all work, and succeeded in producing, when turned of seventy, a well-known volume, — "Dr. Syntax's Tour in Search of the Picturesque."

fortuitous happinesses in which so much of the poetry of common life consists, the prominence which it deserves. It briefly intimates that it was placed there, in its naked unadornedness, "at the particular desire of the Right Honorable George Lyttelton, who died August 22, 1773, aged sixty-four." The poet had willed, like another titled poet of less unclouded reputation, that his "epitaph should be his name alone." Beside the plain slab, — so near that they almost touch, — there is a marble of great elegance, — the monument of the Lady Lucy. It shows that she predeceased her husband, — dying at the early age of twenty-nine, — nearly thirty years. Her epitaph, like the monody, must be familiar to most of my readers; but for the especial benefit of the class whose reading may have lain rather among the poets of the present than of the past century, I give it as transcribed from the marble: —

"Made to engage all hearts and charm all eyes,
Though meek, magnanimous, — though witty, wise;
Polite as she in courts had ever been,
Yet good as she the world had never seen;
The noble fire of an exalted mind,
With gentle female tenderness combined:
Her speech was the melodious voice of love,
Her song the warbling of the vernal grove;
Her eloquence was sweeter than her song,
Soft as her heart, and as her reason strong:
Her form each beauty of the mind expressed;
Her mind was virtue by the graces dressed."

England, in the eighteenth century, saw few better men or better women than Lord Lyttelton and his lady; and it does seem a curious enough fact, that their only son, a boy of many hopes and many advantages, and who possessed quick parts and a vigorous intellect, should have proved, notwithstanding, one of the most flagitious personages of his age. The first

Lord Lyttelton was not more conspicuous for his genius and his virtues, than the second Lord Lyttelton for his talents and his vices.

There are many who, though they do not subscribe to the creed of the phrenologist, are yet unconsciously influenced by its doctrines; and never, perhaps, was the phrenological belief more general than now, that the human race, like some of the inferior races, is greatly dependent, for the development of what is best in it, on what I shall venture to term purity of breed. It has become a sort of axiom, that well-dispositioned intellectual parents produce a well-dispositioned intellectual offspring; and of course, as human history is various enough, when partially culled, to furnish evidence in support of anything, there have been instances adduced in proof of the position, which it would take a long time to enumerate. But were exactly the opposite belief held, the same various history would be found to furnish at least as many evidences in support of it as of the other. The human race, so far at least as the mental and the moral are concerned, comes very doubtfully, if at all, under the law of the inferior natures. David Hume, better acquainted with history than most men, gives what seems to be the true state of the case. "The races of animals," he says, "never degenerate when carefully attended to; and horses in particular always show their blood in their shape, spirit, and swiftness; but a coxcomb may beget a philosopher, as a man of virtue may leave a worthless progeny." It is not uninstructive to observe how strongly the philosophy of the remark is borne out by the facts of Hume's own History. The mean, pusillanimous, foolish John was the son of the wise, dauntless Henry the Second, and the brother of the magnanimous Richard *Cœur de Lion*. His immediate descendant and successor, nearly as weak, though somewhat more honest than himself, was the father of the fearless, politic, unscrupulous Edward the First; and he, of the imbecile Edward the Second; and he, in turn, of the brave, sagacious Edward the Third; and then comes one of those cases which the phrenologist picks out from the general mass, and threads together, as with a string: the heroic Edward the Third was the father of the heroic Black Prince. And thus the record runs on, bearing from beginning to end the same character; save that as *common* men are vastly less rare, as the words imply, than *uncommon* ones, it is inevitable that instances of the ordinary producing the ordinary should greatly predominate over instances of an opposite cast. We see, however, a brutal Henry the Eighth succeeded by his son, a just and gentle Edward the Sixth; and he by his bigoted, weak-minded sister, the bloody Mary; and she by his other sister, the shrewd, politic Elizabeth. But in no history is this independence of man's mental and moral nature of the animal laws of transmission better shown than in the most ancient and authentic of all. The two first brothers the world ever saw,—children of the same father and mother,—were persons of diametrically opposite characters; a similar diversity obtained in the families of Noah and of Jacob: the devout Eli was the father of profligate children; and Solomon, the wise son of a great monarch, a great warrior, and a great author,—he who, according to Cowley, "from best of poets best of kings did grow,"—had much unscrupulous coxcombry and mediocre commonplace among his brethren, and an ill-advised simpleton for his son.

The story of the younger Lyttelton,—better known half a century ago than it is now,—has not a few curious points about it. He was one of three children, two of them girls, apostrophized by the bereaved poet in the Monody:—

"Sweet babes, who, like the little playful fawns
Were wont to trip along these verdant lawns
By your delighted mother's side,
Who now your infant steps shall guide?
Ah! where is now the hand whose tender care
To every virtue would have formed your youth,
And strewed with flowers the thorny ways of truth
O, loss beyond repair!
O, wretched father, left alone
To weep their dire misfortune and thy own!
How shall thy weakened mind, oppressed with woe
And drooping o'er thy Lucy's grave,
Perform the duties that you doubly owe,
Now she, alas! is gone,
From folly and from vice their helpless age to save?

One of the two female children died in infancy; the other lived to contract an advantageous and happy marriage with a very amiable nobleman, and to soothe the dying bed of her father. The boy gave early promise of fine parts and an energetic disposition. He learned almost in childhood to appreciate Milton, mastered his tasks with scarce an effort, spoke and wrote with fluent elegance, and was singularly happy in repartee. It was early seen, however, that his nature was based on a substratum of profound selfishness, and that an uneasy vanity rendered him intensely jealous of all in immediate contact with him, whose claims to admiration or respect he regarded as overtopping his own. All of whom he was jealous it was his disposition to dislike and oppose: his insane envy made war upon them in behalf of self; and, unfortunately, it was his excellent father, — a man possessed of one of the highest and most unsullied reputations of the day, — whom he regarded as most his rival. Had the first Lord Lyttelton been a worse man, the second Lord would possibly have been a better one; for in the moral and the religious, — in all that related to the conduct of life and the government of the passions, — he seemed to regard his father as a sort of reverse standard by which to regulate himself on a principle of contrariety. The elder Lord had produced a treatise on the "Conversion of St. Paul," which continues to hold a prominent place among our works of evidence, and to which, says Johnson, "infidelity has never been able to fabricate a specious answer." It was answered, however, after a sort, by a sceptical foreigner, *Claude Anet*, whose work the younger Lyttelton made it his business diligently to study, and which, as a piece of composition and argument, he professed greatly to prefer to his father's. The elder Lyttelton had written verses which gave him a place among the British poets, and which contain, as he himself has characterized those of Thomson, —

"Not one immoral, one corrupted thought, —
One line which, dying, he could wish to blot."

The younger Lyttelton wrote verses also; but his, though not quite without merit, had to be banished society, like a leper freckled with infection, and they have since perished apart. The elder Lyttelton wrote Dialogues of the Dead; so did the younger; but his dialogues were too blasphemously profane to be given, in a not very zealous age, to the public; and we can but predict their character from their names. The speakers in one were, "King David and Cæsar Borgia;" and in another, "Socrates and Jesus Christ." He gave a loose to his passions, till not a woman of reputation would dare be seen in his company, or permit him, when he waited on her, — heir-apparent as he was to a fine estate and a fair title, — to do more than leave his card. His father, in the hope of awakening him to higher pursuits and a nobler ambition, exerted his influence in getting him returned to Parliament; and he made his début in a brilliant speech, which greatly excited the hopes of the veteran senator and his friends, and was complimented in the House by the opposition, as fraught with the "hereditary ability of the Lytteltons. He subsequently lost his seat, however, in consequence of some irregularities connected with his election, and returned full swing to the gratification of the grosser propensities of his nature. At length, when shunned by high and low, even in the neighborhood of Hagley, he was sent to hide his disgrace in an obscure retreat on the continent.

Meanwhile, the elder Lyttelton was fast breaking up. There was nothing in the nature of his illness, says his physician, in an interesting account of his last moments, to alarm the fears of his friends; but there is a malady of the affections darkly hinted at in the narrative, which had broken his rest and prostrated his strength, and which medicine could not reach. It is sad enough to reflect that he himself had been one of the best of sons. The letter is still extant which his aged father addressed to him, on the publication of his treatise on the "Conversion of St. Paul." After some judicious commendation of the cogency of the arguments and the excellence of the style, the old man goes on to say, "May the King of kings, whose glorious cause you have so well defended, reward your pious labors, and grant that I may be found worthy, through the merits of Jesus Christ, to be an eye-witness of that happiness which I doubt not He will bountifully bestow upon you. In the mean time, I shall never cease glorifying God for having endowed you with such useful talents, and giving me so good a son." And here was the son, in whose behalf this affecting prayer had been breathed, dying broken-hearted, a victim to paternal solicitude and sorrow. But did the history of the species furnish us with no such instances, we would possess one argument fewer than in the existing sta e of things, for a scheme of final retribution, through which every unredressed wrong shall be righted, and every unsettled account receive its appropriate adjustment. Junius, a writer who never praised willingly, had just decided, with reference to his Lordship's long political career, that "the integrity and judgment of Lord Lyttelton were unquestionable;" but the subject of the eulogy was passing to the tribunal of a higher judge. His hopes of immortality rested solely on the revealed basis; and yet it did yield him cause of gratitude on his death-bed, that he had been enabled throughout the probationary course, now at its close, to maintain the character of an honest man. "In politics and in public life," he said to his physician, shortly ere his departure, "I have made public good the rule of my conduct. I never gave counsels which I did not at the time think the best. I have seen that I was sometimes in the wrong; but I did not err designedly. I have endeavored in private life to do all the good in my power; and never for a moment could indulge malicious or unjust designs against any person whatsoever." And so the first Lord Lyttelton slept with his fathers; and Thomas, the second Lord, succeeded him.

He soon attained, in his hereditary seat in the Upper House, to no small consequence as a Parliamentary speaker; and the ministry of the day — the same that lost the colonies to Britain — found it of importance he should be conciliated. His father had long desired, but never could obtain, the government appointment of Chief Justice in Eyre. It was known there was nothing to be gained by conferring a favor of the kind on the first Lord Lyttelton: he would have voted and spoken after exactly the same manner, whether he got the appointment or no. But the second Lord was deemed a man of a different stamp; and the place which the father, after his honest services of forty years, had longed for in vain, the son in the infancy of his peerage, ere he had performed a single service of any kind, received unsolicited. The gift had its effect; and many of his after votes were recorded on the side of ministers, against Chatham and the Americans. No party, however, could calculate very surely on his support: he was frequently drawn aside by some eccentric impulse; and frequently hit right and left in mere wantonness, without caring whether the stroke fell on friend or foe. There were, meanwhile, sad doings at Hagley. In "his father's decent hall," to employ the language of Childe Harold,

> "condemned to uses vile,
> Now Paphian girls were known to sing and smile."

He had been married to a lady, of whom nothing worse has ever been said than that she accepted his hand. Her, however, he had early deserted. But the road he had taken, with all its downward ease and breadth, is not the road which leads to happiness; and enough survives of his private history to show that he was a very miserable man.

> "And none did love him; though to hall and bower
> He gathered revellers from far and near,
> He knew them flatterers of the festal hour,
> The heartless parasites of present cheer;
> Yea, none did love him, — not his lemans dear."

He seems to have been strongly marked by the peculiar heartlessness so generally found to coëxist with the gratuitous and flashy generosity of men of grossly licentious lives; that petrifaction of feeling to which Burns and Byron — both of them unfortunately but too well qualified to decide on the subject — so pointedly refer. But he could feel remorse, however incapable of pity, — and remorse heightened, notwithstanding an ostentatious scepticism, by the direst terrors of superstition. Among the females who had been the objects of his temporary attachment, and had fallen victims to it, there was a Mrs. Dawson, whose fortune, with her honor and reputation, had been sacrificed to her passion, and who, on being deserted by his Lordship for another, did not long survive: she died broken-hearted, bankrupt both in means and character. But though she perished without friend, she was yet fully avenged on the seducer. Ever after, he believed himself haunted by her spectre. It would start up before him in the solitudes of Hagley at noon-day, — at night it flitted round his pillow, — it followed him incessantly during his rustication on the continent, — and is said to have given him especial disturbance when passing a few days at Lyons. In England, when residing for a short time with a brother nobleman, he burst at midnight into the room in which his host slept, and begged, in great horror of mind, to be permitted to pass the night beside him: in his own apartment, he said, he had been strangely annoyed by an unaccountable creaking of the floor. He ultimately deserted Hagley, which he found by much too solitary, and in too close proximity with the parish burying-ground; and removed to a country-house near Epsom, called Pit Place, from its situation in an old chalk-pit. And here, six years after the death of his father, the vital powers suddenly failed him, and he broke down and died in his thirty-sixth year. There were circumstances connected with his death that form the strangest part of his story, — circumstances which powerfully attracted public attention at the time, and which, as they tasked too severely the belief of an incredulous age, have been very variously accounted for. We find Dr. Johnson, whose bias, however, did not incline him to the incredulous side, thus referring to them, in one of the conversations recorded by Boswell. "I mentioned," says the chronicler, "Thomas Lord Lyttelton's vision, — the prediction of the time of his death, and its exact fulfilment." JOHNSON. — "It is the most extraordinary thing that has happened in my day: I heard it with my own ears from his uncle, Lord Westcote. I am so glad to have evidence of the spiritual world, that I am willing to believe it." Dr. ADAMS. — "You have evidence enough; good evidence, which needs not such support." JOHNSON. — "I like to have more."

This celebrated vision, — long so familiar to the British public, that almost all the writers who touch on it, from Boswell to Sir Walter Scott inclusive, deal by the details as too well known to be repeated, — is now getting pretty much out of sight. I shall present the particulars, therefore, as I have been able to collect them from the somewhat varying authorities of the time.* His Lordship, on Thursday, November 5th, 1779, had made the usual opening address to the Sovereign the occasion of a violent attack on the administration; "but this," says Walpole, "was, notwithstanding his government appointment, nothing new to him; he was apt to go point-blank into all extremes, without any parenthesis or decency, nor even boggled at contradicting his own words." In the evening he set out for his house at Epsom, carrying with him, says the same gossiping authority, "a caravan of nymphs." He sat up rather

* Walpole, Wraxall, Warner, and the *Scots Magazine*. Malone, in one of the notes to Boswell's "Johnson," refers the reader for a correct account of "Lyttelton's supposed vision," to "Nash's History of Worcestershire;" and his reference has been reprinted, without alteration, in the elaborate edition of Croker. But the earlier commentator must have been misled in the case by a deceptive memory; and the latter, by taking his predecessor's labors too much on trust. Nash's entire notice consists of but a meagre allusion to his Lordship's death, wound up by the remark, that there were circumstances connected with it well suited to "engage the attention of believers in the second sight."

late after his arrival; and, on retiring to bed, was suddenly awakened from brief slumber a little before midnight, by what appeared to be a dove, which, after fluttering for an instant near the bed-curtains, glided towards a casement-window in the apartment, where it seemed to flutter for an instant longer, and then vanished. At the same moment his eye fell upon a female figure in white, standing at the bed-foot, in which he at once recognized, says Warner, "the spectre of the unfortunate lady that had haunted him so long." It solemnly warned him to prepare for death, for that within three days he should be called to his final account; and, having delivered its message, immediately disappeared. In the morning his Lordship seemed greatly discomposed, and complained of a violent headache. "He had had an extraordinary dream," he said, "suited, did he possess even a particle of superstition, to make a deep impression on his mind;" and in afterwards communicating the particulars of the vision, he remarked, rather, however, in joke than earnest, that the warning was somewhat of the shortest, and that really, after a course of life so disorderly as his, three days formed but a brief period for preparation. On Saturday, he began to recover his spirits; and told a lady of his acquaintance at Epsom, that as it was now the third and last day, he would, if he escaped for but a few hours longer, fairly "jockey the ghost." He became greatly depressed, however, as the evening wore on; and one of his companions, as the critical hour of midnight approached, set forward the house-clock, in the hope of dissipating his fears, by misleading him into the belief that he had entered on the fourth day, and was of course safe. The hour of twelve accordingly struck; the company, who had sat with him till now, broke up immediately after, laughing at the prediction; and his Lordship retired to his bed-room, apparently much relieved. His valet, who had mixed up at his desire a dose of rhubarb, followed him a few minutes after, and he sat up in bed, in apparent health, to take the medicine; but, being in want of a tea-spoon, he despatched the servant, with an expression of impatience, to bring him one. The man was scarce a minute absent. When he returned, however, his master was a corpse. He had fallen backwards on the pillow, and his outstretched hand still grasped his watch, which exactly indicated the fatal hour of twelve. It has been conjectured that his dissolution might have been an effect of the shock he received, on ascertaining that the dreaded hour had not yet gone by: at all events, explain the fact as we may, ere the fourth day had arrived, Lyttelton was dead. It has been further related, as a curious coincidence, that on the night of his decease, one of his intimate acquaintance at Dartford, in Kent, dreamed that his Lordship appeared to him, and, drawing back the bed-curtains, said, with an air of deep melancholy, "My dear friend, it is all over; you see me for the last time."*

* The reader may be curious to see the paragraph in which, sixty-seven years ago, the details of this singular incident were first communicated to the British public through the various periodicals of the day. I quote from the *Scots Magazine* for December 1779:—"On Thursday night, November 25th, Lord Lyttelton sat up late, after the vote on the Address in the House of Lords. He complained of a violent headache next morning, seemed much discomposed, and recited a very striking dream, which, he said, would have made a deep impression on his mind had he been possessed of even the least particle of superstition. He had started up from midnight sleep, on perceiving a bird fluttering near the bed-curtains, which vanished suddenly, when a female spectre, in white raiment, presented herself, and charged him to depend on his dissolution within three days. He lamented jocosely the shortness of the warning; and observed, it was a short time for preparation after so disorderly a life. On the Saturday morning, he found himself in spirits; and when at Epsom, told Mrs. F—— (wife of the Hon. Mr. F——) that he should jockey the ghost if he escaped a few hours, for it was the third and last day. He was

The story has been variously accounted for. Some have held, as we learn from Sir Walter Scott in his "Demonology," that his Lordship, weary of life, and fond of notoriety, first invented the prediction, with its accompanying circumstances, and then destroyed himself to fulfil it. And it is added, in a note furnished by a friend of Sir Walter's, that the whole incident has been much exaggerated. "I heard Lord Fortescue once say," says the writer of the note, "that he was in the house with Lord Lyttelton at the time of the supposed visitation, and he mentioned the following circumstances as the only foundation for the extraordinary superstructure at which the world has wondered: — 'A woman of the party had one day lost a favorite bird, and all the men tried to recover it for her. Soon after, on assembling at breakfast, Lord Lyttelton complained of having passed a very bad night, and having been worried in his dreams by a repetition of the chase of the lady's bird. His death followed, as stated in the story.'" Certainly, had this been all, it would be scarce necessary to infer that his Lordship destroyed himself. But the testimony of Lord Fortescue does not amount to more than simply that at first Lord Lyttelton told but a part of his dream; while the other evidence goes to show that he subsequently added the rest. Nor does the theory of the premeditated suicide seem particularly happy.

seized with convulsions in the evening, and expired, putting off his clothes to go into bed. These circumstances are not only verified by Charles Wal—y, Esq., a captain in the royal navy, and many other respectable characters, witnesses of his Lordship's conversation and exit, but are remarkably impressed by the additional circumstance of a very intimate friend of Lord Lyttelton, at Dartford, in Kent, dreaming on the night of this evening (Saturday, November 27) that his Lordship had appeared to him towards daybreak, and, drawing back the curtain, said, 'My dear friend, it is all over; you see me for the last time,' -- or words to that effect."

If we must indeed hold that the agency of the unseen world never sensibly mingles with that of the seen and the tangible,

"To shame the doctrine of the Sadducee,"

we may at least deem it not very improbable that such a vision should have been conjured up by the dreaming fancy of an unhappy libertine, ill at ease in his conscience, sensible of sinking health, much addicted to superstitious fears, and who, shortly before, had been led, through a sudden and alarming indisposition, to think of death. Nor does it seem a thing beyond the bounds of credibility or coincidence, that in the course of the three following days, when prostrated by his ill-concealed terrors, he should have experienced a second and severer attack of the illness from which, only a few weeks previous, he had with difficulty recovered.*

* Certain it is, — and the circumstance is a curious one, — there were no firmer believers in the truth of the story than Lyttelton's own nearer relatives. It was his uncle, a man of strong sense, to whom Johnson referred as his authority, and on whose direct evidence he built so much; and we are told by Sir Nathaniel Wraxall, that the Lady Dowager Lyttelton, — the younger Lord's stepmother, whom, however, the knight represents as "a woman of a very lively imagination,"— was equally a believer. "I have frequently seen, at her house in Portugal Street, Grosvenor Square," says Sir Nathaniel, "a painting which she herself executed in 1780, expressly to commemorate the event. It hung in a conspicuous part of her drawing-room. There the dove appears at the window; while a female figure, habited in white, stands at the bed-foot, announcing to Lord Lyttelton his dissolution. Every part of the picture was faithfully designed after the description given her by his Lordship's valet, to whom his master related all the circumstances." "About four years after, in the year 1783," adds the knight, "when dining at Pit Place, I had the curiosity to visit Lord Lyttelton's bed-chamber, where the casement-window at which, as his Lordship asserted, the dove appeared to flutter, was pointed out to me." The reader will perhaps remember that Byron refers to the apparition of the bird as a precedent for the passage in the "Bride of Abydos" in which he introduces the spirit of Selim as pouring out its

I returned to Stourbridge, where I baited to get some refreshment, and wait the coach for Hales Owen, in an old-fashioned inn, with its overhanging gable of mingled beam and brick fronting the street, and its some six or seven rooms on the ground-floor, opening in succession into each other like the rattles of a snake's tail. Three solid-looking Englishmen, two of them farmers evidently, the third a commercial traveller, had just sat down to a late dinner; and, on the recommendation of the hostess, I drew in a chair and formed one of the party. A fourth Englishman, much a coxcomb apparently, greatly excited, and armed with a whip, was pacing the floor of the room in which we sat; while in an outer room of somewhat inferior pretensions, there was another Englishman, also armed with a whip, and also pacing the floor; and the two, each from his own apartment, were prosecuting an angry and noisy dispute together. The outer-room Englishman was a groom, — the inner-room Englishman deemed himself a gentleman. They had both got at the races into the same gig, the property of the innkeeper, and quarrelled about who should drive. The groom had argued his claim on the plea that he was the better driver of the two, and that driving along a crowded race-ground was difficult and dangerous: the coxcomb had insisted on driving, because he liked to drive, and because, he said, he did n't choose to be driven in such a public place by a groom. The groom retorted, that though a groom, he was as good a man as he was, for all his fine coat, — perhaps a better man; and so the

sorrows, in the form of a nightingale, over the tomb of Zuleika. "For a belief that the souls of the dead inhabit birds," says the poet, "we need not travel to the east: Lord Lyttelton's ghost story, and many other instances, bring this superstition nearer home." The Lord Westcote, Lord Lyttelton's uncle, who related the story to Johnson, succeeded to the title and estate, and the present Lord Lyttelton is, I believe, Lord Westcote's grandson.

controversy went on, till the three solid Englishmen, worried at their meal by the incessant noise, interfered in behalf of the groom. "Thou bee'st a foolish man," said one of the farmers to the coxcomb; "better to be driven by a groom than to wrangle with a groom."—"Foolish man!" iterated the other farmer, "thou's would have broken the groom's neck and thee's own." —"Ashamed," exclaimed the commercial gentleman, "to be driven by a groom, at such a time as this,—the groom a good driver too, and, for all that appears, an honest man! I don't think any one should be ashamed to be driven by a groom; I know I would n't."—"The first un-English thing I have seen in England," said I: "I thought you English people were above littlenesses of that kind."—"Thank you, gentlemen, thank you," exclaimed the voice from the other room; "I was sure I was right. He 's a low fellow: I would box him for sixpence." The coxcomb muttered something between his teeth, and stalked into the apartment beyond that in which we sat; the commercial gentleman thrust his tongue into his cheek as he disappeared; and we were left to enjoy our pudding in peace. It was late and long this evening ere the *six o'clock* coach started for Hales Owen. At length, a little after eight, when the night had fairly set in, and crowds on crowds had come pouring into the town from the distant race-ground, away it rumbled, stuck over with a double fare of passengers, jammed on before and behind, and occupying to the full every square foot atop.

Though sorely be-elbowed and be-kneed, we had a jovial ride. England was merry England this evening in the neighborhood of Stourbridge. We passed cart, and wagon, and gig, parties afoot and parties on horseback; and there was a free interchange of gibe and joke, hail and halloo. There seemed to be more hearty mirth and less intemperance afloat than I have seen in Scotland on such occasions; but the whole appeared just foolish enough notwithstanding; and a knot of low blackguard gamblers, who were stuck together on the coach front, and conversing with desperate profanity on who they *dia* and by whom they were *done*, showed me that to the foolish there was added not a little of the bad. The Hales Owen road runs for the greater part of the way within the southern edge of the Dudley coal-field, and, lying high, commands a downward view of its multitudinous workings for many miles. It presented from the coach-top this evening a greatly more magnificent prospect than by day. The dark space, — a nether firmament, — for its gray wasteful desolation had disappeared with the vanished daylight, — was spangled bright by innumerable furnaces, twinkling and star-like in the distance, but flaring like comets in the foreground. We could hear the roaring of the nearer fires; here a tall chimney or massy engine peered doubtfully out, in dusky umber, from amid the blackness; while the heavens above glowed in the reflected light, a blood-red. It was near ten o'clock ere I reached the inn at Hales Owen; and the room into which I was shown received, for more than an hour after, continual relays of guests from the races, who turned in for a few minutes to drink gin and water, and then took the road again. They were full of their backings and their bets, and animated by a life-and-death eagerness to demonstrate how Sir John's gelding had distanced my Lord's mare.

CHAPTER VIII.

Abbotsford and the Leasowes. — The one place naturally suggestive of the other. — Shenstone. — The Leasowes his most elaborate Composition. – The English Squire and his Mill. — Hales Owen Abbey; interesting, as the Subject of one of Shenstone's larger Poems. — The old anti-Popish Feeling of England well exemplified by the Fact. — Its Origin and History. — Decline. — Infidelity naturally favorable to the Resuscitation and Reproduction of Popery. — The two Naileresses. — Cecilia and Delia. — Skeleton Description of the Leasowes. — Poetic filling up. — The Spinster. — The Fountain.

I HAD come to Hales Owen to visit the Leasowes, the patrimony which poor Shenstone converted into an exquisite poem, written on the green face of nature, with groves and thickets, cascades and lakes, urns, temples, and hermitages, for the characters. In passing southwards, I had seen from the coach-top the woods of Abbotsford, with the turrets of the mansion-house peeping over; and the idea of the trim-kept desolation of the place suggested to me that of the paradise which the poet of Hales Owen had, like Sir Walter, ruined himself to produce, that it, too, might become a melancholy desert. Nor was the association which linked Abbotsford to the Leasowes by any means arbitrary: the one place may be regarded as having in some degree arisen out of the other. "It had been," says Sir Walter, in one of his prefaces, "an early wish of mine to connect myself with my mother earth, and prosecute those experiments by which a species of creative power is exercised over the face of nature. I can trace, even to childhood, a pleasure derived from Dodsley's account of Shenstone's Leasowes; and I envied the poet much more for the pleasure of accomplishing the objects detailed in his friend's sketch of his grounds, than for the possession of pipe, crook, flock, and Phillis to boot." Alas!

"Prudence sings to thoughtless bards in vain."

In contemplating the course of Shenstone, Sir Walter could see but the pleasures of the voyage, without taking note of the shipwreck in which it terminated; and so, in pursuing identically the same track, he struck on identically the same shoal.

I had been intimate from a very immature period with the writings of Shenstone. There are poets that require to be known early in life, if one would know them at all to advantage. They give real pleasure, but it is a pleasure which the mind outgrows; they belong to the "comfit and confectionary-plum" class; and Shenstone is decidedly one of the number. No mind ever outgrew the "Task," or the "Paradise Lost," or the dramas of Shakspeare, or the poems of Burns: they please in early youth; and, like the nature which they embody and portray, they continue to please in age. But the Langhorns, Wartons, Kirke Whites, Shelleys, Keatses, — shall I venture to say it? — Byrons, are flowers of the spring, and bear to the sobered eye, if one misses acquainting one's self with them at the proper season, very much the aspect of those herbarium specimens of the botanist, which we may examine as matters of curiosity, but scarce contemplate, — as we do the fresh uncropped flowers, with all their exquisite tints and delicious odors vital within them, — as the objects of an affectionate regard. Shenstone was one of the ten or twelve English poets whose works I had the happiness of possessing when a boy, and which, during some eight or ten years of my life, — for books at the time formed luxuries of difficult procurement, and I had to make the most of those I had, — I used to read over and over at the rate of about twice in the twelvemonth. And every time I read the poems, I was sure also to read Dodsley's appended description of the Leasowes. I could never form from it any idea of the place as a whole: the imagery seemed broken up into detached slips, like the imagery of a magic lantern; but then nothing could be finer than the insulated slips; and my mind was filled with gorgeous pictures, all fresh and bright, of "sloping groves," "tufted knolls," "wooded valleys," "sequestered lakes," and "noisy rivulets," — of rich grassy lawns, and cascades that come bursting in foam from bosky hill-sides, — of monumental urns, tablets, and temples, — of hermitages and priories; and I had now come to see in what degree my conceptions, drawn from the description, corresponded with the original, if, indeed, the original still maintained the impress given it by the genius of Shenstone. His writings, like almost all poetic writings that do not please equally at sixteen and sixty, had stood their testing century but indifferently well. No one at least would now venture to speak of him as the "celebrated poet, whose divine elegies do honor to our nation, our language, and our species;" though such, sixty years ago, was the estimate of Burns, when engaged in writing his preface to an uncouth volume of poems first published at Kilmarnock, that promise to get over *their* century with much greater ease. On the "Leasowes,"—by far the most elaborate of all the compositions of its author, — the ingenious thinking of full twenty years had been condensed; and I was eager to ascertain whether it had not stood its testing century better, under the skyey influences, than "Ophelia's Urn," or "the Song of Colin, a discerning Shepherd," under those corresponding influences of the literary heavens which freshen and preserve whatever has life in it, and wear down and dilapidate whatever is dead.

A little after ten o'clock, a gentleman, who travelled in his own carriage, entered the inn, — a frank, genial Englishman, who seemed to have a kind word for every one, and whom the inn-people addressed as the Squire. My Scotch tongue revealed my country; and a few questions on the part of the Squire, about Scotland and Scotch matters, fairly launched us into conversation. I had come to Hales Owen to see the Leasowes, I said: when a very young man, I used to dream about them full five hundred miles away, among the rocks and hills of the wild north; and I had now availed myself of my first opportunity of paying them a visit. The Squire, as he in turn informed me, had taken the inn in his way to rusticate for a few days at a small property of his in the immediate neighborhood of the Leasowes: and if I but called on him on the morrow at his temporary dwelling,— Squire Eyland's Mill,—all the better if I came to breakfast,— he would, he said, fairly enter me on the grounds, and introduce me, as we went, to the old ecclesiastical building which forms the subject of one of Shenstone's larger poems, "The Ruined Abbey." He knew all the localities,— which one acquainted with but the old classic descriptions would now find it difficult to realize, for the place had fallen into a state of sad dilapidation; and often acted the part of *cicerone* to his friends. I had never met with anything half so frank in Scotland from the class who travel in their own carriages; and, waiving but the breakfast, I was next morning at the Mill,— a quiet, rustic dwelling, at the side of a green lane,— a little before ten. It lies at the bottom of a flat valley, with a small stream, lined by many a rich meadow, stealing between its fringes of willows and alders; and with the Leasowes on the one hand, and the Clent Hills, little more than an hour's walk away, on the other, it must form, in the season of green fields and clear skies, a delightful retreat.

The Squire led me through the valley adown the course of the stream for nearly a mile, and then holding to the right for nearly a quarter of a mile more, we came full upon the ruins of Hales Owen Abbey. The mace of the bluff Harry had fallen heavy upon the pile: it had proved, in after times, a convenient quarry for the neighboring farm-houses, and the repair of roads and fences for miles around; and so it now consists of but a few picturesque fragments cut apart by wide gaps, in which we fail to trace even the foundations,—fragments that rise insulated and tall,—here wrapt up in ivy,—there bristling with wall-flower,—over hay-ricks and antique farm-offices, and moss-grown fruit-trees, and all those nameless appurtenances which a Dutchman would delight to paint, of a long-established barn-yard, farm-house, and orchard. I saw, resting against one of the walls, the rudely-carved lid of a stone coffin, which exhibits in a lower corner a squat figure in the attitude of adoration; and along the opposite side and upper corner, an uncouth representation of the crucifixion, in which the figure on the cross seems that of a gaunt ill-proportioned skeleton. Covered over, however, with the lichens of ages, and garnished with a light border of ground ivy,—a plant which greatly abounds amid the ruins,—its antique misproportions seem quite truthful enough, and impress more than elegance. One tall gable, that of the chancel, which forms the loftiest part of the pile, still remains nearly entire; and its great window, once emblazoned with the arms of old Judge Lyttelton, but now stripped of stained glass and carved mullion, is richly festooned with ivy. A wooden pigeon-house has been stuck up in the opening, and half a dozen white pigeons were fluttering in the sunshine this morning, round the ivied gable-top. The dust of the old learned lawyer lies under the hay-ricks below, with that of nameless warriors and forgotten churchmen: and when the spade turns up the soil, fragments of human bones are found, thickly mingled with bits of painted tiles and stained glass.

It may be thought I am but wasting words in describing so

broken a ruin, seeing I must have passed many finer ones undescribed; but it will, I trust, be taken into account that I had perused the "Ruined Abbey" at least twice every twelvemonth, from my twelfth to my twentieth year, and that I had now before me the original of the picture. The poem is not a particularly fine one. Shenstone's thinking required rhyme, just as Pope's weakly person needed stays, to keep it tolerably erect; and the "Ruined Abbey" is in blank verse. There is poetry, however, in some of the conceptions, such as that of the peasant, in the days of John, returning listless from his fields after the Pope had pronounced his dire anathema, and seeing in every dark overbellying cloud

"A vengeful angel, in whose waving scroll
He read damnation."

Nor is the following passage, — descriptive of the same gloomy season of terror and deprivation, — though perhaps inferior in elegance and effect to the parallel passage in the prose of Hume, without merit: —

"The wretch, — whose hope, by stern oppression chased
From every earthly bliss, still as it saw
Triumphant wrong, took wing and flew to heaven,
And rested there, — now mourned his refuge lost,
And wonted peace. The sacred fane was barred;
And the lone altar, where the mourners thronged
To supplicate remission, smoked no more;
While the green weed luxuriant rose around.
Some from their deathbed, in delirious woe,
Beheld the ghastly king approach, begirt
In tenfold terrors, or, expiring, heard
The last loud clarion sound, and Heaven's decree
With unremitting vengeance bar the skies.
Nor light the grief, — by Superstition weighed, —
That their dishonored corse, shut from the verge
Of hallowed earth or tutelary fane,
Must sleep with brutes, their vassals, in the field,
Beneath some path in marle unexorcised."

The chief interest of the poem, however, does not lie in its poetry. It forms one of the most curious illustrations I know of the strong anti-Popish zeal, apart from religious feeling, which was so general in England during the last century, and which, in the Lord-George-Gordon mobs, showed itself so very formidable a principle when fairly aroused. Dickens' picture, in "Barnaby Rudge," of the riots of 1780, has the merit of being faithful; — his religious mobs are chiefly remarkable for being mobs in which there is no religion; but his picture would be more faithful still, had he made them in a slight degree Protestant. Shenstone, like the Lord-George-Gordon mob, was palpably devoid of religion, — "an elegant heathen, rather than a Christian," whose poetry contains verses in praise of almost every god except the true one; and who, when peopling his Elysium with half the deities of Olympus, saw nymphs and satyrs in his very dreams. But though only an indifferent Christian, he was an excellent Protestant. There are passages in the "Ruined Abbey" that breathe the very spirit of the English soldiery, whose anti-Popish huzzas, on the eve of the Revolution, deafened their infatuated monarch in his tent. Take, for instance, the following: —

"Hard was our fate while Rome's director taught
Of subjects born to be their monarch's prey;
To toil for monks, — for gluttony to toil, —
For vacant gluttony, extortion, fraud,
For avarice, envy, pride, revenge, and shame!
O, doctrine breathed from Stygian caves! exhaled
From inmost Erebus!"

Not less decided is the passage in which he triumphs over the suppression of the Monasteries, "by Tudor's wild caprice."

"Then from its towering height, with horrid sound,
Rushed the proud Abbey. Then the vaulted roofs,
Torn from their walls, disclosed the wanton scene

Of monkish chastity! Each angry friar
Crawled from his bedded strumpet, muttering low
An ineffectual curse. The pervious nooks,
That ages past conveyed the guileful priest
To play some image on the gaping crowd,
Imbibe the novel daylight, and expose
Obvious the fraudful engin'ry of Rome."

Even with all his fine taste, and high appreciation, for the purposes of the landscape-gardener, of *bona fide* pieces of antiquity, rich in association, it is questionable, from the following passage, whether his anti-Popish antipathies would not have led him to join our Scotch iconoclasts in their stern work of dilapidation.

"Henceforth was plied the long-continued task
Of *righteous havoc*, covering distant fields
With the wrought remnants of the shattered pile;
Till recent, through the land, the pilgrim sees
Rich tracts of brighter green, and in the midst
Gray mouldering walls, with nodding ivy crowned,
Or Gothic turret, pride of ancient days,
Now but of use to grace a rural scene,
To bound our vistas, and to glad the sons
Of George's reign, reserved for fairer times."

In "The Schoolmistress," the most finished and pleasing of Shenstone's longer poems, we find one of the sources of the feeling somewhat unwittingly exhibited. "Shenstone learned to read," says Johnson, in his biography, "of an old dame, whom his poem of 'The Schoolmistress' has delivered to posterity." "The house of my old schooldame Sarah Lloyd," we find the poet himself saying, in one of his earlier letters (1741), "is to be seen as thou travellest towards the native home of thy faithful servant. But she sleeps with her fathers, and is buried with her fathers; and Thomas her son reigneth in her stead." Of the good Sarah Lloyd we learn from the poem,—a piece of information suited to show how shrewd a part Puseyism is acting in possessing itself of the humbler schools of the country, — that

"She was just, and friend to virtuous lore,
And passed much time in truly virtuous deed,
And in her elfins' ears would oft deplore
The times when truth by Popish rage did bleed,
And tort'rous death was true devotion's meed,
And simple Faith in iron chains did mourn,
That nould on wooden image place her creed,
And lawny saints in smouldering flames did burn:
O, dearest Lord, forfend thilk days should e'er return!"

The anti-Popish feeling of England, which existed, as in Shenstone, almost wholly apart from doctrinal considerations seems to have experienced no diminution till after the suppression of the rebellion of 1745. A long series of historic events had served first to originate, and then to fill with it to saturation every recess of the popular mind. The horrors of the Marian persecution, rendered patent to all by the popular narratives of Fox, — the Invincible Armada and its thumb-screws, — the diabolical plot of the time of James, — the Irish Massacre of the following reign, — the fierce atrocities of Jeffries in the Monmouth rising, intimately associated, in the Protestant mind of the country, with the Popery of his master, — the imprisonment of the bishops, — and the influence of the anti-Romish teaching of the English Church after the Revolution, with the dread, for many years, of a Popish Pretender, — had all united to originate and develop the sentiment which, in its abstract character, we find so adequately represented in Shenstone. Much about the time of the poet's death, however, a decided reäction began to take place. The Pretender died; the whigs originated their scheme of Roman Catholic Emancipation; atheistic violence had been let loose on the clergy of France, not in their character as Popish, but in their character as Christian; and both the genius of Burke and the piety of Hall had appealed to the Protestant sympathies of England in their behalf. The singularly anomalous position and palpable inefficiency of the Irish Establishment had created a very general diversion in favor of the Popish majority of Ireland; the Voluntary controversy united Evangelistic Dissent and Roman Catholicism by the bonds of a common cause, — at least Evangelistic Dissent was fond enough to believe the cause a common one, and learned to speak with respect and regard of "*Roman* Catholic brethren;" the spread of Puseyism in the English Establishment united, by sympathies of a different but not weaker kind, the Papist and the High Churchman; the old anti-Popish feeling has been gradually sinking under the influence of so many reäctive causes; and not since the times of the Reformation was it at so low an ebb as in England at the present day. It would seem as if every old score was to be blotted off, and Popery to be taken a second time on trial. But it will ultimately be found wanting, and will, as in France and Germany, have just to be condemned again. The stiff rigidity of its unalterable codes of practice and belief, — inadequately compensated by the flexibility of its wilier votaries, — has incapacitated it from keeping up with the human mind in its onward march. If it be the sure destiny of man to rise, it must be the as inevitable fate of Popery to sink. The excesses of fifteen hundred years have vitiated and undermined its constitution, intellectual and moral; its absurder beliefs have become incompatible with advanced knowledge, — its more despotic assumptions with rational freedom; and were it not for the craving vacuum in the public mind which infidelity is continually creating for superstition to fill, and into which Popery is fitfully rushing like steam into the condenser of an engine, again and again to be annihilated, and again and again to flow in, its day, in at least the more enlightened portions of the empire, would not be long.

There seems to be a considerable resemblance at bottom between the old English feeling exemplified in Shenstone, and that which at present animates the Ronge movement in Germany. We find the English poet exclaiming,

> "Hail, honored Wickliffe, enterprising sage!
> *An Epicurus in the cause of truth!!*"

And the continental priest, — occupying at best but a half-way position between Luther and Voltaire, and who can remark in his preachings that "if Roman Catholics have a Pope at Rome, the Protestants have made their Pope of a book, and that that book is but a dead letter," — apostrophizes in a similar spirit the old German reformers. I can, however, see nothing inconsistent in the zeal of such men. It does not greatly require the aid of religion to enable one to decide that exhibitions such as that of the holy coat of Treves are dishonest and absurd, or to warm with indignation at the intolerance that would make one's liberty or life pay the penalty of one's freedom of opinion. Shenstone, notwithstanding his indifference to the theological, was quite religious enough to have been sabred or shot, had he been at Paris on the eve of St. Bartholomew, or knocked on the head if in Ulster at the time of the Irish massacre. What, apart from religious considerations, is chiefly to be censured and regretted in the zeal of the Ronges and Shenstones, Michelets and Eugene Sues, is, not that it is inconsistent, but that it constitutes at best but a vacuum-creating power. It forms a void where, in the nature of things, no void can permanently exist, and which superstition is ever rushing in to fill; and so the progress of the race, wherever it is influentially operative, instead of being conducted onwards in its proper line of march, becomes a weary cycle, that ever returns upon itself. The human intellect, under its influence, seems as if drawn within the ceaselessly-revolving eddies of a giddy maelstrom, or as if it had become obnoxious to the remarkable curse pronounced of old by the Psalmist: I quote from the version of Milton,

"My God! *oh, make them as a wheel;*
No quiet let them find;
Giddy and restless let them reel
Like stubble from the wind."

History is emphatic on the point. Nearly three centuries have elapsed since the revived Christianity of the Reformation supplanted Roman Catholicism in Scotland. But there was no vacuum created; the space previously taken up in the popular mind by the abrogated superstition was amply occupied by the resuscitated faith; and, as a direct consequence, whatever reäction in favor of Popery may have taken place among the people is of a purely political, not religious character. With Popery as a religion the Presbyterian Scotch are as far from closing now as they ever were. But how entirely different has been the state of matters in France! There are men still living who remember the death of Voltaire. In the course of a single lifetime, Popery has been twice popular and influential in that country, and twice has the vacuum-creating power, more than equally popular and influential for the time, closed chill and cold around it, to induce its annihilation. The literature of France for the last half-century is curiously illustrative of this process of action and reäction, — of condensation and expansion. It exhibits during that period three distinct groups of authors. There is first a group of vacuum-creators, — a surviving remnant of the Encyclopedists of the previous half-century — adequately represented by Condorcet and the Abbé Raynal; next appears a group of the reäctionists, represented equally well by Chateaubriand and Lamartine; and then — for Popery has again become monstrous, — we see a second group of vacuum-creators in the Eugene Sues and Michelets, the most popular French writers of the present day. And thus must the cycle revolve, "unquiet and giddy as a wheel," until France shall find rest in the Christianity of the New Testament.

I spent so much time among the ruins, that my courteous conductor the Squire, who had business elsewhere to attend to, had to leave me, after first, however, setting me on my way to the Leasowes, and kindly requesting me to make use of his name, if the person who farmed the grounds demurred, as sometimes happened with strangers, to give me admission to them. I struck up the hill, crossed a canal that runs along its side, got into a cross road between sheltered belts of planting, and then, with the Leasowes full in front, stopped at a small nailery, to ask at what point I might most easily gain access to them. The sole workers in the nailery were two fresh-colored, good-looking young girls, whose agile, well-turned arms were plying the hammer with a rapidity that almost eluded the eye, and sent the quick glancing sparks around them in showers. Both stopped short in their work, and came to the door to point out what they deemed the most accessible track. There was no gate, they said, in this direction, but I would find many gaps in the fence: they were in doubt, however, whether the people at the "white house" would give me leave to walk over the grounds: certainly the nailer lads were frequently refused; and they were sorry they could n't do anything for me: I would be sure of permission if they could give it me. At all events, said I, I shall take the longest possible road to the white house, and see a good deal of the grounds ere I meet with the refusal. Both the naileresses laughed, and one of them said she had always heard the Scotch were "long-headed." Hales Owen and its precincts are included in the great iron district of Birmingham; and the special branch of the iron trade which falls to the share of the people is the manufacture of nails. The suburbs of the town are formed chiefly of rows of little brick-houses, with a nail-shop in each; and the quick, smart patter of hammers sounds incessantly, in one encircling girdle of din, from early morning till late night. As I passed through, on my way to the Squire's Mill, I saw whole families at work together, — father, mother, sons, and daughters; and met in streets young girls, not at all untidily dressed considering the character of their vocation, trundling barrowfuls of coal to their forges, or carrying on their shoulders bundles of rod-iron. Of all our poets of the last century, there was scarce one so addicted to the use of those classic nicknames which impart so unreal an air to English poetry, when bestowed on English men and women, as poor Shenstone. We find his verses dusted over with Delias, and Cecilias, and Ophelias, Flavias, and Fulvias, Chloes, Daphnes, and Phillises; and, as if to give them the necessary prominence, the printer, in all the older editions, has relieved them from the surrounding text by the employment of staring capitals. I had read Shenstone early enough to wonder what sort of looking people his Delias and Cecilias were; and now, ere plunging into the richly-wooded Leasowes, I had got hold of the right idea. The two young naileresses were really very pretty. Cecilia, a ruddy blonde, was fabricating tackets; and Delia, a bright-eyed brunette, engaged in heading a double-double.

Ere entering on the grounds, however, I must attempt doing what Dodsley has failed to do, — I must try whether I cannot give the reader some idea of the Leasowes as a whole, in their relation to the surrounding country. Let us, then, once more return to the three Silurian eminences that rise island-like from the basin of the Dudley coal-field, and the parallel line of trap hills that stretches away amid the New Red Sandstone. I have described the lines as parallel, but, like the outstretched sides of a parallel-ruler, not opposite. There joins on, however, to the Silurian line, — like a prolongation of one of the right lines of the mathematician indicated by dots, — an extension of the chain, not Silurian, which consists of eminences of a flatter and humbler character than either the Wren's Nest or the Castle Hill, and which runs opposite to the trap chain for several miles. One of these supplementary eminences — the one adjoining the Castle Hill — is composed of the trap to which the entire line owes its elevation; and a tall, cairn-like group of apparent boulders, that seem as if they had been piled up by giants, but are mere components of a partially disintegrated projection from the rock below, occupies its summit. In the flat hill directly beyond it, though the trap does not appear, it has tilted up the Lower Coal Measures, amid the surrounding New Red Sandstone, saddlewise on its back; the strata shelve downwards on both sides from the anticlinal line atop, like the opposite sides of a roof from the ridge; and the entire hill, to use a still humbler illustration, resembles a huge blister in new plaster, formed by the expansion of some fragment of unslaked lime in the ground-coating beneath. Now, it is with this hill of the Lower Coal Measures — this huge blister of millstone grit — that we have chiefly to do.

Let the reader imagine it of soft swelling outline, and ample base, with the singularly picturesque trap range full in front, some four miles away, and a fair rural valley lying between. Let him further imagine the side of the hill furrowed by a transverse valley, opening at right angles into the great front valley, and separating atop into two forks, or branches, that run up, shallowing as they go, to near the hill-top. Let him, in short, imagine this great valley a broad right line, and the transverse forked valley a gigantic letter Y resting on it. And this forked valley on the hill-side — this gigantic letter Y — is the Leasowes. The picturesqueness of such a position can be easily appreciated. The forked valley, from head to gorge, is a reclining valley, partaking along its bottom of the slope of the eminence on which it lies, and thus possessing, what is by no means common among the valleys of England, true down-hill water-courses, along which the gathered waters may leap in a chain of cascades; and commanding, in its upper recesses, though embraced and sheltered on every side by the surrounding hill, extended prospects of the country below. It thus combines the scenic advantages of both hollow and rising ground, — the quiet seclusion of the one, and the expansive landscapes of the other. The broad valley into which it opens is rich and well wooded. Just in front of the opening we see a fine sheet of water, about twenty acres in extent, the work of the monks; immediately to the right stand the ruins of the abbey; immediately to the left, the pretty compact town of Hales Owen lies grouped around its fine old church and spire; a range of green swelling eminences rises beyond; beyond these, fainter in the distance, and considerably bolder in outline, ascends the loftier range of the trap hills, — one of the number roughened by the tufted woods, and crowned by the obelisk at Hagley; and, over all, blue and shadowy on the far horizon, sweeps the undulating line of the mountains of Cambria. Such is the character of the grounds which poor Shenstone set himself to convert into an earthly paradise, and such the outline of the surrounding landscape. But to my hard anatomy of the scene I must add the poet's own elegant filling up: —

"Romantic scenes of pendent hills,
And verdant vales and falling rills,

And mossy banks the fields adorn,
Where Damon, simple swain, was born.
The Dryads reared a shady grove,
Where such as think, and such as love,
Might safely sigh their summer's day,
Or muse their silent hours away.
The Oreads liked the climate well,
And taught the level plains to swell
In verdant mounds, from whence the eye
Might all their larger works descry.
The Naiads poured their urns around
From nodding rocks o'er vales profound;
They formed their streams to please the view,
And bade them wind as serpents do;
And having shown them where to stray,
Threw little pebbles in their way."

I got ready permission at the house of the Leasowes — a modern building erected on the site of that in which Shenstone resided — to walk over the grounds; and striking upwards directly along the centre of the angular tongue of land which divides the two forks of the valley, I gained the top of the hill, purposing to descend to where the gorge opens below along the one fork, and to reäscend along the other. On the hill-top, a single field's breadth beyond the precincts of the Leasowes, I met a tall middle-aged female, whose complexion, much embrowned by the sun, betrayed the frequent worker in fields, and her stiff angularity of figure, the state of single blessedness, and "maiden meditation, fancy free," which Shakspeare complimented in Elizabeth. I greeted her with fair good day, and asked her whether the very fine grounds below were not the Leasowes? or, as I now learned to pronounce the word, *Lisos*, — for when I gave it its long Scotch sound, no one in the neighborhood seemed to know what place I meant. "Ah, yes," said she, "the *Lisos!* — they were much thought of long ago in Squire Shenstone's days; but they are all ruinated now;

and, except on Sundays, when the nailer lads get into them, when they can, few people come their way. Squire Shenstone was a poet," she added, "and died for love." This was not quite the case: the Squire, who might have married his Phillis had he not been afraid to incur the expense of a wife, died of a putrid fever at the sober age of forty-nine; but there would have been little wit in substituting a worse for a better story, and so I received without challenge the information of the spinster. In descending, I took the right-hand branch of the valley, which is considerably more extended than that to the left. A low cliff, composed of the yellow gritty sandstone of the Lower Coal Measures, and much overhung by stunted alder and hazel bushes, stands near the head of the ravine, just where the Leasowes begin; and directly out of the middle of the cliff, some three or four feet from its base, there comes leaping to the light, as out of the smitten rock in the wilderness, a clear and copious spring, — one of the "health-bestowing" fountains,

"All bordered with moss,
Where the harebells and violets grew."

Alas! moss, and harebells, and violets, were gone, with the path which had once led to the spot, and the seat which had once fronted it; the waters fell dead and dull into a quagmire, like young human life leaping out of unconscious darkness into misery, and then stole away through a boggy strip of rank grass and rushes, along a line of scraggy alders. All was changed, save the full-volumed spring, and it, —

"A thousand and a thousand years,
'T will flow as now it flows."

CHAPTER IX.

Detour. — The Leasowes deteriorated wherever the Poet had built, and improved wherever he had planted. — View from the Hanging Wood. — Stratagem of the Island Screen. — Virgil's Grave. — Mound of the Hales Owen and Birmingham Canal; its sad Interference with Shenstone's Poetic Description of the Infancy of the Stour. — Vanished Cascade and Root-house. — Somerville's Urn. — "To all Friends round the Wrekin." — *River* Scenery of the Leasowes; their great Variety. — Peculiar Arts of the Poet; his Vistas, when seen from the wrong end, Realizations of Hogarth's Caricature. — Shenstone the greatest of Landscape Gardeners. — Estimate of Johnson. — Goldsmith's History of the Leasowes; their after History.

The water creeps downwards from where it leaps from the rock, to form a chain of artificial lakes, with which the bottom of the dell is occupied, and which are threaded by the watercourse, like a necklace of birds' eggs strung upon a cord. Ere I struck down on the upper lake, however, I had to make a detour of a few hundred yards to the right, to see what Dodsley describes as one of the finest scenes furnished by the Leasowes, — a steep terrace, commanding a noble prospect, — a hanging wood, — an undulating pathway over uneven ground, that rises and falls like a snake in motion, — a monumental tablet, — three rustic seats, — and a temple dedicated to Pan. The happy corner which the poet had thus stuck over with so much bravery is naturally a very pretty one. The hill-side, so gentle in most of its slopes, descends for about eighty feet, — nearly at right angles with the forked valley, and nearly parallel to the great valley in front, — as if it were a giant wave on the eve of breaking; and it is on this steep rampart-like declivity, —

this giant wave, — that the hanging wood was planted, the undulating path formed, and the seats and temple erected. But all save the wood has either wholly vanished, or left behind but the faintest traces, — traces so faint that, save for the plan of the grounds appended to the second edition of Dodsley's description, they would have told me no distinct story.

Ere descending the rampart-like acclivity, but just as the ground begins gradually to rise, and when I should be passing, according to Dodsley, through the "Lover's Walk," a sequestered arboraceous lane, saddened by the urn of "poor Miss Dolman," — "by the side of which" there had flowed "a small bubbling rill, forming little peninsulas, rolling over pebbles, or falling down small cascades, all under cover, and taught to murmur very agreeably," — I found myself in a wild tangled jungle, with no path under foot, with the "bubbling rill" converted into a black, lazy swamp, with thickets of bramble all around, through which I had to press my way, as I best could, breast-high, — "poor Miss Dolman's" urn as fairly departed and invisible as "poor Miss Dolman;" in short, everything that had been done undone, and all in readiness for some second Shenstone to begin *de novo*. As the way steepened, and the rank aquatic vegetation of the swamp, once a runnel, gave place to plants that affect a drier habitat, I could detect in the hollow of the hill some traces of the old path; but the place forms a receptacle into which the gusty winter winds sweep the shorn leafage of the hanging wood above, and so I had to stalk along the once trimly-kept walk, through a stratum of decayed leaves, half-leg deep. In the middle of the hanging wood I found what had been once the temple of Pan. There is a levelled space on the declivity, about half the size of an ordinary sitting parlor: the winds had swept it bare; and there, distinctly visible on three sides of the area, are the foundations of a thin brick wall, that, where least broken, rises some six or eight inches above the level. A little further on, where the wood opens on one of the loveliest prospects I ever beheld, I found a decayed oak-post remaining, to indicate the *locale* of a seat that had once eulogized the landscape which it fronted in a classic Latin inscription. But both seat and inscription are gone. And yet, maugre this desolation, not in the days of Shenstone did the Leasowes look so nobly from this elevation as they did this day. I was forcibly reminded of one of the poet's own remarks, and the completeness of its realization: "The works of a person that builds," he says, "begin immediately to decay; while those of him who plants begin directly to improve. In this, planting promises a more lasting pleasure than building." The trees of the Leasowes, when the Leasowes formed the home and furnished the employment of the poet, seem to have been mere saplings. We find him thus writing to a friend in the summer of 1743: — "A malignant caterpillar has demolished the beauty of all our large oaks. Mine are secured by their littleness. But I guess Hagley Park suffers, — a large wood near me being a winter-piece for nakedness." More than a hundred years have since elapsed, and the saplings of a century ago have expanded into the dignity of full-grown treehood. The hanging wood, composed chiefly of very noble beeches, with a sprinkling of grace ful birches on its nether skirt, raises its crest so high as fully to double the height of the eminence which it crowns; while the oaks on the finely varied ground below, of imposing size, and exhibiting in their grouping the hand of the master, compose such a scene as the finest of the landscapes designed by Martin in illustration of Milton's "Paradise Lost." The day was warm, calm, cloudless; the lights and shadows lay clear and transparent on lake and stream, dell and dingle, green swelling lawn and tall forest tree; and the hanging wood, and the mossy escarpment over which it hangs, were as musical in the bright sunshine, with the murmur of bees, as when, exactly a hundred and two years before, Shenstone was penning his pastoral ballad.

Quitting the hanging wood, I struck athwart the declivity, direct on the uppermost lake in the chain which I have described as lying, like a string of birds' eggs, along the bottom of the valley. I found it of small extent, — a pond or lochan, rather than a lake, — darkly colored, — its still, black surface partially embroidered by floats of aquatic plants, among which I could detect the broad leaves of the water-lily, though the flowers were gone, — and overhung on all sides by careless groups of trees, that here and there dip their branches in the water. In one striking feature of the place we may still detect the skill of the artist. There is a little island in the upper part of the lake, by much too small and too near the shore to have any particular interest as such; or, indeed, viewed from below, to seem an island at all. It is covered by a thick clump of alders of low growth, just tall enough and thick enough to conceal, screen-like, the steep bank of the lake behind. The top of the bank is occupied by several lofty oaks; and as the screen of alders hides the elevation on which they stand, they seem to rise direct from the level of the water to the giant stature of a hundred feet. The giants of the theatre are made by setting one man on the shoulders of another, and then throwing over both a large cloak; — the giant trees here are made by setting them upon the shoulders of a hill, and making the thick island-screen serve the purpose of the concealing mantle.

The second lake in the chain — a gloomier and smaller piece of water than the first, and much hidden in wood — has in its present state no beauty to recommend it: it is just such an inky pool, with rotten *snags* projecting from its sluggish surface, as a murderer would select for concealing the body of his victim. A forlorn brick ruin, overflooded by the neighboring streamlet, and capped with sickly ivy, stands at the upper end at the lower, the waters escape by a noisy cascade into a secluded swampy hollow, overshadowed by stately oaks and ashes, much intermixed by trees of a lower growth, — yew, holly, and hazel, — and much festooned with ivy. We find traces of an untrodden pathway on both sides the stream, with the remains of a small, mouldering, one-arched bridge, now never crossed over, and divested of both its parapets; and in the centre of a circular area, surrounded by trees of loftiest stature, we may see about twice as many bricks as an Irish laborer would trundle in a wheel-barrow, arranged in the form of a small square. This swampy hollow is the "Virgil's Grove," so elaborately described by Dodsley, and which so often in the last age employed the pencil and the burin; and the two barrowfuls of brick are all that remain of the obelisk of Virgil. I had run not a few narrow chances of the kind before; but I now fairly sunk half to the knees in the miry bottom, and then pressing onwards, as I best could,

> "Quenched in a boggy Syrtis, neither sea
> Nor good dry land, nigh foundered, on I fared,
> Treading the crude consistence half on foot,
> Half flying,"

till I reached a drier soil beside yet another lake in the chain, scarce less gloomy, and even more sequestered, than the last. There stick out along its edges a few blackened stumps, on which several bushy clusters of fern have taken root, and which, overshadowed by the pendent fronds, seem so many small tree-ferns. I marked here, for the first time, the glance of scales and the splash of fins in the water; but they belonged not to the "fishes of gold" sung by the poet, but to some half-dozen pike that I suppose have long since dealt by the fishes of gold as the bulkier contemporaries of the famous Jack the Giant Killer used to deal by their guests. A further walk of a few hundred yards through the wooded hollow brought me to the angle where the forks of the dell unite and form one valley. A considerable piece of water — by much the largest on the grounds — occupies the bottom of the broad hollow which they form by their union, — the squat stem, to use a former illustration, of the letter Y; and a long narrow bay runs from the main body of the lake up each of the two forks, losing itself equally in both, as it contracts and narrows, amid the over-arching trees.

There is a harmony of form as certainly as of sound, — a music to the eye in the one, as surely as to the ear in the other. I had hitherto witnessed much dilapidation and decay, but it was dilapidation and decay on a small scale; I had seen merely the wrecks of a few artificial toys, scattered amid the sublime of nature; and there were no sensible jarrings in the silent concert of the graceful and the lovely, which the entire scene served to compose. Here, however, all of a sudden, I was struck by a harsh discord. Where the valley should have opened its noble gateway into the champaign, — a gateway placed half-way between the extended magnificence of the expanse below, and the more closely concentrated beauties of the twin dells above, — there stretches, from bank to bank, a stiff, lumpish, rectilinear mound, some seventy or eighty feet in height, by some two or three hundred yards in length, that bars out the landscape, — deals, in short, by the wanderer along the lake or through the lower reaches of the dell, as some refractory land-steward deals by some hapless railway surveyor, when, squatting dow full before him, he spreads out a broad extent of coat-tail, and eclipses the distant sight. Poor Shenstone! — it would have broken his heart. That unsightly mound conveys along its flat, level line, straight as that of a ruler, the Birmingham and Hales Owen Canal. Poor Shenstone once more! With the peculiar art in which he excelled all men, he had so laid out his lakes, that the last in the series seemed to piece on to the great twenty-acre lake dug by the monks, and so to lose itself in the general landscape. And in one of his letters we find him poetical on the course of the vagrant streams, — those of his own grounds, — that feed it. "Their first appearance," he says, "well resembles the playfulness of infancy; they skip from side to side with a thousand antic motions, that answer no other purpose than the mere amusement of the proprietor. They proceed for a few hundred yards, and then their severer labors begin, resembling the graver toils of manhood. They set mills in motion, turn wheels, and ply hammers for manufactures of all kinds; and in this manner roll on under the name of the Stour, supplying works for casting, forging, and shaping iron for every civil and military purpose. Perhaps you may not know that my rills are the principal sources of this river; or that it furnishes the propelling power to more iron-works than almost any other single river in the kingdom." The dull mound now cuts off the sportive infancy of the Stour from its sorely-tasked term of useful riverhood. There is so cruel a barrier raised between the two stages, that we fail to identify the hard-working stream below with the playful little runnels above. The water comes bounding all obscurely out of the nether side of the mound, just as it begins its life of toil, — a poor thing without a pedigree, like some hapless child of quality stolen by the gypsies, and sold to hard labor.

Passing upwards along the opposite branch of the valley, I

found a succession of the same sort of minute desolations as I had met in the branch already explored. Shenstone's finest cascades lay in this direction; and very fine, judging from the description of Dodsley, they must have been. "The eye is here presented," says the poetic bibliopole, "with a fairy vision, consisting of an irregular and romantic fall of water, one hundred and fifty yards in continuity; and a very striking and unusual scene it affords. Other cascades may have the advantage of a greater descent and a larger stream; but a more wild and romantic appearance of water, and at the same time strictly natural, is difficult to be met with anywhere. The scene, though small, is yet aggrandized with so much art, that we forget the quantity of water which flows through this close and overshadowed valley, and are so much pleased with the intricacy of the scene, and the concealed height from whence it flows, that we, without reflection, add the idea of magnificence to that of beauty. In short, it is only upon reflection that we find the stream is not a Niagara, but rather a waterfall in miniature; and that by the same artifice upon a larger scale, were there large trees in place of small ones, and a river instead of a rill, a scene so formed would exceed the utmost of our ideas." Alas for the beautiful cascade! Here still was the bosky valley, dark and solitary, with its long withdrawing bay from the lake speckled by the broad leaves of the waterlily; old gnarled stems of ivy wind, snake-like, round the same massy trunks along which they had been taught to climb in the days of the poet; but for the waterfall, the main feature of the scene, I saw only a long dark trench, — much crusted by mosses and liverworts, and much overhung by wood, — that furrows the side of the hill; and for the tasteful root-house, erected to catch all the beauties of the place, I found only a few scattered masses of brick, bound fast together by the integrity of the cementing lime, and half-buried in a brown stratum of decayed leaves. A little further on, there lay across the runnel a huge monumental urn of red sandstone, with the base elevated and the neck depressed. It dammed up enough of the little stream to form a reservoir at which an animal might drink, and the clayey soil around it was dibbled thick at the time by the tiny hoofs of sheep. The fallen urn had been inscribed to the memory of Somerville the poet.

This southern fork of the valley is considerably shorter than the northern one; and soon rising on the hill-side, I reached a circular clump of firs, from which the eye takes in the larger part of the grounds at a glance, with much of the surrounding country. We may see the Wrekin full in front, at the distance of about thirty miles; and here, in the centre of the circular clump, there stood, says Dodsley, an octagonal seat, with a pedestal-like elevation in the middle, that served for a back, and on the top of which there was fixed a great punch-bowl, bearing as its appropriate inscription the old country toast, "To all friends round the Wrekin." Seat and bowl have long since vanished, and we see but the circular clump. At the foot of the hill there is a beautiful piece of water, narrow and long, and skirted by willows, with both its ends so hidden in wood, and made to wind so naturally, that instead of seeming what it is, — merely a small pond, — it seems one of the reaches of a fine river. We detect, too, the skill of the poet in the appearance presented from this point by the chain of lakes in the opposite fork of the valley. As seen through the carefully disposed trees, they are no longer detached pieces of water, but the reaches of a great stream, — a sweeping inflection, we may suppose, of the same placid river that we see winding through the willows, immediately at the hill-foot. The Leasowes, whose collected waters would scarce turn a mill, exhibit, from this cir cular clump, their fine river scenery. The background beyond rises into a magnificent pyramid of foliage, the apex of which is formed by the tall hanging wood on the steep acclivity, and which sweeps downwards on each side in graceful undulations, now rising, now falling, according to the various heights of the trees or the inequalities of the ground. The angular space between the two forks of the valley occupies the foreground. It sinks in its descent towards the apex, — for the pyramid is of course an inverted one, — from a scene of swelling acclivities, fringed with a winding belt of squat, broad-stemmed beeches, into a soft sloping lawn, in the centre of which, deeply embosomed in wood, rise the white walls of the mansion-house. And such, as they at present exist, are the Leasowes, — the singularly ingenious composition inscribed on an English hill-side, which employed for twenty long years the taste and genius of Shenstone. An eye accustomed to contemplate nature merely in the gross, and impressed but by vast magnitudes or by great multiplicity, might not find much to admire in at least the more secluded scenes, — in landscapes a furlong or two in extent, and composed of merely a few trees, a few slopes, and a pond, or in gloomy little hollows, with interlacing branches high over head, and mossy runnels below. But to one not less accustomed to study the forms than to feel the magnitudes, — who can see spirit and genius in even a vignette, beauty in the grouping of a clump, in the sweep of a knoll, in the convexity of a mossy bank, in the glitter of a half-hidden stream, or the blue gleam of a solitary lochan, — one who can appreciate all in nature that the true landscape-painter admires and develops, — will still find much to engage him amid the mingled woods and waters, sloping acclivities, and hollow valleys, of the Leasowes. I have not yet seen a piece of ground of equal extent that exhibits a tithe of its variety, or in which a few steps so completely alters a scene. In a walk of half a mile one might fill a whole portfolio with sketches, all fine and all various.

It was chiefly in the minuter landscapes of the place that I missed the perished erections of the poet. The want of some central point on which the attention might first concentrate, and then, as it were, let itself gradually out on the surrounding objects, served frequently to remind me of one of the poet's own remarks. "A rural scene to me is never perfect," he says, "without the addition of some kind of building. I have, however, known a scar of rock in great measure supplying the deficiency." Has the reader observed how unwittingly Bewick seems to have stumbled on this canon, and how very frequently the scar of rock — somewhat a piece of mannerism, to be sure, but always fine, and always picturesquely overhung with foliage — is introduced as the great central object into his vignettes? In nature's, too, the effect, when chance embodied in some recluse scene, must have been often remarked. I have seen a huge rock-like boulder, roughened by lichens, giving animation and cheerfulness to the wild solitude of a deep forest-clearing; and a gray undressed obelisk, reared many centuries ago over the savage dead, imparting picturesqueness and interest to a brown sterile moor.

With the poet's erections, every trace of his lesser ingenuities has disappeared from the landscape, — his peculiar art, for instance, of distancing an object to aggrandize his space, or in contriving that the visiter should catch a picturesque glimpse of it just at the point where it looked best; and that then, losing sight of it, he should draw near by some hidden path, over which the eye had not previously travelled. The artist, with his many-hued pigments at command, makes one object seem near and another distant, by giving to the one a deeper and to the other a fainter tinge of color. Shenstone, with a palette much less liberally furnished, was skilful enough to produce similar effects with his variously-tinted shrubs and trees. He made the central object in his vista some temple or root-house, of a faint retiring color; planted around it trees of a diminutive size and a "blanched fady hue," such as the "almond willow" and "silver osier;" then, after a blank space, he planted another group of a deeper tinge, — trees of the average hue of the forest, such as the ash and the elm; and then, last of all, in the foreground, after another blank space, he laid down trees of deep-tinted foliage, such as the dark glossy holly, and the still darker yew. To the aërial, too, he added the linear perspective. He broadened his avenues in the foreground, and narrowed them as they receded; and the deception produced he describes — and we may well credit him, for he was not one of the easily satisfied — as very remarkable. The distance seemed greatly to increase, and the grounds to broaden and extend. We may judge, from the nature of the device, of the good reason he had to be mortally wroth with members of the Lyttelton family, when, as Johnson tells us, they used to make a diversion in favor of Hagley, somewhat in danger of being eclipsed at the time, by bringing their visiters to look up his vistas from the wrong end. The picture must have been set in a wofully false light, and turned head-downwards to boot, when the *distant* willows waved in the foreground beside the dimly-tinted obelisk or portico, and the *nearer* yews and hollies rose stiff, dark, and diminutive, in an avenue that broadened as it receded, a half-dozen bow-shots behind them. Hogarth's famous caricature on the false perspective of his contemporary brethren of the easel would in such a case be no caricature at all, but a truthful representation of one of Shenstone's vistas viewed from the wrong end.

Some of the other arts of the poet, are, however, as I have already had occasion to remark, still very obvious. It was one of his canons, that when "an object had been once viewed from its proper point, the foot should never travel to it by the same path which the eye had travelled over before." The visiter suddenly lost it, and then drew near obliquely. We can still see that all his pathways, in order to accommodate themselves to this canon, were covered ways, which winded through thickets and hollows. Ever and anon, whenever there was aught of interest to be seen, they emerged into the open day, like moles rising for a moment to the light, and then straightway again buried themselves from view. It was another of his canons, that "the eye should always look down upon water." "Customary nature," he remarks, "made the thing a necessary requisite." "Nothing," it is added, "could be more sensibly displeasing than the breadth of flat ground," which an acquaintance, engaged, like the poet, though less successfully, in making a picture-gallery of his property, had placed "between his terrace and his lake." Now, in the Leasowes, wherever water is made to enter into the composition of the landscape, the eye looks down upon it from a commanding elevation, — the visiter never feels, as he contemplates it that he is in danger of being carried away by a flood, should an embankment give way. It was yet further one of Shenstone's canons, that "no mere slope from the one side to the other can be agreeable ground: the eye requires a balance," not however, of the kind satirized by Pope, in which

> "Each alley has its brother,
> And half the platform just reflects the other;"

but the kind of balance which the higher order of landscape-painters rarely fail to introduce into their works. "A building, for instance, on one side may be made to contrast with a group of trees, a large oak, or a rising hill, on the other." And in meet illustration of this principle, we find that all the scenes of the Leasowes are at least well balanced, though most of their central points are unluckily away: the eye never slides off the landscape, but cushions itself upon it with a sense of security and repose; and the feeling, even when one fails to trace it to its origin, is agreeable. "Whence," says the poet, 'does this taste proceed, but from the love we bear to regularity in perfection? But, after all, in regard to gardens, the shape of the ground, the disposition of the trees, and the figure of the water, must be sacred to nature, and no forms must be allowed that make a discovery of art."

England has produced many greater poets than Shenstone, but she never produced a greater landscape-gardener. In at least this department he stands at the head of his class, unapproachable and apart, whether pitted against the men of his own generation, or those of the three succeeding ones. And in any province in which mind must be exerted, it is at least something to be first. The estimate of Johnson cannot fail to be familiar to almost every one. It is, however, so true in itself, and so exquisitely characteristic of stately old Samuel, that I must indulge in the quotation. "Now was excited his [Shenstone's] delight in rural pleasures, and his ambition of rural elegance. He began to point his prospects, to diversify his surface, to entangle his walks, and to wind his waters; which he did with such judgment and such fancy as made his little domain the envy of the great and the admiration of the skilful, — a place to be visited by travellers and copied by designers. Whether to plant a walk in undulating curves, and to place a bench at every turn where there is an object to catch the view, — to make water run where it will be heard, and to stagnate where it will be seen, — to leave intervals where the eye will be pleased, and to thicken the plantation where there is something to be hidden, — demand any great powers of mind, I will not inquire: perhaps a surly and sullen spectator may think such performances rather the sport than the business of human reason. But it must be at least confessed, that to embellish the form of Nature is an innocent amusement; and some praise must be allowed, by the most supercilious observer, to him who does best what such multitudes are contending to do well."

But though England had no such landscape-gardener as Shenstone, it possessed denizens not a few who thought more highly of their own taste than of his; and so the history of the Leasowes, for the ten years that immediately succeeded his death, is a history of laborious attempts to improve what he had rendered perfect. This history we find recorded by Goldsmith in one of his less known essays. Considerable allowance must be made for the peculiar humor of the writer, and its exaggerative tendency; for no story, real or imaginary, ever lost in the hands of Goldsmith; but there is at least an air of truth about its general details. "The garden," he says, "was completely grown and finished: the marks of every art were covered up by the luxuriance of nature, — the winding walks were grown dark, — the brooks assumed a natural selvage, — and the rocks were covered with moss. Nothing now remained but to enjoy the beauties of the place, when the poor poet died, and his garden was obliged to be sold for the benefit of those who had contributed to its embellishment.

"The beauties of the place had now for some time been celebrated as well in prose as in verse; and all men of taste wished for so envied a spot, where every turn was marked with the poet's pencil, and every walk awakened genius and meditation. The first purchaser was one Mr. Truepenny, a button-maker who was possessed of three thousand pounds, and was willing also to be possessed of taste and genius.

"As the poet's ideas were for the natural wildness of the landscape, the button-maker's were for the more regular productions of art. He conceived, perhaps, that as it is a beauty in a button to be of a regular pattern, so the same regularity ought to obtain in a landscape. Be that as it will, he employed the shears to some purpose; he clipped up the hedges, cut down the gloomy walks, made vistas on the stables and hog-sties, and showed his friends that a man of true taste should always be doing.

"The next candidate for taste and genius was a captain of a ship, who bought the garden because the former possessor could find nothing more to mend; but unfortunately he had taste too. His great passion lay in building, — in making Chinese temples and cage-work summer-houses. As the place before had the appearance of retirement, and inspired meditation, he gave it a more peopled air; every turning presented a cottage or icehouse, or a temple; the garden was converted into a little city, and it only wanted inhabitants to give it the air of a village in the East Indies.

"In this manner, in less than ten years the improvement has gone through the hands of as many proprietors, who were all willing to have taste, and to show their taste too. As the place had received its best finishing from the hands of the first possessor, so every innovator only lent a hand to do mischief. Those parts which were obscure have been enlightened; those walks which led naturally have been twisted into serpentine windings. The color of the flowers of the field is not more various than the variety of tastes that have been employed here, and all in direct contradiction to the original aim of its first improver. Could the original possessor but revive, with what a sorrowful heart would he look upon his favorite spot again! He would scarcely recollect a dryad or a wood nymph of his former acquaintance; and might perhaps find himself as much a stranger in his own plantation as in the deserts of Siberia."

The after history of the Leasowes is more simple. Time, as certainly as taste, though much less offensively, had been busy with seat and temple, obelisk and root-house; and it was soon found that, though the poet had planted, he had not built, for posterity. The ingenious antiquary of Wheatfield discovered in the parsonage-house garden of his village, some time about the middle of the last century, a temple of lath and plaster, which had been erected, he held, by the old Romans, and dedicated to Claudius Cæsar; but the lath and plaster of these degenerate days do not last quite so long. The progress of dilapidation was further accelerated by the active habits of occasional visiters. Young men tried their strength by setting their shoulders to the obelisks; and old women demonstrated their wisdom by carrying home pieces of the seats to their fires: a robust young fellow sent poor Mr. Somerville's urn a spinning down the hill; a vigorous iconoclast beheaded the piping fawn at a blow. There were at first large additions made to the inscriptions, of a kind which Shenstone could scarce have anticipated; but anon inscriptions and additions too began to disappear; the tablet in the dingle suddenly failed to compliment Mr. Spence; and Virgil's Grove no longer exhibited the name of Virgil. "The ruinated Priory wall" became too thoroughly a ruin; the punch-bowl was shivered on its stand; the iron ladle wrenched from beside the ferruginous spring; in short, much about the time when young Walter Scott was gloating over Dodsley, and wishing he, too, had a property of which to make a plaything, what Shenstone had built and inscribed on the Leasowes could be known but from Dodsley alone. His artificialities had perished, like the artificialities of another kind of the poets his contemporaries; and nothing survived in his more material works, as in their writings, save those delightful portions in which he had but given body and expression to the harmonies of nature.

CHAPTER X.

Shenstone's Verses. — The singular Unhappiness of his Paradise. — English Cider. — Scotch and English Dwellings contrasted. — The Nailers of Hales Owen; their Politics a Century ago. — Competition of the Scotch Nailers; unsuccessful, and why. — Samuel Salt, the Hales Owen Poet. — Village Church. — Salt Works at Droitwich; their great Antiquity. — Appearance of the Village. — Problem furnished by the Salt Deposits of England; various Theories. — Rock Salt deemed by some a Volcanic Product; by others the Deposition of an overcharged Sea; by yet others the Produce of vast Lagoons. — Leland. — The Manufacture of Salt from Sea-water superseded, even in Scotland, by the Rock Salt of England.

It was now near sunset, and high time that I should be leaving the Leasowes, to "take mine ease in mine inn." By the way, one of the most finished among Shenstone's lesser pieces is a paraphrase on the apophthegm of old Sir John. We find Dr. Samuel Johnson, as exhibited in the chronicle of Boswell, conning it over with meikle glee in an inn at Chapelhouse; and it was certainly no easy matter to write verse that satisfied the doctor.

"To thee, fair Freedom! I retire,
From flattery, cards, and dice, and din;
Nor art thou found in mansions higher
Than the low cot or humble inn.

"'T is here with boundless power I reign;
And every health which I begin
Converts dull port to bright champagne;
Such freedom crowns it at an inn.

"I fly from pomp, I fly from plate,
I fly from falsehood's specious grin;
Freedom I love, and form I hate,
And choose my lodgings at an inn.

"Here, waiter, take my sordid ore,
Which lacqueys else might hope to win;
It buys what courts have not in store, —
It buys me freedom at an inn.

"Whoe'er has travelled life's dull round,
Where'er his stages may have been,
May sigh to think he still has found
The warmest welcome at an inn."

Ere, however, quitting the grounds to buy freedom a the "Plume of Feathers," I could not avoid indulging in a natural enough reflection on the unhappiness of poor Shenstone. Never, as we may see from his letters, was there a man who enjoyed life less. He was not vicious; he had no overpowering passion to contend with; he could have had his Phillis, had he chosen to take her; his fortune, nearly three hundred a-year, should have been quite ample enough, in the reign of George the Second, to enable a single man to live, and even, with economy, to furnish a considerable surplus for making gimcracks in the Leasowes; he had many amusements, — he drew tastefully, had a turn, he tells us, for natural history, wrote elegant verse and very respectable prose; the noble and the gifted of the land honored him with their notice; above all, he lived in a paradise, the beauties of which no man could better appreciate; and his most serious employment, like that of our common ancestor in his unfallen state, was "to dress and to keep it. And yet, even before he had involved his affairs, and the dun came to the door, he was an unhappy man. "I have lost my road to happiness," we find him saying ere he had completed his thirty-fourth year. Nay, we even find him quite aware of the *turning* at which he had gone wrong. "Instead," he adds, "of pursuing the way to the fine lawns and venerable oaks which distinguish the region of happiness, I am got into the pitiful parterre-garden of amusement, and view the nobler scenes at a distance. I think I can see the road, too, that leads the better way, and can show it to others; but I have got many miles to measure back before I can get into it myself, and no kind of resolution to take a single step. My chief amusements at present are the same they have long been, and lie scattered about my farm. The French have what they call a *parque ornée*, — I suppose, approaching about as near to a garden as the park at Hagley. I give my place the title of a *ferme ornée*." Still more significant is the frightful confession embodied in the following passage, written at a still earlier period: — "Every little uneasiness is sufficient to introduce a whole train of melancholy considerations, and to make me utterly dissatisfied with the life I now lead, and the life which I foresee I shall lead. I am angry, and envious, and dejected, and frantic, and disregard all present things, just as becomes a madman to do. I am infinitely pleased, though it is a gloomy joy, with the application of Dr. Swift's complaint, 'that he is forced to die in a rage, like a poisoned rat in a hole.'" Amusement becomes, I am afraid, not very amusing when rendered the exclusive business of one's life. All that seems necessary in order to render fallen Adams thoroughly miserable, is just to place them in paradises, and, debarring them serious occupation, to give them full permission to make themselves as happy as they can. It was more in mercy than in wrath that the first father of the race, after his nature had become contaminated by the fall, was driven out of Eden. Well would it have been for poor Shenstone had the angel of stern necessity driven him also, early in the day, out of his paradise, and sent him into the work-day world beyond, to eat bread in the sweat of his brow. I quitted the Leasowes in no degree saddened by the consideration that I had been a hard-working man all my life, from boyhood till now; and that the future, in this respect, held out to me no brighter prospect than I had realized in the past.

When passing through York, I had picked up at a stall a good old copy of the poems of Philips, — John, not Ambrose; and in railway carriages and on coach-tops I had revived my acquaintance, broken off for twenty years, with "Cider, a Poem," "Blenheim," and the "Splendid Shilling;" and now, in due improvement of the lessons of so judicious a master, I resolved, when taking my ease in the "Plume of Feathers," that, for one evening at least, I should drink only cider.

"Fallacious drink! ye honest men, beware,
Nor trust its smoothness; the third circling glass
Suffices virtue."

The cider of the "Plume" was, however, scarce so potent as that sung by Philips. I took the third permitted glass, after a dinner transposed far into the evening by the explorations of the day, without experiencing a very great deal of the exhilarating feeling described, —

"Or lightened heart,
Dilate with fervent joy, or eager soul,
Keen to pursue the sparkling glass amain."

Nor was the temptation urgent to make up in quantity what was wanting in strength: "the third circling glass sufficed virtue." Here, as at the inns in which I had baited, both at Durham and York, I was struck by the contrast which many of the older English dwelling-houses furnish to our Scotch ones of the same age. In Scotland the walls are of solid stone-work, thick and massy, with broad-headed, champer-edged rybats, and ponderous soles and lintels, selvaging the opening; whereas the wood-work of the interior is almost always slight and fragile, formed of spongy deal or moth-hollowed fir rafters. After the lapse of little more than a century, there are few of our Scotch floors on which it is particularly safe to tread. In the older English dwellings we generally find a reverse condition of things: the outsides, constructed of slim brick-work, have a toy-like fragility about them: whereas inside we find strong oaken beams, and long-enduring floors and stairs of glossy wainscot. We of course at once recognize the great scarcity of good building-stone in the one country, and of well-grown forest-wood in the other, as the original and adequate cause of the peculiarity. Their dwelling-houses seem to have had different starting points; those of the one being true lineal descendants of the old Pict's house, complete from foundation to summit without wood, — those of the other, lineal descendants of the old forest-dwellings of the Saxon, formed ship-like in their unwieldy oaken strength, without stone. Wood to the one class was a mere subordinate accident, of late introduction, — stone to the other; and were I sent to seek out the half-way representatives of each, I would find those of England in its ancient beam-formed houses of the days of Elizabeth, in which only angular interstices in the walls are occupied by brick, and those of Scotland in its time-shattered fortalices of the type of the old castle of Craig-house, in Ross-shire, where floor rises above floor in solid masonry, or of the type of Borthwick-castle, near Edinburgh, stone from foundation to ridge.

I spent some time next morning in sauntering among the cross lanes of Hales Owen, now and then casting vague guesses, from the appearance of the humbler houses, — for what else lies within reach of the passing traveller? — regarding the character and condition of the inmates; and now and then looking in through open windows and doors at the nailers, male and female, engaged amid their intermittent hammerings and fitful showers of sparks. As might be anticipated of a profession fixed very much down to the corner of a country, and so domestic in its nature, nail-making is hereditary in the families that pursue it. The nailers of Hales Owen in the present day are the descendants of the nailers who, as Shenstone tells us, were so intelligent in the cause of Hanover during the outburst of 1745. "The rebellion," he says, in writing a friend just two months after the battle of Prestonpans, "is, as you may guess, the subject of all conversation. Every individual nailer here takes in a newspaper, and talks as familiarly of kings and princes as ever Master Shallow did of John of Gaunt." Scarcely a century had gone by, and I now found, from snatches of conversation caught in the passing, that the nailers of Hales Owen were interested in the five points of the Charter and the success of the League, and thought much more of what they deemed their own rights, than of the rights of either monarchs *de facto* or monarchs *de jure*. There was a nail-manufactory established about seventy years ago at Cromarty, in the north of Scotland, which reared not a few Scotch nailers; but they seemed to compete on unequal terms with those of England; and after a protracted struggle of rather more than half a century, the weaker went to the wall, and the Cromarty nail-works ceased. There is now only a single nail-forge in the town; and this last of the forges is used for other purposes than the originally intended one. I found in Hales Owen the true key to the failure of the Cromarty manufactory, and saw how it had come to be undersold in its own northern field by the nail-merchants of Birmingham. The Cromarty nailer wrought alone, or, if a family man, assisted but by his sons:

whereas the Hales Owen nailer had, with the assistance of his sons, that of his wife, daughters, and maiden sisters to boot; and so he bore down the Scotchman in the contest, through the aid lent him by his female auxiliaries, in the way his blue-painted ancestors, backed by not only all the fighting men, but also all the fighting women of the district, used to bear down the enemy.

In passing a small bookseller's shop, in which I had marked on the counter an array of second-hand books, I dropped in to see whether I might not procure a cheap edition of Shenstone, with Dodsley's description, and found a tidy little woman behind the counter, who would fain, if she could, have suited me to my mind. But she had no copy of Shenstone, nor had she ever heard of Shenstone. She well knew Samuel Salt, the Hales Owen tee-total poet, and could sell me a copy of *his* works; but of the elder poet of Hales Owen she knew nothing. I bought from her two of Samuel's broadsheets, — the one a wrathful satire on the community of Odd-Fellows; the other, "A Poem on Drunkenness."

"O, how silly is the drinker!
  Swallowing what he does not need ·
In the eyes of every thinker
  He must be a fool indeed.
How he hurts his constitution!
All for want of resolution
  Not to yield to drink at first!"

Such is the verse known within a mile of the Leasowes, while that of their poet is forgotten. Alas for fame! Poor Shenstone could scarce have anticipated that the thin Castalia of tee-totalism was to break upon his writings, like a mill-dam during a thunder-storm, to cover up all their elegances from the sight where they should be best known, and present instead but a turbid expanse of water.

I got access to the parish church, a fine old pile of red sandstone, which dates, in some of its more ancient portions, beyond the Norman conquest. One gorgeous marble, sentineled by figures of Benevolence, Fidelity, and Major Halliday, all very classic and fine, and which cost, as my guide informed me, a thousand pounds, failed greatly to excite my interest: I at least found that a simple pedestal in front of it, surmounted by a plain urn, impressed me more. The pedestal bears a rather lengthy inscription, in the earlier half of which there is a good deal of verbiage; but in the concluding half the writer seems to have said nearly what he intended to say.

* * * *

"Reader, if genius, taste refined,
A native elegance of mind, —
If virtue, science, manly sense,
If wit that never gave offence,
The clearest head, the tenderest heart,
In thy esteem e'er claimed a part, —
O ! smite thy breast, and drop a tear,
For know, thy Shenstone's dust lies here."

The Leasowes engaged me for the remainder of the day; and I again walked over them a few weeks later in the season, when the leaf hung yellow on the tree, and the films of gray silky gossamer went sailing along the opener glades in the clear frosty air. But I have already recorded my impressions of the place, independently of date, as if all formed at one visit. I must now take a similar liberty with the chronology of my wendings in another direction; and, instead of passing direct to the Clent Hills in my narrative, as I did in my tour, describe, first a posterior visit paid to the brine-springs at Droitwich. I shal by and by attempt imparting to the reader, from some commanding summit of the Clent range, a few general views regarding the geology of the landscape; and by first bearing me company on my visit to Droitwich, he will be the better able to keep pace with me in my after survey.

The prevailing geological system in this part of England is the New Red Sandstone, Upper and Lower. It stretches for many miles around the Dudley coal-basin, much in the way that the shires of Stirling and Dumbarton stretch around the waters of Loch Lomond, or the moors of Sutherland or the hills of Inverness-shire encircle the waters of Loch Shin or Loch Ness. In the immediate neighborhood of the basin we find only the formations of the lower division of the system, and these are of comparatively little economic value: they contain, however, a calcareous conglomerate, which represents the magnesian limestone of the northern counties, and which in a very few localities is pure enough to be wrought for its lime: they contain, too, several quarries of the kind of soft building sandstone which I found the old stone-mason engaged in sawing at Hagley. But while the lower division of the New Red is thus unimportant, its upper division is, we find, not greatly inferior in economic value to the Coal Measures themselves. It forms the inexhaustible storehouse of our household salt, — all that we employ in our fisheries, in our meat-curing establishments for the army and navy, in our agriculture, in our soda manufactories, — all that fuses our glass and fertilizes our fields, imparts the detergent quality to our soap, and gives us salt herrings and salt pork, and everything else salt that is the better for being so, down to our dinner celery and our breakfast eggs; it forms, in short, to use a Scoticism, the great *salt-backet* of the empire; and the hand, however frequently thrust into it, never finds an empty corner. By pursuing southwards, for seven or eight miles, the road which, passing through Hales Owen, forms the principal street of the village, we rise from the lower incoherent marls, soft sandstones, and calcareous conglomerates of the system, to the equally incoherent marls, and nearly equally soft sandstones, of its upper division ; and, some five or six miles further on, reach the town of Droitwich, long famous for its salt springs. There were salt-works at Droitwich in the times of the Romans, and ever *since* the times of the Romans. In the age of the Heptarchy, Kenulph, King of Mercia, after cutting off the hands and putting out the eyes of his brother-king, Egbert of Kent, squared his accounts with Heaven by giving ten salt-furnaces in Droitwich to the church of Worcester. Poor Edwy of England, nearly two centuries after, strove, though less successfully, to purchase the Church's sanction to his union with his second cousin, the beautiful Elgiva, by giving it five salt-furnaces more. In all probability, the salt that seasoned King Alfred's porridge, when he lived with the neat-herd, was supplied by the works at Droitwich. And still the brine comes welling up, copious as ever. I saw one powerful spring boiling amid the twilight gloom of its deep pot, like a witch's cauldron in a cavern, that employs a steam-engine night and day to pump it to the surface, and furnishes a thousand tons of salt weekly. In 1779, says Nashe, in his History of Worcestershire, the net salt duties of the empire amounted to about two hundred and forty thousand pounds, and of that sum not less than seventy-five thousand pounds were derived from the salt-works at Droitwich.

The town lies low. There had been much rain for several days previous to that of my visit, — the surrounding fields had the dank blackened look so unlovely in autumn to the eye of the farmer, and the roads and streets were dark with mud. Most of the houses wore the dingy tints of a remote and somewhat neglected antiquity. Droitwich was altogether as I saw it, a sombre-looking place, with its gray old church looking down upon it from a scraggy wood-covered hill; and what struck me as peculiarly picturesque was, that from this dark centre there should be passing continually outwards, by road or canal, wagons, carts, track-boats, barges, all laden with pure white salt, that looked in the piled-up heaps like wreaths of drifted snow. There could not be two things more unlike than the great staple of the town, and the town itself. There hung, too, over the blackened roofs, a white volume of vapor, — the steam of the numerous salt-pans, driven off in the course of evaporation by the heat, — which also strikingly contrasted with the general blackness. The place has its two extensive salt-works, — the old and the new. To the new I was denied access; but it mattered little, as I got ready admittance to the old. The man who superintended the pumping engine, though he knew me merely as a curious traveller somewhat mud-bespattered, stopped the machine for a few seconds, that I might see undisturbed the brine boiling up from its secret depths; and I was freely permitted to take the round of the premises, and to examine the numerous vats in their various stages of evaporation. It is pleasant to throw one's self, unknown and unrecommended, on the humanity of one's fellows, and to receive kindness simply as a man!

As I saw the vats seething over the furnaces, some of them more than already half-filled with the precipitated salt, and bearing atop a stratum of yellowish-colored fluid, the grand problem furnished by the saline deposits of this formation rose before me in all its difficulty. Geology propounds many a hard question to its students, — questions quite hard and difficult enough to keep down their conceit, unless, indeed, very largely developed; and few of these seem more inexplicable than the problem furnished by the salt deposits. Here, now, are these briny springs welling out of this Upper New Red Sandstone of central England, — springs whose waters were employed in making salt two thousand years ago, and which still throw up that mineral at the rate of a thousand tons apiece weekly, without sign of diminution in either their volume or their degree of saturation! At Stoke Prior, about three miles to the east of Droitwich, a shaft of four hundred and sixty feet has been sunk in the Upper New Red, and four beds of rock-salt passed through, the united thickness of which amount to eighty-five feet. Nor does this comprise the entire thickness, as the lower bed, though penetrated to the depth of thirty feet, has not been perforated. In the salt-mines of Cheshire, the beds are of still greater thickness, — an upper bed measuring in depth seventy-eight feet, and an under bed, to which no bottom has yet been found, a hundred and twenty feet. And in Poland and Spain there occur salt deposits on a larger scale still. The saliferous district of Cordova, for instance, has its solid hills of rock-salt, which nearly equal in height and bulk Arthur's Seat taken from the level of Holyrood House. How, I inquired, beside the flat steaming cauldrons, as I marked the white crystals arranging their facets at the bottom, — how were these mighty deposits formed in the grand laboratory of Nature? Formed they must have been, in this part of the world, in an era long posterior to that of the Coal; and in Spain, where they belong to the cretaceous group, in an era long posterior to that of the Oolite. They are more immediately underlaid in England by a sandstone constituting the base of the Upper New Red, which is largely charged with vegetable remains of a peculiar and well-marked character; and the equally well-marked flora of the carboniferous period lies entombed many hundred feet below. All the rock-salt in the kingdom must have been formed since the more recent vegetation of the Red Sandstone lived and died, and was entombed amid the smooth sands of some deep-sea bottom.

But how formed? Several antagonist theories have been promulgated in attempted resolution of the puzzle. By some the salt has been regarded as a volcanic product ejected from beneath; by some, as the precipitate of a deep ocean over-charged with saline matter; by some, as a deposit of salt-water lakes cut off from the main sea, like the salt lagoons of the tropics, by surf-raised spits or bars, and then dried up by the heat of the sun. It seems fatal to the first theory, that the eras of Plutonic disturbance in this part of the kingdom are of a date anterior to the era of the Saliferous Sandstone. The Clent Hills belong to the latest period of trappean eruption traceable in the midland counties; and they were unquestionably thrown up, says Murchison, shortly after the close of the Carboniferous era, — many ages ere the Saliferous era began. Besides, what evidence have we derived from volcanoes, either recent or extinct, that rock-salt, in deposits so enormously huge, is a volcanic product? Volcanoes in the neighborhood of the sea — and there are but few very active ones that have not the sea for their neighbor — deposit not unfrequently a crust of salt on the rocks and lavas that surround their craters; but we never hear of their throwing down vast saliferous beds, continuous for great distances, like those of the New Red Sandstone of England. And further, even were salt in such huge quantity an unequivocally volcanic production, how account for its position and arrangement here? How account for the occurrence of a volcanic product, spreading away in level beds and layers for nearly two hundred miles, in one of the least disturbed of the English formations, and forming no inconsiderable portion of its strata? As for the second theory, it seems exceedingly difficult to conceive how, in an open sea, subject, of course, like all open seas, to such equalizing influences as the ruffling of the winds and the deeper stirrings of the tides, any one tract of water should become so largely saturated as to throw down portions of its salt, when the surrounding tracts, less strongly impregnated, retained theirs. I have seen a fish-curer's vat throwing down its salt when surcharged with the mineral, but never any one stronger patch of the brine doing so ere the general mixture around it had attained to the necessary degree of saturation. And the lagoon theory, though apparently more tenable than any of the others, seems scarce less enveloped in difficulty. The few inches, at most few feet, of salt which line the bottoms and sides of the lagoons of the tropics, are but poor representatives of deposits of salt like those of the Upper Old Red of Cheshire; and Geology, as has been already indicated, has its deposits huger still Were one of the vast craters of the moon — Tycho or Copernicus — to be filled with sea-water to the brim, and the fires of twenty Ætnas to be lighted up under it, we could scarce expect as the result a greater salt-making than that of Cordova or Cracow. A bed of salt a hundred feet in thickness would demand for its salt-pan a lagoon many hundred feet in depth; and lagoons many hundred feet in depth, in at least the present state of things, are never evaporated.*

* Dr. Friedrich Parrot, the Russian traveller, gives a brief account, in his "Journey to Ararat" (1836), of the salt lakes that now mark the site of the inland sea which seems to have once occupied a large portion of the central basin of Asia. Their salt, however, though abundant and valuable regarded as an article of traffic and a source of revenue, would form, we find, but an inconsiderable geologic deposit, — a stratum scarce equal to the thinnest of the unworkable seams at Stoke Prior or Northwich. "At the western extremity of the expansion of the river Manech, on its northern shore," says the traveller, "are a number of salt lakes,

The salt-works at Droitwich were visited, in the reign of Henry the Eighth, by Leland the antiquary. He "asked a salter," he tells us, "how many furnaces they had in all; and the salter numbered them to an eighteen score, saying, that every one paid yearly to the king six shillings and eightpence." "Making salt," the antiquary adds, "is a notable destruction of wood, — six thousand loads of the young pole-wood, easily cloven, being used twelvemonthly; and the lack of wood is now perceivable in all places near the Wyche, on as far as Worcester." The Dudley coal-field seems to have been broached just in time to preserve to the midland districts their iron and salt trade. The complaint that the old forests were well-nigh gone was becoming general, when, in 1662, a Dudley miner took out a patent for smelting his ironstone with coke instead of charcoal; and the iron trade of England has been

the largest of which, there called Grusnoe Azore, is probably the same that is distinguished in our maps by the name of the new salt lake, and is five miles long, and two-thirds of a mile wide. These lakes have the property, in common with others of the same kind, that during the hottest season of the year, which, in these parts, is from May to the end of August, the surface of the water becomes covered with a crust of salt nearly an inch thick, which is collected with shovels into boats, and piled away. This is managed by private individuals, who rent the privilege from the government of the Don, on condition of paying a tenth of the produce. On this occasion I was much interested in being able to prove to my own satisfaction, that in such lakes it is nothing more than the rapid evaporation from the heat of the sun, and the consequent supersaturation of the water with salt, that effects the crystallization of the latter; for these lakes are so shallow that the little boats in which the salt is gathered are generally trailing on the bottom, and leave a long furrow behind them on it; so that the lake is consequently to be regarded as a wide pan of enormous superficial extent, in which the brine can easily reach the degree of concentration required; while, on the other hand, if the summer prove cold or rainy, the superfluous water must necessarily militate against the crystallization of the salt, or even prevent it altogether."

on the increase ever since. And only a few years later, the salters of Droitwich became equally independent of the nearly exhausted forests, by lighting up their "eighteen score furnaces" with coal. The railways and canals of the country have since spread the rock-salt of the New Red Sandstone over the empire and it is a curious fact, that some of our old established Scotch saltworks — works so old that they were in existence for centuries before the Scotch salter had ceased to be a slave — are now engaged in crystallizing, not sea-water, as formerly, but rock-salt, from the midland counties of England. I picked up, about a twelvemonth ago, on a cart-road in the neighborhood of Prestonpans, a fragment of rock-salt, and then, a few yards nearer the town, a second fragment; and curious to know where the mineral could have come from, in a district that has none of its own, I went direct to one of the more ancient salt-works of the place to inquire. But the large reservoir of salt water attached to the works for supplying the boilers, and which communicates by a pipe with the profounder depths of the sea beyond, of itself revealed the secret. There, against one of the corners, lay a red, half-molten pile of the rock-salt of Cheshire; while the enveloping sea-water — of old the only source of the salt manufactured in the village — constituted but a mere auxiliary source of supply, and a solvent.

CHAPTER XI.

Walk to the Clent Hills. — Incident in a Fruit Shop. — St. Kenelm's Chapel. — Legend of St. Kenelm. — Ancient Village of Clent; its Appearance and Character. — View from the Clent Hills. — Mr. Thomas Moss. — Geologic Peculiarities of the Landscape; Illustration. — The Scotch Drift. — Boulders; these transported by the Agency of Ice Floes. — Evidence of the Former Existence of a broad Ocean Channel. — The Geography of the Geologist. — Aspect of the Earth ever Changing. — Geography of the Palæozoic Period; of the Secondary; of the Tertiary. — Ocean the great Agent of Change and Dilapidation.

Let us now return to Hales Owen, and thence pass on to the Clent Hills, — famous resorts, in those parts, of many a summer pic-nic party from the nearer villages, and of pale-faced artizans and over-labored clerks, broken loose for a few happy days from the din and smoke of the more distant Birmingham. I was fortunate in a pleasant day, — rather of the warmest for walking along the low, dusty roads, but sufficiently cool and breezy on the grassy slopes of the hills. A humble fruit-shop stood temptingly open among the naileries in the outer skirts of Hales Owen, and I stepped in to purchase a few pears: a sixpenceworth would have been by no means an overstock in Scotland to one who had to travel several miles up hill in a warm day; and so I asked for no less here. The fruitman began to fill a capacious oaken measure, much like what, in Scotland, we would term a meal lippy, and to pile up the fruit over it in a heap. "How much is that?" I asked. — "Why, only fivepenn'orth," replied the man; "but I'll give thee the other penn'orth arter." — "No, no, stop," said I; "give me just the half of fivepenn'orth; you are much more liberal here than the fruit-dealers in my country; and I find the half will be quite as much as I can manage." The incident reminded me of the one so good-humoredly related by Franklin. When fresh from Boston, where food was comparatively high, he went into a baker's shop in Philadelphia to purchase threepence worth of bread on which to breakfast, and received, to his astonishment, for the money, three huge loaves, two of which he had to carry through the streets stuck under his arms, while satiating his hunger to the full on the third.

When little more than a mile out of town, I struck off the high road through a green lane, flanked on both sides by extensive half-grown woods, and overhung by shaggy hedges, that were none the less picturesque from their having been long strangers to the shears, and much enveloped in climbing, berry-bearing plants, honeysuckles, brambles, and the woody night-shade. As the path winds up the acclivity, the scene assumes an air of neglected wildness, not very common in England: the tangled thickets rise in irregular groups in the foreground; and, closing in the prospect behind, I could see through the frequent openings the green summits of the Clent Hills, now scarce half-a-mile away. I was on historic ground, — the "various wild," according to Shenstone, "for Kenelm's fate renowned;" and which, at a still earlier period, had formed one of the battle-fields on which the naked Briton contended on unequal terms with the mail-enveloped Roman. Half-way up the ascent, at a turning in the lane, where the thicket opens into a grassy glade, there stands a fine old chapel of dark red sandstone, erected in the times of the Heptarchy, to mark the *locale* of a tragedy characteristic of the time, — the murder of the boy-king St. Kenelm, at the instigation of his sister Kendrida. I spent some time in tracing the half-obliterated carvings on the squat Saxon door-way, — by far the most ancient part of the edifice, — and in straining hard to find some approximation to the human figure in the rude effigy of a child sculptured on the wall, with a crown on its head and a book in its hand, intended, say the antiquaries, to represent the murdered prince, but at present not particularly like anything. The story of Kenelm we find indicated, rather than told, in one of Shenstone's elegies: —

"Fast by the centre of yon various wild,
Where spreading oaks embower a Gothic fane,
Kendrida's arts a brother's youth beguiled;
There Nature urged her tenderest pleas in vain.
Soft o'er his birth, and o'er his infant hours,
The ambitious maid could every care employ;
And with assiduous fondness crop the flowers,
To deck the cradle of the princely boy.

"But soon the bosom's pleasing calm is flown;
Love fires her breast; the sultry passions rise;
A favored lover seeks the Mercian throne,
And views her Kenelm with a rival's eyes.
See, garnished for the chase, the fraudful maid
To these lone hills direct his devious way:
The youth, all prone, the sister-guide obeyed;
Ill-fated youth! himself the destined prey."

The minuter details of the incident, as given by William of Malmesbury and Matthew of Westminster, though admirably fitted for the purpose of the true ballad-maker, are of a kind which would hardly have suited the somewhat lumbrous dignity of Shenstone's elegiacs. Poor Kenelm, at the time of his death, was but nine years old. His murderer, the favored lover of his sister, after making all sure by cutting off his head with a long-bladed knife, had buried head, knife, and body, under a bush in a "low pasture" in the forest, and the earth concealed its dead. The deed, however, had scarce been perpetrated, when a white dove came flying into old St. Peters, at Rome, a full thousand miles away, bearing a scroll in its bill, and, dropping the scroll on the high altar, straightway disappeared. And on the scroll there was found inscribed in Saxon characters the following couplet: —

> "In Clent, in Caubage, Kenelm, kinge-born,
> Lyeth under a thorne, his hede off shorne."

So marvellous an intimation, — miraculous, among its other particulars, in the fact, that rhyme of such angelic origin should be so very bad, — though this part of the miracle the monks seem to have missed, — was, of course, not to be slighted. The Churchmen of Mercia were instructed by the pontiff to make diligent search after the body of the slain prince; and priests, monks and canons, with the Bishop of Mercia at their head, proceeded forthwith in long procession to the forest. And there, in what Milton, in telling the story terms a "mead of kine," they found a cow lowing pitifully beside what seemed to be a newly-laid sod. The earth was removed, the body of the murdered prince discovered, the bells of the neighboring churches straightway began "to rongen a peale without mannes helpe;" and a beautiful spring of water, the resort of many a pilgrim for full seven centuries after, burst out of the excavated hollow. The chapel was erected immediately beside the well; and such was the odor of sanctity which embalmed the memory of St. Kenelm, that there was no saint in the calendar on whose day it was more unsafe to do anything useful. There is a furrow still to be seen, scarce half a mile to the north of the chapel, from which a team of oxen, kept impiously at work during the festival of the saint ran away, and were never after heard of; and the owner lost not only his cattle, but, shortly after, his eyes to boot. The chapel received gifts in silver, and gifts in gold, — "crouns," and "ceptres," and "chalysses:" there grew up around it, mainly through the resort of pilgrims, a hamlet, which, in the times of Edward the First, contained a numerous population, and to which Henry the Third granted an annual fair. At length the age of the Reformation arrived; Henry the Eighth seized on the gold and silver; Bishop Latimer broke down the well; the pilgrimages ceased; the hamlet disappeared; the fair, after lingering on till the year 1784, disappeared also; and St. Kenelm's, save that the ancient chapel still survived, became exactly such a scene of wild woodland solitude as it had been ere the boy-prince fell under the knife of the assassin. The drama of a thousand years was over when, some time about the close of the last century, a few workmen, engaged in excavating the foundations of the ruined monastery of Winchcomb, in which, according to the monkish chroniclers, the body of the young prince had been interred near that of his father, lighted on a little stone coffin, beside a larger, which lay immediately under the great eastern window of the church. They raised the lid. There rested within, a little dust, a few fragments of the more solid bones, a half-grown human skull tolerably entire, and beside the whole; and occupying half the length of the little coffin, lay a long-bladed knife, converted into a brittle oxide, which fell in pieces in the attempt to remove it. The portion of the story that owed its existence to the monks had passed into a little sun-gilt vapor; but here was there evidence corroborative of its truthful nucleus surviving still.

I reached the nearest summit in the Clent range, and found it an oblong grassy level, many acres in extent, bounded on the right by a secluded valley that opens among the hills, with a sma.. stream running through it, The gieen slopes on both sides of the hollow, fc.. half their heights, from the summits downwards, retain all their old irregularities of surface, unscarred by plough or harrow: a few green fields, and a few picturesque cottages environed by hedge-rows, with an old mill and mill-pond, occupy the lower declivities and the bottom; and just where the valley opens into the level country we find the little ancient village of Clent, one of the prettiest and most characteristic of all old English villages. It stands half enwrapped in tall wood, and half embraced by the outstretched arms of the valley, with its ancient, time-eaten church rising in the midst, like the central obelisk in a Druidic circle, and its old, venerable dwellings betimbered with dark oak and belatticed with lead, and much beshrouded in ivy and honeysuckle, scattered irregularly around. There were half-a-dozen children at play in the grass-grown street as I passed; and a gentleman, who seemed the clergyman of the place, stood in earnest talk, at one of the cottage doors, with an aged matron in a black gown and very white cap; but I saw no other inhabitants, and scarce any mark of more: no noisy workshops — no stir of business, — nothing doing, or like to be done. Clent, for the last nine hundred years, seems to have had a wonderfully easy life of it, — an indolent, dreamy, uncaring summer-day sort of life. It was much favored by Edward the Confessor, as a curious charter, exempting its inhabitants from the payment of tolls at fairs, and from serving as jurors still survives to show; and, regarding itself as a village fairly provided for, it seems to have thrust its hands into its pockets at the time, and to have kept them there ever since. Its wood-embosomed churchyard, as might be anticipated from its years, seems vastly more populous than its cottages. According to the practice of this part of the country, the newer tombstones are all in deep black, and the lettering in gold; the stones rise thick around the gray old church, half-concealing the sward; and the sun, gleaming partially through openings in the tall trees, that run hedge-like round the whole, glistens here and there with a very agreeable effect on the bright letters. It would seem as if the tomb, less gloomy here than elsewhere, was smiling in hope, amid the general quiet. I had come down on the left-hand side of the valley to visit the village, which I now quitted by ascending the hill on the right, through long hollow lanes, rich in blackberries and ivy, and over which aged trees shoot out their gnarled branches, roughly bearded with moss. The hill-top I found occupied, like that on the other side of the valley, by an uneven plain, covered by a short sward, and thinly mottled with sheep; and all around to the dim horizon lay, spread out as in a map, the central districts of England.

One half the prospect from this hill-top is identically that which Thomson described from the eminence over Hagley. There stretches away along the horizon a blue line of hills, from the Wrekin and the Welsh mountains on the north, to the steep Malverns and the hills that surround Worcester on the south. The other half of the prospect embraces the iron and coal districts, with their many towns and villages, their smelting furnaces, forges, steam-engines, tall chimneys, and pit-fires innumerable; and beyond the whole lies the huge Birmingham, that covers its four square miles of surface with brick. No day, however bright and clear, gives a distinct landscape in this direction; all is dingy and dark; the iron furnaces vomit smoke night and noon, Sabbath-day and week-day; and the thick reek rises ceaselessly to heaven, league beyond league, like the sulphurous cloud of some never-ending battle. The local antiquary can point out, amid the haze, a few scenes of historic and literary interest. Yonder church, due north, in the middle distance, that seems to lead so unquiet and gloomy a life among the furnaces, — a true type of the Church militant, — had for its minister, many years ago, one Mr. Thomas Moss, who wrote, amid the smoke, a little poem known to every English reader, — "The Beggar's Petition." In an opposite direction there may be seen, when the sun shines, an old building, in which the conspirator Garnet, whose head wrought miracles on the straw amid which it was cast,* and several of the other Gunpowder Plot conspirators, secreted themselves for many days in a cavity in the wall. I have already referred to the scene of the old British battle, and of the assassination of St. Kenelm, both full in view; and to the literary recollections that linger around Hagley and the Leasowes, both full in view also. But the prospect is associated with an immensely more ancient history than that of the

* The miracle of the straw seems to have been considerably less remarkable than the belief in it. A young Jesuit-presumptive, attached to his reverend brother the "Martyr Garnet," had possessed himself, by way of relic, of one of the bloody ears of straw, stained by contact with the gory head, and stored it up in a bottle. Looking at it shortly after, he saw through the glass, on one of the chaff sheathes, the miniature semblance of a human head surrounded by a glory, and called on several of his co-religionists to admire the miracle. It was, however, unsafe in those days for Jesuits to work miracles in England. Tidings of the prodigy got abroad; law proceedings were instituted at the instance of the Privy Council; and though straw, bottle and Jesuit, had prudently disappeared, witnesses were cited to give evidence in court regarding it; among the rest, a painter named Bowen. And the painter's testimony was very amusing, and much to the point. He had seen the miniature head on the straw, he said; there could be no doubt of that; but then he had quite as little doubt that he could make as good, or even a better head, on an ear of straw, himself. And such was the miracle on the faith of which it was held that either Garnet was innocent of the Gunpowder Plot, or the Gunpowder Plot laudable in itself.

days of the Romans or of the Heptarchy, and with a literature considerably more modern than that of Lord Lyttelton or Mr. Moss; and it is on this more ancient history, as recorded in this more modern literature, that I shall attempt fixing the attention of the reader. When Signor Sarti exhibits his anatomical models, he takes up one cover after another, — first the skin, then the muscles, then the viscera, then the greater blood-vessels and deeper nerves, — until at length the skeleton is laid bare. Let us, in the same way, strip the vast landscape here of its upper integuments, coat after coat, beginning first with the vegetable mould, — the scarf-skin of the country, — wherein its beauty lies, with all its fields and hedge-rows, houses and trees; and proceed downwards, cover after cover, venturing a few remarks on the anatomy of each covering as we go, till we reach those profound depths which carry within their blank folds no record of their origin or history.

The vegetable mould is stripped away, with all its living inhabitants, animal and vegetable; man himself has disappeared, with all that man has built or dug, erected or excavated; and the vast panorama, far as the eye can reach, presents but a dreary wilderness of diluvial clays and gravels, with here a bare rock sticking through, and there a scattered group of boulders. Now mark a curious fact. The lower clays and gravels in this desert are chiefly of local origin; they are formed mainly of the rock on which they rest. These quartz pebbles, for instance, so extensively used in this part of the country in causewaying footways, were swept out of the magnesian conglomerate of the *Lower* New Red; these stiff clays are but re-formations of the saliferous marls of the *Upper* Red; these darkened gravels are derived from the neighboring coal-field; and yonder gray, mud-colored stratum, mixed up with fragments of limestone, is a deposit from the rather more distant Silurians. But not such the character of the widely-spread upper stratum, with its huge granitic boulders. We may see within the range of the landscape whence all the lower beds have come from; but no powers of vision could enable us to descry whence the granitic boulders and gravels have come from. Strange as the circumstance may seem, they are chiefly Scotch, — travellers, in the remote past, from the granitic rocks of Dumfries and Kirkcudbright. They lie amid sea-shells of the existing species, — the common oyster, the edible cockle and periwinkle, island-cyprina, rock-whelk (*purpura lapillus*), and a host of others of the kind we may any day pick on our shores. Now mark the story which they tell. This region of central England was once a broad ocean sound, that ran nearly parallel to St. George's Channel; there rose land on both sides of it: Wales had got its head above water; so had the Cotteswold Hills in Gloucestershire; and not a particle of the Scotch drift is to be found on either side, where the ancient land lay. But the drift marks the entire course of the central channel, lying thick in Lancashire, Cheshire, Staffordshire, and Worcestershire, in some localities to the depth of a hundred and fifty feet. And in its present elevation it averages in its course from fifty to five hundred feet over the existing sea. This ancient sound seems to have narrowed towards the south, where it joined on to the Bristol Channel; but such was its breadth where we now stand, that the eye would have failed to discover the eastern shore. Its waves beat against the Malverns on the one side, and the Cotteswold Hills on the other; it rose high along the flanks of the Wrekin; the secluded dells of Hagley were but the recesses of a submarine rock, shaggy with seaweed, that occupied its central tide-way; while the Severn, exclusively a river of Wales in those days, emptied its waters into the sea at the Breidden

Hills in Montgomeryshire, a full hundred miles from where it now falls into the Bristol Channel. Along this broad sound, every spring, when the northern ice began to break up, — for its era was that of the British glacier and iceberg, — huge ice-floes came drifting in shoals from the Scottish coast, loaded underneath with the granitic blocks which they had enveloped when forming in friths and estuaries; and, as they floated along, the loosened boulders dropped on the sea-bottom beneath. Here lie scores in the comparatively still water, and there lie hundreds where the conflicting tides dashed fierce and strong. "In the tract extending from the hamlet of Trescot to the village of Trysull, in the south-western parts of Staffordshire," says Sir Roderick Murchison, "the quantity, and occasionally gigantic dimensions, of these northern boulders (several tons in weight) may well excite surprise, seeing that they there occupy one of the most central districts of England. Here the farmer is incessantly laboring to clear the soil, either by burying them, or by piling them up into walls or hedge-banks; and his toil, like that of Sisyphus, seems interminable; for in many spots new crops of them, as it were, appear as fast as the surface is relieved from its sterilizing burden. So great, indeed, is their abundance, that an observer unacquainted with the region would feel persuaded he was approaching the foot of some vast granitic range; and yet the source of their origin is one hundred and fifty miles distant."

There are few things that speak more powerfully to the imagination of the geologist than the geography of his science. It seems natural to man to identify the solid globe which he inhabits by its great external features, particularly by its peculiar arrangement of continent and ocean. We at once recognize it in the prints of our popular astronomical treatises, as seen from the moon, or through the telescope from some of the more distant planets, by the well-known disposition of its land and water; and were that disposition made greatly different in the representation, we would at once fail to regard it as the earth on which we ourselves reside. It might be some of the other planets, we would say, but not ours. And yet these great features are exceedingly evanescent, compared with the enduring globe which they diversify and individualize, — mere changing mist-wreaths on the surface of an unchanging firmament. The up-piled clouds of one sunset, all gorgeous with their tints of bronze and fire, are not more diverse, in place, arrangement and outline, from the streaked and mottled cloudlets of another, radiant in their hues of gold and amber, than the lands and oceans of any one great geologic system, from the lands and oceans of the system that had preceded or come after it. Every geologic era has had a geography of its own. The earth, like a child's toy, that exhibits a dozen different countenances peeping out in succession from under the same hood, has presented with every revolution a new face. The highest lands of Asia and continental Europe formed ocean-beds in the times of the Oolite: the highest lands of our own country were swam over by the fish of the Old Red Sandstone.

There is much to exercise the imagination in facts such as these, whether one views in fancy the planet as a whole, ever changing its aspect amid the heavens, or calls up more in detail the apparition of vanished states of things amid existing scenes of a character altogether diverse, — buried continents, for instance, on the blue open sea, or long evanished oceans far inland, amid great forests and mighty hills. I can well understand the feeling experienced by Dr. Friedrich Parrot, as he travelled day after day in his journey to Ararat along the flat banks of the Manech, and saw in the salt marshes and brine lakes of the district irrefragable evidence that a great inland sea, of which the Caspian and the Sea of Aral are but minute fragments, — mere detached pools, left amid the general ebb, — had once occupied that vast central basin of Asia into which the Volga and the Oxus fall. He was ever realizing to himself — and deriving much quiet enjoyment from the process — a time when a sea without visible shore occupied, league beyond league, the surrounding landscape, and picturing in fancy the green gleam of the waves, interposed, cloud-like, between him and the sun. Very similar must be the feelings of the voyager on the great Pacific. We find trace in this ocean of a sinking continent, — a continent once of greater area than all Europe, — in the act of foundering, with but merely its mast-heads above the water. Great coral reefs that whiten the green depths league after league and degree after degree, for hundreds and thousands of miles, with here and there a tall mountain-peak existing as a surf-engirdled island, are all that remain to show where a "wide continent bloomed," that had existed as such myriads of ages after the true geologic *Atlantis* had been engulfed.

It seems more than questionable whether we shall ever arrive at a knowledge approximating to correct, regarding the distribution of ocean and continent in the earlier, or even secondary geologic formations. The Silurian and Old Red Sandstone systems give but few indications of land at all, and certainly no indications whatever of its place or extent. The Coal Measures, on the other hand, puzzle with the multiplicity of their alternations of land and water, — in some instances, of sea and land. We know little more than that an ocean-deposit forms very generally the base of the system, and that the deep bottom occupied by the sea came afterwards to be a platform, on which great forests sprang up and decayed; and that amid the broken stumps of these forests, when again submerged, the *Holoptychius* and *Megalichthys* disported. The same sort of obscurity hangs over the geography of the New Red Sandstone: we but know that land and water there were, from finding, wrapped up in the strata, the plants and reptiles of the one, and the fish and shells of the other. A few insulated facts dawn upon us in the Oolite. We ascertain that the Jurasic Alps formed in those early times the bottom of the sea, — nay, that the cuttle-fish discharged its ink, and the ammonite reared its sail, over the side of the gigantic Himalaya range; whereas, from the disposition of the Oolitic patches on both the eastern and western coasts of Scotland, it seems at least probable that in that remote period this ancient country, — "*Old* Scotland," — had got its head and shoulders above water. From the Weald we merely learn that a great river entered the sea somewhere near what now forms the south of England or north of France, — a river which drained the waters of some extensive continent, that occupied, it is probable, no small portion of the space now covered up by the Atlantic. It is not at all impossible that the long trails of sea-weed, many fathoms in length, which undulate in mid ocean to the impulses of the Gulf Stream, and darken the water over an area hundreds of miles in extent, are anchored beneath, to what once formed the *Rocky Mountains* of this submerged America. The Cretaceous system, as becomes its more modern origin, tells a somewhat more distinct story. It formed the bed of a great ocean, which extended from central England to at least the shores of the Red Sea, and included within its area considerable portions of France, Spain, Italy, Dalmatia, Albania, and the Morea, — a considerable part of Syria, as indicated in the ichthyolitic strata of Lebanon, — and large tracts of the great valley of Egypt, as shown by the nummulitic limestone of the pyramids. But the geography of these older formations, whether Palæozoic or Secondary, cannot be other than imperfect. Any one system, as shown on the geologic map, is but a thing of shreds and patches. Here it occurs as a continuous belt, — there as a detached basin, — yonder as an insulated outlier; and it is only on these shreds and patches that the geography of each system can be traced, when we can trace it at all. The field of the map in each instance resembles one of those dilapidated frescoes of Pompeii, in which by much the greater part of the plaster has fallen from the wall, and we can trace but broken fragments of the picture on the detached bits that remain. The geologic geographer finds himself in the circumstances of the cod-fishing skipper, who, in going one day, when crossing the Atlantic, to consult his charts, found them reduced to detached tatters, and came on deck in a paroxysm of consternation, to tell his crew that they might put about ship when they pleased, for the rats had eaten Newfoundland.

With the dawn of the Tertiary ages the fragments greatly extend, and tolerably adequate notions of the arrangements of land and water over wide areas may be formed.* The reader

* One of the most ingenious pieces of geologic geography to be anywhere met with in the literature of the science, may be found in Mr. Charles Maclaren's well-known "Sketch of the Geology of Fife and the Lothians." It occurs as part of a theory of the diluvial phenomena of "Crag and Tail," and appeals with equal effect to the reason and imagination of the reader. "If there has been a good deal of denudation on the east side of Scotland," says Mr. Maclaren, "there has been much more on the west. The absence of sand-banks on the west coast; the greater depth of the ocean there; the numerous and profound indentations of the land, in the shape of bays, estuaries, and lakes; the rocky islands, which had once been parts of the mainland; the removal of so large a part of the red sandstone of Ross and Sutherland, which had once covered a hundred miles of the western coast to the depth of two or three thousand feet, and is now reduced to a few isolated cones, — all these facts, with the familiar examples of Crag and Tail, indicate that the surface of Scotland has been swept by powerful denuding currents coming

must have seen Lyell's map of Europe, as Europe existed in the Eocene period, — a map constructed mainly on the geologic data of M. A. Boué. The land which it exhibits exists as

from the west. The west coast of England and Ireland also exhibits deep indentations in high rocky land. We find the same appearances in a less marked degree on the coast of Normandy and Brittany in France, and on a still smaller scale upon the west coasts of Spain and Portugal. The west coast of Norway is one long line of islands, promontories, and deep fiords, — showing that the primary rocks, in spite of their hardness, have been breached in a thousand places by powerful currents. The western coasts of Denmark, Holland and Belgium, having the British Isles before them as a breakwater, have few indentations, except where laid open by the rivers. An effect so general should have a general cause, and perhaps physical geography may afford a clue to it. If the land rose in detached portions, and by successive lifts, from the sea, we may suppose that there was a time when the surface of the globe consisted of a great expanse of ocean studded with islands. Such Adolphe Brongniart supposes its condition to have been, at least in Europe, when the Coal Measures were deposited. In this state of things there would be three great and constant currents, — one within the tropics, running westward ; and two running eastward between the tropics and the poles. The trade-winds in the torrid zone, and the prevailing westerly winds in the extra-tropical regions, would alone account for these currents. But to these causes must be added the southward course of an under-current, from the pole, of *cold water*, with a low velocity of revolution, and the northward course of an upper current, from the equator, of *warm water*, with a high velocity of revolution. The first would become a westerly current when it reached the tropics, and the second an easterly current when it reached the temperate zone. Such would be the state of an open ocean from the equator to the north pole ; and, *mutatis mutandis*, the same description applies to the southern hemisphere. All the three currents, in truth, exist at this day, but enfeebled and metamorphosed by the transverse position of the two great continents. Now, if these currents were acting permanently, and with the force which they would have if little obstructed, their operation, when tracts of land rose above the sea, would be thus : — They would form deep indentations on the *east side* of intertropical, and on the *west side* of extratropical lands ; and, when acting in very favorable circumstances, would form islands, by making breaches through continents, or separating their prominent parts. The detached groups of islands. There is, first, the British group, little different in form and extent from what it is now, save that the south-eastern corner of England is cut off diagonally, from the Wash to the Isle of Wight; next the Swedish and Norwegian group, consisting mainly of one great island: and then a still larger group than either, scattered over the existing area of France, Southern Austria, part of Turkey in Europe, and part of Italy. Running through the midst, there is a broad ocean sound, that stretches across, where it opens into the German Sea, from Norway to Dover, and that then expands in breadth, and sweeps eastwards, — covering in its course the beds of the Black and the Caspian Seas, — into the great Asiatic basin. And in this Europe of shreds and fragments, — of detached clusters of islets, with broad ocean channels flowing between,

boundary between the opposite currents would be between the latitudes of 28° and 30°, where a zone of still water would exist; and their *maximum* effort would be near the equator, and within the polar circle. When the land was rising, and near the surface of the water, or partially above it, the currents would produce the phenomena of Crag and Tail. The crag or head would point to the east within the tropics, and to the west in the temperate regions. The current would of course not flow invariably in one precise direction, but be occasionally deflected by high lands to the north or south of its true direction. We must keep in mind also, that though not perhaps very strong, it would be constant; and that transitory storms and hurricanes would generally incorporate themselves with it, and augment its force. A temporary current evidently would not explain the facts. If the same agent swept away the solid rocks which once environed and covered Arthur's Seat and North Berwick Law, and also deposited the tail of clay and gravel lying behind these mountains, it must have acted for thousands of years. But it is more probable that there were two or more currents at distant epochs. Perhaps New Holland, New Guinea, Borneo, the Philippines, and Spice Islands, may be the remnants of what was once the southern prolongation of the Asiatic continent, and which had been breached and divided by the tropical current before Africa and South America rose from the deep to arrest its free course. The idea, however, is thrown out merely as a conjecture on a subject requiring much additional investigation."

— the strange existences described by Cuvier enjoyed life during the earlier ages of the Tertiary. As we descend towards the present state of things, and lands and seas approximate to their existing relations, the geographic data become more certain. One side of the globe has, we find, its vanishing continent, — the other its disappearing ocean. The northern portion of our own country presents almost the identical outline which the modern geographer transfers to his atlas, save that there is here and there a narrow selvage clipped off and given to the sea, and that while the loftier headlands protrude as far as now into the ocean, the friths and bays sweep further inland: but in the southern part of the island the map is greatly different; a broad channel sweeps onwards through the middle of the land; and the Highlands of Wales, south and north, exist as a detached, bold-featured island, placed half-way between the coasts of England and Ireland. I found it exceedingly pleasant to lie this day on the soft short sward, and look down through the half-shut eye, as the clouds sailed slowly athwart the landscape, on an apparition of this departed sea, now in sunshine, now in shadow. Adventurous keel had never ploughed it, nor had human dwelling arisen on its shores; but I could see, amid its deep blue, as the light flashed out amain, the white gleam of wings around the dark tumbling of the whale and the grampus: and now, as the shadows rested on it dim and sombre, a huge shoal of ice-floes came drifting drearily from the north, — the snow-laden rack brushing their fractured summits, and the stormy billows chafing angrily below.

Was it the sound of the distant surf that was in mine ears, or the low moan of the breeze, as it crept through the neighboring wood? O, that hoarse voice of Ocean, never silent since time first began, — where has it not been uttered! There is stillness amid the calm of the arid and rainless desert, where no spring rises and no streamlet flows, and the long caravan plies its weary march amid the blinding glare of the sand, and the red unshaded rays of the fierce sun. But once and again, and yet again, has the roar of Ocean been there. It is *his* sands that the winds heap up; and it is the skeleton remains of his vassals — shells, and fish, and the stony coral — that the rocks underneath enclose. There is silence on the tall mountain-peak, with its glittering mantle of snow, where the panting lungs labor to inhale the thin bleak air, — where no insect murmurs and no bird flies, — and where the eye wanders over multitudinous hill-tops that lie far beneath, and vast dark forests that sweep on to the distant horizon, and along long hollow valleys where the great rivers begin. And yet once and again, and yet again, has the roar of Ocean been there. The effigies of his more ancient denizens we find sculptured on the crags, where they jut from beneath the ice into the mist-wreath; and his later beaches, stage beyond stage, terrace the descending slopes. Where has the great destroyer not been, — the devourer of continents, — the blue foaming dragon, whose vocation it is to eat up the land? His ice-floes have alike furrowed the flat steppes of Siberia and the rocky flanks of Schehallion; and his nummulites and fish lie imbedded in great stones of the pyramids, hewn in the times of the old Pharaohs, and in rocky folds of Lebanon still untouched by the tool. So long as Ocean exists there must be disintegration, dilapidation, change; and should the time ever arrive when the elevatory agencies, motionless and chill, shall sleep within their profound depths, to awaken no more, — and should the sea still continue to impel its currents and to roll its waves, — every continent and island would at length disappear, and again, as of old, "when the fountains of the great deep were broken up,"

"A shoreless ocean tumble round the globe."

Was it with reference to this principle, so recently recognized, that we are so expressly told in the Apocalypse respecting the tenovated earth, in which the state of things shall be fixed and eternal, that "there shall be no more sea"? or are we to regard the revelation as the mere hieroglyphic — the pictured shape — of some analogous moral truth? "Reasoning from what we know," — and what else remains to us? — an earth without a sea would be an earth without rain, without vegetation, without life, — a dead and doleful planet of waste places, such as the telescope reveals to us in the moon. And yet the Ocean does seem peculiarly a creature of time, — of all the great agents of vicissitude and change, the most influential and untiring; and to a state in which there shall be no vicissitude and no change, — in which the earthquakes shall not heave from beneath, nor the mountains wear down and the continents melt away, — it seems inevitably necessary that there should be "no more sea."

But, carried away by the speculation, I lag in my geological survey.

CHAPTER XII.

Geological Coloring of the Landscape. — Close Proximity in this Neighborhood of the various Geologic Systems. — The Oolite; its Medicinal Springs; how formed. — Cheltenham. — Strathpeffer. — The Saliferous System; its Organic Remains and Foot-prints. — Record of Curious Passages in the History of the Earlier Reptiles. — Salt Deposits. — Theory. — The Abstraction of Salt from the Sea on a large Scale probably necessary to the continued Existence of its Denizens. — Lower New Red Sandstone. — Great Geologic Revolution. — Elevation of the Trap. — Hills of Clent; Era of the Elevation. — Coal Measures; their three Forests in the Neighborhood of Wolverhampton. — Comparatively small Area of the Birmingham Coal-field. — Vast Coal-fields of the United States. — Berkeley's Prophecy. — Old Red Sandstone. —Silurian System. — Blank.

Let us now raise from off the landscape another integument, — let us remove the boulder clays and gravels, as we formerly removed the vegetable mould, and lay the rock everywhere bare. There is no longer any lack of color in the prospect; it resembles, on the contrary, a map variously tinted by the geographer, to enable the eye to trace his several divisions, natural or arbitrary. The range of trap-hills which furnishes our peak of survey is of a deep olive-green; the New Red Sandstone that spreads out so widely around it, of a bright brick-red. There is a coal-field on either hand, — the barren field of the Forest of Wyre, and the singularly productive field of Dudley; and they both are irregularly checkered black, yellow, and gray. Beyond the Wyre field lies an immense district of a deep chocolate-red tint, — a huge development of the Old Red Sandstone. Still further beyond, we may discern in the distance a bluish-gray province of great extent, much broken into hills, which consists of an at least equally huge development of the Silurian; while, rising over the red saliferous marls in an opposite direction, we may see a series of flat, low-lying rocks of the Oolitic system, passing from a pale neutral tint into a smoky brown and a light straw-yellow. In such close proximity are the geological systems in this part of the country, that the geologist who passes the night in Birmingham on the Lower New Red Sandstone, may go and take an early breakfast on the Silurian, the Old Red, the Carboniferous, the Saliferous, or the Oolitic systems, just as he inclines. Good sections, such as our northern sea-coasts furnish, are all that are wanting to render the locality one of the finest in the kingdom to the student of the stony science: but these he misses sadly; and he, alas! cannot deal with the stubborn integuments of the country in reality, as we are dealing with them so much at our ease in imagination, on one of the summits of the Clent Hills.

The integument that falls to be examined first in order, after the boulder drift and the gravels, is the Oolitic one; but it occupies merely a corner on the verge of the horizon, and need not engage us long. One remark regarding it, however, though rendered familiar to the geologic reader by the writings of Murchison and Mantell, I shall venture to repeat. We have seen how this central district of the kingdom has its storehouses of coal, iron, salt, lime, — liberal donations to the wants of the human animal, from the Carboniferous, Saliferous, and Silurian systems; and to these we must now add its inexhaustible deposits of medicine, — contributions to the general stock by the Oolitic system. Along the course of the Lias, medicinal springs abound; there is no other part of England where they rise so thickly, or of a quality that exerts a more powerful influence on the human frame. The mineral waters of Cheltenham, for instance, so celebrated for their virtues, are of the number; and the way in which they are elaborated in such vast quantities seems to be simply as follows: — They all rise in the Lias, — a formation abounding in sulphate of iron, lime, magnesia, lignite, and various bituminous matters; but they have their origin far beneath, in the saliferous marls of the Upper New Red, which the Lias overlies. In the inferior formation they are simply brine springs: but brine is a powerful solvent; passing through the Lias, it acts upon the sulphur and the iron; becomes, by means of the acid thus set free and incorporated with it, a more powerful solvent still; operates upon the lime, upon the magnesia, upon the various lignites and bitumens; and at length rises to the surface, a brine-digested extract of Liasic minerals. The several springs yield various analyses, according to the various rocks of the upper formation which they pass through, — some containing more, some less lime, sulphur, iron, magnesia; but in all the dissolving menstruum is the same. And such, it would appear, is the mode in which Nature prepares her simples in this rich district, and keeps her medicine-chest ever full.

Let us trace the progress of a single pint of the water thus elaborated, from where it first alights on the spongy soil in a wintry shower, till where it sparkles in the glass in the pump-room at Cheltenham. It falls among the flat hills that sweep around the ancient city of Worcester, and straightway buries itself, all fresh and soft, in the folds of the Upper New Red Sandstone, where they incline gently to the east. It percolates, in its downward progress, along one of the unworkable seams of rock-salt that occur in the superior marls of the formation; and, as it pursues, furlong after furlong, its subterranean journey, savors more and more strongly of the company it keeps; becomes in succession hard, brackish, saline, briny; and then many fathoms below the level at which it had entered, escapes from the sa.iferous stratum, tnrough a transverse fissure, into an inferior Liasic bed. And here it trickles, for many hundred yards, through a pyritiferous shale, on which its biting salts act so powerfully, that it becomes strongly tinctured by the iron oxide, and acidulated by the sulphur. And now it forces its upward way through the minute crevices of a dolomitic limestone, which its salts and acids serve partially to decompose; so that to its salt, iron and sulphur, it now adds its lime and its magnesia. And now it flows through beds of organic remains, animal and vegetable, — now through a stratum of belemnites, and now a layer of fish, — now beside a seam of lignite, and now along a vein of bitumen. Here it carries along with it a dilute infusion of what had been once the muscular tissue of a crocodile, and here the strainings of the bones of an ichthyosaurus. And now it comes gushing to the light in an upper Liasic stratum, considerably higher in the geologic scale than the saliferous sandstones into which it had at first sunk, but considerably lower with reference to the existing levels. And now take it and drink it off at once, without pause or breathing space. It is not palatable, and it smells villanously; but never did apothecary mix up a more curiously-compounded draught; and if it be not as salutary as it is elaborate, the faculty are sadly in error.

The underground history of the mineral springs of Great Britain would form an exceedingly curious chapter. I visited, a few weeks since, the springs at Strathpeffer, and explored, as carefully as rather imperfect sections and rather limited time permitted, the geology of the valley. The lower hills that rise around it are composed of the great conglomerate base of the Old Red Sandstone system. The denudation of ages has swept every trace of the superior strata from their sides and summits; but in the sheltered trough of the valley at least one of the overlying beds has escaped. We find laid at length along the hollow bottom, like a pancake in a platter, the lower ichthyolitic bed of the formation, so rich in other parts of the country in animal remains, but which exists in this locality as a gray brecciated rock, devoid of visible fossils, but so largely saturated with the organic matter into which they have been resolved, that, when struck by the hammer, the impalpable dust set loose affects very sensibly the organs of taste, and appeals scarce less strongly to those of smell than the swine-stones of England. And it is through this saturated bed that the mineral waters take their course. Even the upper springs of the valley, as they pass over it, contract, in a sensible degree, its peculiar taste and odor. The dweller on the sea-coast is struck, on entering the pump-room, by the familiarity of the powerful smell which fills the place. It is that of a muddy sea-bottom when uncovered by the ebb. He finds that, whatever else may have changed within the rock since the times of the Lower Old Red Sandstone, the scent of the ancient ooze of this system is exactly what it ever was; and he drinks the water, convinced, if a geologist, that if man did not come early enough in the day to breakfast on the fish of the Old Red,—*Acanthodiens*, *Dipteriens*, *Coccostei*, and *Pterichthyes*,—he has at least come quite in time enough to gulp down as medicine an infusion of their juices and their bones.

We strip off the Liasic integument, "as ye peel the fig when its fruit is fresh;" and it is with the Upper New Red formation, on which the Lias rests,—its saliferous marls and vast beds of rock-salt,—that we have now to deal. There occurs among the superior strata of the formation a bed of variously-colored sandstone, of little depth, but great horizontal extent, remarkable for containing, what in England at least is comparatively rare in the New Red, organic remains. We find it chiefly characterized by an inequilateral bivalve, not larger than a small pea, which conchologists term the *Posidónomya*; and by the teeth and ichthyodorulites of fishes: on the surface, too, of some of its ripple-marked slabs, curious records lie inscribed of the doings of the earlier reptiles. On one large slab in the Warwick Museum, figured by Sir Roderick Murchison, we may see the footprints of some betailed batrachian, that went waddling along, greatly at its leisure, several hundred thousand years ago, like the sheep of the nursery rhyme, "trailing its tail behind it." There is a double track of footprints on the flag, — those of the right and left feet: in the middle, between the two, lies the long groove formed by the tail, — a groove continuous, but slightly zig-zagged, to indicate the waddle. The creature half-way in its course lay down to rest, having apparently not much to do, and its abdomen formed a slight hollow in the sand beneath. In again rising to its feet, it sprawled a little; and the hinder part of its body, in getting into motion, fretted the portion of the surface that furnished the main fulcrum of the movement, into two wave-like curves. The marks on another slab of the same formation compose such a notice of the doings of one of the earlier chelonians as a provincial editor would set into type for his newspaper, were the reptile My Lord Somebody, his patron. The chelonian journeyed adown a moist sandy slope, furrowed by ripple-markings, apparently to a watering-place. He travelled leisurely, as became a reptile of consequence, set down his full weight each step he took, and left a deep-marked track in double line behind him. And yet, were his nerves less strong, he *might* have bestirred himself; for the southern heavens were dark with tempest at the time, and a thunderous-like shower, scarce a mile away, threatened to wet him to the skin. On it came: and the large round drops, driven aslant by a gale from the south, struck into the sand like small shot, at an angle of sixty. How the traveller fared on the occasion has not transpired; but clear and palpable it is that he must have been a firm fellow, and that the heavy globular drops made a much less marked impression on the sand consolidated by his tread, than when they fell elsewhere on the incoherent surface around him. Such are two of the curious old-world stories recorded on this upper bed of New Red Sandstone; and there are many more of the same class. A lower bed of light-colored stone occupies the base of the saliferous system, forming its pavement, and separating it from the inferior New Red. And this bed has also its organisms, chiefly vegetable,—flabelliform palm-leaves,—narrow, slender spikes, resembling those of the grasses,—and a peculiarly formed ear-like cone or catkin, termed the echinostachys. And these constitute some of the earliest remains known to the geologist of a flora specifically different from that of the Coal Measures. Interposed between this pavement and the fossiliferous sandstone band above, there occurs a vast thickness of saliferous marls, interstratified with those enormous beds of rock-salt, continuous over wide areas, in which all the salt-mines of England have been excavated, and which now forces upon us, a second time, the problem of the saliferous deposits. The wind-bound ship-master, detained in port long after the specified day of sailing, takes instruments in the hands of a legal official, and, "protesting against the weather," frees himself from all risk of prosecution from passenger or supercargo. I have already, in like manner, entered my protest against the difficulties which environ this subject; and shall now launch into it, shielded by the document against the responsibility of failure, or the odium consequent on entering a wrong port.

If in the existing state of things we seek for phenomena

similar in *kind* to those which produced the Coal Measures, we shall not be disappointed; but we shall be greatly disappointed if we seek for phenomena not only similar in kind, but also equal in *power*. An American swamp or a Scotch morass gives us but the equivalent of a single thin seam of coal; a submarine peat-moss, based on a layer of vegetable mould, and topped by a bed of sea-sand, the equivalent merely of a single thin seam, resting on an earthy shale, and overlaid by a shelly sandstone. Swamp, morass, submerged peat-moss, nay, even if we add to these some river delta, which, like that of the Mississippi, receives the spoils of a wide forest-covered continent, are but slender representatives of even our Scottish coal-field, with its three hundred and eighty-seven successive beds, of which eighty-four are seams of coal. We must be content, in our illustrations drawn from the present scene of things, with phenomena similar in kind, without looking for aught corresponding in extent. Even had we now the Carboniferous vegetation, the stiff and rigid earth, grown old, would not exhibit the ever-recurring sinkings, with occasional risings, of surface, which buried the lower beds of the Carboniferous system full four thousand feet beneath its upper deposits. Now, in dealing with the Saliferous system, let us content ourselves, as in dealing with the Coal Measures, with simply illustrating the foregone phenomena by phenomena of the existing state of things apparently similar in kind, though palpably dissimilar in extent and degree. Let us take for granted, as we do in the case of the Carboniferous period, a comparatively flexible state of the earth's crust, — frequent sinkings of the surface, with occasional risings and progressive depositions of matter, that keep pace with the general subsidence. And let us then refer to some of the salt formations of the present time, as illustrative of the way in which, amid greatly more active energies of nature, vastly more enormous deposits of this mineral came to be formed; just as our writers on the Coal Measures refer, on a similar understanding, to existing swamps and mosses.

We are told by Major Harris, in his "Highlands of Ethiopia," that when on his journey, he reached, with his party, near the Abyssinian frontier, a desert valley, occupied by a salt lake, the *Bahr Assal*, which forms a prolongation of the Gulf of Tadjura. A broad bar of lava had cut off its waters from those of the gulf; and, fed by no rivers, and exposed in a burning climate to the unmitigated rays of the sun, intensified by reflection from hot rocky mountains, they had shrunk into "an elliptical basin, seven miles in its transverse axis, half-filled with smooth water of the deepest cerulean hue, and half with a solid sheet of glittering, snow-white salt, the offspring of evaporation." Here, at least, was one extensive bed of salt in the forming; nor is it difficult to conceive how: the work of evaporation completed, and the entire lake rendered a white, solid mass, some general sinking of the surface continued, till the waves of the outer gulf toppled for a time over the lava bar, and then, succeeded, as such sinkings so often were during the Carboniferous period, by a slight elevatory movement, might give to it a second supply of brine with which to double its thickness. We find no lava bars in the saliferous sandstone; but sand-bars raised by the surf on a flat arenaceous coast during a slow and equable sinking of the surface, would meet the emergencies of our theory less clumsily, and better. Let us conceive, then, along a range of flat coast extending from the northern parts of Lancashire to the Bristol Channel, a chain of lagoons, some of lesser, some of larger extent, and separated from the main sea by sand spits or bars raised by the surf; let us suppose the climate to be at least as warm as that on the African shore of the Red Sea, in which the salt of the *Bahr Assal* is forming; let us imagine a subsidence of the land going on so exceedingly slow and gradual as to be counterbalanced by the deposition of earthy matter taking place in the sea on the one hand, — by the crystallization of the salt in the lagoons, fed by occasional supplies of salt water, on the other, — and by the rise of the bar, ever operated upon by the surf, in the line between. A paroxysm of sudden subsidence would, of course, bring the formation of the salt-bed to a close, and cover it up with a stratum of sand or marl; a slight elevatory movement succeeding the paroxysm would have the effect of rendering the superimposed stratum the foundation of a second lagoon and second bed of salt. According as the periods between the elevatory movements and the paroxysms of subsidence were long or short, the beds of salt would be thick or thin. Among the five beds that occur at Stoke Prior, in the vicinity of Droitwich, there is one more than thirty feet in depth, and one not more than six inches. According as the duration of the term of submergence was extended or brief, would be the thickness or thinness of the bars by which the salt-beds were separated. At Stoke Prior, one of these separating bars falls short of three feet, while another somewhat exceeds twenty-four. As the lagoons chanced to be well or ill protected from the introduction of extraneous matter, the salt which formed in them would be pure or impure. One of the Stoke Prior beds contains full twenty-five per cent. of reddish marl, while another is so unmixed with earthy matter that it might be used, without any previous refining preparation, for the purpose of the fish-curer. And thus deposition after deposition would take place, and, as in the Coal Measures, subsidence succeed subsidence, until the entire Saliferous system would come to be formed. It has been started as an objection to the lagoon theory, that the salt-beds contain no organic remains, which, it is held, they would have done had they owed their origin to sea-water. I am, however, not sure that the objection is particularly strong. Let us remember that the organisms of the entire system in England are but few and ill preserved, and that the marls which alternate with the salt have failed to preserve organisms at all; while the shells of the superior band occur but as mere casts in an incoherent clay. Let us further remember what takes place in the upper pots and hollows of our rocky shores, when, at the height of a stream-tide, they receive their fill of sea-water mingled with sea-wrack, and are then left during the neaps to present their festering contents undisturbed and undiluted to the influence of the sun. Their waters assume a turbid blue color and a strong fetid odor, and become in this state so powerful a dissolvent, that a few warm days converts the wrack which they contain into an impalpable mud. Further, it may be deemed a fact worthy of consideration, as at least not hostile to the sea-water theory, that the rock-salt of England contains, like the bilge-water of these tide-forsaken pots, a considerable admixture of iodine, — a substance which enters largely into the composition of the sponges and marine algæ.

Single masses of salt, like those of Cordova, might come to be elaborated by a greatly more simple process. The Mediterranean is not an intertropical sea; but what, notwithstanding, would be the probable result, were it to be cut off from the Atlantic by some such bar of rock as severed the *Bahr Assal* from the Gulf of Tadjura? There is no other inland sea that, in proportion to its extent of surface, receives such scanty contributions of river water; and, to supply the waste of evaporation from its million of square miles of surface, its deep throat is continually gulping up the waters of the Atlantic at the rate of many thousand tons hourly. A powerful current flows incessantly inwards through the Straits of Gibraltar, and yet the level within is not more than maintained. Were the Atlantic excluded, the inland sea would of course gradually dry up, until its area had so considerably lessened that its rivers would be of themselves sufficient to counterbalance its waste of surface; and were its rivers wanting, as might well be the case had it a Desert of Sahara on its northern, as on its southern side, even its profounder depths of more than a thousand fathoms would in time evaporate, and but enormous beds of salt remain behind. It seems not improbable, that the loose arenaceous materials of the New Red Sandstone may have existed, ere they formed an ocean bottom, as the incoherent sands of some geologic Sahara that encircled the inland seas and lagoons of this system, and that a consequent lack of rivers may have operated influentially in the formation of the salt. By the way, may not this process of separating huge deposits of this mineral from the sea,—a process which has been going on, we find, in every formation, from the Onondaga salt group of the Upper Silurian, as developed in the United States of America, down to the recent salt-lakes of the Asiatic basin,—be a provision in nature for preserving to the ocean its proper degree of density and saturation? In the natural course of things, the sea would necessarily be growing salter and heavier. The waves wash out of every shore, and receive from every river, minute supplies of salt, which evaporation has scarce any tendency to dissipate, and which, in the lapse of ages, would be necessarily accumulating in the waters, till the delicate gills and branchiæ of the various inmates, formed with reference to a rarer medium, would labor amid the dense and briny fluid, and their bodies, heretofore of a gravity exactly proportioned to that of their element, but now grown too light for it, would float helplessly atop.* True, the salt seems in every instance to have been abstracted and locked up by accident; but then the recurrence of the accident in every geologic formation demonstrates it to be one of those on which the adept in the doctrine of chances might safely calculate. It seems an accident of the fixed class on which Goldsmith bases his well-known reflection in the "Vicar of Wakefield." "To what a fortuitous concurrence," he remarks, "do we not owe every pleasure and convenience of our lives! How many seeming accidents must unite before we can be clothed or fed! The peasant must be disposed to labor, the shower must fall, the wind fill the merchant's sail, or numbers must want the usual supply."

And now we strip off the thick saliferous integument of the Upper New Red, with all its marls, rock-salts and sandstones, and lay bare the lower formation. Within at least the range of our prospect, we shall find in it few marks of organic existence, and these few doubtful and indistinct. Some of the red incoherent sandstones which form its base contain carbonaceous markings, but of a character too obscure to be interpreted; and we may occasionally detect in the calcareous conglomerate above — its upper member — shells and encrinital stems; but they occur in merely the enclosed fragments, and belong to the older rocks. And yet there attaches no little geologic interest to this barren formation: it marks the era of a great change. The rugged conglomerate, which rises so high along the flanks of the hill on which we stand, represents in this

* Indisposition prevented me from hearing Professor Fleming lecture last spring on the saliferous deposits; but the idea started here belongs, I am inclined to suspect, to the professor, notwithstanding. I think I must have received it in conversation, from some attendant on the course, who had enjoyed the pleasure which I unluckily missed.

locality the Magnesian Limestone,—the formation with which the long-derived and darkly-antique Palæozoic systems end and on whose upper platform the first of the Secondary systems begins. A strange shifting of scenes took place on that rough stratum at our feet; but it would seem as if the theatre had been darkened when the alterative process was going on. The lamps burnt low, and concealed the machinery of the stage. In the long course of geologic history there have been many medals struck,—many previous to the time of this revolution, and many after it; but none records the nature of the revolution itself; nor is there geology enough in the world to fill up the gap. It yawns in the middle of the forum, and no one has dared to fling even a plausible conjecture into it. Up till the deposition of that Magnesian stratum had taken place, all the fish of which we possess specimens sufficiently well-preserved to indicate the fact were characterized by the heterocercal tail, —the vertebral column was prolonged into the upper lobe of the caudal fin;* but with that stratum the peculiarity ceased, and fishes with the homocercal tail of our common osseous varieties took their place. In that Magnesian formation, too, just ere the occurrence of the revolution, we find the first trace of reptiles. The long drama of the Palæozoic period, with all its distinct acts, ended with the dethronement of the huge sauroid fish,—for untold ages the master existence of creation;

* At the annual general meeting of the Geological Society, held in February last (1846), it was stated by the president, Mr. Horner, in his admirable address, that certain highly characteristic genera of the fishes of the Old Red Sandstone, such as the *Coccosteus* and *Pterichthys*, do not possess the heterocercal tail. It should have perhaps been added, however, to prevent misconception, that neither do they possess tails of the homocercal type. The form of tail in both cases is quite as unique among the ancient Ganoid order, as that of the tail of the Ray family among existing Placoids.

and the ew-born reptile reigned in its stead. We find, too, numerous well-known types of shells, familiar in the older rocks, appearing in this formation for the last time. So far as is yet known, the Magnesian Limestone contains the last-created species of Producta, and the last-created Spirifer. We ascertain that these shells continued to exist up till the breaking out of this great geologic revolution, and that then, like some of the extinct French noblesse cut short by the guillotine, they disappear forevermore. And now, raising from off the landscape this curious integument, and setting it aside, as Signor Sarti removes to a side-table one of the bits of his figure, — a piece of the external skin, mayhap, thickened by its adipose lining or a well-compacted sheet of muscle and sinew, — we lay bare the coal-fields, and the range of trappean eminences that broke them up as with wedges, just as their upper strata had been consolidated, and they had received their first thin covering of the Lower New Red.

I must, I find, employ, though with considerable modifications, an illustration which I have used at least once before. Here is a small shallow pond, covered over with a thick cake of ice, and with a line of boulders rising in its centre. There have been two frosts and an intervening thaw. Just as the first frost set in, the boulder tops lay under the surface, and the earlier-formed crust of ice stretched over them; but, as frequently happens when the temperature sinks suddenly below the freezing point, a great shrinking of the water took place: the ice, unsupported from beneath, leaned for a little while on the boulders, and then giving way on both sides, half-way between their summits and the shore, and, as a direct consequence, cracking also directly over them, the summits came through, and the ice-sheets lay reclining in masses against them, broken by faults, and shivered by transverse cuttings. At this stage, however, the thaw came on, and encircled with a shallow ring of water, that rose over the depressed surface, the central patch of shivered ice, and the boulders in the midst; and then the second frost set in, and the shallow liquefied ring became a solid. Now, let us mark the phenomena exhibited. There, first, in the centre of the pond, rises the line of boulders. There is an isolated area all around them, — a formation of the earlier frost, much broken by faults; and these radiate from the stones rudely and irregularly, but still, on the whole, distinctly enough to indicate the boulder-line as a producing cause of the fracturing and dislocation. And then, around this broken and disjointed area, we find an encircling formation of the later frost, — the solidified ring, — in which there are no faults or cuttings, but in which all is undisturbed and entire. Our geological model is now complete; that row of boulders represents the chain of Trap and Silurian hills which runs along the Dudley coal-field, and whose elevation from below has so broken up the formation with long lines of radiating faults and transverse fractures. The fractured, insulated area of the ice of the first frost represents the coal-field itself; the unbroken enveloping ring of the second, the surrounding New Red Sandstone.

Now, there are several points worthy of notice in this model. Observe, first, that we can ascertain with great certainty, relatively at least, at what period the dislocations and fracturings of the central area took place. They occurred at the close, or not long after the close, of the first ice formation, and not later; for had they taken place during the time of the second ice formation, it also would have been broken up, whereas we find it entire. Observe, next, that under the shallow solidified ring of the second frost we may naturally expect to find existing, as a nether stratum, a prolongation of the shattered ice of the first.

And founding on exactly this simple principle, the New Red Sandstone of this part of the country, *i. e.* the unfractured ice of the second frost, has been lately pierced through, to get at the Coal Measures, *i. e.* the fractured ice of the first; and very valuable though deeply-seated seams of coal have repaid the boldness of the search, and confirmed the justness of the reasoning. Observe, further, that this broken condition of the coal-field, if its surface were bared in the style we have dared to uncover it from our hill-top, as Asmodeus uncovered the houses of Madrid, would present, viewed from above, a very striking appearance. Of the twelve panes in the window opposite to which I write, by far the most conspicuous is the pane through the centre of which an unlucky urchin sent yesterday a stone. There is a little hole in the middle, from which some fifteen or twenty bright rays proceed, star-like, to every part of the astragal frame. The ray-like cracks of the coal-field are, of course, wholly obscured by the diluvium and the vegetable mould. A shower of snow — to return to our first illustration — has covered up, with a continuous veil, central boulders, flawed area, and encircling ring, reducing them all to one aspect of blank uniformity; and we can but dip down upon the cracks and flaws, here the point of a finger, there the end of a stick; and so, after many soundings have thus been taken, piece out a plan of the whole. It would seem as if, in at least one of the planets to which we point the telescope, there is no such enveloping integument; and the starred and fractured surface remains exposed and naked, like that of the ice of the pond ere the snow-shower came on. Those who have enjoyed the luxury of hearing Professor Nichol, of Glasgow, lecture on the lunar phenomena, must remember his graphic description of the numerous ray-like lines, palpable as the cracks in a damaged pane, that radiate in every direction, some of them extending for hundreds of miles, from all the larger craters of the moon.

There are not a few interesting appearances in this Dudley coal-field. Its seams, like those of every other coal-field yet known, have been formed under very various conditions: some of them must have been deposits of vegetable matter washed by rivers into seas or lakes; some of them seem to have formed in marshy hollows, like our existing peat-mosses, or, if we must seek out analogies from somewhat warmer climates than those in which peat is elaborated, like the Dismal Swamp of the United States; and some evidently covered as great forests the sites which they now occupy as coal-seams. There is a colliery about a mile and a half to the south of Wolverhampton, where an outcrop of what is termed the *bottom coal* is wrought in the open air. The surface, in consequence, has been bared of the debris and diluvium, and in one corner the upper plane of a thin seam of coal exposed for about a quarter of an acre. It is found to present exactly the appearance of a moor on which a full-grown fir wood had been cut down a few months before, and only the stumps left behind. Stump rises beside stump, to the number of seventy-three in all: the thickly-diverging roots strike out on every side into what had been once vegetable mould, but which now exists as an indurated, brownish-colored shale. Many trunks, sorely flattened, lie recumbent on the coal, some of them full thirty feet in length, while some of the larger stumps measure rather more than two feet in diameter. There lie thick around, stigmaria, lepidodendra, calamites, and fragments of ulodendra; and yet, with all the assistance which these lent, the seam of coal formed by this ancient forest does not exceed five inches in thickness. It must have required no little vegetable matter to consolidate into the mineral which supplies us, year after year, with our winter fuel; the coal which loads a single large collier would, when it existed as wood, have built many large colliers. Not a few of the stumps in this area are evidently water-worn; and there have been found immediately over them scales of *Megalichthys*, and the shells of an Unio, somewhat resembling in form the common pearl muscle of our rivers, but considerably smaller. The prostrate forest had been submerged, and molluscs lived and fishes swam over it. It is further worthy of notice, that this upper forest is underlaid, at the depth of a few feet, by a second forest, in which the stumps lie as thickly and are of as great a size, as in the first; and that this second forest is underlaid, in turn, by the remains of yet a third. We find three full-grown forests closely packed up in a depth of not more than twelve feet.

Once more, ere we wrap up this Carboniferous integument of the landscape, and lay bare the Old Red Sandstone, let us mark to how small a coal-field central England has, for so many years, owed its flourishing trade. Its area, as I have already had occasion to remark, scarcely equals that of one of our larger Scottish lakes; and yet how many thousand steam-engines has it set in motion, — how many railway trains has it propelled across the country, — how many thousand wagon-loads of salt has it elaborated from the brine, — how many million tons of iron has it furnished, raised to the surface, smelted, and hammered! It has made Birmingham a great city, — the first iron depot of Europe; and filled the country with crowded towns and busy villages. And if one small field has done so much, what may we not expect from those vast basins, laid down by Lyell in the geological map of the United States, prefixed to his recent singularly interesting work of travels? When glancing, for the first time, over the three huge coal fields of the States, each surrounded by its ring of Old Red

Sandstone, like patches of mineral bitumen floating in their clay-tinged pools, I called to mind the prophecy of Berkeley, and thought I could at length see, what Berkeley could not, the *scheme* of its fulfilment. The metaphysical bishop marked the *westward* course of empire: he saw Persia resigning the sceptre to Macedonia, and Macedonia yielding it, in turn, to Rome, and to those western nations of Europe that abut on the Atlantic. And at a time when North America was still covered with the primeval forests, he anticipated an age in which that country would occupy as preëminent a place among the nations as had been occupied in other ages by Assyria or Rome. Its enormous coal-fields — equal in extent, some of them, to all England, and whose dark seams, exposed to the light for miles, inlay the landscape as with ebony, and impart to it its most striking peculiarity of feature — seem destined to form no mean element in its greatness. If a patch containing but a few square miles has done so much for central England, what may not fields containing many hundred square leagues do for the United States?

"Westward the course of empire takes its way;
The four first acts already past,
A fifth shall close the drama with the day:
Time's noblest offspring is the last."

And now, stripping off the dark Coal Measures like a pall, we expose the chocolate-colored beds of the Old Red Sandstone. In our immediate neighborhood there is a hiatus in the geologic series, — the Carboniferous system rests on the Silurian; but westwards, and on to the south-west, we may see the Old Red Sandstone stretching away in enormous development. As estimated by a practised eye, — that of Sir Roderick Murchison, — its entire thickness in this part of the country falls little short of ten thousand feet. Here, as everywhere else, it seems chiefly remarkable for its strange forms of the vertebrate animals, exclusively fish. The Upper Old Red formation, so rich in Scotland in the remains of *Holoptychius*, *Platygnathus Bothriolepis*, and their contemporaries, is comparatively barren in England. The middle formation, however, we find mottled with ichthyolitic fragments, representative of the two great orders of fish in which, at this early period, and for long ages after, all vertebrate existence was comprised. Fragments of the ichthyodorulites of Placoids are not unfrequent; and the occipital plates of the Ganoid Cephalaspides abound. The true fish seems to have overspread and taken full possession of the seas during the deposition of this system, as the Trilobite had taken possession of them in the preceding one. But we hasten on: the thick Old Red coils up and away, like a piece of old elastic parchment that had been acquiring for ages the *set* of the roll; and now the still more ancient Silurian system occupies the entire prospect. In this system the remains of the vertebrate animals first appear, — few and far between, and restricted, so far as is yet known, to its great upper division exclusively. We pass hurriedly downwards. The vertebrata vanish from creation. We have traced the dynasty to its first beginnings; and now an ignobler, though more ancient, race of kings occupy the throne.* We have reached, in our explora

* Of course, in all cases in which the evidence is negative, the decision must be given under protest, as not in its nature irreversible, but dependent on whatever positive evidence the course of discovery may yet serve to evolve. In February last (1846), when this chapter was written, no trace of reptiles had been found earlier than the Lower New Red Sandstone, — the Permian system of Sir Roderick Murchison. I find, however, from a report of the proceedings of the meeting of the British Association, held last September at Southampton, that Mr. Lyell having examined certain footprints, the discovery of Dr. King, of the United States, which occur in Pennsylvania in the middle of the Coal Measures, he has determined them to be those of a large reptilion. It does seem strange enough that the

tions, the dynasty of the crustacea. In all creation, as it exists in this period of dusk antiquity, we see nothing that overtops the Trilobite, with his jointed mail of such exquisite workman

prints of this eldest of reptiles should be found so far in advance of what has been long deemed the vanguard of its order, — the thecodent Saurians of the Permian, — and this, too, in a system so carefully explored as the Coal Measures ; and yet the occurrence is not without a parallel in the geologic scheme. The mammal of the Stonesfield Slate stands as much alone, and still further in advance of its fellows. I do not find that I have anything to alter in my statement regarding the introduction of the fish. In Professor Silliman's American Journal for January 1846, it is stated, that an ichthyodorulite had been just discovered in the Onondago Limestone of New York, and an imperfectly-preserved fish-bone in the Oriskany Sandstone of the same state. There seems, however, to be no reason to conclude from their contemporary organisms, — chiefly shells and corals, which closely approximate to those of the Wenlock Limestone, — that either of them belonged to a more ancient fish than the ichthyodorulite described by Mr. Sedgwick, to which I have already had occasion to refer. It seems not unworthy of remark, that while among the fish of the Old Red Sandstone considerably more than three-fourths of the species, and greatly more than nineteen-twentieths of the individuals, are of the Ganoid order, all the fish of the Silurian system yet discovered are Placoids. [The statement here regarding the absence of fish in the Lower Silurian, which I retain in a second edition, as it may serve to indicate the onward march of geological science, was in accordance, only a few months ago, when the first edition of this work appeared, with what was known of the more ancient rocks and their fossils. But it also illustrates, like my statement respecting the reptiles of the Permian, the unsolid character of negative evidence, when made the basis of positive assertion. It is now determined that the Lower, like the Upper Silurian, has its fish. "Alas for one of my generalizations, founded on negative evidence, on which you build!" says Sir Roderick Murchison, in a communication which I owe to his kindness. "The Lower Silurian is no longer to be viewed as an invertebrate period ; for the Onchus (species not yet decided) has been found in Llandeilo Flags, and in the Lower Silurian Rocks of Bala. In one respect I am gratified by the discovery ; for the form is so very like that of the *Onchus Murchisoni* of the Ludlow Rocks, that it is clear the Silurian system is one great natural-history series, as proved, indeed, by all its other organic remains." — *Second Edition.*]

ship, and his prominent eye of many facets, that so capriciously refuses to admit the light through more or less than just its four hundred and ten spherical lenses. The Cephalopoda indeed, may have held with him a divided empire; but the Brachiopoda, the Pteropoda, the Gasteropoda, and the Acephala, must have been unresisting subjects, and all must have been implicit deference among the Crinoidea, the Pennularia, the Corals, and the Sponges. As we sink lower and lower, the mine of organic existence waxes unproductive and poor: a few shells now and then appear, a few graptolites, a few sponges. Anon we reach the outer limits of life: a void and formless desert stretches beyond, and dark night comes down upon the landscape.

CHAPTER XIII.

Birmingham; incessant Clamor of the Place. — Toy-shop of Britain; Serious Character of the Games in which its Toys are chiefly employed. — Museum. — Liberality of the Scientific English. — Musical Genius of Birmingham. — Theory. — Controversy with the Yorkers. — Anecdote. — The English Language spoken very variously by the English, in most cases spoken very ill. — English Type of Person. — Attend a Puseyite Chapel. — Puseyism a feeble Imitation of Popery. — Popish Cathedral. — Popery the true Resting-place of the Puseyite. — Sketch of the Rise and Progress of the Puseyite Principle; its purposed Object not attained; Hostility to Science. — English Funerals.

THE sun had set ere I entered Birmingham through a long low suburb, in which all the houses seem to have been built during the last twenty years. Particularly tame-looking houses they are; and I had begun to lower my expectations to the level of a flat, mediocre, three-mile city of brick, — a sort of manufactory in general, with offices attached, — when the coach drove up through New-street, and I caught a glimpse of the Town Hall, a noble building of Anglesea marble, of which Athens in its best days might not have been ashamed. The whole street is a fine one. I saw the lamps lighting up under a stately new edifice, — the Grammar School of King Edward the Sixth, which, like most recent erections of any pretension, either in England or among ourselves, bears the mediæval stamp: still further on I could descry, through the darkening twilight, a Roman-looking building that rises over the market-place; and so I inferred that the humble brick of Birmingham, singularly abundant, doubtless, and widely spread, represents merely the business necessities of the place; and that, when on any occasion its taste comes to be displayed, it proves to be a not worse taste than that shown by its neighbors. What first struck my ear as peculiar among the noises of a large town, — and their amount here is singularly great, — was what seemed to be somewhat irregular platoon-firing, carried on, volley after volley, with the most persistent deliberation. The sounds came, I was told, from the "proofing-house," — an iron-lined building, in which the gunsmith tests his musket-barrels, by giving them a quadruple charge of powder and ball, and then, after ranging them in a row, firing them from outside the apartment by means of a train. Birmingham produces on the average a musket per minute, night and day, throughout the year: it, besides, furnishes the army with its swords, the navy with its cutlasses and pistols, and the busy writers of the day with their steel pens by the hundredweight and the ton; and thus it labors to deserve its name of the "Great Toy-shop of Britain," by fashioning toys in abundance for the two most serious games of the day, — the game of war and the game of opinion-making.

On the morrow I visited several points of interest connected with the place and its vicinity. I found at the New Cemetery, on the north-western side of the town, where a party of Irish laborers were engaged in cutting deep into the hill-side, a good section, for about forty feet, of the Lower New Red Sandstone; but its only organisms — carbonized leaves and stems, by much too obscure for recognition — told no distinct story; and so incoherent is the enclosing sandstone matrix, that the laborers dug into it with their mattocks as if it were a bank of clay. I glanced over the Geological Museum attached to the Birmingham Philosophical Institution, and found it, though small, beautifully kept and scientifically arranged. It has its few specimens of New Red Sandstone fossils, chiefly *Posidonomya*.

from the upper sandstone band which overlies he saliferous marls; but their presence in a middle place here between the numerous fossils of the Carboniferous and Oolotic systems serves but to show the great poverty in organic remains of the intermediate system, as developed in England. Though of course wholly a stranger, I found free admission to both the Dudley and Birmingham Museums, and experienced, with but few exceptions, a similar liberality in my visits to all the other local collections of England which fell in my way. We have still great room for improvement in this respect in Scotland. We are far behind at least the laymen of England, — its liberal mechanicians and manufacturers, and its cultivators of science and the arts, — in the generosity with which they throw open their collections; and resemble rather that portion of the English clergy who make good livings better by exhibiting their consecrated places, — not too holy, it would seem, to be converted into show-boxes, — for paltry twopences and groats. I know not a museum in Edinburgh or Glasgow, save that of the Highland Society, to which a stranger can get access at once so readily and so free as that which I obtained, in the course of my tour, to the Newcastle, Dudley, Birmingham and British Museums.

Almost all the larger towns of England manifest some one leading taste or other. Some are peculiarly literary, some decidedly scientific; and the taste paramount in Birmingham seems to be a taste for music. In no town in the world are the mechanical arts more noisy: hammer rings incessantly on anvil; there is an unending clang of metal, an unceasing clank of engines; flame rustles, water hisses steam roars, and from time to time, hoarse and hollow over all, rises the thunder of the proofing-house. The people live in an atmosphere continually vibrating with clamor; and it would seem as if their amusements had caught the general tone, and become noisy, like their avocations. The man who for years has slept soundly night after night in the neighborhood of a foundery, awakens disturbed, if by some accident the hammering ceases: the imprisoned linnet or thrush is excited to emulation by even the screeching of a knife-grinder's wheel, or the din of a coppersmith's shop, and pours out its soul in music. It seems not very improbable that the two principles on which these phenomena hinge — principles as diverse as the phenomena themselves — may have been influential in inducing the peculiar characteristic of Birmingham; that the noises of the place, grown a part of customary existence to its people, — inwrought, as it were, into the very staple of their lives, — exert over them some such unmarked influence as that exerted on the sleeper by the foundery; and that, when they relax from their labors, they seek to fill up the void by modulated noises, first caught up, like the song of the bird beside the cutler's wheel or coppersmith's shop, in unconscious rivalry of the clang of their hammers and engines. Be the truth of the theory what it may, there can be little doubt regarding the fact on which it hinges. No town of its size in the empire spends more time and money in concerts and musical festivals than Birmingham, no small proportion of its people are amateur performers; almost all are musical critics; and the organ in its great Hall, the property of the town, is, with scarce the exception of that of York, the largest in the empire, and the finest, it is said, without any exception. But on this last point there hangs a keen controversy.

The Yorkers contend that *their* organ is both the greater and the finer organ of the two; whereas the Birminghamers assert, on the contrary, that *theirs*, though it may not measure more, plays vastly better. "It is impossible," retort the Yorkers, "that it can play even equally well; nay, were it even as large and as fine an organ,—which it is not,—it would be inferior by a half and more, unless to an instrument such as ours you could add a Minster such as ours also."—"Ah," rejoin the Birminghamers, "fair play! organ to organ: you are coming *Yorkshire* over us now: the building is not in the case at issue. You are surely conscious your instrument, single-handed, is no match for ours, or you would never deem it necessary to back it in this style by so imposing an auxiliary." But the argument of the York controversialists I must give in their own words:—"It is worse than idle in the Birmingham people," say the authors of the "Guide to York Minster," "to boast of their organ being *unrivalled*: we will by and by show how much it *falls short* of the York organ in actual size. But even were their instrument a *fac simile* of ours, it would not avail in a comparison; for it would still lack the building, which, in the case of our magnificent cathedral, is the better half of the organ, after all. In this, old Ebor stands unrivalled among all competitors in this kingdom. Even in the noble cathedrals that are dispersed through the country, no equal can be found to York Minster in dimensions, general proportions, grandeur of effect to the eye, and the sublimity and mellowness which it imparts to sound. It is true, indeed, that such a building requires an instrument of vast power to fill it with sound; but when it is filled, as with its magnificent organ *it now is*, the effect is grand and affecting in the highest degree; and yet there are in this organ *many* solo stops of such beautifully vocal, soft, and varied qualities of tone, as actually to *require* (as they fascinatingly claim) the closest attention of the listener. We beg it to be clearly understood, that we have not the slightest intention of depreciating the real merits of the Birmingham organ, as it is confessedly a very complete and splendid instrument; but when we notice such unscrupulous violations of truth as have been so widely disseminated, we deem it a duty incumbent upon us to set the public right."

That I might be the better able to take an intelligent part in so interesting a controversy, — a controversy in which, considering the importance of the point at issue, it is really no wonder though people should lose temper, — I attended a musical meeting in the Town Hall, and heard the great organ. The room — a very large one — was well filled, and yet the organ was the sole performer; for so musical is the community, that night after night, though the instrument must have long since ceased to be a novelty, it continues to draw together large audiences, who sit listening to it for hours. I have unluckily a dull ear, and, in order to enjoy music, must be placed in circumstances in which I can draw largely on the associative faculty; I must have airs that breathe forth old recollections, and set me a dreaming; and so, though neither Yorker nor Birminghamer, I may be deemed no competent authority in the organ controversy. I may, however, at least venture to say, that the Birmingham instrument makes a considerably louder noise in its own limited sphere than that of York in the huge Minster; and that I much preferred its fine old Scotch melodies, — though a country maiden might perhaps bring them out more feelingly in a green holm at a *claes-lifting*, — to the "great Psalm-tune" of its rival. When listening, somewhat awearied, to alternations of scientific music and the enthusiastic plaudits of the audience, I bethought me of a Birmingham musical meeting which held rather more than a century ago, and of the especial plaudit through which its memory has been embalmed in an anecdote. One of the pieces performed on the occasion was the "Il Penseroso" of Milton set to music; but it went on heavily, till the well-known couplet ending

"Iron tears down Pluto's cheek"

at once electrified the meeting. "Iron tears!" "Iron tears!" Could there be anything finer or more original? Tears made of iron were the only kind of iron articles not manufactured in Birmingham.

I visited the Botanic Gardens in the neighborhood, but found them greatly inferior to those of Edinburgh; and made several short excursions into the surrounding country, merely to ascertain, as it proved, that unless one extends one's walk some ten or twelve miles into the Dudley, Hagley, Droitwich, or Hales Owen districts, there is not a great deal worth seeing to be seen. Still, it was something to get the eye familiarized with the externals of English life, and to throw one's self in the way of those chance opportunities of conversation with the common people, which loiterings by the lanes and road-sides present. My ear was now gradually becoming acquainted with the several varieties of the English dialect, and my eye with the peculiarities of the English form and countenance. How comes it that in Great Britain, and, I suppose, everywhere else, every six or eight square miles of area, nay, every little town or village, has its own distinguishing intonations, phrases, modes of pronunciation, in short, its own style of speaking the general language, almost always sufficiently characteristic to mark its inhabitants? There are not two towns or counties in Scotland that speak Scotch after exactly the same fashion; and I now found, in the sister country, varieties of English quite as marked, parcelled out into geographical patches as minute. In workmen's barracks, where parties of mechanics, gathered from all parts of the country, spend the greater part of a twelvemonth together at a time, I have, if I mistake not, marked these colloquial peculiarities in the forming. There are few men who have not their set phrases and forms of speech, acquired inadvertently, in most cases at an early period, when the habit of giving expression to their ideas is in the forming, — phrases and set forms which they learn to use a good deal oftener than the necessities of their thinking require; and I have seen, in the course of a few months, the peculiarities of this kind of some one or two of the more intelligent and influential mechanics of a party, caught all unwittingly by almost all its members, and thus converted, to a considerable extent, into peculiarities of the party itself; and peculiar tones, inflections, modes of pronunciation, at first, mayhap, chance-derived, seem at least equally catching. A single stuttering boy has been known to infect a whole class; and no young person, with the imitative faculty active within him, ever spent a few months in a locality distant from his home, without bringing back with him, on his return, a sensible twang of its prevalent intonations and idioms. Of course, when the language of a town or district differs greatly from that of the general standard of the country, or very nearly approximates to it, there must have been some original cause of the peculiarity, which imparted aim and object to the imitative faculty. For instance, the Scotch spoken in Aberdeen differs more from the pure English standard than that of any other town in Scotland; whereas the Scotch spoken in Inverness, if Scotch it may be called, most nearly approximates to it; and we may detect a producing cause in both cases. The common dialect of Inverness, though now acquired by the ear, was originally, and that at no very remote period, the book-taught English of an educated Celtic people, to whom Gaelic was the mother tongue; while in Aberdeen — one of the old seats of learning in the country, and which seems to have been brought, in comparatively an early age, under the influence of the ancient Scotch literature — the language of Barbour* and Dunbar got a firm lodgment among the educated classes, which, from the remoteness of the place, the after influence of the English court served but tardily to affect. Obviously, in some other cases, the local peculiarity, when it involves a marked departure from the existing standard, has to be traced, not to literature, but to the want of it. But at least the great secondary cause of all such peculiarities — the invariable, ever-operative cause in its own subordinate place — seems to be that faculty of unconscious imitation universally developed in the species, which the philosophic Hume deemed so actively operative in the formation of national character, and one of whose special vocations it is to transfer personal traits and characteristics from leading, influential individuals, to septs and communities. Next to the degree of surprise that a stranger feels in England that the language should be spoken so variously by the people, is that of wonder that it should in most cases be spoken so ill. Lord Nugent, in remarking, in his "Lands Classical and Sacred," that "the English language is the one which in the present state of the habitable globe — what with America, India, and Australia — is spoken by the greatest number of people," guards his statement by a sly proviso; that is, he adds, if we recognize as English "what usually passes for such in most parts of Scotland and the United States." Really, his lordship might not have been so particular. If the rude dialects of Lancashire, Yorkshire and Northumberland, stand muster as part and parcel of the language written by Swift and Addison, and spoken by Burke and Bolingbroke, that of Old Machar and Kentucky may be well suffered to pass.

I had entered a considerable way into England ere I was

* Barbour was Archdeacon of Aberdeen.

struck by the peculiarities of the English face and figure. There is no such palpable difference between the borderers of Northumberland and those of Roxburghshire as one sometimes marks in the inhabitants of contiguous counties in Scotland itself; no such difference, for instance, as obtains between the Celtic population of Sutherland, located on the southern side of the Ord Hill, and the Scandinavian population of Caithness, located on its northern side. But, as the traveller advances on the midland counties, the English cast of person and countenance becomes very apparent. The harder frame and thinner face of the northern tribes disappear shortly after one leaves Newcastle; and one meets, instead, with ruddy, fleshy, compactly-built Englishmen, of the true national type. There is a smaller development of bone; and the race, on the average, seem less tall: but the shoulders are square and broad, the arms muscular, and the chest full; and if the lower part of the figure be not always in keeping with the upper, its inferiority is perhaps rather an effect of the high state of civilization at which the country has arrived, and the consequent general pursuit of mechanical arts that have a tendency to develop the arms and chest, and to leave the legs and thighs undeveloped, than an original peculiarity of the English as a race. The English type of face and person seems peculiarly well adapted to the female countenance and figure; and the proportion of pretty women to the population — women with clear, fair complexions, well-turned arms, soft features, and fine busts — seems very great. Even the not very feminine employment of the naileresses of Hales Owen, though hereditary in their families for generations, has failed to render their features coarse or their forms masculine. To my eye, however, my countrymen — and I have now seen them in almost every district of Scotland — present an appearance of rugged strength, which the

English, though they take their place among the more robust European nations, do not exhibit; and I find the carefully-constructed tables of Professor Forbes, based on a large amount of actual experiment, corroborative of the impression. As tested by the *dynamometer*, the average strength of the full-grown Scot exceeds that of the full-grown Englishman by about one-twentieth, — to be sure, no very great difference, but quite enough, in a prolonged contest, hand to hand, and man to man, with equal skill and courage on both sides, decidedly to turn the scale. The result of the conflict at Bannockburn, where, according to Barbour, steel rung upon armor in hot, close fight for hours, and at Otterburn, where, according to Froissart, the English fought with the most obstinate bravery, may have a good deal hinged on this purely physical difference.

I attended public worship on the Sabbath, in a handsome chapel in connection with the Establishment, which rises in an outer suburb of the town. There were many conversions taking place at the time from Puseyism to Popery: almost every newspaper had its new list; and as I had learned that the clergyman of the chapel was a high Puseyite, I went to acquaint myself, at first hand, with the sort of transition faith that was precipitating so much of the altered Episcopacy of England upon Rome. The clergyman was, I was told, a charitable, benevolent man, who gave the poor proportionally much out of his little, — for his living was a small one, — and who was exceedingly diligent in the duties of his office; but his congregation, it was added, had sadly fallen away. The high Protestant part of it had gone off when he first became decidedly a Puseyite; and latterly, not a few of his warmer friends had left him for the Popish cathedral on the other side of the town. The hive ecclesiastical had cast off its two swarms, — its best Protestants and its best Puseyites. I saw the clergyman go through the service of the day, and deemed his various Puseyistic emendations rather poor things in a pictorial point of view. They reminded me — for the surrounding atmosphere was by much too clear — of the candle-light decorations of a theatre, when submitted to the blaze of day, in all the palpable rawness of size and serge, ill-jointed carpentry, and ill ground ochre. They seemed sadly mistimed, too, in coming into being in an age such as the present; and reminded one of maggots developed into flies by artificial heat amid the chills of winter. The altar stood in the east end of the building; there was a golden crucifix inwrought in the cloth which covered it; and directly over, a painting of one of our Saviour's miracles, and a stained window. But the *tout ensemble* was by no means striking; it was merely fine enough to make one miss something finer. The clergyman prayed with his back to the people; but there was nothing grand in the exhibition of a back where a face should be. He preached in a surplice, too; but a surplice is a poor enough thing in itself, and in no degree improves a monotonous discourse. And the appearance of the congregation was as little imposing as that of the service: the great bulk of the people seemed drowsily inattentive. The place, like a bed of residuary cabbage-plants twice divested of its more promising embryos, had been twice thinned of its earnestness, — first of its Protestant earnestness, which had flowed over to the meeting-house and elsewhere, — next of its Puseyite earnestness, which had dribbled out into the cathedral; and there had been little else left to it than a community of what I shall venture to term *cat*-Christians, — people whose attachments united them, not to the clergyman or his doctrines, but simply, like those of the domestic cat, to the walls of the building. The chapel contained the desk from which their banns had been proclaimed, and the font in which their children had been baptized: and the corner in which they had sat for so many years was the only corner anywhere in England in which they could fairly deem themselves "at church." And so *there* were they to be found, Sabbath after Sabbath, regardless of the new face of doctrine that flared upon them from the pulpit. The sermon, though by no means striking as a piece of composition or argument, was fraught with its important lesson. It inscribed the "Do this and live" of the abrogated covenant, so congenial to the proud confidence of the unsubdued human heart, on a substratum of that lurking fear of unforgiving trespass, not less natural to man, which suggests the mediation of the merely human priest, the merit of penance, and the necessity of the confessional. It represented man as free to will and work out his own salvation; but exhibited him also as a very slave, because he had failed to will and to work it. It spoke of a glorious privilege, in which all present had shared, — the privilege of being converted through baptism; but left every one in doubt whether, in *his* individual case, the benefit had not been greatly more than neutralized by transgression since committed, and whether he were not now in an immensely more perilous state of reprobation than if he had never been *converted*. Such always is the vaulting liberty of a false theology, when held in sincerity. Its liberty invariably "overleaps itself, and falls on the other side." It is a liberty which "gendereth to bondage."

I next visited the Popish cathedral, and there I found in perfection all that Puseyism so palpably wanted. What perhaps first struck was the air of real belief — of credulity all awake and earnest — which characterized the congregation. The mind, as certainly as the body, seemed engaged in the kneelings, the bowings, the responses, the crossings of the person, and the dippings of the finger-tip in the holy water. It was the harvest season, and the passages of the building were crowded with Irish reapers, — a ragged and many-patched assemblage. Of the corresponding class in England and Scotland, Protestantism has no hold, — they have broken loose from her control; but Popery in Ireland has been greatly more fortunate: she is peculiarly strong in the ignorant and the reckless, and formidable in their possession. In the services of the cathedral everything seemed in keeping. The altar, removed from the congregation by an architectural screen, and enveloped in a dim obscurity, gave evidence, in its picturesque solemnity, — its twinkling lights and its circling incense, — that the church to which it belonged had fully mastered the principles of effect. The musically modulated prayer, sounding in the distance from within the screen, — the imposing procession, — the mysterious genuflections and frequent kneelings, — the sudden music, rising into paroxysms of melody in the crises of the passing ceremony, — the waving of the smoking censer, — the tolling of the great bell at the elevation of the host, — all spoke of the accumulative art of more than a thousand years. The trick of scenic devotion had been well caught, — the theatric religion that man makes for himself had been skilfully made. The rites of Puseyism seem but poor shadows in comparison, — mere rudimentary efforts in the way of design, that but serve to beget a taste for the higher style of art. I did not wonder that such of the Puseyites of the chapel as were genuine admirers of the picturesque in religion should have found their way to the cathedral.

In doctrine, however, as certainly as in form and ceremony the Romish church constitutes the proper resting-place of the Puseyite. The ancient Christianity, as it exists in the Anglican Church, is a mere inclined slide, to let him down into it It furnishes him with no doctrinal resting-place of its own. In every form of Christianity in which men are earnest there must exist an *infallibility* somewhere. By the Episcopalian Protestant, as by the Presbyterian, that infallibility is recognized as resting in the Scriptures; and by the consistent Papist that infallibility is recognized as resting in the Church. But where does the infallibility of the Puseyite rest? Not in the Scriptures; for, repudiating the right of private judgment, he is necessarily ignorant of what the Scriptures truly teach. Not in tradition; for he has no trustworthy guide to show him where tradition is right, or where wrong. Not in his Church; for his Church has no voice; or, what amounts to exactly the same thing, her voice is a conflicting gabble of antagonist sounds. Now one bishop speaks after one fashion, — now another bishop speaks after another, — and anon the queen speaks, through the ecclesiastical courts, in tones differing from them all. Hence the emphatic complaint of Mr. Ward, in the published letter in which he assigns his reasons for entering the communion of Rome: — "He can find," he says, "no teaching" in the English Church; and repudiating, as he does, the right of private judgment, there is logic in his objection. "If we reverence," he argues, "the fact of the apostolicity of creeds on the authority of the English Church, so far as we do not believe the English Church to be infallibly directed, exactly so far we do not believe the creeds to be infallibly true." Consistent Puseyism can find its desiderated infallibility in Rome only.

The rise and progress of this corruption in the Church of England promises to form a curious episode in the ecclesiastical history of the age. It is now rather more than ten years since Whigism, yielding to the pressure of reïnvigorated Popery, suppressed the ten Irish bishoprics, and a body of politic churchmen met to deliberate how best, in the future, such deadly aggressions on their Church might be warde l off. They saw her unwieldy bulk lying in a state of syncope before the spoiler; and concluded that the only way to save was to rouse and animate her, by breathing into her some spirit of life. Unless they succeeded in stirring her up to defend herself, they found defence would be impracticable: it was essential to the protection of her goods and chattels that she should become a living soul, too formidable to be despoiled; and, in taking up their line of policy, they seem to have set themselves as coolly to determine respecting the nature and kind of spirit which they should breathe into her, as if they were a conclave of chemists deliberating regarding the sort of gas with which a balloon was to be inflated. They saw two elements of strength in the contemporary Churches, and but two only, — the Puritanic and the Popish element; and making their choice between them, they selected the Popish one as that with which the Church of England should be animated.* On some such principle, it would seem, as that through which the human body is enabled to resist, by means of the portion of the atmospheric air within, the enormous pressure of the atmospheric air without, strength was sought in an internal Popery, from the pressure of the aggressive Popery outside. An extensive and multifarious machinery was set in motion, in consequence of the determination, with the scarce concealed design, of "unprotestantizing the English Church." Ceremonies less imposing than idle were introduced into her services; altars displaced at

* I am far from asserting here that they had it as much in their power to avail themselves of the Puritanic as of the Popish element; or yet that if they had, any mere considerations of policy would have led them to adopt it. As shown by such publications as "Keble's Sacred Year," and "Froud's Remains," the current of tendency in the English Church had begun to flow for several years previous in the mediæval channel, and the members of this meeting had already got afloat on the stream

the Reformation were again removed to their prescribed site in the east; candles were lighted at noon-day; crucifixes erected; the clergyman, after praying with his back to the people, ascended the pulpit in his surplice to expatiate on the advantages of the confessional, and the real presence in the sacrament; enticing pictures were held up to the suffering poor, of the comforts and enjoyments of their class in the middle ages; and the pew-battle was fought for them, that they might be brought under the influence of the revived doctrines. To the aristocracy hopes were extended of a return to the old state of implicit obedience on the part of the people, and of absolute authority on the part of the people's lords: the whole artillery of the press was set in requisition, — from the novelette and poem for the young lady, and the tale for the child, to the high-priced review for the curious theologian, and the elaborate "Tract for the Times." Nay, the first journal in the world was for a season engaged in advocating the designs of the party. And the exertions thus made were by no means fruitless. The unprotestantizing leaven introduced into the mass of the English Establishment began to ferment, and many of the clergy, and not a few of the laity, were infected.

But there was a danger in thus animating with the Popish spirit the framework of the English Church, on which the originators of the scheme could not have fully calculated. It has been long held in Scotland as one of the popular superstitions of the country, that it is a matter of extreme danger to simulate death, or personate the dead. There is a story told in the far north of a young fellow, who, going out one night, wrapped in a winding-sheet, to frighten his neighbors, was met, when passing through the parish churchyard, by a real ghost, that insisted, as their vocation was the same, on their walking together; and so terrible, says the story, was the shock which the young fellow received, that in a very few days he had become a real ghost too. There is another somewhat similar story told of a lad who had, at a lyke wake, taken the place of the corpse, with the intention of rising in the middle of the night to terrify the watchers, and was found, when a brother wag gave the agreed signal, deaf to time; for in the interval he had become as true a corpse as the one whose stretching board he had usurped. Now, the original Puseyites, in dressing out their clerical brethren in the cerements of Popery, and setting them a-walking, could hardly have foreseen that many of them were to become the actual ghosts which they had decked them to simulate. They did not know that the old Scotch superstition, in at least its relation to them, was not an idle fancy, but a sober fact; and that these personators of the dead were themselves in imminent danger of death. Some suspicion of the kind, however, does seem to have crossed them. Much that is peculiar in the ethics of the party appears to have been framed with an eye to the uneasinesses of consciences not quite seared, when bound down by the requirements of their position to profess beliefs of one kind, and by the policy of their party to promulgate beliefs of another, — to be ostensibly Protestant, and yet to be instant in season and out of season in subverting Protestantism; in short, in the language of Mr. Ward, "to be Anglican clergymen, and yet hold Roman Catholic doctrine." But the moral sense in earnest Puseyism is proving itself a too tender and sensitive thing to bear with the morality which politic Puseyism, ere it gathered heat and life, had prepared for its use. It finds that the English Church is not the Church of Rome, — that the Convocation is not the Vatican, nor Victoria the Pope, — that it is not honest to subvert Protestantism under cloak of the Protestant name, nor to muster in its ranks, and eat its bread, when in the service of the enemy. And so Puseyism, in its more vital sections, is fast ceasing to be Puseyism. The newspapers still bear their lists of conversions to Rome; and thus the means so invidiously resorted to of strengthening the English Establishment against Popery is fast developing itself into a means of strengthening Popery at the expense of the English Establishment.

The influence on science of this mediæval Christianity, so strangely revived, forms by no means the least curious part of its history. It would appear as if the doctrine of authority, as taught by Puseyism and Popery, — the doctrine of a human infallibility in religious matters, whether vested in Popes, Councils, or Churches, — cannot coëxist in its integrity, as a real belief, with the inductive philosophy. It seems an antagonist force; for, wherever the doctrine predominates, the philosophy is sure to decline. The true theologic counterpart to the inductive scheme of Bacon is that Protestant right of private judgment, which, dealing by the word of God as the inductive philosophy deals by the works of God, involves as its principle what may be termed the inductive philosophy of theology. There is certainly nothing more striking in the history of the resuscitation of the mediæval faith within the English Church, than its marked hostility to scientific truth, as exhibited in the great educational institutions of England. Every product of a sound philosophy seems disappearing under its influence, like the fruits and flowers of the earth when the chilling frosts of winter set in. But it is impossible to state the fact more strongly than it has been already stated by Mr. Lyell, in his lately published "Travels in America." "After the year 1839," he says, "we may consider three-fourths of the sciences still nominally taught at Oxford to have been virtually exiled from the university. The class-rooms of the professors were some of them entirely, others nearly deserted.

Chemistry and botany attracted, between the years 1840 and 1844, from three to seven students; geometry, astronomy, and experimental philosophy, scarcely more; mineralogy and geology, still taught by the same professor who, fifteen years before, had attracted crowded audiences, from ten to twelve; political economy, still fewer; even ancient history and poetry scarcely commanded an audience; and, strange to say, in a country with whose destinies those of India are so closely bound up, the first of Asiatic scholars gave lectures to one or two pupils, and these might have been absent, had not the cherished hope of a Boden scholarship for Sanscrit induced them to attend." I may state, in addition, on the best authority, that the geological professor here referred to, — Dr. Buckland, — not only one of the most eminent masters of his science, but also one of the most popular of its exponents, — lectured, during his last course, to a class of three. Well may it be asked whether the prophecy of Pope is not at length on the eve of fulfilment: —

> "She comes! she comes! the sable throne behold,
> Of Night primeval and of Chaos old,
> As, one by one, at dread Medea's strain,
> The sickening stars fade off the ethereal plain, —
> As Argus' eyes, by Hermes' wand oppressed,
> Close one by one in everlasting rest.
> Thus, at her felt approach and secret might,
> Art after art goes out, and all is night."

The anti-scientific influences of the principle have, however, not been restricted to the cloisters of the university. They have been creeping of late over the surface of English society as that sulphurous fog into which the arch-fiend in Milton transformed himself when he sought to dash creation into chaos crept of old over the surface of Eden. The singularly extended front of opposition presented last autumn by the newspaper press of England to the British Association, when holding its sittings at Southampton, and the sort of running fire kept up for weeks after on its more distinguished members, — men such as Sir Roderick Murchison, Dr. Buckland, and Mr. Lyell, — seem to have been an indirect consequence of a growing influence in the country on the part of the revived superstition. One of the earliest assaults made on the Association, as hostile in its nature and tendencies to religion, appeared several years ago in the leading organ of Tractarianism, the "British Critic;" but the "Critic" in those days stood much alone. Now, however, though no longer in the field, it has got not a few successors in the work, and its party many an active ally. The mediæval miasma, originated in the bogs and fens of Oxford, has been blown aslant over the face of the country; and not only religious, but scientific truth, is to experience, it would seem, the influence of its poisonous blights and rotting mildews.

It is not difficult to conceive how the revived superstition of the middle ages should bear no good will to science or its institutions. Their influences are naturally antagonistic. The inductive scheme of interrogating nature, that takes nothing for granted, and the deferential, submissive scheme, that, in ecclesiastical matters, yields wholly to authority, and is content though nothing should be proved, cannot well coëxist in one and the same mind. "I believe because it is impossible," says the devout Mediævalist; "I believe because it is demonstrable," says the solid Baconian. And it is scarce in the nature of things that one and the same individual should be a Baconian in one portion of his mind and a Mediævalist in another, — that in whatever relates to the spiritual and ecclesiastical, he should take all on trust, and in whatever relates to the visible and material, believe nothing without evidence. The Baconian state of mind is decidedly anti-mediæval; and hence the avowed Puseyite design of unprotestantizing the English Church finds a scarce more determined enemy in the truth elicited by the enlightened and well-directed study of the word of God, than in the habit of mind induced by the enlightened and well-directed study of the works of God. Nor is it in any degree matter of wonder that modern Tractarianism should on this principle be an especial enemy of the British Association, — an institution rendered peculiarly provoking by its peripatetic propensities. It takes up the empire piecemeal, by districts and squares, and works its special efforts on the national mind much in the way that an agriculturist of the modern school, by making his sheepfold-walk bit by bit over the area of an entire moor, imparts such fertility to the soil, that the dry unproductive heaths and mosses wear out and disappear, and the succulent grasses spring up instead. A similar association located in London or Edinburgh would be, to borrow from Dr. Chalmers, a scientific institute on merely the *attractive* scheme: men in whom the love of science had been already excited would seek it out, and derive profit and pleasure in that communion of congenial thought and feeling which it created; but it could not be regarded as a great intellectual machine for the *production* of men of science, and the general formation of habits of scientific inquiry. But the peripatetic character of the Association constitutes it a scientific institute on the *aggressive* system. It sets itself down every year in a new locality; excites attention; awakens curiosity; furnishes the provincial student with an opportunity of comparing the fruits of his researches with those of labors previously directed by resembling minds to similar walks of exploration enables him to test the value of his discoveries, and ascertain their exact degrees of originality; above all, brings hundreds around him to experience an interest they never felt before, in questions of science; imparts facts to them never to be forgotten, and habits of observation not to be relinquished; in short, communicates to all its members a disposition of mind exactly the reverse of that indolent and passive quiescence of mood which Puseyism so strongly inculcates by homily and novelette, on at least its lay adherents. Truly, it is by no means strange that the revived principle, and those organs of the public press which it influences, should be determined enemies of the British Association. It is, however, but just to add, that Tractarianism and its myrmidons have not been the only assailants. Tractarianism first raised the fog, but not a few good simple people of the opposite party have since got bewildered in it; and, through the confusion incident on losing their way, they have fallen in the quarrel into the ranks of their antagonists, and have been doing battle in their behalf.*

On quitting the Puseyite chapel, I met a funeral, the first I had seen in England. It was apparently that of a person in the middle walks, and I was a good deal struck with its dissimilarity, in various points, to our Scotch funerals of the same class. The coffin of planed elm, finished off with all the care usually bestowed on pieces of household furniture made of the commoner forest hardwood, was left uncolored, save on the edges, which, like those of a mourning card, were belted with black. There was no pall covering it; and, instead of being borne on staves, or on the shoulders, it was carried, basket-like, by the handles. An official, bearing a gilded baton, marched in front; some six or eight gentlemen in black paced slowly beside the bearers; a gentleman and lady, in deep

* As shown by the assaults on the Association of such organs of the Low Church party as the Dublin "Statesman" and London "Record."

mourning, walked arm-in-arm at the coffin-head; and a boy and girl, also arm-in-arm, and in mourning, came up behind them. Such was the English funeral, — one of those things which, from their familiarity, are not described by the people of the country to which they belong, and which prove unfamiliar, in consequence, to the people of other countries. On the following Monday I took an outside seat on a stage-coach, for Stratford-on-Avon.

CHAPTER XIV.

Drive from Birmingham to Stratford rather tame. — Ancient Building in a modern-looking Street; of rude and humble Appearance. — "The Immortal Shakspeare born in this House." — Description of the Interior. — The Walls and Ceiling covered with Names. — Albums. — Shakspeare, Scott, Dickens; greatly different in their Intellectual Stature, but yet all of one Family. — Principle by which to take their Measure. — No Dramatist ever draws an Intellect taller than his own. — Imitative Faculty. — The *Reports* of Dickens. — Learning of Shakspeare. — New Place. — The Rev. Francis Gastrall. — Stratford Church. — The Poet's Grave; his Bust; far superior to the idealized Representations. — The Avon. — The Jubilee, and Cowper's Description of it. — The true Hero Worship. — Quit Stratford for Olney. — Get into bad Company by the way. — Gentlemen of the Fancy. — Adventure.

THE drive from Birmingham, for the greater part of the way, is rather tame. There is no lack of fields and hedge-rows, houses and trees; but, from the great flatness of the country, they are doled out to the eye in niggardly detail, at the rate of about two fields and three hedge-rows at a time. Within a few miles of Stratford-on-Avon, however, the scenery improves. We are still on the Upper New Red Sandstone, and on this formation the town is built: but the Lias beyond shoots out, just in the line of our route, into a long promontory, capped by two insulated outliers, that, projected far in advance, form the outer piquets of the newer and higher system; and for some four or five miles ere we enter the place, we coast along the tree-mottled shores of this green headland and its terminal islands. A scattered suburb introduces us to a rather commonplace-looking street of homely brick houses, that seem as if they had all been reared within the last half century; all, at least, save one, a rude, unsightly specimen of the oak framed domicile of the days of Elizabeth and James. Its walls are incrusted with staring white-wash, its beams carelessly daubed over with lamp-black; a deserted butcher's shop, of the fifth-rate class, with the hooks still sticking in the walls, and the sill-board still spread out, as if to exhibit the joints, occupies the ground-floor; the one upper story contains a single rickety casement, with a forlorn flower-pot on the sill; and directly in front of the building there is what seems a rather clumsy sign-board, hung between two poles, that bears on its weather-beaten surface a double line of white faded letters on a ground of black. We read the inscription, and this humblest of dwellings — humble, and rather vulgar to boot — rises in interest over the palaces of kings: — "The immortal Shakspeare was born in this house." I shall first go and see the little corner his birth-place, I said, and then the little corner his burial-place: they are scarce half a mile apart; nor, after the lapse of more than two centuries, does the intervening modicum of time between the two events, his birth and his burial, bulk much larger than the modicum of space that separates the respective scenes of them; but how marvellously is the world filled with the cogitations which employed that one brain in that brief period! Could it have been some four pounds' weight of convoluted matter, divided into two hemispheres, that, after originating these buoyant immaterialities, projected them upon the broad current of time, and bade them sail onwards and downwards forever? I cannot believe it: the sparks of a sky-rocket survive the rocket itself but a very few seconds. I cannot believe that these thoughts of Shakspeare, "that wander through eternity," are the mere sparks of an exploded rocket, — the mere scintillations of a little galvanic battery, made of fibre and albumen, like that of the torpedo, and whose ashes would now lie in the corner of a snuff-box.

I passed through the butcher's shop, over a broken stone pavement, to a little gloomy kitchen behind, and then, under charge of the guide, up a dark narrow stair, to the low-browed room in which the poet was born. The floor of old oak, much worn in the seams, has apparently undergone no change since little Bill, be-frocked and be-booted in woolen prepared from the rough material by the wool-comber his father, coasted it along the walls, in bold adventure, holding on, as he went, by tables and chairs. The ceiling, too, though unluckily covered up by modern lath and plaster, is in all probability that which stretched over the head of the boy. It presents at least no indication of having been raised. A man rather above the middle size may stand erect under its central beam with his hat on, but with certainly no room to spare; and it seems more than probable that, had the old ceiling been changed for another, the new one would have been heightened. But the walls have been sadly altered. The one window of the place is no longer that through which Shakspeare first saw the light; nor is the fireplace that at which he stealthily lighted little bits of stick, and twirled them in the air, to see the fiery points converted into fiery circles. There are a few old portraits and old bits of furniture, of somewhat doubtful lineage, stuck round the room; and, on the top of an antique cabinet, a good plaster cast of the monumental bust in the church, in which, from its greater accessibility, one can better study than in the original the external signs affixed by nature to her mind of largest calibre. Every part of the walls and ceiling is inscribed with names. I might add mine, if I chose, to the rest, the woman told me; but I did not choose it. Milton and Dryden would have added theirs: he, the sublimest of poets, who, ere criticism had taken the altitude of the great writer whom he so fervently loved and admired, could address him in the fondness of youthful enthusiasm as "my Shakspeare;" and he, the sympathetic critic, who first dared to determine that "of all modern, and perhaps ancient poets, Shakspeare had the largest and most comprehensive soul." Messrs. Wiggins and Tims, too, would have added *their* names; and all right. They might not exactly see for themselves what it was that rendered Shakspeare so famous; but their admiration, entertained on trust, would be at least a legitimate *echo* of his renown; and so their names would have quite a right to be there as representatives of the outer halo — the *second* rainbow, if I may so express myself — of the poet's celebrity. But I was ashamed to add mine. I remembered that I was a *writer;* that it was my *business* to write, — to cast, day after day, shavings from off my mind, — the figure is Cowper's, — that went rolling away, crisp and dry, among the vast heap already on the floor, and were never more heard of; and so I did n't add my name. The woman pointed to the album, or rather set of albums, which form a record of the visiters, and said her mother could have turned up for me a great many names that strangers liked to look at; but the old woman was confined to her bed, and she, considerably less at home in the place, could show me only a few. The first she turned up was that of Sir Walter Scott; the second, that of Charles Dickens. "You have done remarkably well," I said "your mother could n't have done better. Now, shut the book."

It was a curious coincidence. *Shakspeare*, Scott Dickens! The scale is a descending one; so is the scale from the lion to the leopard, and from the leopard to the tiger-cat; but cat, leopard, and lion, belong to one great family; and these three poets belong unequivocally to one great family also. They are genericaly one; masters, each in his own sphere, not simply of the art of exhibiting character in the truth of nature, — for that a Hume or a Tacitus may possess, — but of the rarer and more difficult *dramatic* art of making characters exhibit themselves. It is not uninstructive to remark how the peculiar ability of portraying character in this form is so exactly proportioned to the general intellectual power of the writer who possesses it. No dramatist, whatever he may attempt, ever draws taller men than himself: as water in a bent tube rises to exactly the same height in the two limbs, so intellect in the character produced rises to but the level of the intellect of the producer. Milton's fiends, with all their terrible strength and sublimity, are but duplicates of the Miltonic intellect united to vitiated moral natures; nor does that august and adorable Being, who perhaps should not have been *dramatically* introduced into even the "Paradise Lost," excel as an intelligence the too daring poet by whom he is exhibited. Viewed with reference to this simple rule, the higher characters of Scott, Dickens, and Shakspeare, curiously indicate the intellectual stature of the men who produced them. Scott's higher characters possess massive good sense, great shrewdness, much intelligence: they are always very superior, if not always great men; and by a careful arrangement of drapery, and much study of position and attitude, they play their parts wonderfully well. The higher characters of Dickens do not stand by any means so high; the fluid in the original tube rests at a lower level: and no one seems better aware of the fact than Dickens himself. He knows his proper walk; and, content with expatiating in a comparatively humble province of human life and character, rarely stands on tiptoe, in the vain attempt to portray an intellect taller than his own. The intellectual stature of Shakspeare rises, on the other hand, to the highest level of man. His range includes the loftiest and the lowest characters, and takes in all between. There was no human greatness which he could not adequately conceive and portray; whether it was a purely intellectual greatness, as in Hamlet; or a purely constitutional greatness, — forceful and massive, — as in Coriolanus and Othello; or a happy combination of both, as in Julius Cæsar. He could have drawn with equal effect, had he flourished in an after period, the Lord Protector of England and the Lord Protector's Latin secretary; and men would have recognized the true Milton in the one, and the genuine Cromwell in the other.

It has frequently occurred to me, that the peculiar dramatic faculty developed so prominently in these three authors, that, notwithstanding their disparities of general intellect, we regard it as constituting their generic stamp, and so range them together in one class, seems, in the main, rather a humble one, when dissociated from the auxiliary faculties that exist in the mind of genius. Like one of our Scotch pebbles, so common in some districts, in their rude state, that they occur in almost every mole-hill, it seems to derive nearly all its value and beauty from the cutting and the setting. A Shakspeare without genius would have been merely the best mimic in Stratford. He would have caught every peculiarity of character exhibited by his neighbors, — every little foible, conceit, and awkwardness, — every singularity of phrase, tone, and gesture. However little heeded when he spoke in his own character, he would be deemed worthy of attention when he spoke in the character of others; for whatever else his *viva voce* narratives might want, they would be at least rich in the dramatic; men would recognize in his imitations peculiarities which they had failed to remark in the originals, but which, when detected by the keen eye of the mimic, would delight them, as "natural though not obvious;"

and though, perhaps, regarded not without fear, he would at all events, be deemed a man of infinite amusement. But to this imitative faculty, — this mere perception of the peculiarities that confer on men the stamp of individuality, — there was added a world-wide invention, an intellect of vastest calibre, depths unsounded of the poetic feeling, with a breadth of sympathy which embraced all nature; and the aggregate was a Shakspeare. I have seen this imitative ability, so useless in the abstract, rendered valuable by being set in even very humble literary attainment, — that of the newspaper reporter; and have had to estimate at a different rate of value the respective reports of gentlemen of the press, equal in their powers of memory and in general acquirement, and unequal merely in the degree in which they possessed the imitative faculty. In the reports of the one class I have found but the meaning of the speakers; in those of the other, both the meaning and the speakers too. Dickens, ere he became the most popular of living English authors, must have been a first-class reporter; and the faculty that made him so is the same which now leads us to speak of him in the same breath with Shakspeare. Bulwer is evidently a man of great reflective power; but Bulwer, though a writer of novels and plays, does not belong to the Shakspearian genus. Like those dramatists of English literature that, maugre their play-writing propensities, were not dramatic, — the Drydens and Thomsons of other days, — he lacks the imitative power. By the way, in this age of books, I marvel no bookseller has ever thought of presenting the public with the Bow-street reports of Dickens. They would form assuredly a curious work, — not less so, though on a different principle, than the Parliamentary reports of Dr. Samuel Johnson.

No one need say what sort of a building the church of Stratford-on-Avon is: no other edifice in the kingdom ha half so often employed the pencil and the burin. I may just remark, however, that it struck me at a little distance, rising among its graceful trees, beside its quiet river, as one of the finest old English churches I had yet seen. One passes, in approaching it from the poet's birthplace, through the greater part of Stratford. We see the town-hall, a rather homely building, — the central point of the bizarre Jubilee Festival of 1769, — with a niche in front occupied by a statue of Shakspeare presented to the town by David Garrick, the grand master of ceremonies on the occasion. We then pass a lane, which leads down to the river, and has a few things worth looking at on either hand. There is an old Gothic chapel on the one side, with so ancient a school attached to it, that it existed as such in the days of the poet's boyhood; and in this school, it is supposed, he may have acquired the little learning that served fairly to enter him on his after-course of world-wide attainment. Little, I suppose, would have served the purpose: a given knowledge of the alphabet, and of the way of compounding its letters into words, as his premises, would have enabled the little fellow to work out the rest of the problem for himself. There has been much written on the learning of Shakspeare, but not much to the purpose: one of our old Scotch proverbs is worth all the dissertations on the subject I have yet seen. "God's bairns," it says, "are *eath* to *lear*," *i. e.* easily instructed. Shakspeare must, I suppose, have read many more books than Homer (we may be sure, every good one that came in his way, and some bad ones), and yet Homer is held to have known a thing or two: the more ancient poet was unquestionably as ignorant of English as the more modern one of Greek; and as the one produced the "Iliad" without any acquaintance with "Hamlet," I do not see why the other might not have produced "Hamlet" without any acquaintance with the "Iliad." John son was quite in the right in holding that, though the writings of Shakspeare exhibit "much knowledge, it is often such knowledge as books did not supply." He might have added further, that the knowledge they display, which books *did* supply, is of a kind which might be all found in *English* books at the time, — fully one-half of it, indeed, in the romances of the period. Every great writer, in the department in which he achieves his greatness, whether he be a learned Milton or an unlearned Burns, is self-taught. One stately vessel may require much tugging ere she gets fairly off the beach, whereas another may float off, unassisted, on the top of the flowing tide; but when once fairly prosecuting their voyage in the open sea, both must alike depend on the spread sail and the guiding rudder, on the winds of heaven and the currents of the deep.

On the opposite side of the lane, directly fronting the chapel, and forming the angle where lane and street unite, there is a plain garden-wall, and an equally plain dwelling-house; and these indicate the site of Shakspeare's domicile, — the aristocratic mansion, — one of the "greatest," it is said, in Stratford, — which the vagrant lad, who had fled the country in disgrace, returned to purchase for himself, when still a young man, — no longer a vagrant, however, and "well to do in the world." The poet's wildnesses could not have lain deep in his nature, or he would scarce have been a wealthy citizen of Stratford in his thirty-third year. His gardens extended to the river side, — a distance of some two or three hundred yards; and doubtless the greater part of some of his later dramas must have been written amid their close green alleys and straight-lined walks, — for they are said to have been quaint, rich, and formal, in accordance with the taste of the period; and so comfortable a mansion was the domicile that, in 1643, Queen Henrietta, when at Stratford with the royalist army, made it her place of residence for three weeks. I need scarce tell its subsequent story. After passing through several hands, it was purchased, about the middle of the last century, by the Rev. Francis Gastrall, — a nervous, useless, ill-conditioned man, much troubled by a bad stomach and an unhappy temper. The poet's mulberry-tree had become ere now an object of interest; and his reverence, to get rid of the plague of visiters, cut it down and chopped it into fagots. The enraged people of the town threw stones and broke his reverence's windows; and then, to spite them still more, and to get rid of a poor-rate assessment to boot, he pulled down the poet's house. And so his reverence's name shares, in consequence, in the celebrity of that of Shakspeare, — "pursues the triumph and partakes the gale." The Rev. Francis Gastrall must have been, I greatly fear, a pitiful creature; and the clerical prefix in no degree improves the name.

The quiet street gets still quieter as one approaches the church. We see on either side a much greater breadth of garden-walls than of houses, — walls with the richly-fruited branches peeping over; and at the churchyard railing, thickly overhung by trees, there is so dense a mass of foliage, that of the church, which towers so high in the distance, we can discern no part save the door. A covered way of thick o'erarching limes runs along the smooth flat gravestones from gateway to doorway. The sunlight was streaming this day in many a fantastic patch on the lettered pavement below, though the checkering of shade predominated; but at the close of the vista the Gothic door opened dark and gloomy, in the midst of broad sunshine. The Avon flows past the churchyard wall. One may drop a stone at arm's length over the edge of the parapet into four feet water, and look down on shoals of tiny fish in play around the sedges. I entered the silent church, and passed along its rows of old oak pews, on to the chancel. The shadows of the trees outside were projected dark against the windows, and the numerous marbles of the place glimmered cold and sad in the thickened light. The chancel is raised a single step over the floor, — a step some twelve or fourteen inches in height; and, ranged on end along its edge, just where the ascending foot would rest, there lie three flat tombstones. One of these covers the remains of "William Shakspeare, Gentleman;" the second, the remains of his wife, Anne Hathaway; while the third rests over the dust of his favorite daughter Susanna, and her husband John Hall. And the well-known monument — in paley tints of somewhat faded white lead — is fixed in the wall immediately above, at rather more than a man's height from the floor.

At the risk of being deemed sadly devoid of good taste, I must dare assert that I better like the homely monumental bust of the poet, low as is its standing as a work of art, than all the idealized representations of him which genius has yet transferred to marble or canvas. There is more of the true Shakspeare in it. Burns complained that the criticisms of Blair, if adopted, would make his verse "too fine for either warp or woof;" and such has been the grand defect of the artistic idealisms which have been given to the world as portraits of the dramatist. They make him so pretty a fellow, all redolent of poetic odors, "shining so brisk" and "smelling so sweet," like the fop that annoyed Hotspur, that one seriously asks if such a person could ever have got through the world. No such type of man, leaving Stratford penniless in his twenty-first year, would have returned in his thirty-third to purchase the "capital messuage" of New Place, "with all the appurtenances," and to take rank amid the magnates of his native town. The poet of the artist would never have been "William Shakspeare *Gentleman*, nor would his burying-ground have lain in the chancel of his parish church. About the Shakspeare of the stone bust, on the contrary, there is a purpose-like strength and solidity. The head, a powerful mass of brain, would require all Dr. Chalmers' hat; the forehead is as broad as that of the doctor, considerably taller, and of more general capacity; and the whole countenance is that of a shrewd, sagacious, kindly-tempered man, who could, of course, be poetical when he willed it, — vastly more so, indeed, than anybody else, — but who mingled wondrous little poetry in the management of his every-day business. The Shakspeare of the stone bust could, with a very slight training, have been Chancellor of the Exchequer; and in opening the budget, his speech would embody many of the figures of Cocker, judiciously arranged, but not one poetical figure.

On quitting the church, I walked for the better part of two miles upwards along the Avon, — first on the Stratford side to the stone bridge, which I crossed, and then on the side opposite, through quiet, low-lying meadows, bordered by fields. Up to the bridge the stream is navigable, and we may see the occasional sail gleaming white amid the green trees, as it glides past the resting-place of the poet. But on the upper side there are reaches through which even a slight shallop would have difficulty in forcing her way. The bulrush attains, in the soft oozy soil that forms the sides and bottom of the river, to a great size: I pulled stems from eight to ten feet in height; and in the flatter inflections, where the current stagnates, it almost chokes up the channel from side to side. Here it occurs in tall hedge-like fringes that line and overtop the banks, — there, in island-like patches, in the middle of the stream, — yonder, in diffused transverse thickets, that seem to connect the fringes on the one side with the fringes on the other. I have rarely seen anything in living nature — nature recent and vital —

that better enabled me to realize the luxuriant aquatic vegeta tion of the Coal Measures. The unbroken stream dimples amid the rushes; in the opener depths we may mark, as some burnished fly flutters along the surface, the sullen plunge of the carp; the eel, startled by the passing shadow, wriggles outward from its bank of mud; while scores of careless gudgeons, and countless shoals of happy minnows, dart hither and thither, like the congregated midges that dance unceasingly in the upper element, but a few inches over them. For the first mile or so, the trees which line the banks are chiefly old willow pollards, with stiff rough stems and huge bunchy heads. Shrubs of various kinds, chiefly, however, the bramble and the woody nightshade, have struck root atop into their decayed trunks, as if these formed so many tall flower-pots; and we may catch, in consequence, the unwonted glitter of glossy black and crimson berries from amid the silvery leaves. The scenery improves as we ascend the stream. The willow pollards give place to forest trees, carelessly grouped, that preserve, unlopped and unmutilated, their proper proportions. But the main features of the landscape remain what they were. A placid stream, broadly befringed with sedges, winds in tortuous reaches through rich meadows; and now it sparkles in open sun light, for the trees recede; and anon it steals away, scarce seen, amid the gloom of bosky thickets. And such is the Avon, — Shakspeare's own river. Here must he have wandered in his boyhood, times unnumbered. That stream, with its sedges, and its quick glancing fins, — those dewy banks, with their cowslips and daffodils, — trees chance-grouped, exactly such as these, and to which these have succeeded, — must all have stamped their deep impress on his mind; and, when an unsettled adventurer in London, they must have risen before him in all their sunshiny peacefulness, to inspire feelings of sadness and regret; and when, in after days, he had found his true vocation, their loved forms and colors must have mingled with the tissue of his poetry. And here must he have walked in sober middle life, when fame and fortune had both been achieved, happily to feel amid the solitude that there is but little of solid good in either, and that, even were it otherwise, the stream of life glides away to its silent bourn, from their gay light and their kindly shelter, to return no more forever. What would his thoughts have been, if, after spending in these quiet recesses his fiftieth birth-day, he could have foreseen that the brief three score and ten annual revolutions, — few as certainly as evil, — which have so long summed up the term of man's earthly existence, were to be mulcted, in his case, of full seventeen years!

How would this master of human nature have judged of the homage that has now been paid him for these two centuries? and what would have been *his* theory of "Hero Worship"? Many a bygone service of this inverted religion has Stratford-on-Avon witnessed. The Jubilee devised by Garrick had no doubt much of the player in it; but it possessed also the real devotional substratum, and formed the type, on a splendid scale, not less in its hollowness than in its groundwork of real feeling, of those countless acts of devotion of which the poet's birth and burial places have been the scene. "Man praises man;" Garrick, as became his occupation, was a little more ostentatious and formal in his Jubilee services, — more studious of rich ceremonial and striking forms, — more *High Church* in spirit, — than the simpler class of hero-devotees who are content to worship extempore; but that was just all.

"He drew the Liturgy, and framed the rites
And solemn ceremonial of the day,
And called the world to worship on the banks

> Of Avon, famed in song. Ah! pleasant proof
> That piety has still in human hearts
> Some place, a spark or two not yet extinct.
> The mulberry-tree was hung with blooming wreaths;
> The mulberry-tree stood centre of the dance;
> The mulberry-tree was hymned with dulcet airs;
> And from his touchwood trunk the mulberry-tree
> Supplied such relics as devotion holds
> Still sacred, and preserves with pious care.
> So 't was a hallowed time; decorum reigned,
> And mirth without offence. No few returned
> Doubtless much edified, and all refreshed."

Such was Cowper's estimate — to be sure, somewhat sarcastically expressed — of the services of the Jubilee. What would Shakspeare's have been of the deeply-based sentiment, inherent, it would seem, in human nature, in which the Jubilee originated? An instinct so widely diffused and so deeply implanted cannot surely be a mere accident; it must form, however far astray of the proper mark it may wander, one of the original components of the mental constitution, which we have not given ourselves. What would it be in its integrity? It must, it would appear, have humanity on which to rest, — a nature identical with our own; and yet, when it finds nothing higher than mere humanity, it is continually running, as in the case of the Stratford Jubilee, into grotesque idolatry. Did Shakspeare, with all his vast knowledge, know where its aspirations could be directed aright? The knowledge seems to have got, somehow, into his family; nay, she who appears to have possessed it was the much-loved daughter on whom his affections mainly rested,

> "Witty above her sexe; but that 's not all, —
> Wise to salvation was good Mistress Hall."

So says her epitaph in the chancel, where she sleeps at the

feet of her father. There is a passage in the poet's will, too, written about a month ere his death, which may be, it is true, a piece of mere form, but which may possibly be something better. "I commend my soul into the hands of God my Creator, hoping, and assuredly believing, through the only merits of Jesus Christ, my Saviour, to be made partaker of life everlasting." It is, besides, at least something, that this play-writer and play-actor, with wit at will, and a shrewd appreciation of the likes and dislikes of the courts and monarchs he had to please, drew for their amusement no Mause Headriggs or Gabriel Kettledrummles. Puritanism could have been no patronizer of the Globe Theatre. Both Elizabeth and James hated the principle with a perfect hatred, and strove hard to trample it out of existence; and such a laugh at its expense as a Shakspeare could have raised would have been doubtless a high luxury; nay, Puritanism itself was somewhat sharp and provoking in those days, and just a little coarse in its jokes, as the Martin Mar-Prelate tracts survive to testify; but the dramatist, who grew wealthy under the favor of Puritan-detesting monarchs was, it would seem, not the man to make reprisals. There are scenes in his earlier dramas, from which, as eternity neared upon his view, he could have derived little satisfaction; but there is no "Old Mortality" among them. Had the poor player some sense of what his beloved daughter seems to have clearly discovered, — the true "Hero Worship"? In his broad survey of nature and of man, did he mark one solitary character standing erect amid the moral waste of creation, untouched by taint of evil or of weakness, — a character infinitely too high for even his vast genius to conceive, or his profound comprehension to fathom? Did he draw near to inquire, and to wonder, and then fall down humbly to adore?

I took the evening coach for Warwick, on my way to Olney.

and passed through the town for the railway station, a few minutes before sunset. It was a delightful evening, and the venerable castle and ancient town, with their surrounding woods and quiet river, formed in the red light a gorgeous picture. I could fain have waited for a day to explore Guy's Cliff, famous of old for its caves and its hermits, and to go over the ancient castle of king-making Warwick, — at once the most extensive and best preserved monument in the kingdom of the bygone feudal grandeur. The geology of the locality, too, is of considerable interest. From Stratford to the western suburbs of Warwick, the substratum of the landscape is composed, as every fallow-field which we pass certifies, in its flush of chocolate red, of the saliferous marls. Just, however, where the town borders on the country, the lower pavement of sandstone, on which the marls rest, comes to the surface, and stretches away northward in a long promontory, along which we find cliffs and quarries, and altogether bolder features than the denuding agents could have sculptured out of the incoherent marls. Guy's Cliff, and the cliff on which Warwick Castle stands, are both composed of this sandstone. It is richer, too, in remains of vertebrate animals, than the Upper New Red anywhere else in England. It has its bone bed, containing, though in a sorely mutilated state, the remains of fish, chiefly teeth, and the remains of the teeth and vertebræ of saurians. The saurian of Guy's Cliff, with the exception of the saurian of the Dolomitic Conglomerate, near Bristol, is the oldest British reptile known to geologists. Time pressed, however; and leaving behind me the antiquities of Warwick, geologic and feudal, I took my seat in the railway train for the station nearest Olney, — that of Wolverton. And the night fell ere we had gone over half the way.

I had now had some little experience of railway travelling

in England, and a not inadequate idea of the kind of quiet, comfortable-looking people whom I might expect to meet in a second-class carriage. But my fellow-passengers this evening were of a different stamp. They were chiefly, almost exclusively indeed, of the male sex, — vulgar, noisy, ruffian-like fellows, full of coarse oaths and dogged asseverations, and singularly redolent of gin; and I was quite glad enough, when the train stopped at the Wolverton station, that I was to get rid of them. At the station, however, they came out *en masse.* All the other carriages disgorged similar cargoes; and I found myself in the middle of a crowd that represented very unfairly the people of England. It was now nine o'clock. I had intended passing the night in the inn at Wolverton, and then walking on in the morning to Olney, a distance of nine miles; but when I came to the inn, I found it all ablaze with light, and all astir with commotion. Candles glanced in every window; and a thorough Babel of sound — singing, quarrelling, bell-ringing, thumping, stamping, and the clatter of mugs and glasses — issued from every apartment. I turned away from the door, and met, under the lee of a fence which screened him from observation, a rural policeman. "What is all this about?" I asked. — "Do you not know?" was the reply. — "No; I am quite a stranger here." — "Ah, there are many strangers here. But do you not know?" — "I have no idea whatever," I reiterated: "I am on my way to Olney, and had intended spending the night here; but would prefer walking on, to passing it in such a house as that." — "O, beg pardon; I thought you had been one of themselves: Bendigo of Nottingham has challenged Caunt of London to fight for the championship. The battle comes on to-morrow, somewhere hereabouts; and we have got all the blackguards in England, south and north, let loose upon us. If you walk on to Newport Pagnell, — just four miles, —

you will no doubt get a bed; but the way is lonely, and there have been already several robberies since nightfall." — "I shall take my chance of that," I said. —" Ah, —well, — your best way, then, is to walk straight forwards, at a smart pace, keeping the middle of the highway, and stopping for no one." · I thanked the friendly policeman, and took the road. It was a calm, pleasant night; the moon, in her first quarter, was setting dim and lightless in the west; and an incipient frost, in the form of a thin film of blue vapor, rested in the lower hollows.

The way was quite lonely enough; nor were the few straggling travellers whom I met of a kind suited to render its solitariness more cheerful. About half way on, where the road runs between tall hedges, two fellows started out towards me, one from each side of the way. "Is this the road," asked one, "to Newport Pagnell?" — "Quite a stranger here," I replied, without slackening my pace; "don't belong to the kingdom even." — "No!" said the same fellow, increasing his speed, as if to overtake me; "to what kingdom, then?" — "Scotland," I said, turning suddenly round, somewhat afraid of being taken from behind by a bludgeon. The two fellows sheered off in double quick time, the one who had already addressed me muttering, "More like an Irishman, I think;" and I saw no more of them. I had luckily a brace of loaded pistols about me, and had at the moment a trigger under each fore-finger; and though the ruffians — for such I doubt not they were — could scarcely have been cognizant of the fact, they seemed to have made at least a shrewd approximation towards it. In the autumn of 1842, during the great depression of trade, when the entire country seemed in a state of disorganization, and the law in some of the mining districts failed to protect the lieges, I was engaged in following out a course of geologic exploration in our Lothian Coal Field; and, unwilling to suspend my labors, had got the pistols, to do for myself, if necessary, what the authorities at the time could not do for me. But I had fortunately found no use for them, though I had visited many a lonely hollow and little-frequented water-course, — exactly the sort of places in which, a century ago, one would have been apt to raise footpads as one now starts hares; and in crossing the borders, I had half resolved to leave them behind me. They gave confidence, however, in unknown neighborhoods, or when travelling alone in the night-time; and so I had brought them with me into England, to support, if necessary, the majesty of the law and the rights of the liege subject; and certainly did not regret this evening that I had.

I entered Newport Pagnell a little after ten o'clock, and found all its inns exactly such scenes of riot and uproar as the inn at Wolverton. There was the same display of glancing lights in the windows, and the same wild hubbub of sound. On I went. A decent mechanic, with a white apron before him, whom I found in the street, assured me there was no chance of getting a bed in Newport Pagnell, but that I might possibly get one at Skirvington, a village on the Olney road, about three miles further on. And so, leaving Newport Pagnell behind me, I set out for Skirvington. It was now wearing late, and I met no more travellers: the little bit of a moon had been down the hill for more than an hour, the fog rime had thickened, and the trees by the wayside loomed through the clouds like giants in dominos. In passing through Skirvington, I had to stoop down and look between me and the sky for sign-posts. There were no lights in the houses, save here and there in an upper casement; and all was quiet as in a churchyard. By dint of sky-gazing, I discovered an inn, and rapped hard at the door. It was opened by the landlord, *sans* coat and waist-coat. There was no bed to be had there, he said; the beds were all occupied by travellers who could get no accommodation in Newport Pagnell; but there was another inn in the place further on, though it was n't unlikely, as it did n't much business, the family had gone to bed. This was small comfort. I had, however, made up my mind, that if I failed in finding entertainment at inn the second, I should address myself to hay-rick the first; but better fortune awaited me. I sighted my way to the other sign-post of the village: the lights within had gone up stairs to the attics; but as I tapped and tapped, one of them came trippingly down; it stood pondering behind the door for half a second, as if in deliberation, and then bolt and bar were withdrawn, and a very pretty young Englishwoman stood in the door-way. "Could I get accommodation there for a night, — supper and bed?" There was a hesitating glance at my person, followed by a very welcome "yes;" and thus closed the adventures of the evening. On the following morning I walked on to Olney. It was with some little degree of solicitude that, in a quiet corner by the way, remote from cottages, I tried my pistols, to ascertain what sort of defence I would have made had the worst come to the worst in the encounter of the previous evening. Pop, pop! — they went off beautifully, and sent their bullets through an inch board; and so in all probability I would have succeeded in astonishing the "fancy-men."

CHAPTER XV.

Cowper; his singular Magnanimity of Character; Argument furnished by his latter Religious History against the Selfish Philosophy. — Valley of the Ouse. — Approach to Olney. — Appearance of the Town. — Cowper's House; Parlor; Garden. — Pippin-tree planted by the Poet. — Summer-house written within and without. — John Tawell. — Delightful Old Woman. — Weston-Underwood. — Thomas Scott's House. — The Park of the Throckmortons. — Walk described in "The Task." — Wilderness. — Ancient Avenue. — Alcove; Prospect which it commands, as drawn by Cowper. — Colonnade. — Rustic Bridge. — Scene of the "Needless Alarm." — The Milk Thistle.

OLNEY! Weston-Underwood! Yardley-Chase! the banks of the Ouse, and the park of the Throckmortons! Classic ground once more, — the home and much-loved haunts of a sweet and gentle, yet sublimely heroic nature, that had to struggle on in great unhappiness with the most terrible of all enemies, — the obstinate unreasoning despair of a broken mind. Poor Cowper! There are few things more affecting in the history of the species than the Heaven-inspired magnanimity of this man. Believing himself doomed to perish everlastingly, — for such was the leading delusion of his unhappy malady, — he yet made it the grand aim of his enduring labors to show forth the mercy and goodness of a God who, he believed, had no mercy for him, and to indicate to others the true way of salvation, — deeming it all the while a way closed against himself. Such, surely, is not the character or disposition of the men destined to perish. We are told by his biographers that the well-known hymn in which he celebrates the "mysterious way" in which "God works" to "perform his wonders," was written at the close of the happy period which intervened between the first and second attacks of his cruel malady; and that what suggested its composition were the too truly interpreted indications of a relapse. His mind had been wholly restored to him; he had been singularly happy in his religion: and he had striven earnestly, as in the case of his dying brother, to bring others under its influence. And now, too surely feeling that his intellect was again on the eve of being darkened, he deemed the providence a frowning one, but believed in faith that there was a "smiling face" behind it. In his second recovery, though his intellectual stature was found to have greatly increased, — as in some racking maladies the person of the patient becomes taller, — he never enjoyed his whole mind. There was a missing faculty, if faculty I may term it: his well-grounded hope of salvation never returned. It were presumptuous to attempt interpreting the real scope and object of the afflictive dispensation which Cowper could contemplate with such awe; and yet there does seem a key to it. There is surely a wondrous sublimity in the lesson which it reads. The assertors of the selfish theory have dared to regard Christianity itself, in its relation to the human mind, as but one of the higher modifications of the self-aggrandizing sentiment. May we not venture to refer them to the grief-worn hero of Olney, — the sweet poet who first poured the stream of Divine truth into the channels of our literature, after they had been shut against it for more than a hundred years, — and ask them whether it be in the power of sophistry to square *his* motives with the ignoble conclusions of their philosophy?

Olney stands upon the Oolite, on the northern side of the valley of the Ouse, and I approached it this morning from the south, across the valley. Let the reader imagine a long green ribbon of flat meadow, laid down in the middle of the land scape like a web on a bleaching green, only not quite so straightly drawn out. It is a ribbon about half a mile in breadth, and it stretches away lengthwise above and below, far as the eye can reach. There rises over it on each side a gentle line of acclivity, that here advances upon it in flat promontories, there recedes into shallow bays, and very much resembles the line of a low-lying but exceedingly rich coast; for on both sides, field and wood, cottage and hedge-row, lie thick as the variously tinted worsteds in a piece of German needlework; the flat ribbon in the midst is bare and open, and through it there winds, from side to side, in many a convolution, as its appropriate pattern, a blue sluggish stream, deeply fringed on both banks by an edging of tall bulrushes. The pleasantly grouped village directly opposite, with the long narrow bridge in front, and the old handsome church and tall spire rising in the midst, is Olney; and that other village on the same side, about two miles further up the stream, with the exceedingly lofty trees rising over it, — trees so lofty that they overhang the square tower of its church, as a churchyard cypress overhangs a sepulchral monument, — is Weston-*Underwood.* In the one village Cowper produced "The Task;" in the other he translated "Homer."

I crossed the bridge, destined, like the "Brigs of Ayr," and the "Bridge of Sighs," long to outlive its stone and lime existence; passed the church, — John Newton's; saw John Newton's house, a snug building, much garnished with greenery; and then entered Olney proper, — the village that was Olney a hundred years ago. Unlike most of the villages of central England, it is built, not of brick, but chiefly at least of a calcareous yellow stone from the Oolite, which, as it gathers scarce any lichen or moss, looks clean and fresh after the lapse of centuries; and it is not until the eye catches the dates on the peaked gable points, 1682, 1611, 1590, that one can regard the place as no hastily run up town of yesterday, but as a place that had a living in other times. The main street, which is also the Bedford road, broadens towards the middle of the village into a roomy angle, in shape not very unlike the capacious pocket of a Scotch housewife of the old school: one large elm tree rises in the centre; and just opposite the elm, among the houses which skirt the base of the angle, — *i. e.* the bottom of the pocket, — we see an old-fashioned house, considerably taller than the others, and differently tinted; for it is built of red brick, somewhat ornately bordered with stone. And this tall brick house was Cowper's home for nineteen years. It contains the parlor, which has become such a standard paragon of snugness and comfort, that it will need no repairs in all the future; and the garden behind is that in which the poet reared his cucumbers and his Ribston pippins, and in which he plied hammer and saw to such excellent purpose, in converting his small greenhouse into a summer sitting-room, and in making lodging-houses for his hares. He dated from that tall house not a few of the most graceful letters in the English language, and matured, from the first crude conceptions to the last finished touches, "Truth," "Hope," "The Progress of Error," "Retirement," and "The Task." I found the famed parlor vocal with the gabble of an infant school: carpet and curtains were gone, sofa and bubbling urn: and I saw, instead, but a few deal forms, and about two dozen chubby children, whom all the authority of the thin old woman, their teacher, could not recall to diligence in the presence of the stranger. The walls were sorely soiled, and the plaster somewhat broken; there was evidence, too, that a partition had been removed, and that the place was roomier by one-half than when Cowper and Mrs. Unwin used to sit down in it to their evening tea

But at least one interesting feature had remained unchanged. There is a small port-hole in the plaster, framed by a narrow facing of board; and through this port-hole, cut in the partition for the express purpose, Cowper's hares used to come leaping out to their evening gambols on the carpet. I found the garden, like the house, much changed. It had been broken up into two separate properties; and the proprietors having run a wall through the middle of it, one must now seek the pippin-tree which the poet planted in one little detached bit of garden, and the lath-and-plaster summer-house, which, when the weather was fine, used to form his writing-room in another. The Ribston pippin looks an older-like tree, and has more lichen about it, though far from tall for its age, than might be expected of a tree of Cowper's planting; but it is now seventy-nine years since the poet came to Olney, and in less than seventy-nine years young fruit-trees become old ones. The little summer-house, maugre the fragility of its materials, is in a wonderfully good state of keeping: the old lath still retains the old lime; and all the square inches and finger-breadths of the plaster, inside and out, we find as thickly covered with names as the space in our ancient Scotch copies of the "Solemn League and Covenant." Cowper would have marvelled to have seen his little summer-house, — for little it is, — scarce larger than a four-posted bedstead, — written, like the roll described in sacred vision, "within and without." It has still around it, in its green old age, as when it was younger and less visited, a great profusion of flowering shrubs and hollyhocks; we see from its window the back of honest John Newton's house, much enveloped in wood, with the spire of the church rising over; and on either side there are luxuriant orchards, in which the stiffer forms of the fruit-trees are relieved by lines of graceful poplars. Some of the names on the plaster are not particularly classical. My conductress pointed to one signature, in especial, which was, she said, an object of great curiosity, and which a "most respectable person," — "*just after the execution*," — had come a day's journey to see. It was that of the hapless "John Tawell, Great Birkenstead, Hants," who about two years ago was hung for the murder of his mistress. It had been added to the less celebrated names, for so the legend bore, on the "21st day of seventh month 1842;" and just beside it some kind friend of the deceased had added, by way of postscript, the significant hieroglyphic of a minute human figure, suspended on a gibbet, with the head rather uncomfortably twisted awry.

I had made several unsuccessful attempts to procure a guide acquainted with the walks of the poet, and had inquired of my conductress (an exceedingly obliging person, I may mention, — housekeeper of the gentleman to whom the outermost of the two gardens belongs), as of several others, whether she knew any one at once willing and qualified to accompany me for part of the day in that capacity. But she could bethink herself of nobody. Just, however, as we stepped out from the garden into the street, there was an old woman in a sad-colored cloak, and bearing under the cloak a bulky basket, passing by. "O!" said the housekeeper, "there is just the person that knows more about Cowper than any one else. She was put to school, when a little girl, by Mrs. Unwin, and was much about her house at Weston-Underwood. Gossip, gossip! come hither." And so I secured the old woman as my guide; and we set out together for Weston and the pleasure-grounds of the Throckmortons. She was seventy-one, she said; but she walked every day with her basket from Weston-Underwood to Olney, — sometimes, indeed, twice in the day, — to shop and market for her neighbors. She had now got a basket of fresh herrings, which were great rarities in these parts, and it behooved her to get them delivered: but she would then be quite free to accompany me to all the walks in which she had seen Squire Cowper a hundred and a hundied times, — to the "Peasant's Nest," and the "alcove," and the "avenue," and the "rustic bridge," and the "Wilderness," and "Yardley oak," and, in short, anywhere or everywhere. I could not have been more in luck: my delightful old woman had a great deal to say: she would have been equally garrulous, I doubt not, had Cowper been a mere country squire, and Mrs. Unwin his housekeeper; but as he chanced to be a great poet, and as his nearer friends had, like the planets of a central sun, become distinctly visible, from their proximity, by the light which he cast, and were evidently to remain so, her gossip about him and them I found vastly agreeable. The good Squire Cowper! she said, — well did she remember him, in his white cap, and his suit of green turned up with black. She knew the Lady Hesketh too. A kindly lady was the Lady Hesketh; there are few such ladies now-a-days: she used to put coppers into her little velvet bag every time she went out, to make the children she met happy; and both she and Mrs. Unwin were remarkably kind to the poor. The road to Weston-Underwood looks down upon the valley of the Ouse. "Were there not water-lilies in the river in their season?" I asked; "and did not Cowper sometimes walk out along its banks?" — "O yes," she replied; "and I remember the dog Beau, too, who brought the lily ashore to him. Beau was a smart, petted little creature, with silken ears, and had a good deal of red about him."

My guide brought me to Cowper's Weston residence, a handsome, though, like the Olney domicile, old-fashioned house, still in a state of good repair, with a whitened many-windowed front, and tall steep roof flagged with stone; and I whiled away some twenty minutes or so in the street before it, while my old woman went about dispersing her herrings. Weston-Underwood, as villages go, must enjoy a rather quiet, do-nothing sort of existence, for in all that time not a passenger went by. The houses — steep-roofed, straw-thatched, stone-built erections, with the casements of their second stories lost in the eaves — straggle irregularly on both sides of the road, as if each house had an independent will of its own, and was somewhat capricious in the exercise of it. There is a profusion of well-grown, richly-leaved vines, trailed up against their walls: the season had been unfavorable, and so the grapes, in even the best bunches, scarcely exceeded in size our common red currants; but still they were *bona fide* vines and grapes, and their presence served to remind one of the villages of sunnier climates. A few tall walls and old gateway columns mingle with the cottages, and these are all that now remain of the mansion-house of the Throckmortons. One rather rude-looking cottage, with its upper casement half hid in the thatch, is of some note, as the scene of a long struggle in a strong rugged mind, — honest, but not amiable, — which led ultimately to the production of several useful folios of solid theology. In that cottage a proud Socinian curate studied and prayed himself, greatly against his will, into one of the soundest Calvinists of modern times: it was for many years the dwelling-place of Thomas Scott; and his well-known narrative, "The Force of Truth," forms a portion of his history during the time he lived in it. The road I had just travelled over with the woman was that along which John Newton had come, in the January of 1774, to visit, in one of these cottages, two of Scott's parishioners, — a dying man and woman; and the Socinian, who had *not* visited them, was led to think seriously, for the first time, that he had a duty as a clergyman which he failed to perform.

It was along the same piece of road, some three years later, that Scott used to steal, when no longer a Socinian, but still wofully afraid of being deemed a Methodist, to hear Newton preach. There were several heaps of stones lying along the street, — the surplus materials of a recent repair, — that seemed to have been gathered from the neighboring fields, but had been derived, in the first instance, from some calcareous grit of the Oolite; and one of these lay opposite the windows of Cowper's mansion. The first fragment I picked up contained a well-marked Plagiostoma; the second, a characteristic fragment of a Pecten. I bethought me of Cowper's philippic on the earlier geologists, which, however, the earlier geologists too certainly deserved, for their science was not good, and their theology wretched; and I indulged in, I dare say, something approaching to a smile. Genius, when in earnest, can do a great deal; but it cannot put down scientific truth, save now and then for a very little time, and would do well never to try.

My old woman had now pretty nearly scattered over the neighborhood her basket of herrings; but she needed, she said, just to look in upon her grandchildren, to say she was going to the woodlands, lest the poor things should come to think they had lost her; and I accompanied her to the cottage. It was a humble low-roofed hut, with its earthen floor sunk, as in many of our Scottish cottages, a single step below the level of the lane. Her grandchildren, little girls of seven and nine years, were busily engaged with their lace bobbins: the younger was working a piece of narrow edging, for her breadth of attainment in the lace department extended as yet over only a few threads; whereas the elder was achieving a little belt of open-work, with a pattern in it. They were orphans, and lived with their poor grandmother, and she was a widow. We regained the street, and then, passing through a dilapidated gateway, entered the pleasure-grounds, — the scene of the walk so enchantingly described in the opening book of "The Task." But, before taking up in detail the minuter features of the place, I must attempt communicating to the reader some conception of it as a whole.

The road from Olney to Weston-Underwood lies parallel to the valley of the Ouse, at little more than a field's breadth up the slope. On its upper side, just where it enters Weston, there lies based upon it (like the parallelogram of a tyro geometrician, raised on a given right line) an old-fashioned rectangular park, — that of the Throckmortons, — about half a mile in breadth by about three-quarters of a mile in length. The sides of the enclosure are bordered by a broad belting of very tall and very ancient wood; its grassy area is mottled by numerous trees, scattered irregularly; its surface partakes of the general slope; it is traversed by a green valley, with a small stream trotting along the bottom, that enters it from above, nearly about the middle of the upper side, and that then, cutting it diagonally, passes outwards and downwards towards the Ouse through the lower corner. About the middle of the park this valley sends out an off-shoot valley, or dell rather, towards that upper corner furthest removed from the corner by which it makes its exit; the off-shoot dell has no stream a-bottom, but is a mere grassy depression, dotted with trees. It serves, however, with the valleys into which it opens, so to break the surface of the park that the rectangular formality of the lines of boundary almost escape notice. Now, the walk described in "The Task" lay along three of the four sides of this parallelogram. The poet, quitting the Olney road at that lower corner where the diagonal valley finds egress, struck up along the side of the park, turned at the nearer upper corner, and passed through the belting of wood that runs along the top; turned again at the further upper corner, and, coming down on Weston, joined the Olney road just where it enters the village. After first quitting the highway, a walk of two furlongs or so brought him abreast of the "Peasant's Nest;" after the first turning atop, and a walk of some two or three furlongs more, he descended into the diagonal valley, just where it enters the park, crossed the rustic bridge which spans the stream at the bottom, marked the doings of the mole, and then ascended to the level on the other side. Near the second turning he found the alcove, and saw the trees in the streamless dell, as if "sunk, and shortened to their topmost boughs;" then, coming down upon Weston, he passed under the "light and graceful arch" of the ancient avenue; reached the "Wilderness" as he was nearing the village; and, emerging from the thicket full upon the houses, saw the "thrasher at his task," through the open door of some one of the barns of the place. Such is a hard outline, in road-map fashion, of the walk which, in the pages of Cowper, forms such exquisite poetry. I entered it somewhat unluckily to-day at the wrong end, commencing at the western corner, and passing on along its angles to the corner near Olney, thus reversing the course of Cowper, for my old woman had no acquaintance with "The Task," or the order of its descriptions; but, after mastering the various scenes in detail, I felt no difficulty in restoring them to the integrity of the classic arrangement.

On first entering the park, among the tall forest-trees that, viewed from the approach to Olney, seem to overhang the village and its church, one sees a square, formal corner, separated from the opener ground by a sunk dry-stone fence, within which the trees, by no means lofty, are massed as thickly together as saplings in a nursery-bed run wild, or nettles in a neglected burying-ground. There are wha seem sepulchral urns among the thickets of this enclosure; and sepulchral urns they are, — raised, however, to commemorate the burial-places, not of men, but of beasts. Cowper in 1792 wrote an epitaph for a favorite pointer of the Throckmortons; and the family, stirred up by the event, seem from that period to have taken a dog-burying bias, and to have made their Wilderness the cemetery; for this square enclosure in the corner, with its tangled thickets and its green mouldy urns, is the identical Wilderness of "The Task,"

> "Whose well-rolled walks,
> With curvature of slow and easy sweep, —
> Deception innocent, — give ample space
> To narrow bounds."

One wonders at the fortune that assigned to so homely and obscure a corner — a corner which a nursery-gardener could get up to order in a fortnight — so proud and conspicuous a niche in English literature. We walk on, however, and find the scene next described greatly more worthy of the celebrity conferred on it. In passing upwards, along the side of the park, we have got into a noble avenue of limes, — tall as York Minster, and very considerably longer, for the vista diminishes till the lofty arch seems reduced to a mere doorway; the smooth glossy trunks form stately columns, and the branches, interlacing high over head, a magnificent roof.

> "How airy and how light the graceful arch,
> Yet awful as the consecrated roof
> Reëchoing pious anthems! while beneath
> The checkered earth seems restless as a flood
> Brushed by the wind. So sportive is the light
> Shot through the boughs, it dances as they dance,
> Shadow and sunshine intermingling quick,
> And darkening and enlightening, as the leaves
> Play wanton every moment, every spot."

What exquisite description! And who, acquainted with Cowper, ever walked in a wood when the sun shone, and the wind ruffled the leaves, without realizing it! It was too dead a calm to-day to show me the dancing light and shadow where the picture had first been taken: the feathery outline of the foliage lay in diluted black, moveless on the grass, like the foliage of an Indian-ink drawing newly washed in; but all else was present, just as Cowper had described half a century before. Two minutes' walk, after passing through the avenue, brought me to the upper corner of the park, and "the proud alcove that crowns it," — for the "proud alcove" does still crown it. But time, and the weather, and rotting damps, seem to be working double tides on the failing pile, and it will not crown it long. The alcove is a somewhat clumsy erection of wood and plaster, with two squat wooden columns in front, of a hybrid order between the Tuscan and Doric, and a seat within. A crop of dark-colored mushrooms cherished by the damp summer had shot up along the joints of the decaying floor; the plaster, flawed and much stained, dangled from the ceiling in numerous little bits, suspended, like the sword of old, by single hairs; the broad deal architrave had given way at one end, but the bolt at the other still proved true; and so it hung diagonally athwart the two columns, like the middle bar of a gigantic letter N. The "characters uncouth" of the "rural carvers" are, however, still legible; and not a few names have since been added. This upper corner of the park forms its highest ground, and the view is very fine. The streamless dell — not streamless always, however, for the poet describes the urn of its little Naiad as filled in winter — lies immediately in front, and we see the wood within its hollow recesses, as if "sunk, and shortened to the topmost boughs." The green undulating surface of the park, still more deeply grooved in the distance by the diagonal valley, and mottled with trees, stretches away beyond to the thick belting of tall wood below. There is a wide opening, just where the valley opens, — a great gap in an immense hedge, — that gives access to the further landscape; the decent spire of John Newton's church rises, about two miles away, as the central object in the vista thus formed; we see in front a few silvery reaches of the Ouse; and a blue uneven line of woods that runs along the horizon closes in the prospect. The nearer objects within the pale of the park, animate and inanimate, — the sheepfold and its sheep, the hay-wains, empty and full, as they pass and repass to and from the hay-field, — the distinctive characters of the various trees, and their shortened appearance in the streamless valley, — occupy by much the larger part of Cowper's description from the alcove; while the concluding five lines afford a bright though brief glimpse of the remoter prospect, as seen through the opening. But I must not withhold the description itself, — at once so true to nature and so instinct with poetry, — familiar as it must prove to the great bulk of my readers.

"Now roves the eye;
And, posted on this speculative height,
Exults in its command. The sheepfold here
Pours out its fleecy tenants o'er the glebe.
At first, progressive as a stream, they seek
The middle field; but, scattered by degrees,
Each to his choice, soon whiten all the land.
There from the sunburnt hay-field homeward creeps
The loaded wain; while, lightened of its charge,
The wain that meets it passes swiftly by,
The boorish driver leaning o'er his team,
Vociferous and impatient of delay.
Nor less attractive is the woodland scene,
Diversified with trees of various growth,
Alike yet various. Here the gray smooth trunks

Of ash, or lime, or beech, distinctly shine
Within the twilight of their distant shades ;
There, lost behind a rising ground, the wood
Seems sunk, and shortened to its topmost boughs.
No tree in all the grove but has its charms,
Though each its hue peculiar ; paler some,
And of a wannish gray ; the willow such,
And poplar, that with silver lines his leaf,
And ash far stretching his umbrageous arm ;
Of deeper green the elm ; and deeper still,
Lord of the woods, the long-surviving oak.
Some glossy-leaved, and shining in the sun,
The maple, and the beech of oily nuts
Prolific, and the lime at dewy eve
Diffusing odors : nor unnoted pass
The sycamore, capricious in attire,
Now green, now tawny, and, ere autumn yet
Have changed the woods, in scarlet honors bright.
O'er these, but far beyond (a spacious map
Of hill and valley interposed between),
The Ouse, dividing the well-watered land,
Now glitters in the sun, and now retires,
As bashful, yet impatient to be seen."

Quitting the alcove, we skirt the top of the park of the Throckmortons, on a retired grassy walk that runs straight as a tightened cord along the middle of the belting which forms the park's upper boundary, — its enclosing hedge, if I may so speak without offence to the dignity of the ancient forest-trees which compose it. There is a long line of squat broad-stemmed chestnuts on either hand, that fling their interlacing arms athwart the pathway, and bury it, save where here and there the sun breaks in through a gap, in deep shade ; but the roof overhead, unlike that of the ancient avenue already described, is not the roof of a lofty nave in the light, florid style, but of a low-browed, thickly-ribbed Saxon crypt, flanked by ponderous columns, of dwarfish stature, but gigantic strength. And this double tier of chestnuts, extended along the park-top from corner to corner, is the identical "length ot colonnade" eulogized by Cowper in "The Task": —

> "Monument of ancient taste,
> Now scorned, but worthy of a better fate;
> Our fathers knew the value of a screen
> From sultry suns; and, in their shaded walks
> And long-protracted bowers, enjoyed at noon
> The gloom and coolness of declining day.
> Thanks to Benevolus, — he spares me yet
> These chestnuts ranged in corresponding lines;
> And, though himself so polished, still reprieves
> Their obsolete prolixity of shade."

Half-way on, we descend into the diagonal valley, — "but cautious, lest too fast," — just where it enters the park from the uplands, and find at its bottom the "rustic bridge." It was rustic when at its best, — an arch of some four feet span or so, built of undressed stone, fenced with no parapet, and covered over head by a green breadth of turf; and it is now both rustic and ruinous to boot, for one-half the arch has fallen in. The stream is a mere sluggish runnel, much overhung by hawthorn bushes: there are a good many half-grown oaks scattered about in the hollow; while on either hand the old massy chestnuts top the acclivities.

Leaving the park at the rustic bridge, by a gap in the fence, my guide and I struck outwards through the valley towards the uplands. We had left, on crossing the hedge, the scene of the walk in "The Task;" but there is no getting away in this locality from Cowper. The first field we stepped into "adjoining close to Kilwick's echoing wood," is that described in the "Needless Alarm;" and we were on our way to visit "Yardley oak." The poet, conscious of his great wealth in the pictorial, was no niggard in description; and so the field, though not very remarkable for anything, has had its picture drawn.

"A narrow brook, by rushy banks concealed,
Runs in a bottom and divides the field;
Oaks intersperse it that had once a head,
But now wear crests of oven-wood instead;
And where the land slopes to its watery bourn,
Wide yawns a gulf beside a ragged thorn.
Bricks line the sides, but shivered long ago,
And horrid brambles intertwine below;
A hollow scooped, I judge, in ancient time,
For baking earth or burning rock to lime."

The "narrow brook" here is that which, passing downwards into the park, runs underneath the rustic bridge, and flows towards the Ouse through the diagonal valley. The field itself, which lies on one of the sides of the valley, and presents rather a steep slope to the plough, has still its sprinkling of trees; but the oaks, with the oven-wood crests, have nearly all disappeared; and for the "gulf beside the thorn," I could find but a small oblong, steep-sided pond, half overshadowed by an ash-tree. Improvement has sadly defaced the little field since it sat for its portrait; for though never cropped in Squire Cowper's days, as the woman told me, it now lies, like the ordinary work-day pieces of ground beyond and beside it, in a state of careful tillage, and smelt rank at the time of a flourishing turnip crop. "O," said the woman, who for the last minute had been poking about the hedge for something which she could not find, "do you know that the Squire was a beautiful drawer?"—"I know that he drew," I replied; "but I do not know that his drawings were fine ones. I have in Scotland a great book filled with the Squire's letters; and I have learned from it, that ere he set himself to write his long poems, he used to draw 'mountains and valleys, and ducks and dabchicks,' and that he threatened to charge his friends at the rate of a halfpenny a piece for them." — "Ah," said the woman, "but he drew grandly, for all that; and I have just been looking for a kind of thistle that used to grow here, — but the farmer has, I find, weeded it all out, — that he made many fine pictures of. I have seen one of them with Lady Hesketh, that her ladyship thought very precious. The thistle was a pretty thistle, and I am sorry they are all gone. It had a deep red flower, set round with long thorns; and the green of the leaves was crossed with bright white streaks." I inferred from the woman's description that the plant so honored by Cowper's pencil must have been the "milk thistle," famous in legendary lore for bearing strong trace on its leaves of glossy green of the milk of the Virgin Mother, dropped on it in the flight to Egypt.

CHAPTER XVI.

Yardley Oak; of immense Size and imposing Appearance. — Cowper's Description singularly illustrative of his complete Mastery over Language. — Peasant's Nest. — The Poet's Vocation peculiarly one of Revolution. — The School of Pope; supplanted in its unproductive Old Age by that of Cowper. — Cowper's Coadjutors in the Work. — Economy of Literary Revolution. — The old English Yeoman. — Quit Olney. — Companions in the Journey. — Incident. — Newport Pagnell. — Mr. Bull and the French Mystics. — Lady of the Fancy. — Champion of all England. — Pugilism. — Anecdote.

Half an hour's leisurely walking — and, in consideration of my companion's three score and eleven summers, our walking *was* exceedingly leisurely — brought us, through field and dingle, and a country that presented, as we ascended, less of an agricultural and more of a pastoral character, to the woods of Yardley Lodge. We enter through a coppice on a grassy field, and see along the opposite side a thick oak wood, with a solitary brick house, the only one in sight, half hidden amid foliage in a corner. The oak wood has, we find, quite a character of its own. The greater part of its trees, still in their immature youth, were seedlings within the last forty years: they have no associates that bear in their well-developed proportions, untouched by decay, the stamp of solid mid-aged tree hood; but here and there, — standing up among them, like the long-lived sons of Noah, in their old age of many centuries, amid a race cut down to the three score and ten, — we find some of the most ancient oaks in the empire, — trees that were trees in the days of William the Conqueror. These are mere hollow trunks, of vast bulk, but stinted foliage, in which the fox shelters and the owl builds, — mere *struldbrugs* of the forest. The bulkiest and most picturesque among their number we find marked by a white-lettered board: it is a hollow pollard of enormous girth, twenty-eight feet five inches in circumference a foot above the soil, with skeleton stumps, bleached white by the winters of many centuries, stretching out for a few inches from amid a ragged drapery of foliage that sticks close to the body of the tree, and bearing on its rough gray bole wens and warts of astounding magnitude. The trunk, leaning slightly forward, and wearing all its huger globosities behind, seems some fantastic old-world mammoth, seated kangaroo-fashion on its haunches. Its foliage this season had caught a tinge of yellow, when the younger trees all around retained their hues of deep green; and, seen in the bold relief which it owed to the circumstance, it reminded me of Æneas' golden branch, glittering bright amid the dark woods of Cumea. And such is Yardley oak, the subject of one of the finest descriptions in English poetry, — one of the most characteristic, too, of the muse of Cowper. If asked to illustrate that peculiar power which he possessed above all modern poets, of taking the most stubborn and untractable words in the language, and bending them with all ease round his thinking, so as to fit its every indentation and irregularity of outline, as the ship-carpenter adjusts the stubborn planking, grown flexible in his hand, to the exact mould of his vessel, I would at once instance some parts of the description of Yardley oak. But farewell, noble tree! so old half a century ago, when the poet conferred on thee immortality, that thou dost not seem older now!

"Time made thee what thou wast, — king of the woods;
And Time hath made thee what thou art, — a cave
For owls to roost in. Once thy spreading boughs
O'erhung the champaign; and the numerous flocks

That grazed it stood beneath that ample cope
Uncrowded, yet safe sheltered from the storm.
No flock frequents thee now. Thou hast outlived
Thy popularity, and art become
(Unless verse rescue thee a while) a thing
Forgotten as the foliage of thy youth.
While thus through all the stages thou hast pushed
Of treeship, — first a seedling hid in grass ;
Then twig ; then sapling ; and, as century rolled
Slow after century, a giant bulk
Of girth enormous, with moss-cushioned root
Upheaved above the soil, and sides embossed
With prominent wens globose, — till, at the last,
The rottenness, which time is charged to inflict
On other mighty ones, found also thee."

I returned with my guide to the rustic bridge, resumed my walk through the hitherto unexplored half of the chestnut colonnade; turned the corner; and then, passing downwards along the lower side of the park, through neglected thickets, — the remains of an extensive nursery run wild, — I struck outwards beyond its precincts, and reached a whitened dwelling-house that had been once the "Peasant's Nest." But nowhere else in the course of my walk had the hand of improvement misimproved so sadly. For the hill-top cottage,

"Environed with a ring of branchy elms
That overhung the thatch,"

I found a modern hard-cast farm-house, with a square of offices attached, all exceedingly utilitarian, well kept, stiff, and disagreeable. It was sad enough to find an erection that a journeyman bricklayer could have produced in a single month substituted for the "peaceful covert" Cowper had so often wished his own, and which he had so frequently and fondly visited. But those beauties of situation which awakened the admiration, and even half excited the envy, of the poet improvement could not alter; and so they are now what they ever were. The diagonal valley to which I have had such frequent occasion to refer is just escaping from the park at its lower corner: the slope, which rises from the runnel to the level, still lies on the one hand within the enclosure; but it has escaped from it on the other, and forms, where it merges into the higher grounds, the hill-top on which the "Nest" stands; and the prospect, no longer bounded by the tall belting of the park, is at once very extensive and singularly beautiful.

> "Here Ouse, slow winding through a level plain
> Of spacious meads, with cattle sprinkled o'er,
> Conducts the eye along its sinuous course
> Delighted. There, fast-rooted in their bank,
> Stand, never overlooked, our favorite elms,
> That screen the herdsman's solitary hut;
> While far beyond, and overthwart the stream,
> That, as with molten glass, inlays the vale,
> The sloping land recedes into the clouds,
> Displaying on its varied side the grace
> Of hedge-row beauties numberless, square towers,
> Tall spire, from which the sound of cheerful bells
> Just undulates upon the listening ear,
> Groves, heaths, and smoking villages remote."

Leaving the farm-house, I descended into the valley; passed along a tangled thicket of yew, plane and hazel, in which I lingered a while to pick blackberries and nuts, where Cowper may have picked them; came out upon the Olney road by the wicket gate through which he used to quit the highway and strike up to the woodlands; and, after making my old woman particularly happy by a small gratuity, returned to Olney.

I trust it will not be held that my descriptions of this old-fashioned park, with its colonnade and its avenues, its dells and its dingles, its alcove and its wilderness, have been too minute. It has an interest as independent of any mere beauty or picturesqueness which it may possess, as the field of Bannockburn or the meadows of Runnimede. It indicates the fulcrum, if I may so speak, on which the lever of a great original genius first rested, when it upturned from its foundations an effete school of English verse, and gave to the literature of the country a new face. Its scenery, idealized into poetry, wrought one of the greatest literary revolutions of which the history of letters preserves any record. The school of Pope, originally of but small compass, had sunk exceedingly low ere the times of Cowper: it had become, like Nebuchadnezzar's tree, a brass-bound stump, that sent forth no leafage of refreshing green, and no blossoms of pleasant smell; and yet, for considerably more than half a century, it had been the only existing English school. And when the first volume of "Poems by William Cowper, Esq., of the Inner Temple," issued from the press, there seemed to be no prospect whatever of any other school rising to supplant it. Several writers of genius had appeared in the period, and had achieved for themselves a standing in literature; nor were they devoid of the originality, in both their thinking and the form of it, without which no writer becomes permanently eminent. But their originality was specific and individual, and terminated with themselves: whereas the school of Pope, whatever its other defects, was of a generic character. A second Collins, a second Gray, a second Goldsmith, would have been mere timid imitators, — mere mock Paganinis, playing each on the one exquisite string of his master, and serving by his happiest efforts but to establish the fidelity of the imitation. But the poetry of Pope formed an instrument of larger compass and a more extensive gamut, and left the disciples room to achieve for themselves, in running over the notes of their master, a certain amount of originality Lyttelton's "Advice to Belinda," and Johnson's "London," exhibit the stamp of very different minds; and the "Pursuits of Literature" is quite another sort of poem from the "Triumphs of Temper;" but they all alike belong to the school of Pope, and bear the impress of the "Moral Essays," the "Satires," or the "Rape of the Lock." The poetical mind of England had taken an inveterate set; it had grown up into artificial attitudes, like some superannuated posture-maker, and had lost the gait and air natural to it. Like the painter in the fable, it drew its portraits less from the life than from cherished models and familiar casts approved by the connoisseur; and exhibited nature, when it at all exhibited it, through a dim haze of colored conventionalities. And this school, grown rigid and unfeeling in its unproductive old age, it was part of the mission of Cowper to supplant and destroy. He restored to English literature the wholesome freshness of nature, and sweetened and invigorated its exhausted atmosphere, by letting in upon it the cool breeze and the bright sunshine. The old park, with its noble trees and sequestered valleys, were to him what the writings of Pope and of Pope's disciples were to his contemporaries: he renewed poetry by doing what the first poets had done.

It is not uninteresting to mark the plan on which nature delights to operate in producing a renovation of this character in the literature of a country. Cowper had two vigorous coadjutors in the work of revolution; and all three, though essentially unlike in other respects, resembled one another in the preliminary course through which they were prepared for their proper employment. Circumstances had conspired to throw them all outside the pale of the existing literature. Cowper. at the ripe age of thirty-three, when breathing in London the literary atmosphere of the day, amid his friends, — the Lloyds, Colmans, and Bonnel Thorntons, — was a clever and tasteful imitator, but an imitator merely, both in his prose and his verse. His prose in "The Connoisseur" is a feeble echo of that of Addison; while in his verse we find unequivocal traces of Prior, of Philips, and of Pope, but scarce any trace whatever of a poet at least not inferior to the best of them, — Cowper himself. Events over which he had no control suddenly removed him outside this atmosphere, and dropped him into a profound retirement, in which for nearly twenty years he did not peruse the works of any English poet. The chimes of the existing literature had fairly rung themselves out of his head, ere, with a heart grown familiar in the interval with all earnest feeling, — an intellect busied with ever ripening cogitation, — an eye and ear conversant, day after day, and year after year, with the face and voice of nature, — he struck, as the key-notes of his own noble poetry, a series of exquisitely modulated tones, that had no counterparts in the artificial gamut. Had his preparatory course been different, — had he been kept in the busy and literary world, instead of passing, in his insulated solitude, through the term of second education, which made him what we all know, — it seems more than questionable whether Cowper would have ever taken his place in literature as a great original poet.* His two coadjutors in the work of

* Cowper himself seems to have been thoroughly aware that his long seclusion from the world of letters told in his favor. "I reckon it among my principal advantages as a composer of verses," we find him saying, in one of his letters to the younger Unwin, "that I have not read an English poet these thirteen years, and but one these twenty years. Imitation even of the best models is my aversion. It is servile and mechanical, — a trick that has enabled many to usurp the name of author, who could not have written at all, if they had not written upon the pattern of some one indeed original. But when the ear and taste have been much accustomed

literary revolution were George Crabbe and Robert Burns. The one, self-taught, and wholly shut out from the world of letters, laid in his vast stores of observation, fresh from nature in an obscure fishing village on the coast of Suffolk; the other educated in exactly the same style and degree, — Crabbe had a little bad Latin, and Burns a little bad French, — and equally secluded from the existing literature, achieved the same important work on the bleak farm of Mossgiel. And the earlier compositions of these three poets, — all of them true backwoodsmen in the republic of letters, — clearers of new and untried fields in the rich unopened provinces, — appeared within five years of each other — Crabbe's first and Burns' last. This process of renovating a worn-out literature does certainly seem a curious one. Circumstances virtually excommunicated three of the great poetic minds of the age, and flung them outside the literary pale; and straightway they became founders of churches of their own, and carried away with them all the people.

Cowper, however, was better adapted by nature, and more prepared by previous accomplishment, for the work of literary revolution, than either Burns or Crabbe. His poetry — to return to a previous illustration, rather, however, indicated than actually employed — was in the natural what Pope's was in the artificial walk, — of a generic character; whereas theirs was of a strongly specific cast. The writers who have followed Crabbe and Burns we at once detect as imitators; whereas the writers to whom Cowper furnished the starting note have attained to the dignity of originals. He withdrew their attention from the old models, — thoroughly commonplaced by

to the manner of others, it is almost impossible to avoid it; and we imitate in spite of ourselves, just in proportion as we admire." (*Correspondence*, 1781.)

reproduction, — and sent them out into the fields and the woods with greatly enlarged vocabularies, to describe new things in fresh language. And thus has he exercised an indirect but potent influence on the thinking and mode of description of poets whose writings furnish little or no trace of his peculiar style or manner. Even in style and manner, however, we discover in his pregnant writings the half-developed germs of after schools. In his lyrics we find, for instance, the starting notes of not a few of the happiest lyrics of Campbell. The noble ode "On the Loss of the Royal George" must have been ringing in the ears of the poet who produced the "Battle of the Baltic;" and had the "Castaway" and the "Poplar Field" been first given to the world in company with the "Exile of Erin" and the "Soldier's Dream," no critic could have ever suspected that they had emanated from quite another pen. We may find similar traces in his works of the minor poems of the Lake School. "The Distressed Travellers, or Labor in Vain;" "The Yearly Distress, or Tithing-Time;" "The Colubriad;" 'The Retired Cat;" "The Dog and the Water Lily;" and "The Diverting History of John Gilpin," — might have all made their first appearance among the "Lyrical Ballads," and would certainly have formed high specimens of the work. But it is not form and manner that the restored literature of England mainly owes to Cowper, — it is spirit and life; not so much any particular mode of exhibiting nature, as a revival of the habit of looking at it.

I had selected as my inn at Olney a quiet old house, kept by a quiet old man, who, faithful to bygone greatness, continued to sell his ale under the somewat faded countenance of the late Duke of York. On my return, I found him smoking a pipe, in his clean, tile-paved kitchen, with a man nearly as old as himself, but exceedingly vigorous for his years, — a fresh-colored, square-shouldered, deep-chested, English-looking man, with good sense and frank good-humor broadly impressed on every feature. The warm day and the long walk had rendered me exceedingly thirsty: I had been drinking, as I came along, at every runnel; and I now asked the landlord whether he could not get me something to slake my drought less heady than his ale. "O," said his companion, taking from his pocket half a dozen fine jargonelle pears, and sweeping them towards me across the old oak table, "these are the things for your thirst." I thanked him, and picked out of the heap a single pear. "O," he exclaimed, in the same tone of refreshing frankness, "take all, take all; they are all of my own rearing; I have abundance more on my trees at home." With so propitious a beginning, we were soon engaged in conversation. He was, as I afterwards learned from my host, a very worthy man, Mr. Hales, of Pemberton, the last, or nearly the last, of the race of old English yeomen in this part of the country. His ancestors had held their small property of a few fields for centuries, and he continued to hold it still. He well remembered Cowper, he told me; Newton had left Olney before his day, some sixty-five or sixty-six years ago; but of Thomas Scott he had some slight recollection. The connection of these men with the locality had exerted, he said, a marked influence on the theologic opinions and beliefs of the people; and there were few places in England, in consequence, in which the Puseyistic doctrines had made less way. The old parishioners of Newton and Scott, and the town's folk and neighbors of Cowper, had felt, of course, an interest in their writings; and so there were more copies of the "Poems," and the "Cardiphonia," and the "Force of Truth," and the "Essays," scattered over the place, than over perhaps any other locality in England. And so the truth was at least known in Olney, and its neightorhood, whatever use might be made of it. I inquired whether he had ever heard of one Moses Brown, who had been curate in Olney exactly a hundred years before, — a good man, a poet, and a friend of James Hervey, and whose poems, descriptive and devotional, though not equal by a great deal to those of Cowper, had passed through several editions in their day. Mr. Hales had barely heard that such a man there had been, and had some recollection of an aged woman, one of his daughters. I parted from the old frank yeoman, glad I should have seen so fine a specimen of a class fast hastening to extinction. The reader will remember that Gulliver, in the island of the sorcerers, when the illustrious dead were called up to hold converse with him, had the curiosity to summon, among the rest, a few English yeomen of the old stamp, — "once so famous," says the satirist, "for the simplicity of their manners, diet, and dress, — for justice in their dealings, — for their true spirit of liberty and love of their country." And I deemed myself somewhat in luck in having found a representative of the class still in the land of the living, considerably more than a century after Swift had deemed it necessary to study his specimens among the dead.

After exhausting the more interesting walks of the place, I quitted Olney next morning for the railway, by an omnibus that plies daily between Bedford and Wolverton. There were two gentlemen in the vehicle. The one dressed very neatly in black, with a white neck-cloth and somewhat prim-looking beaver hat, I at once set down as a Dissenting minister; the other, of a rather more secular cast, but of staid and sober aspect, might, I inferred, be one of his deacons or elders. They were engaged, as I entered, in discussing some theological question which they dropped, however, as we drove on through the street, and evinced a curiosity to know where

Newton and Thomas Scott had lived. I pointed ou to them the house of Cowper, and the house and church of Newton; and, in crossing the famous bridge over the Ouse, directed their attention to the distant village of Weston-Underwood, in which Scott had officiated for many years as a curate. And so I got fairly into their good graces, and had my share assigned me in the conversation. They discussed Newton and Scott, and characterized as sound and excellent the "Commentary" of the one and the "Letters" of the other; but the labors of Cowper, whose rarer genius, and intellect of finer texture, seemed removed beyond the legitimate range of their appreciation, they regarded apparently as of less mark and importance. I deemed them no inadequate representatives of a worthy section of the English people, and of an obvious power in the country, — a power always honestly and almost always well directed, but rather in obedience to the instincts of a wise religion than the promptings of a nicely-discriminating intelligence. The more secular-looking traveller of the two, on ascertaining that I had come from Edinburgh, and was a citizen of the place, inquired whether I was not a *parishioner* of Dr. Chalmers, — the one Scotchman, by the way, with whose name I found every Englishman of any intelligence in some degree acquainted; and next, whether I was not a member of the Free Church. The Disruption both gentlemen regarded as a great and altogether extraordinary event. They knew almost nothing of the controversy which had led to it; but there was no mistaking the simple fact of which it was an embodiment, namely, that from four to five hundred ministers of the Established Church had resigned their livings on a point of principle. To this effect, at least, the iron tongue of rumor had struck with no uncertain sound; and the tones were of a kind suited not to lower the aspirations of the religious sentiment.

nor to cast a shade of suspicion on its reality as a principle of conduct.

In the middle of a weary ascent immediately over the old yeoman's hamlet of Pemberton, the horse that dragged us fairly stood still: and so we had to get out and walk; and though we paced over the ground quite leisurely enough, both vehicle and driver were left far behind ere we got to the top of the hill. We paused, and paused, and sauntered on for a few hundred yards at a time, and then paused again and again; and still no omnibus. At length, the driver came puffing up behind us afoot, on the way to Newport Pagnell, he said, for another "hanimal," for his "poor hoss" had foundered on that "cussed hill." My fellow-traveller, the presumed deacon, proved considerably more communicative than his companion the minister. He had, I found, notwithstanding his gravity, some town-bred smartness about him, and was just a little conceited withal; or, I should perhaps rather say, was not quite devoid of what constitutes the great innate impression of the true Englishman, — an impression of his own superiority, simply in virtue of his country, over all and sundry who speak his language with an accent not native to the soil. But I never yet quarrelled with a feeling at once so comfortable and so harmless, and which the Scotch — though in a form less personal as it regards the individual entertaining it, and with an eye more to Scotland in the average — cherish as strongly; and so the Englishman and I agreed during our walk excellently well. He had unluckily left his hat in the vehicle, bringing with him instead, what served as his coach-cap, a pinched Glengary bonnet, which, it must be confessed, looked nearly as much out of place on his head as Captain Knockdunder's cocked hat, trimmed with gold lace, when mounted high over philabeg and plaid, on the head of the redoubted captain. And on nearing the village of Skirvington, he seemed to feel that the bonnet was not the sort of head-dress in which a demure Englishman looked most himself. "It might do well enough for a Scotchman like me," he said, "but not so well for him." I wore, by chance, a tolerably good hat, and proposed making a temporary exchange, until we should have passed the village; but fate declared itself against the transaction. The Englishman's bonnet would have lain, we found, like a coronet upon a cushion on the Scotch head; and the Scotch hat, on the other hand, threatened to swallow up the Englishman. I found myself in error in deeming him an acquaintance of our fellow-traveller the minister: he did not even know his name, and was exceedingly anxious to find it out, — quite fidgety on the point; for he was, he said, a profoundly able man, and, he was certain, a person of note. At the inn at Newport Pagnell, however, he succeeded, I know not how, in ferreting the name out; and whispered into my ear, as we went, that he was assured he was in the right in deeming our companion somebody: the gentleman in black beside us was no other than Dr. ———. But the doctor's name was wholly unfamiliar to me, and I have since forgotten it.

Newport Pagnell! I had but just one association with the place, besides the one formed as I had passed through its streets two evenings before, on the night of riot and clamor: it had been for many years the home of worthy, witty, bluff William Bull, — the honest Independent minister who used so regularly to visit poor Cowper in his affliction, ere Cowper had yet become famous, and whom the affectionate poet learned so cordially to love. How strangely true genius does brighten up whatever object it falls upon! It is, to borrow from Sir Walter's illustration, the playful sunbeam, that, capriciously selecting some little bit of glass or earthen ware in the middle of a ploughed field, renders it visible across half a country, by the light which it pours upon it. An old astronomer, ere the heavens had been filled up with their fantastic signs, — crabs, and fish, and scorpions, bulls and rams, and young ladies, and locks of young ladies' hair, — could give a favorite toy or pet companion a place in the sky; but it is only the true poet who possesses an analogous power now. He can fix whatever bauble his fancy rests upon high in the literary heavens; and no true poet ever exercised the peculiar privilege of his order more sportively than Cowper. He has fixed Mr. Bull's tobacco-box and his pipe amid the signs, and elicited many a smile by setting the honest man a-smoking high up in the moon. But even to the moon his affection followed him, as may be seen from the characteristic passage, glittering, as is Cowper's wont, with an embroidery of playful humor, inwrought into a sad-colored groundwork of melancholy, in which he apostrophizes the worthy minister in his new lodgment. "Mon aimable and très chèr ami, — it is not in the power of chaises or chariots to carry you where my affections will not follow you. If I heard that you were gone to finish your days in the moon, I should not love you the less, but should contemplate the place of your abode as often as it appeared in the heavens, and say, 'Farewell, my friend, forever! Lost, but not forgotten! Live happy in thy lantern, and smoke the remainder of thy pipes in peace. Thou art rid of earth, — at least, of all its cares, — and so far can I rejoice in thy removal; and as to the cares that are to be found in the moon, I am resolved to suppose them lighter than those below, — heavier they can hardly be.'"

Cowper's translations of the better devotional poems of Madame Guion were made at the request of Mr. Bull, who, though himself a Calvinist, was yet so great an admirer of the mystic Frenchwoman, — undoubtedly sincere, though not always judicious, in her devotional aspirations, — that he travelled on one occasion twenty miles to see her picture. He urged him, too, during that portion of partial convalescence in which his greater poetical works were produced, again to betake himself to the composition of original hymns; but it was the hour of the power of darkness, and this second request served but to distress the mind of the suffering poet. He had "no objection," he said, "to giving the graces of the foreigner an English dress," but "insuperable ones to affected exhibitions of what he did not feel." — "Ask possibilities," he adds, "and they shall be performed; but ask no hymns from a man suffering from despair, as I do. I could not sing the Lord's song, were it to save my life, banished as I am, not to a strange land, but to a remoteness from His presence, in comparison with which the distance from east to west is no distance, — is vicinity and cohesion." Alas, poor Cowper! — sorely smitten by the archers, and ever carrying about with him the rankling arrow in the wound. It is not improbable that one of the peculiar doctrines of the Mystics, though it could scarce have approved itself to his judgment, may have yet exercised a soothing influence on the leading delusion of his unhappy malady; and that he may have been all the more an admirer of the writings of Madame Guion, — for a great admirer he was, — in consequence of her pointed and frequent allusion to it It was held by the class of Christians to which she belonged, — among the rest, by Fenelon, — that it would be altogether proper, and not impossible, for the soul to acquiesce in even its own destruction, were it to be God's will that it should be destroyed. We find the idea brought strongly out in one of the poems translated by Cowper; but it is in vain now to inquire respecting the mood of strangely-mingled thought and feeling, — of thought solid and sane, and of acute feeling, quickened by madness, — in which he must have given to it its first embodiment in English verse.

"Yet He leaves me, — cruel fate!
Leaves me in my lost estate.
Have I sinned? O, say wherein;
Tell me, and forgive my sin!
King and Lord, whom I adore,
Shall I see thy face no more?
Be not angry; I resign
Henceforth all my will to thine:
I consent that Thou depart,
Though thine absence breaks my heart.
Go, then, and forever too;
All is right that Thou wilt do."

A mile beyond Skirvington, when we had almost resigned ourselves to the hardship of walking over all the ground which we had bargained for being carried over, we were overtaken by the omnibus drawn by the "fresh hoss." It stopped for a few seconds as we entered Newport Pagnell, to pick up a passenger; and a tall, robust, hard-featured female, of some five-and-forty or so, stepped in. Had we heard, she asked, when adjusting herself with no little bustle in a corner of the conveyance, — had we heard how the great fight had gone? No! — my two companions had not so much as heard that a great fight there had been. "O dear!" exclaimed the robust female, "not heard that Bendigo challenged Caunt for the championship! — ay, and he has beaten him too. Three hundred guineas a-side!" — "Bad work, I am afraid," said the gentleman in black. — "Yes," exclaimed the robust female; "bad work, foul work; give 'em fair play, and Bendigo is no match for Caunt. Hard stiff fellow, though! But there he is!" We looked out in the direction indicated, and saw the champion of all England standing at a public-house door, with a large white patch over one eye, and a deep purple streak under the other. He reminded me exceedingly of Bill Sikes, in the illustrations by Cruikshank of Oliver Twist. For two mortal hours had he stood up, under the broiling sun of the previous day, to knock down, and be knocked down in turn, all in a lather of blood and sweat, and surrounded by a ring of the greatest scoundrels in the kingdom. And the ninety-third round had determined him the best man of two, and the champion of all England. I felt convinced, however, like the old king in the ballad, that England holds

> "Within its realme,
> Five hundred as good as hee."

There had been sad doings in the neighborhood, — not a little thieving in the houses, several robberies on the highway, and much pocket-picking among the crowds; in short, as the reporter of a sporting paper, "The Era," who seemed to have got bitten somehow, summed up his notice of the fight,— "had the crowds brought together been transported *en masse* to Botany Bay, they would have breathed forth such a moral pestilence as would have infected the atmosphere of the place. Pugilism has been described as one of the manifestations of English character and manners. I suspect, however, that in the present day it manifests nothing higher than the unmitigated blackguardism of England's lowest and most disreputable men. Regarding the English *ladies* who take an interest in it, I must of course venture nothing untender; indeed, I saw but a single specimen of the class, and that for but twenty minutes or so, for the robust female left us at the first stage.

A pugilist, notwithstanding his pugilism, may be, I doubt not, a brave fellow; the *bottom* he displays is, in most instances, the identical quality which, in the desperate tug of war, so distinguishes, over all the other troops of Europe, the British soldier. But the "science of defence" can have in itself no tendency either to strengthen native courage, or to supply the want of it. It must take its place rather among those artificial means of inspiring confidence, that, like the bladders of the swimmer, serve but to induce a state of prostration and helplessness when they unexpectedly give way; and can be but an indifferent preparation for meeting full in front the bayonet-point that breaks in upon its guards, or the whizzing bullet that beats them down. I have been told by an aged relative, now deceased, who saw much service, that in the first great naval battle in which he was engaged, and the first great storm he experienced, there were two men — one in each instance — whose cowardice was palpable and apparent to the whole crew, and who agreed so far in character, that each was the champion pugilist and bully of his vessel. The dastard in the engagement — that of Camperdown — was detected coiling up his craven bulk in a place of concealment, out of reach of the shot: the dastard in the storm was rendered, by the extremeness of his terror, unfit for duty. The vessel in which my relative sailed at the time — the same relative who afterwards picked up the curious shell amid the whistling of the bullets in Egypt — was one of those old-fashioned, iron-fastened ships of the line that, previous to the breaking out of the first revolutionary war, had been lying in dock for years, and that, carefully kept, so far at least as externals were concerned, looked extremely well when first sent to sea, but proved miserable weather-boats amid the straining of a gale, when their stiff rusty bolting began to slacken and work out. The gale, in this especial instance, proved a very tremendous one; and the *old* Magnificent went scudding before it, far into the Northern Ocean, under bare poles. She began to open in the joints and seams like a piece of basket-work; and though the pumps were plied incessantly by half-hour relays, the water rose fast within the hold, and she threatened to settle down. My relative was stationed in the well-room during one of the night-watches, just as the tempest had reached its crisis, to take note of the state of the leakage; and a man came round every quarter of an hour to receive his report. The water, dimly visible by the lantern of horn, rose fast along the gauge, covering, inch after inch, four feet and a half, — four feet nine, — five feet, — five feet three, — five feet and a half: the customary quarter of an hour had long elapsed, yet no one appeared to report; and the solitary watcher, wondering at the delay, raised the little hatch directly above head, and stepped out upon the orlop, to represent the state of matters below. Directly over the opening, a picture of cold, yellow terror, petrifying into stone, stood the cowed bruiser, with a lantern dangling idly from his finger points. "What make you here?" asked my relative.—"Come to report." — "Report! is that reporting?" — "O!! — how many feet water?" — "Five and a half." — "Five feet and a half!" exclaimed the unnerved bully, striking his hands together, and letting his lantern fall into the open hatch, — "Five feet and a half! Gracious heaven! it's all over with us!" Nothing, I have oftener than once heard my relative remark, so strongly impressed him, during the terrors of the gale, as the dread-impressed features and fear-modulated tones of that unhappy man.

CHAPTER XVII.

Cowper and the Geologists. — Geology in the Poet's Days in a State of great Immaturity. — Case different now. — Folly of committing the Bible to a False Science. — Galileo. — Geologists at one in all their more important Deductions; vast Antiquity of the Earth one of these. — State of the Question. — Illustration. — Presumed Thickness of the Fossiliferous Strata. — Peculiar Order of their Organic Contents; of their Fossil Fish in particular, as ascertained by Agassiz. — The Geologic Races of Animals entirely different from those which sheltered with Noah in the Ark. — Alleged Discrepancy between Geologic Fact and the Mosaic Record not real. — Inference based on the opening Verses of the Book of Genesis. — Parallel Passage adduced to prove the Inference unsound. — The Supposition that Fossils may have been created such examined: unworthy of the Divine Wisdom; contrary to the Principles which regulate Human Belief; subversive of the grand Argument founded on Design. — The profounder Theologians of the Day not Anti-Geologists. — Geologic Fact in reality of a kind fitted to perform important Work in the two Theologies, Natural and Revealed; subversive of the "Infinite-Series" Argument of the Atheist; subversive, too, of the Objection drawn by Infidelity from an Astronomical Analogy. — Counter-objection. — Illustration.

It may have been merely the effect of an engrossing study long prosecuted, but so it was, that of all I had witnessed amid the scenes rendered classic by the muse of Cowper, nothing more permanently impressed me than a few broken fossils of the Oolite which I had picked up immediately opposite the poet's windows. There had they lain, as carelessly indifferent to the strictures in "The Task," as the sun in the central heavens, two centuries before, to the denunciations of the Inquisition. Geology, however, in the days of Cowper had not attained to the dignity of a science. It lacked solid footing as it journeyed amid the wastes of Chaos; and now tipped, as with its toe-points, a "crude consistence" of ill-understood facts, and now rose aloft into an atmosphere of obscure conjecture, on a "tumultuous cloud" of ill-digested theory. In a science in this unformed, rudimental stage, whether it deal with the stars of heaven or the strata of the earth, the old anarch of Infidelity is sure always to effect a transitory lodgment; and beside him stand his auxiliaries,

> "Rumor, and Chance,
> And Tumult, and Confusion, all embroiled,
> And Discord with a thousand various mouths."

And so it is in no degree derogatory to the excellent sense of Cowper, that he should have striven to bring Revelation in direct antithetical collision with the inferences of the geologists.

There exists, however, no such apology for the Dean Cockburns and London "Records" of the present day. Geology, though still a youthful science, is no longer an immature one: it has got firm footing on a continent of fact; and the man who labors to set the doctrines of Revelation in array against its legitimate deductions, is employed, whatever may be his own estimate of his vocation, not on the side of religious truth, but of scepticism and infidelity. His actual work, however excellent his proposed object, is identically that of all the shrewder infidels, — the Humes, Volneys, Voltaires, and Bolingbrokes, — who have compassed sea and land, and pressed every element into their service, in attempting to show that the facts and doctrines of the Bible traverse those great fixed laws which regulate human belief. No scientific question was ever yet settled dogmatically, or ever will. If the question be one in the science of numbers, it must be settled arithmetically; if in the science of geometry, it must be settled mathematically; if in the science of chemistry, it must be settled experimentally. The

Church of Rome strove hard, in the days of Galileo, to settle an astronomical question theologically; and did its utmost to commit the Bible to the belief that the earth occupies a central position in the system, and that the sun performs a daily revolution around it: but the astronomical question, maugre the Inquisition, refused to be settled other than astronomically. And all now believe that the central position is occupied, not by the earth, but by the sun; and that it is the lesser body that moves round the larger, — not the larger that moves round the lesser. What would have been the result, had Rome, backed by the Franciscan, succeeded in pledging the verity of Scripture to a false astronomy? The astronomical facts of the case would have, of course, remained unchanged. The severe truth of geometry would have lent its demonstrative aid to establish their real character. All the higher minds would have become convinced for themselves, and the great bulk of the lower, at second hand, that the Scripture pledge had been given, not to scientific truth, but to scientific error; and the Bible, *to the extent to which it stood committed*, would be justly regarded as occupying no higher a level than the Shaster or Koran. Infidelity never yet succeeded in placing Revelation in a position so essentially false as that in which it was placed by Rome, to the extent of Rome's ability, in the case of Galileo.

Now, ultimately at least, as men have yielded to astronomy the right of decision in all astronomical questions, must they resign to geology the settlement of all geological ones. I do not merely speak of what *ought*, but of what assuredly *must* and will be. The successive geologic systems and formations, with all their organic contents, are as real existences as the sun itself; and it is quite as possible to demonstrate their true place and position, relative and absolute. And so long as certain fixed laws control and regulate human belief, certain inevitable deductions must and will continue to be based on the facts which these systems and formations furnish. Geologists of the higher order differ among themselves, on certain minutiæ of their science, to nearly as great an extent as the Episcopalian differs in matters ecclesiastical from the Presbyterian, or the Baptist or Independent from both. But their differences militate no more against the great conclusions in which they all agree, than the theological differences of the Protestant churches against the credibility of those leading truths of Christianity on which all true churches are united. And one of these great conclusions respects the incalculably vast antiquity of the earth on which we dwell. It seems scarce possible to over-estimate the force and weight of the evidence already expiscated on this point; and almost every new discovery adds to its cogency and amount. That sectional thickness of the earth's crust in which, mile beneath mile, the sedimentary strata are divided into many-colored and variously-composed systems and formations, and which abounds from top to bottom in organic remains, forms but the mere pages of the register. And it is rather the nature and order of the entries with which these pages are crowded, than the amazing greatness of their number, or the enormous extent of the space which they occupy (rather more than five miles), — though both have, of course, their weight, — that compel belief in the remoteness of the period to which the record extends. Let me attempt elucidating the point by a simple illustration.

In a well-kept English register, continuous from a distant antiquity to the present time, there are many marks demonstrative of the remoteness of the era to which it reaches, besides the bulk and number of the volumes which compose it, and the multitude of the entries which they contain. In an earlier volume we find the ancient Saxon character united to that somewhat meagre yet not inexpressive language in which Alfred wrote and conversed. In a succeeding volume, the Saxon, both in word and letter, gives place to Norman French. The Norman French yields, in turn, in a yet succeeding one, to a massive black-letter character, and an antique combination of both tongues, which we term the genuine old English. And then, in after volumes, the old English gradually modernizes and improves, till we recognize it as no longer old: we see, too, the heavy black-letter succeeded by the lighter Italian hand, at first doggedly stiff and upright, but anon bent elegantly forward along the line. And in these various successions of character and language we recognize the marks of a genuine antiquity. Nor, in passing from these, — the mere externals of the register, — to the register itself, are the evidences less conclusive. In reading upwards, we find the existing families of the district preceded by families now extinct, and these, in turn, by families which had become extinct at earlier and still earlier periods. Names disappear, — titles alter, — the boundaries of lands vary as the proprietors change, — smaller estates are now absorbed by larger, and now larger divide into smaller. There are traces not a few of customs long abrogated and manners become obsolete; and we see paroxysms of local revolution indicated by a marked grouping of events of corresponding character, that assume peculiar force and significancy when we collate the record with the general history of the kingdom. Could it be possible, I ask, to believe, regarding such a many-volumed register, — with all its various styles, characters, and languages, — its histories of the rise and fall of families, and its records of conquests, settlements, and revolutions, — that it had been all hastily written at a heat on a Saturday night, some three or four weeks ago, without any intention to deceive on the part of the writer, — nay, without any intention even of making a register at all? The mere bulk and number of the volumes would militate sadly against any such supposition; but the peculiar character and order of their contents would militate against it more powerfully still.

Now, the geologic register far excels any human record, in the number and significancy of the marks of a strictly analogous cast which demonstrate its vast antiquity. As we ascend higher, and yet higher, the characters of the document strangely alter. In the Tertiary ages we find an evident approximation to the existing style. An entire change takes place as we enter the Secondary period. A change equally marked characterizes the Palæozoic eras. Up till the commencement of the Cretaceous system, two great orders of fish, — the *Ctenoid* and *Cycloid*, — fish furnished with horny scales and bony skeletons, — comprise, as they now do, the great bulk of the finny inhabitants of the waters. But immediately beyond the Cretaceous group these two orders wholly disappear, and the *Ganoid* and *Placoid* orders — fish that wear an armature of bone outside, and whose skeletons are chiefly cartilaginous — take their places. Up till the period of the Magnesian Limestone, the *homocercal* or two-lobed type of fish-tail greatly preponderates, as at the present time; but in all the older formations, — those of the immensely extended Palæozoic period, — not a single tail of this comparatively modern type is to be found, and the *heterocercal* or one-sided tail obtains exclusively. Down till the deposition of the Chalk has taken place, all the true woods are coniferæ of the Pine or Araucarian families. After the Chalk has been deposited, hard-wood trees, of the dicotyledonous order, are largely introduced. Down till the times of the Magnesian Limestone, plants of an inferior order — ferns, stigmaria, club-mosses, and calamites — attain to a size so gigantic that they rival the true denizens of the forest whereas with the dawn of the Secondary period we find the immaturities of the vegetable kingdom reduced to a bulk and size that consort better with the palpable inferiority of their rank in creation. And not only are the styles and characters of the several periods of the geologic register thus various, but, as in the English register of my illustration, the record of the rise and fall of septs and families is singularly distinct. The dynasties of the crustacean, the fish, the reptile, and the mammiferous quadruped, succeed each other in an order as definite as the four great empires in the "Ancient History" of Rollin. Nor are the periods when single families arose and sank less carefully noted. The trilobite family came into existence with the first beginnings of the Palæozoic division, and ceased at its close. The belemnite family began and became extinct with the Secondary formations. The ammonite and gryphite, in all their many species, did not outlive the deposition of the Chalk. There is one definite period, — the close of the Palæozoic era, — at which the Brachiopoda, singularly numerous throughout many previous formations, and consisting of many great families, suddenly, with the exception of a single genus, drop off and disappear. There is another definite period, — the close of the Secondary era, — at which the Cephalopoda, with nearly as few exceptions, disappear as suddenly. At this latter period, too, the Enaliosaurians, so long the monster tyrants of the ocean, cease forever, and the Cetacea take their places: the be-paddled reptiles go off the stage, and the be-paddled mammalia come on. But perhaps the most striking series of facts of this nature in the whole range of geological literature, is that embodied in the table affixed by Agassiz to his great work on fossil fish.

This singularly interesting document — which, like the annual balance-sheet of a great mercantile house or banking company, that comprises in its comparatively few lines of figures the result of every arithmetical calculation made by the firm during the twelvemonth — condenses, in a single page, the results of the naturalist's observations in his own peculiar department for many years. It marks at what periods the great families of the extinct fishes began, and when they ceased, and at what periods those great families arose which continue to exist in the present state of things. The facts are exceedingly curious. Some of the families are, we find, of comparatively brief standing, and occupy but small space in the record, — others sweep across well-nigh the whole geological scale. Some come into existence with the beginning of a system, and cease at its close, — others continue to exist throughout almost all the systems together. The salmon and herring families, though the species were different, lived in the ages of the Chalk, and ever since, throughout the periods of the Tertiary; while the cod and haddock family pertains, on the contrary, to but the existing scene of things. The *Cephalaspides* — that family to which the *Pterichthys* and *Coccosteus* belong — were restricted to a single system, the Old Red Sandstone; nor had its contemporaries the *Dipterians* — that family to which the *Osteolepis* and *Diplopterus* belong — a longer term; whereas the *Cœlacanthes*, — the family of the *Holoptychius*, *Glyptolepis*, and *Asterolepis*, — while it began as early, passed down to the times of the Chalk, — and the *Cestracions* — even a more ancient family still — continue to have their living representatives. It is held by the Dean of York that the fact of the Noachian Deluge may be made satisfactorily to account for all the geologic phenomena. Alas! No cataclysm, however great or general, could have produced diversities of style, each restricted to a determinate period, and which become more broadly apparent the more carefully we collate the geologic register as it exists in one country with the same register as it exists in another. No cataclysm could have arranged an infinitude of entries in exact chronological order, or assigned to the tribes and families which it destroyed and interred distinct consecutive periods and formations. It is but common sense to hold that the Deluge could not have produced an ancient church-yard, — such as the Grayfriars of Edinburgh, — with its series of tombstones in all their successive styles, — Gothic, Elizabethan, Roman, and Grecian, — complete for many centuries. It could not have been the author of the old English register of my illustration. Geologists affirm regarding the Flood, merely to the effect that it could not have written Hume's History of England, nor even composed and set into type Mr. Burke's British Peerage.

Such are a few of the difficulties with which the anti-geologist has to contend. That leading fact of the Deluge, — the ark, — taken in connection with the leading geologic fact that the organic remains of the various systems, from the Lower Silurian to the Chalk inclusive, are the remains of extinct races and tribes, forms a difficulty of another kind. The fact of the ark satisfactorily shows that man in his present state has been contemporary with but one creation. The preservation by sevens and by pairs of the identical races amid which he first started into existence superseded the necessity of a creation after the Flood; and so it is the same tribes of animals, wild and domestic, which share with him in his place of habitation now, that surrounded him in Paradise. But the Palæozoic, Secondary, and older Tertiary animals, are of races and tribes altogether diverse. We find among them not even a single species which sheltered in the ark. The races contemporary with man were preserved to bear him company in his pilgrimage, and to minister to his necessities; but those strange races, buried, in many instances, whole miles beneath the surface, and never seen save imbedded in rock and transformed into stone, could not have been his contemporaries. They belong, as their place and appearance demonstrate, to periods long anterior. Nor can it be rationally held, that of those anterior periods revelation should have given us any history. They lie palpably beyond the scope of the sacred record. On what principle, seeing it is silent on the contemporary creations of Mars, Venus, and Jupiter, ought it to have spoken on the consecutive creations of the Silurian, Carboniferous, and Oolitic periods? Why should it promulgate the truths of Geology, seeing that those of Astronomy it has withheld? Man everywhere has entertained the expectation of a book, Heaven-inspired, that should teach him what God is, and what God demands of him. The sacred books of all the false religions, from those of Zoroaster and the Brahmins to those of Mahomet and the Mormons, are just so many evidences that the expectation exists. And the Bible is its fulfilment. But man has entertained no such expectation of a revelation from God of the truths of science; nor is it according to the economy of Providence, — the economy manifested in the slow and gradual development of the species, — that any such expectation should be realized. The "Principia" of Newton is an uninspired volume; and only the natural faculties were engaged in the discovery of James Watt.

But it is not urged, it may be said, that the Scriptures reveal geologic truth as such; it is merely urged that geologists must not traverse Scripture statements respecting the age of the earth, as revealed for purely religious purposes by God to Moses. But *did* God reveal the earth's age to Moses? Not directly, surely, or else men equally sound in the faith would not be found lengthening or shortening the brief period which intervenes between Adan and Abraham, just as they adopt the Hebrew or Septuagint chronology, by nearly a thousand years. Here, however, it may be said that we are in doubt regarding the real chronology, not because God has not *indirectly* revealed it, but because man, in either the Hebrew or Samaritan record, has vitiated the revelation. Most true: still, however, the doubt *is* doubt. But did God reveal the earth's *age*, either directly or otherwise? Let us examine the narrative. "In the beginning God created the heaven and the earth. And the earth was without form and void; and darkness was upon the face of the deep. And the Spirit of God moved upon the face of the waters. And God said, Let there be light, and there was light." Now, let it be admitted, for the argument's sake, that the earth existed in the dark and void state described here only six days, *of twenty-four hours each*, before the creation of man; and that the going forth of the Spirit and the breaking out of the light, on this occasion, were events immediately introductory to the creation to which we ourselves belong. And what then? It is evident, from the continuity of the narrative in the passage, say the anti-geologists, that there could have been no creations on this earth prior to the present one. Nay, not so: for aught that appears in the narrative, there might have been many. Between the creation of the matter of which the earth is composed, as enunciated in the first verse, and the earth's void and chaotic state, as described in the second, a *thousand* creations might have intervened. As may be demonstrated from even the writings of Moses himself, the continuity of a narrative furnishes no evidence whatever that the facts which it records were continuous.

Take, for instance, the following passage. "There went out a man of the house of Levi, and took to wife a daughter of Levi. And the woman conceived and bare a son; and when she saw him that he was a goodly child, she hid him three months. And when she could not longer hide him, she took for him an ark of bulrushes, and daubed it with slime and with pitch, and put the child therein; and she laid it in the flags by the river's brink."* The narrative here is quite as continuous as in the first three verses of Genesis. In the order of the relation, the marriage of the parents is as directly followed in the one case by the birth of a son, as the creation of matter is followed in the other by the first beginnings of the existing state of things. The reader has as slight grounds to infer, in the one case, that between the marriage of the parents and the birth of the child the births of several other children of the family had taken place, as to infer, in the other, that between the creation of matter and the subsisting creation there had taken place several other creations. And if the continuity of the narrative would not justify the inference in the one case, just as little can it justify it in the other. We know, however, from succeeding portions of Scripture, that the father and mother of this child *had* several other children born to them in the period that intervened between their marriage and his birth. They had a son named Aaron, who had been born at least two years previous; and a daughter, Miriam, who was old enough at the time to keep sedulous watch over the little ark of bulrushes, and to suggest to Pharaoh's daughter that it might be well for her to go and call one of the Hebrew women

*I owe this passage, in its bearing on the opening narrative in Genesis, to the Rev. Alexander Stewart, of Cromarty, — for fifteen years my parish minister, and one of decidedly the most original-minded men and most accomplished theologians his country has ever produced. And he, I may add, like all careful students of Scripture of the higher calibre, can see no irreconcilable difference between Bible truth and the great facts of the geologist.

to be nurse to the child. It was essential, in the course of Scripture narrative, that we should be introduced to personages so famous as Aaron and Miriam, and who were destined to enact parts so important in the history of the Church; and so we *have* been introduced to them. And had it been as necessary for the purposes of revelation that reference should have been made to the intervening creations in the one case, as to the intervening births in the other, we would doubtless have heard of them too. But, as has been already said, it was not so necessary; it was not necessary at all. The ferns and lepidodendra of the Coal Measures are as little connected with the truths which influence our spiritual state, as the vegetable productions of Mercury or of Pallas; the birds and reptiles of the Oolite, as the unknown animals that inhabit the plains or disport in the rivers of Saturn or Uranus. And so revelation is as silent on the geological phenomena as on the contemporary creations, — on the periods and order of systems and formations, as on the relative positions of the earth and sun, or the places and magnitudes of the planets.

But organic remains may, it is urged, have been created such; and the special miracle through which the gourd of Jonah, though it must have seemed months old, sprung up in a single night, and the general miracle through which the trees of Paradise must have appeared, even on the first evening of their creation, half a century old, have been adduced to show that the globe, notwithstanding its marks of extreme antiquity, may have been produced with all these marks stamped upon it, as if in the mint. "The very day when the ocean dashed its first waves on the shore," says Chateaubriand, "it bathed, let us not doubt, rocks already worn by the breakers, and beaches strewn with the wrecks of shells." — "For aught that appears in the bowels of the earth," said the "Record" newspaper, some two years ago, in adopting this peculiar view, as expressed by a worthy Presbyterian minister, "the world might have been called into existence yesterday." Let us just try whether, as creatures to whom God has given reason, and who cannot acquire facts without drawing inferences, we can believe the assertion; and ascertain how much this curious principle of explaining geologic fact actually involves.

"The earth, for anything that appears to the contrary, may have been made yesterday!" We stand in the middle of an ancient burying-ground in a northern district. The monuments of the dead, lichened and gray, rise thick around us; and there are fragments of mouldering bones lying scattered amid the loose dust that rests under them, in dark recesses impervious to the rain and the sunshine. We dig into the soil below: here is a human skull, and there numerous other well-known bones of the human skeleton, — vertebræ, ribs, arm and leg bones, with the bones of the breast and pelvis. Still, as we dig, the bony mass accumulates; — we disinter portions, not of one, but of many skeletons, some comparatively fresh, some in a state of great decay; and with the bones there mingle fragments of coffins, with the wasted tinsel-mounting in some instances still attached, and the rusted nails still sticking in the joints. We continue to dig, and, at a depth to which the sexton almost never penetrates, find a stratum of pure sea-sand, and then a stratum of the sea-shells common on the neighboring coast, — in especial, oyster, muscle, and cockle shells. It may be mentioned, in the passing, that the churchyard to which I refer, though at some little distance from the sea, is situated on one of the raised beaches of the north of Scotland; and hence the shells. We dig a little further, and reach a thick bed of sandstone, which we penetrate, and beneath which we find a bed of impure lime, richly charged with the remains of fish of strangely antique forms. "The earth, for anything that appears to the contrary, might have been made yesterday!" Do appearances such as these warrant the inference? Do these human skeletons, in all their various stages of decay, appear as if *they* had been made yesterday? Was that bit of coffin, with the soiled tinsel on the one side, and the corroded nail sticking out of the other, made yesterday? Was yonder skull, instead of having ever formed part of a human head, created yesterday, exactly the repulsive-looking sort of thing we see it? Indisputably not. Such is the nature of the human mind, — such the laws that regulate and control human belief, — that in the very existence of that churchyard we do and must recognize positive proof that the world was *not* made yesterday.

But can we stop in our process of inference at the mouldering remains of the churchyard? Can we hold that the skull was not created a mere skull, and yet hold that the oyster, muscle, and cockle shells beneath are not the remains of molluscous animals, but things originally created in exactly their present state, as empty shells? The supposition is altogether absurd. Such is the constitution of our minds, that we must as certainly hold yonder oyster-shell to have once formed part of a mollusc, as we hold yonder skull to have once formed part of a man. And if we cannot stop at the skeleton, how stop at the shells? Why not pass on to the fish? The evidence of design is quite as irresistible in them as in the human or the molluscous remains above. We can still see the scales which covered them occupying their proper places, with all their nicely-designed bars, hooks, and nails of attachment. the fins which propelled them through the water, with the multitudinous pseudo-joints, formed to impart to the rays the proper elasticity, lie widely spread on the stone; the sharp-pointed teeth, constructed like those of fish generally, rather for the purpose of holding fast slippery substances than of mastication, still bristle in their jaws; nay, the very plates, spines, and scales of the fish on which they had fed, still lie undigested in their abdomens. We cannot stop short at the shells: if the human skull was not created a mere skull, nor the shell a mere dead shell, then the fossil fish could not have been created a mere fossil. There is no broken link in the chain at which to take our stand; and yet, having once recognized the fishes as such, — having recognized them as the remains of animals, and not as stones that exist in their original state, — we stand committed to all the organisms of the geological scale.

But we limit the Divine power, it may be said: could not the Omnipotent First Cause have created all the fossils of the earth, vegetable and animal, in their fossil state? Yes, certainly; the act of their creation, regarded simply as an act of power, does not and cannot transcend his infinite ability. He could have created all the burying-grounds of the earth, with all their broken and wasted contents, brute and human. He could have created all the mummies of Mexico and of Egypt as such, and all the skeletons of the catacombs of Paris. It would manifest, however, but little reverence for his character to compliment his infinite power at the expense of his infinite wisdom. It would be doing no honor to his name to regard him as a creator of dead skeletons, mummies, and church-yards. Nay, we could not recognize him as such, without giving to the winds all those principles of common reason which in his goodness he has imparted to us for our guidance in the ordinary affairs of life. In this, as in that higher sense adduced by our Saviour, "God is not the God of the dead, but of the living." In the celebrated case of Eugene Aram, the skeleton of his victim, the murdered Clark, was found in a cave; but how, asked the criminal, in his singularly ingenious and eloquent defence, could that skeleton be known to be Clark's? The cave, he argued, had once been a hermitage; and in times past hermitages had been places not only of religious retirement, but of burial also. "And it has scarce or ever been heard of," he continued, "but that every cell now known contains or contained those relics of humanity, — some mutilated, some entire. Give me leave to remind the Court that here sat solitary sanctity, and here the hermit and the anchorite hoped that repose for their bones when dead, they here enjoyed when living. Every place conceals such remains. In fields, on hills, on highway sides, on wastes, on commons, lie frequent and unsuspected bones. But must some of the living be made answerable for all the bones that earth has concealed and chance exposed?" Such were the reasonings, on this count, of Eugene Aram; and it behooved the jury that sat upon him in judgment to bestow upon them their careful consideration. But how very different might not his line of argument have been, had the conclusions of the anti-geologist squared with the principles of human belief! If the fossil exuviæ of a fish, or the fossil skeleton of a reptile, may have never belonged to either a reptile or a fish, then the skeleton of a man may have never belonged to a man. No more could be argued, Aram might have said, from the finding of a human skeleton in the floor of a cave, than from the finding of a pebble or a piece of rock in the floor of a cave. So far from being justified in inferring from it that a murder had been perpetrated, a jury could not have so much as inferred from it that a human creature had existed.

Is the anti-geologist, I would fain ask, prepared to give up the great argument founded on design, as asserted and illustrated by all the master-minds who have written on the

Evidences? Is he resolved, in the vain hope of bearing down the geologist, to make a full surrender to the infidel? Let us mark how Paley's well-known illustration of the watch found on the moor would apply in this controversy. From the design exhibited in the construction of the watch, the existence of a designer is inferred; whereas, from a stone found on the same moor, in which no such marks of design are apparent, the Archdeacon urges that no such inference regarding the existence of a designer could be drawn. But what would be thought of the man who could assert that the watch, with all its seeming design, was not a watch, but a stone; and that, notwithstanding its spring, its wheels, and its index, it had never been intended to measure time? What could be said of a sturdily avowed belief in a *design* not *designed*, and not the work of a *designer*, — in a watch furnished with all the parts of a watch, that is, notwithstanding, a mere stone, and occupies just its proper place when lying among the other stones of a moor? What could be said of such a belief, paraded not simply *as* a belief, but actually as of the *nature of reasoning*, and fitted to bear weight in controversy? And yet, such is the position of the anti-geologist, who sees in the earth, with all its fossils, no evidence that it might not have been created yesterday. For obvious it is, that in whatever has been designed, fitness of parts bears reference to the purposed object which the design subserves; and that if there be no purposed object, there can exist no fitness of parts in relation to it, and, in reality, no design. The *analogy* drawn in the case from the miracle of creation is no analogy at all. It is not *contrary* to the laws which control human belief, that the first races of every succeeding creation should have been called into existence in a state of full development; nay, it is in palpable and harmonious *accordance* with these laws. It is necessary that the anima which had no parents to care or provide for it should come into existence in a state of maturity sufficient to enable it to care and provide for itself; it is equally necessary that the contemporary vegetable, its food, should be created in a condition that fitted it for *being* food. Had the first man and first woman been created mere infants, they would, humanly speaking, have shared the fate of the "babes in the wood." Had the productions of the vegetable kingdom been created in an analogous state of immaturity, "the horse," to borrow from an old proverb, "would have died when the grass was growing." But *it is* contrary to the laws which control human belief, that the all-wise Creator should be a maker of churchyards full of the broken debris of carcasses,—of skeletons never purposed to compose the framework of animals, — of watches never intended to do aught than perform the part of stones.*

* In the pages of no writer is the argument drawn from the miracle of creation — if argument it may be termed — at once so ingeniously asserted and so exquisitely adorned, as in the pages of Chateaubriand. The passage is comparatively little known in this country, and so I quote it entire from the translation of a friend.

"We approach the last objection concerning the modern origin of the globe. 'The earth,' it is said, 'is an old nurse, whose decrepitude everything announces. Examine its fossils, its marbles, its granites, and you will decipher its innumerable years, marked by circle, by stratum, or by branch, like those of the serpent by his rattles, the horse by his teeth, or the stag by his horns.'

"This difficulty has been a hundred times solved by this answer, — 'God *should* have created, and without question has created, the world, with all the marks of antiquity and completeness which we now see.'

"Indeed, it is probable that the Author of nature at first planted old forests and young shoots, — that animals were produced, some full of days, others adorned with all the graces of infancy. Oaks, as they pierced the fruitful soil, would bear at once the forsaken nest of the crow and the young posterity of the dove; the caterpillar was chrysalis and butterfly; the insect, fed on the herb, suspended its golden egg amid the forests, or trembled in the wavy air; the bee which had lived but a single morning

I confess it grieves me more than if Puseyism were the offender, to see a paper such as the London "Record,"— the organ of no inconsiderable section of the Evangelical Episco-

reckoned its ambrosia by generations of flowers. We must believe that the sheep was not without its young, the fawn without its little ones,— that the thickets hid nightingales, astonished with their own first music, in warming the fleeting hopes of their first loves. If the world had not been at once young and old, the grand, the serious, the moral, would disappear from nature; for these sentiments belong essentially to the antique. Every scene would have lost its wonders. The ruined rock could not have hung over the abyss; the woods, despoiled of every chance appearance, would not have displayed that touching disorder of trees bending over their roots, and of trunks leaning over the courses of the rivers. Inspired thoughts, venerable sounds, magic voices, the sacred gloom of forests, would vanish with the vaults which served them for retreats; and the solitudes of heaven and earth would remain naked and disenchanted, in losing those columns of oak which unite them. The very day when the ocean dashed its first waves on the shores, it bathed—let us not doubt—rocks already worn by the breakers, beaches strewn with the wrecks of shells, and headlands which sustained against the assaults of the waters the crumbling shores of earth. Without this inherent old age, there would have been neither pomp nor majesty in the work of the Eternal; and, what could not possibly be, nature in its innocence would have been less beautiful than it is to-day amid its corruption. An insipid infancy of plants, animals, and elements, would have crowned a world without poetry. But God was not so tasteless a designer of the bowers of Eden as infidels pretend. The man king was himself born thirty years old, in order to accord in his majesty with the ancient grandeur of his new kingdom; and his companion reckoned sixteen springs which she had not lived, that she might harmonize with flowers, birds, innocence, love, and all the youthful part of the creation."

This is unquestionably fine writing, and it contains a considerable amount of general truth. But not a particle of the true does it contain in connection with the one point which the writer sets himself to establish. There exists, as has been shown, a reason, palpable in the nature of things, why creation, in even its earliest dawn, should not have exhibited an insipid infancy of plants and animals; the animals, otherwise, could not have survived, and thus the great end of creation would have been defeated. But though there exists an obvious reason for the creation of ɿacy of England, — committing itse.f to the anti-geologists on this question. At the meeting of the British Association which

the full-grown and the mature, there exists no reason whatever for the creation of the ruined and the broken. It is a very indifferent argument to allege that the poetic sentiment demanded the production of fractured shells on the shores, or of deserted crows' nests in the trees. If sentiment demanded the creation of broken shells that had never belonged to molluscous animals, how much more imperatively must it have demanded the creation of broken human skeletons that had never belonged to men! or, if it rendered necessary the creation of deserted crows' nests, how much more urgent the necessity for the creation of deserted palaces and temples, sublime in their solitude, or of desolate cities partially buried in the sands of the desert! There is a vast deal more of poetry in the ancient sepulchres of Thebes and of Luxor, with their silent millions of the em balmed dead, than in the comminuted shells of sea-beaches; and in Palmyra and the pyramids, than in deserted crows' nests. Nor would the creation of the one class of productions be in any degree less probable, or less according to the principles of human belief, than the other. And mark the inevitable effects on human conduct! The man who honestly held with Chateaubriand in this passage, and was consistent in following out to their legitimate consequences the tenets which it embodies, could not sit as a juryman in either a coroner's inquest or a trial for murder, conducted on circumstantial evidence. If he held that an old crow's nest might have been called into existence as such, how could he avoid holding that an ancient human dwelling might not have been called into existence as such? If he held that a broken patella or whelk-shell might have been created a broken shell, how could he avoid holding that a human skull, fractured like that of the murdered Clark, might not have been created a broken skull? To him Paley's watch, picked up on a moor, could not appear as other than merely a curious stone, charged with no evidence, in the peculiarity of its construction, that it had been intended to measure time. The entire passage is eminently characteristic of that magnificent work of imagination, "The Genius of Christianity," in which Chateaubriand sets himself to reconvert to Romanism the infidelity of France. He ever attempts dealing by the reasoning faculty in his countrymen, as the Philistines of old dealt by the Jewish champion: instead of meeting it in the open field, and with the legitimate weapons, he sends forth the exquisitely beautiful Delilah of his fancy to cajole and set it asleep, and then bind it as with green withes.

held at York in 1844, the puerilities of Dean Cockburn were happily met with and exposed by the Rev. Mr. Sedgwick; and it was on that occasion that the "Record," after pronouncing it no slight satire on this accomplished man of science, that one of the members present should have eulogized his "boldness as a clergyman," adopted the assertion, — can it be called belief? — that for aught which appears to the contrary, "the world might have been made yesterday." Attempts to support the true in religion by the untrue in science, manifest, I am afraid, exceedingly little wisdom. False witnesses, when engaged in just causes, serve but to injure them; and certainly neither by anti-geologists nor at the Old Bailey should "kissing the book" be made a preliminary to supporting the untrue. I do not find that the truly great theologians of the day manifest any uneasy jealousy of geological discovery. Geologists, expatiating in their proper province, have found nothing antagonistic in the massive intellect and iron logic of Dr. Cunningham, of Edinburgh, nor in the quick comprehensiveness and elastic vigor of Dr. Candlish. Chalmers has already given his deliverance on this science, — need it be said after what manner? — and in a recent number of the "North British Review" may be found the decision regarding it of a kindred spirit, the author of the "Natural History of Enthusiasm." "The reader," says this distinguished man, in adverting to certain influential causes that in the present day widely affect theologic opinion and the devotional feeling, "will know that we here refer to that indirect modification of religious notions and sentiments, that results insensibly from the spread and consolidation of the modern sister sciences, Astronomy and Geology, which, immeasurably enlarging, as they do, our conceptions of the universe in its two elements of space and time, expel a congeries of narrow errors, heretofore regarded as unquestionable truths, and open before us at once a Chart and a History of the Dominions of Infinite Power and Wisdom. We shall hasten to exclude the supposition," he continues, "that, in thus mentioning the relation of the modern sciences to Christianity we are thinking of anything so small and incidental as are the alleged discrepancies between the terms of Biblical history, in certain instances, and the positive evidence of science. All such discordances, whether real or apparent, will find the proper means of adjustment readily and finally in due time. We have no anxieties on the subject. Men 'easily shaken in mind' will rid themselves of the atoms of faith which perhaps they once possessed, by the means of 'difficulties' such as these. But it is not from causes so superficial that serious danger to the faith of a people is to be apprehended." The passages which follow this very significant one are eminently beautiful and instructive; but enough is here given to indicate the judgment of the writer on the point at issue.

There is, I doubt not, a day coming, when writers on the evidences of the two Theologies, Natural and Revealed, will be content to borrow largely from the facts of the geologist. Who among living men may anticipate the thinking of future generations, or indicate in what direction new avenues into the regions of thought shall yet be opened up by the key of unborn genius? The births of the human intellect, like those which take place in the human family, await their predestined time. There are, however, two distinct theologic vistas on the geologic field, that seem to open up of themselves. Infidelity has toiled hard to obviate the necessity of a First Great Cause, by the fiction of an Infinite Series; and Metaphysic Theology has labored hard, in turn, to prove the fiction untenable and absurd. But metaphysicians, though specially assisted in the work by such men as Bentley and Robert Hall, have not been successful. They have, indeed, shown that an infinite series is, from many points of view, wholly *inconceivable*, but they have not shown that it is *impossible;* and its inconceivability merely attaches to it in its character as *an infinity contemplated entire.* Exactly the same degree of inconceivability attaches to "the years of the Eternal," if we attempt comprehending the eternity of Deity otherwise than in the progressive mode which Locke so surely demonstrates to be the only possible one: we can but take our stand at some definite period, and realize the possibility of measuring backwards, along the course of His existence for ever and ever, and have at every succeeding stage an undiminished infinitude of work before us. Metaphysic Theology furnishes no real argument against the "Infinite Series" of the atheist. But Geology supplies the wanting link, and laughs at the idle fiction of a race of men without beginning. Infinite series of human creatures! Why, man is but of yesterday. The fish enjoyed life during many creations, — the bird and reptile during not a few, — the marsupial quadruped ever since the times of the Oolite, — the sagacious elephant in at least the latter ages of the Tertiary. But man belongs to the present creation, and to it exclusively. He came into being *late on the Saturday evening.* He has come, as the great moral instincts of his nature so surely demonstrate, to prepare for the sacred to-morrow. In the chariot of God's providence, as seen by the prophet in vision, there are wheels within wheels, — a complex duality of type and symbol: and there may possibly exist a similar complexity of arrangement, — a similar duality of typical plan, — in the Divine institution of the Sabbath. Its place, as the seventh day, may bear reference, not only to that special subordinate week in which the existing scene of things was called into being, but also to that great geologic week, within which is comprised the entire scheme of creation.

The second theological vista into the geologic field opens up a still more striking prospect. There is a sad oppressiveness in that sense of human littleness which the great truths of astronomy have so direct a tendency to inspire. Man feels himself lost amid the sublime magnitudes of creation, — a mere atom in the midst of infinity; and trembles lest the scheme of revelation should be found too large a manifestation of the Divine care for so tiny an ephemera. Now, I am much mistaken if the truths of Geology have not a direct tendency to restore him to his true place. When engaged some time since in perusing one of the sublimest philosophic poems of modern times, — the "Astronomical Discourses" of Dr. Chalmers, — there occurred to me a new argument that might be employed against the infidel objection which the work was expressly written to remove. The infidel points to the planets; and, reasoning from an analogy which, on other than geologic data, the Christian cannot challenge, asks whether it be not more than probable that each of these is, like our own earth, not only a scene of creation, but also a home of rational, accountable creatures. And then follows the objection, as fully stated by Dr. Chalmers: — "Does not the largeness of that field which astronomy lays open to the view of modern science throw a suspicion over the truth of the Gospel history? and how shall we reconcile the greatness of that wonderful movement which was made in heaven for the redemption of fallen man, with the comparative meanness and obscurity of our species? Geology, when the doctor wrote, was in a state of comparative infancy. It has since been largely developed, and we have been introduced, in consequence, to the knowledge of some five or six different creations, of which this globe was the successive scene ere the present creation was called into being. At the time the "Astronomical Discourses" were published, the infidel could base his analogy on his knowledge of but one creation, — that to which we ourselves belong; whereas we can now base our analogy on the knowledge of at least six creations, the various productions of which we can handle, examine, and compare. And how, it may be asked, does this immense extent of basis affect the objection with which Dr. Chalmers has grappled so vigorously? It annihilates it completely. You argue — may not the geologist say to the infidel — that yonder planet, because apparently a scene of creation like our own, is also a home of accountable creatures like ourselves? But the extended analogy furnished by geologic science is full against you. Exactly so might it have been argued regarding our own earth during the early creation represented by the Lower Silurian system, and yet the master-existence of that extended period was a crustacean. Exactly so might it have been argued regarding the earth during the term of the creation represented by the Old Red Sandstone, and yet the master-existence of that not less extended period was a fish. During the creation represented by the Carboniferous period, with all its rank vegetation and green reflected light, the master-existence was a fish still. During the creation of the Oolite, the master-existence was a reptile, a bird, or a marsupial animal. During the creation of the Cretaceous period, there was no further advance. During the creation of the Tertiary formations, the master-existence was a mammiferous quadruped. It was not until the creation to which we ourselves belong was called into existence, that a rational being, born to anticipate a hereafter, was ushered upon the scene. Suppositions such as yours would have been false in at least five out of six instances; and if in five out of six *consecutive* creations there existed no accountable agent, what shadow of reason can there be for holding that a different arrangement obtains in five out of six *contemporary* creations? Mercury, Venus, Mars, Jupiter, Saturn, and Uranus, may have all their plants and animals; and yet they may be as devoid of rational, accountable creatures, as were the creations of the Silurian, Old Red Sandstone, Carboniferous, Oolitic, Cretaceous, and Tertiary periods. They may be merely some of the "many mansions" prepared in the "Father's house" for the immortal creature of kingly destiny, made in the Father's own image, to whom this little world forms but the cradle and the nursery.

But the effect of this extended geologic basis may be neutralized, — the infidel may urge, — by extending it yet a little further. Why, he may ask, since we draw our analogies regarding what obtains in the other planets from what obtains in our own, — why not conclude that each one of them has also had its geologic eras and revolutions, — its Silurian, Old Red Sandstone, Carboniferous, Oolitic, Cretaceous, and Tertiary periods; and that now, contemporary with the creation of which man constitutes the master-existence, they have all their fully matured creations headed by rationality? Why not carry the analogy thus far? Simply, it may be unhesitatingly urged in reply, because to carry it so far would be to carry it beyond the legitimate bounds of analogy; and because analogy pursued but a single step beyond the limits of its proper province, is sure always to land the pursuer in error. Analogy is not identity. It is safe when it deals with generals; very unsafe when it grapples with particulars.

Analogy, I repeat, is not identity. Let me attempt illustrating the fact in its bearing on this question. We find reason to conclude, as Isaac Taylor well expresses it, that "the planetary stuff is all one and the same." And we know to a certainty, that human nature, wherever it exists in the present state of things, "is all one and the same" also. But when reasoning analogically regarding either, we can but calculate on generals, not particulars. Man being all over the world a constructive, house-making animal, and, withal, fond of ornament, one would be quite safe in arguing analogically from an acquaintance with Europe alone, that wherever there is a civilized nation, architecture must exist as an art. But analogy is not identity; and he would be egregiously in error who would conclude that nations, civilized or semi-civilized, such as the Chinese, Hindoos, or ancient Mexicans, possess not only an ornate architecture, but an architecture divided into two great schools; and that the one school has its Doric, Ionic, and Corinthian orders, and the other school its Saxon, Norman, and Florid styles. In like manner, man's nature being everywhere the same, it may be safely inferred that man will everywhere be an admirer of female beauty. But analogy is not identity; and it would be a sad mistake to argue, just as one chanced to be resident in Africa or England, that man everywhere admired black skins and flat noses, or a fair complexion and features approximating to the Grecian type. And instances of a resembling character may be multiplied without end. Analogy, so sagacious a guide in its own legitimate field, is utterly blind and senseless in the precincts that lie beyond it: it is nicely correct in its generals, — perversely erroneous in its particulars; and no sooner does it quit its proper province, the general, for the particular, than there start up around it a multitude of solid objections, sternly to challenge it as a trespasser on grounds not its own. How infer, we may well ask the infidel, — admitting, for the argument's sake, that all the planets come under the law of geologic revolution, — how infer that they have all, or any of them save our own earth, arrived at the stage of stability and ripeness essential to a fully-developed creation, with a reasoning creature as its master-existence? Look at the immense mass of Jupiter, and at that mysterious mantle of cloud, barred and streaked in the direction of his *trade winds*, that forever conceals his face. May not that dense robe of cloud be the ever-ascending steam of a globe that, in consequence of its vast bulk, has not sufficiently cooled down to be a scene of life at all? Even the analogue of our Silurian creation may not yet have begun in Jupiter. Look, again, at Mercury, where it bathes in a flood of light, — enveloped within the sun's halo, like some forlorn smelter sweltering beside his furnace-mouth. A similar state of things may obtain on the surface of that planet, from a different, though not less adequate cause. But it is unnecessary to deal further with an analogy so palpably overstrained, and whose aggressive place and position in a province not its own so many unanswerable objections start up to elucidate and fix.

The subject, however, is one which it would be difficult to exhaust. The Christian has nothing to fear, the infidel nothing to hope, from the great truths of geology. It is assuredly not through any enlargement of man's little apprehension of the Infinite and the Eternal that man's faith in the scheme of salvation by a Redeemer need be shaken. We are incalculably more in danger from one unsubdued passion of our lower nature, even the weakest and the least, than from all that the astronomer has yet discovered in the depths of heaven, or the geologist in the bowels of the earth. If one's heart be right, it is surely a good, not an evil, that one's view should be expanded; and geology is simply an expansion of view in the direction of the eternity that hath gone by.

It is not less, but more sublime, to take one's stand on the summit of a lofty mountain, and thence survey the great ocean over many broad regions, — over plains, and forests, and undulating tracts of hills, and blue remote promontories, and far-seen islands, — than to look forth on the same vast expanse from the level champaign, a single field's breadth from the shore. It can indeed be in part conceived from either point how truly sublime an object that ocean is, — how the voyager may sail over it day after day, and yet see no land rise on the dim horizon, — how its numberless waves roll, and its great currents ceaselessly flow, and its restless tides ever rise and fall, — how the lights of heaven are mirrored on its solitary surface, solitary, though the navies of a world be there, — and how, where plummet-line never sounded, and where life and light alike cease, it reposes with marble-like density, and more than Egyptian blackness, on the regions of a night on which there dawns no morning. But the larger view inspires the profounder feeling. The emotion is less overpowering, the conception less vivid, when from the humble flat we see but a band of water rising to where the sky rests, over a narrow selvage of land, than when, far beyond an ample breadth of foreground, and along an extended line of coast, and streaked with promontories and mottled with islands, and then spreading on and away in an ample plain of diluted blue, to the far horizon, we see the great ocean in its true character, wide and vast as human ken can descry. And such is the sublime prospect presented to the geologist, as he turns him towards the shoreless ocean of the upper eternity. The mere theologian views that boundless expanse from a flat, and there lies in front of him but the narrow strip of the existing creation, — a green selvage of a field's breadth, fretted thick by the tombs of dead men; while to the eye purged and strengthened by the euphrasy of science, the many vast regions of other creations,

— promontory beyond promontory, — island beyond island, — stretch out in sublime succession into that boundless ocean of eternity, whose sumless, irreducible area their vast extent fails to lessen by a single handbreadth, — that awful, inconceivable eternity, — God's *past* lifetime in its relation to God's finite creatures, — with relation to the infinite I AM himself, the indivisible element of the eternal *now*. And there are thoughts which arise in connection with the ampler prospect, and analogies, its legitimate produce, that have assuredly no tendency to confine man's aspirations, or cramp his cogitative energies, within the narrow precincts of mediocre unbelief. What mean the peculiar place and standing of our species in the great geologic week? There are tombs everywhere: each succeeding region, as the eye glances upwards towards the infinite abyss, is roughened with graves; the pages on which the history of the past is written are all tombstones; the inscriptions. epitaphs: we read the characters of the departed inhabitants in their sepulchral remains. And all these unreasoning creatures of the bygone periods — these humbler pieces of workmanship produced early in the week — died, as became their natures, without intelligence or hope. They perished ignorant of the past, and unanticipative of the future, — knowing not of the days that had gone before, nor recking of the days that were to come after. But not such the character of the last born of God's creatures, — the babe that came into being late on the Saturday evening, and that now whines and murmurs away its time of extreme infancy during the sober hours of preparation for the morrow. Already have the quick eyes of the child looked abroad upon all the past, and already has it noted why the passing time should be a time of sedulous diligence and expectancy. The work-day week draws fast to its close, and to-morrow is the Sabbath!

CHAPTER XVIII.

The Penny-a-mile Train and its Passengers. — *Aunt* Jonathan. — London by Night. — St. Paul's; the City as seen from the Dome. — The Lord Mayor's Coach. — Westminster Abbey. — The Gothic Architecture a less exquisite Production of the Human Mind than the Grecian. — Poets' Corner. — The Mission of the Poets. — The Tombs of the Kings. — The Monument of James Watt. — A humble Coffee-house and its Frequenters. — The Woes of Genius in London. — Old 110, Thames-street. — The Tower. — The Thames Tunnel. — Longings of the True Londoner for Rural Life and the Country; their Influence on Literature. — The British Museum; its splendid Collection of Fossil Remains. — Human Skeleton of Guadaloupe. — The Egyptian Room. — Domesticities of the Ancient Egyptians. — Cycle of Reproduction. — The Mummies.

I MUST again take the liberty, as on a former occasion, of ante-dating a portion of my tour: I did not proceed direct to London from Olney; but as I have nothing interesting to record of my journeyings in the interval, I shall pursue the thread of my narrative as if I had.

For the sake of variety, I had taken the penny-a-mile train; and derived some amusement from the droll humors of my travelling companions, — a humbler, coarser, freer, and, withal, merrier section of the people, than the second-class travellers, whose acquaintance, in at least my railway peregrinations, I had chiefly cultivated hitherto. We had not the happiness of producing any very good jokes among us; but there were many laudable attempts; and, though the wit was only tolerable, the laughter was hearty. There was an old American lady of the company, fresh from Yankee-land, who was grievously teased for the general benefit; but aunt Jonathan, though only indifferently furnished with teeth, had an effective tongue; and Mister Bull, in most of the bouts, came off but second best. The American, too, though the play proved now and then somewhat of a horse character, was evidently conscious that her country lost no honor by her, and seemed rather gratified than otherwise. There were from five-and-twenty to thirty passengers in the van; among the rest, a goodly proportion of town-bred females, who mingled in the fun at least as freely as was becoming, and were smart, when they could, on the American; and immediately beside the old lady there sat a silent, ruddy country girl, who seemed travelling to London to take service in some family. The old lady had just received a hit from a smart female, to whom she deigned no reply; but, turning round to the country girl, she patted her on the shoulder, and tendered her a profusion of thanks for some nameless obligation which, she said, she owed to her. "La! to me, ma'am?" said the girl. — "Yes, to you, my pretty dear," said the American: "it is quite cheering to find one modest Englishwoman *among so few.*" The men laughed outrageously; the females did not like the joke half so well, and bridled up. And thus the war went on. The weather had been unpromising, — the night fell exceedingly dark and foul, — there were long wearisome stoppages at almost every station, — and it was within an hour of midnight, and a full hour and a half beyond the specified time of arrival, ere we entered the great city. I took my place in an omnibus, beside a half-open window, and away the vehicle trundled for the Strand.

The night was extremely dreary; the rain fell in torrents; and the lamps, flickering and flaring in the wind, threw dismal gleams over the half-flooded streets and the wet pavement, revealing the pyramidal rain-drops as they danced by myriads in the pools, or splashed against the smooth slippery flagstones.

The better shops were all shut, and there were but few lights in the windows: sober, reputable London seemed to have gone to its bed in the hope of better weather in the morning; but here and there, as we hurried past the opening of some lane or alley, I could mark a dazzling glare of light streaming out into the rain from some low cellar, and see forlorn figures of ill-dressed men and draggled women flitting about in a style which indicated that London not sober and not reputable was still engaged in drinking hard drams. Some of the objects we passed presented in the uncertain light a ghostly-like wildness, which impressed me all the more, that I could but guess at their real character. And the guesses, in some instances, were sufficiently wide of the mark. I passed in New Road a singularly picturesque community of statues, which, in the uncertain light, seemed a parliament of spectres, held in the rain and the wind, to discuss the merits of the "Interment in Towns" Commission, somewhat in the style the two ghosts discussed, in poor Ferguson's days, in the Greyfriars' churchyard, the proposed investment of the Scotch Hospital funds in the Three per Cents. But I found in the morning that the picturesque parliament of ghosts were merely the chance-grouped figures of a stone-cutter's yard. The next most striking object I saw were the long ranges of pillars in Regent-street. They bore about them an air that I in vain looked for by day, of doleful, tomb-like grandeur, as the columns came in sight, one after one, in the thickening fog, and the lamps threw their paley gleams along the endless architrave. Then came Charing Cross, with its white jetting fountains, sadly disturbed in their play by the wind, and its gloomy, shade-like equestrians. And then I reached a quiet lodging-house in Hungerford-street, and tumbled, a little after midnight, into a comfortable bed. The morning arose as gloomily as the evening had closed; and the first sounds I heard, as I awoke, were the sharp patter of rain drops on the panes, and the dash of water from the spouts on the pavement below.

Towards noon, however, the rain ceased, and I sallied out to see London. I passed great and celebrated places,—Warren's great blacking establishment, and the great house of the outfitting Jew and his son, so celebrated in "Punch," and then the great "Punch's" own office, with great "Punch" himself, pregnant with joke, and larger than the life, standing sentinel over the door. And after just a little uncertain wandering, the uncertainty of which mattered nothing, as I could not possibly go wrong, wander where I might, I came full upon St. Paul's, and entered the edifice. It is comfortable to have only twopence to pay for leave to walk over the area of so noble a pile, and to have to pay the twopence, too, to such grave, clerical-looking men as the officials at the receipt of custom. It reminds one of the blessings of a religious establishment in a place where otherwise they might possibly be overlooked: no private company could afford to build such a pile as St. Paul's, and then show it for twopences. A payment of eighteenpence more opened my way to the summit of the dome, and I saw, laid fairly at my feet, all of London that the smoke and the weather permitted, in its existing state of dishabille, to come into sight. But though a finer morning might have presented me with a more extensive and more richly-colored prospect, it would scarce have given me one equally striking. I stood over the middle of a vast seething cauldron, and looked down through the blue reek on the dim indistinct forms that seemed parboiling within. The denser clouds were rolling away, but their huge volumes still lay folded all around on the outskirts of the prospect. I could see a long reach of the river, with its gigantic bridges striding across; but both ends of the tide, like those of the stream seen by Mirza, were enveloped in darkness; and the bridges, gray and unsolid-looking themselves, as if cut out of sheets of compressed vapor, seemed leading to a spectral city. Immediately in the foreground there lay a perplexed labyrinth of streets and lanes, and untraceable ranges of buildings, that seemed the huddled-up fragments of a fractured puzzle, — difficult enough of resolution when entire, and rendered altogether unresolvable by the chance that had broken it. As the scene receded, only the larger and more prominent objects came into view, — here a spire, and there a monument, and yonder a square Gothic tower; and as it still further receded, I could see but the dim fragments of things, — bits of churches inwrought into the cloud, and the insulated pediments and columned fronts of public buildings, sketched off in diluted gray. I was reminded of Sir Walter Scott's recipe for painting a battle: a great cloud to be got up as the first part of the process; and as the second, here and there an arm or a leg stuck in, and here and there a head or a body. And such was London, the greatest city of the world, as I looked upon it this morning, for the first time, from the golden gallery of St. Paul's.

The hour of noon struck on the great bell far below my feet; the pigmies in the thoroughfare of St. Paul's Yard, still further below, were evidently increasing in number and gathering into groups; I could see faces that seemed no bigger than fists thickening in the windows, and dim little figures starting up on the leads of houses; and then, issuing into the Yard from one of the streets, there came a long line of gay coaches, with the identical coach in the midst, all gorgeous and grand, that I remembered to have seen done in Dutch gold, full five-and-thirty years before, on the covers of a splendid sixpenny edition of "Whittington and his Cat." Hurrah for Whittington, Lord Mayor of London! Without having once ba gained for such a thing, — all unaware of what was awaiting me, — I had ascended St. Paul's to see, as it proved, the Lord Mayor's procession. To be sure, I was placed rather high for witnessing with the right feeling the gauds and the grandeurs. All human greatness requires to be set in a peculiar light, and does not come out to advantage when seen from either too near or too distant a point of view; and here the sorely-diminished pageant at my feet served rather provokingly to remind one of Addison's ant-hill scene of the *Mayor* emmet, with the bit of white rod in its mouth, followed by the long line of *Aldermanic* and *Common Council* emmets, all ready to possess themselves of the bit of white rod in their own behalf, should it chance to drop. Still, however, there are few things made of leather and prunello really grander than the Lord Mayor's procession. Slowly the pageant passed on and away; the groups dispersed in the streets, the faces evanished from the windows, the figures disappeared from the house-tops; the entire apparition and its accompaniments melted into thin air, like the vision seen in the midst of the hollow valley of Bagdad; and I saw but the dim city parboiling amid the clouds, and the long leaden-colored reach of the river bounding half the world of London, as the monstrous ocean snake of the Edda more than half encircles the globe.

My next walk led to Westminster Abbey and the New Houses of Parliament, through St. James' Park. The unpromising character of the day had kept loungers at home; and the dank trees dripped on the wet grass, and loomed large through the gray fog, in a scene of scarce less solitude, though the roar of the city was all around, than the trees of Shenstone at the Leasowes. I walked leisurely once and again along the Abbey, as I had done at St. Paul's, to mark the general aspect and effect, and fix in my mind the proportions and true contour of the building. And the conclusion forced upon me was just that at which, times without number, I had invariably arrived before. The Gothic architecture, with all its solemn grandeur and beauty, is a greatly lower and less exquisite production of the human intellect than the architecture of Greece. The saintly legends of the middle ages are scarce less decidedly inferior to those fictions of the classic mythology which the greater Greek and Roman writers have sublimed into poetry. I have often felt that the prevailing bias in favor of everything mediæval, so characteristic of the present time, from the theology and legislation of the middle ages, to their style of staining glass and illuminating manuscripts, cannot be other than a temporary eccentricity, — a mere cross freshet, chance-raised by some meteoric accident, — not one of the great permanent ocean-currents of tendency ; but never did the conviction press upon me more strongly than when enabled on this occasion to contrast the *new* architecture of St. Paul's with the *old* architecture of Westminster. *New! Old! Modern! Ancient!* The merits of the controversy lie summed up in these words. The new architecture is the truly ancient architecture, while the old is comparatively modern: but the immortals are always young; whereas the mortals, though their term of life may be as extended as that of Methuselah, grow old apace. The Grecian architecture will be always the new architecture; and, let fashion play whatever vagaries it pleases, the Gothic will be always old. There is a wonderful amount of genius exhibited in the contour and filling up of St. Paul's. In passing up and down the river, which I did frequently during my short stay in London, my eye never wearied of resting on it: like all great works that have had the beautiful inwrought into their essence by the persevering touches of a master, the more I dwelt on it, the more exquisite it seemed to become. York Minster, the finest of English Gothic buildings, is perhaps equally impressive on a first survey; but it exhibits no such soul of beauty as one dwells upon it, — it lacks the halo that forms around the dome of St. Paul's. I was not particularly struck by the New Houses of Parliament. They seem prettily got up to order, on a rich pattern, that must have cost the country a vast deal per yard; and have a great many little bits of animation in them, which remind one of the communities of lives that dwell in compound corals, or of the divisible life, everywhere diffused and nowhere concentrated, that resides in poplars and willows; but they want the one animating soul characteristic of the superior natures. Unlike the master-erection of Wren, they will not breathe out beauty into the minds of the future, as pieces of musk continue to exhale their odor for centuries.

I walked through Poets' Corner, and saw many a familiar name on the walls: among others, the name of Dryden, familiar because he himself had made it so; and the name of Shadwell, familiar because he had quarrelled with Dryden. There also I found the sepulchral slab of old cross John Dennis, famous for but his warfare with Pope and Addison; and there, too, the statue of Addison at full length, not far from the periwigged effigy of the bluff English admiral that had furnished him with so good a joke. There, besides, may be seen the marble of the ancient descriptive poet Drayton; and there the bust of poor eccentric *Goldie*, with his careless Irish face, who thought Drayton had no claim to such an honor, but whose own claim has been challenged by no one. I had no strong emotions to exhibit when pacing along the pavement in this celebrated place, nor would I have exhibited them if I had: and yet I did feel that I had derived much pleasure in my time from the men whose names conferred honor on the wall. There was poor Goldsmith: he had been my companion for thirty years; I had been first introduced to him through the medium of a common school collection, when a little boy in the humblest English class of a parish school; and I had kept up the acquaintance ever since. There, too, was Addison, whom I had known so long, and, in his true poems, his prose ones, had loved as much; and there were Gay, and Prior, and Cowley, and Thomson, and Chaucer, and Spenser, and Milton; and there, too, on a slab on the floor, with the freshness of recent interment still palpable about it, as if to indicate the race at least not *long* extinct, was the name of Thomas Campbell. I had got fairly among my patrons and benefactors. How often, shut out for months and years together from all literary converse with the living, had they been almost my only companions,— my unseen associates, who, in the rude work-shed, lightened my labors by the music of their numbers, and who, in my evening walks, that would have been so solitary save for them, expanded my intellect by the solid bulk of their thinking, and gave me eyes, by their exquisite descriptions, to look at nature! How thoroughly, too, had they served to break down in my mind at least the narrower and more illiberal partialities of country, leaving untouched, however, all that was worthy of being cherished in my attachment to poor old Scotland! I learned to deem the English poet not less my countryman than the Scot, if I but felt the true human heart beating in his bosom; and the intense prejudices which I had imbibed when almost a child, from the fiery narratives of Blind Harry and of Barbour, melted away, like snow-wreaths from before the sun, under the genial influences of the glowing poesy of England. It is not the harp of Orpheus that will effectually tame the wild beast which lies ambushing in human nature, and is ever and anon breaking forth on the nations, in cruel, desolating war. The work of giving peace to the earth awaits those divine harmonies which breathe from the Lyre of Inspiration when swept by the Spirit of God. And yet the harp of Orpheus does exert an auxiliary power. It is of the nature of its songs, — so rich in the human sympathies, so charged with the thoughts, the imaginings, the hopes, the wishes, which it is the constitution of humanity to conceive and entertain, — it is of their nature to make us feel that the nations are all of one blood, — that man is our brother, and the world our country.

The sepulchres of the old English monarchs, with all their obsolete grandeur, impressed me more feebly, though a few rather minute circumstances have, I perceive, left their stamp Among the royal cemeteries we find the tombs of Mary of Scotland, and her great rival Elizabeth, with their respective effigies lying atop, cut in marble. And though the sculptures exhibit little of the genius of the modern statuary, the great care of their finish, joined to their unideal, unflattering individuality, afford an evidence of their truth which productions of higher talent could scarce possess. How comes it, then, I would fain ask the phrenologist, that by far the finer head of the two should be found on the shoulders of the weaker woman? The forehead of Mary — poor Mary, who had a trick of falling in love with "*pretty men*," but no power of governing them — is of very noble development, — broad, erect, powerful; while that of Elizabeth, — of queenly, sagacious Elizabeth, — who could both fall in love with men and govern them too, and who was unquestionably a great monarch, irrespective of sex, — is a poor, narrow, pinched-up thing, that rises tolerably erect for one-half its height, and then slopes abruptly away. The next things that caught my eye were two slabs of Egyptian porphyry — a well-marked stone, with the rich purple ground spotted white and pink, — inlaid as panels in the tomb of Edward the First. Whence, in the days of Edward, could the English stone-cutter have procured Egyptian porphyry? I was enabled to form at least a guess on the subject, from possessing a small piece of exactly the same stone, which had been picked up amid heaps of rubbish in the deep rocky ravine of Siloam, and which, as it does not occur *in situ* in Judea, was supposed to have formed at one time a portion of the Temple. Is it not probable that these slabs, which, so far as is yet known, Europe could not have furnished, were brought by Edward, the last of the crusading princes of England, from the Holy Land, to confer sanctity on his place of burial, — mayhap originally, — though Edward himself never got so far, — from that identical ravine of Siloam which supplied my specimen? It was not uncommon for the crusader to take from Palestine the earth in which his body was to be deposited; and if Edward succeeded in procuring a genuine bit of the true Temple, and an exceedingly pretty bit to boot, it seems in meet accordance with the character of the age that it should have been borne home with him in triumph, to serve a similar purpose. I was a good deal struck, in one of the old chapels, — a little gloomy place, filled with antique regalities sorely faded, and middle-age glories waxed dim, — by stumbling, very unexpectedly, on a noble statue of James Watt. The profoundly contemplative countenance — so happily described by Arago as a very personification of abstract thought — contrasted strongly with the chivalric baubles and meaningless countenances on the surrounding tombs. The new and the old governing forces — the waxing and the waning powers — seemed appropriately typified in that little twilight chapel.

My next free day — for, of the four days I remained in London, I devoted each alternate one to the British Museum —

spent in wandering everywhere, and looking at everything,— in going up and down the river in steamboats, and down and athwart the streets on omnibuses. I took my meals in all sorts of odd-looking places. I breakfasted one morning in an exceedingly poor-looking coffee-house, into which I saw several people dressed in dirty moleskin enter, just that I might see how the people who dress in dirty moleskin live in London. Some of them made, I found, exceedingly little serve as a meal. One thin-faced, middle-aged man brought in a salt herring with him, which he gave to the waiter to get roasted; and the roasted salt herring, with a penny's worth of bread and a penny's worth of coffee, formed his breakfast. Another considerably younger and stouter man, apparently not more a favorite of fortune, brought in with him an exceedingly small bit of meat, rather of the bloodiest, stuck on a wooden pin, which he also got roasted by the waiter, and which he supplemented with a penny's worth of coffee and but a halfpenny's worth of bread. I too, that I might experience for one forenoon the sensations of the London poor, had my penny's worth of coffee, and, as I had neither meat nor herring, my three-halfpenny worth of bread; but both together formed a breakfast rather of the lightest, and so I dined early. There is a passage which I had read in Goldsmith's "History of the Earth and Animated Nature" many years before, which came painfully into my mind on this occasion. The poor poet had sad experience in his time of the destitution of London; and when he came to discourse as a naturalist on some of the sterner wants of the species, the knowledge which he brought to bear on the subject was of a deeply tragic cast. "The lower race of animals," he says, "when satisfied, for the instant moment are perfectly happy; but it is otherwise with man. His mind anticipates distress, and feels the pangs of want even before they arrest him. Thus, the mind being continually harassed by the situation, it at length influences the constitution, and unfits it for all its functions. Some cruel disorder, but nowise like hunger, seizes the unhappy sufferer; so that almost all those men who have thus long lived by chance, and whose every day may be considered as a happy escape from famine, are known at last to die in reality of a disorder caused by hunger, but which, in the common language, is often called a broken heart. Some of these I have known myself when very little able to relieve them; and I have been told by a very active and worthy magistrate, that the number of such as die in London for want is much greater than one would imagine, — I think he talked of two thousand in a year."

Rather a curious passage this to occur in a work of Natural History. It haunted me a while this morning: the weather, though no longer wet, was exceedingly gloomy; and I felt depressed as I walked along the muddy streets, and realized, with small effort, the condition of the many thousands who, without friends or home, money or employment, have had to endure the mingled pangs of want and anxiety in London. I remembered, in crossing Westminster Bridge to take boat on the Surrey side, that the poet Crabbe walked on it all night, when, friendless, in distress and his last shilling expended, he had dropped, at the door of Edmund Burke, the touching letter on which his last surviving hope depended. The Thames was turbid with the rains, — the tide was out, — and melancholy banks of mud, here and there overtopped by thickets of grievously befouled sedges, lay along its sides. One straggling thicket, just opposite the gloomy Temple Gardens, — so solitary in the middle of a great city, — had caught a tattered jacket; and the empty sleeve, stretched against the taller sedges seemed a human arm raised above the unsolid ooze.

The scene appeared infinitely better suited than that drawn by the bard of Rhysdale, to remind one

"Of mighty poets in their misery dead."

Here it was that Otway perished of hunger, — Butler, in great neglect, — starving Chatterton, of poison. And these were the very streets which Richard Savage and Samuel Johnson had so often walked from midnight till morning, having at the time no roof under which to shelter. Pope summons up old Father Thames, in his "Windsor Forest," to tell a silly enough story: how strangely different, how deeply tragic, would be the real stories which Father Thames could tell! Many a proud heart, quenched in despair, has forever ceased to beat beneath his waters. Curiously enough, the first thing I saw, on stepping ashore at London Bridge, was a placard, intimating that on the previous night a gentleman had *fallen* over one of the bridges, and offering a reward of twenty shillings for the recovery of the body.

There was a house in Upper Thames-street which I was desirous to see. I had had no direct interest in it for the last five-and-twenty years: the kind relative who had occupied it when I was a boy had long been in his grave, — a far distant one, beyond the Atlantic; and 110 Upper Thames-street might, for aught I knew, be now inhabited by a Jew or a Mahometan. But I had got some curious little books sent me from it, at a time when my books were few and highly valued; and I could not leave London without first setting myself to seek out the place they had come from. Like the tomb of the lovers, however, which Tristram Shandy journeyed to Lyons to see, and saw, instead, merely the place where the tomb had been, I found that old 110 had disappeared: and a tall modern erection, the property of some great company, occupied its site. I next walked on through the busiest streets I had ever seen,

"With carts, and cars, and coaches, roaring all,"

to Tower Hill; and saw the crown jewels of England, and the English history done in iron, — for such is the true character of the old armory, containing the mailed effigies of the English kings. I saw, too, the cell in which imprisoned Raleigh wrote his "History of the World;" and the dark narrow dungeon, with its rude stone arch, and its bare walls, painfully lettered, as with a nail-point, furnished me with a new vignette, by which to illustrate in imagination some of the most splendid poetry ever written in prose. From the Tower I walked on to explore that most ingenious work and least fortunate undertaking of modern times, — the Thames Tunnel; and found it so extremely like the ordinary prints given of it in the "Penny Magazine" and elsewhere, that I could scarcely believe I had not seen it before. There were a good many saunterers, like myself, walking up and down along the pavement, now cheapening some of the toys exhibited for sale in the cross arches, and now listening to a Welsh harper who was filling one of the great circular shafts with sound; but not a single passenger did I see. The common English have a peculiar turn for possessing themselves of *almost*-impossibilities of the reel-in-the-bottle class; and a person who drew rather indifferent profiles in black seemed to be driving a busy trade among the visiters. The great charm appeared to lie in the fact that the outlines produced were outlines of their very selves, taken under the Thames. I spent the rest of the day in riding along all the greater streets on the tops of omnibuses, and in threading some of the more characteristic lanes on foot. Nothing more surprised me, in my peripatetic wanderings, than to find, when I had now and then occasion to inquire my way, that the Londoners do not know London. The monster city of which they are so proud seems, like other very great ones of the earth, to have got beyond the familiarities of intimate acquaintance with even the men who respect it most.

I learned not to wonder, as I walked along the endless labyrinth of streets, and saw there was no such thing for a pedestrian as getting fairly into the country, that the literature of London — its purely indigenous literature — should be of so rural a character. The mere wayside beauties of nature, — green trees, and fresh grass, and soft mossy hillocks sprinkled over with harebells and daisies, and hawthorn bushes gray in blossom, and slender woodland streamlets, with yellow primroses looking down upon them from their banks, — things common and of little mark to at least the ordinary men that live among them, — must be redolent of poetry to even the ordinary Londoner, who, removed far from their real presence, contemplates them in idea through an atmosphere of intense desire. There are not a few silly things in what has been termed the Cockney school of poetry: in no other school does a teasing obscurity hover so incessantly on the edge of no meaning, or is the reader so much in danger of embracing, like one of the old mythologic heroes, a cloud for a goddess. But I can scarce join in the laugh raised against its incessant "babble about green fields," or marvel that, in its ceaseless talk of flowers, its language should so nearly resemble that of Turkish love-letters composed of nosegays. Its style is eminently true to London nature, — which, of course, is simply human nature in London, — in the ardent desire which it breathes for rural quiet, and the green sunshiny solitude of the country. "Shapes of beauty" according to one of its masters, — poor Keats, —

"Move away the pall
From the tired spirit."

And then he tells us what some of those shapes of beauty are,—

"Such the sun, the moon,
Trees old and young, sprouting a shady boon
For simple sheep; and such are daffodils
With the green world they live in; and clear rills,
That for themselves a cooling covert make
'Gainst the hot season; the mid-forest brake,
Rich with a sprinkling of fair musk-rose blooms."

Keats, the apprentice of a London surgeon, was an overtoiled young man in delicate health, cooped up by his employment the whole week round for years together; and in this characteristic passage,—puerile enough, it must be confessed, and yet poetical too,—we have the genuine expression of the true city calenture under which he languished. But perhaps nowhere in the compass of English poetry is there a more truthful exhibition of the affection than in Wordsworth's picture of the hapless town girl, poor Susan. She is in the heart of the city, a thoughtless straggler along the busy streets, when a sudden burst of song from an encaged thrush hung against the wall touches the deeply-seated feeling, and transports her far and away into the quiet country, where her days of innocency had been spent.

"What ails her? She sees
A mountain ascending, a vision of trees;
Bright volumes of vapor through Lothbury glide,
And a river flows on through the vale of Cheapside.
Green pastures she views in the midst of the vale,
Down which she so often has tripped with her pail ·
And a single small cottage, a nest like a dove's,
The only one dwelling on earth that she loves."

It is an interesting enough fact that from the existence of this strong appetite for the rural intensified into poetry by those circumstances which render all attempts at its gratification mere tantalizing snatches, that whet rather than satisfy, the influence of great cities on the literature of a country should be, not to enhance the artificia., but to impart to the natural prominence and value. The "Farmer's Boy" of Bloomfield was written in a garret in the midst of London; and nowhere perhaps in the empire has it been read with a deeper relish than by the pale country-sick artisans and clerks of the neighboring close courts and blind alleys. Nowhere have Thomson, Cowper, and Crabbe, with the poets of the Lake School, given a larger amount of pleasure than in London; and when London at length came to produce a school of poetry exclusively its own, it proved one of the graver faults of its productions, that they were too incessantly descriptive, and too exclusively rural.

I spent, as I have said, two days at the British Museum, and wished I could have spent ten. And yet the ten, by extending my index acquaintance with the whole, would have left me many more unsettled points to brood over than the two. It is an astonishing collection; and very astonishing is the history of creation and the human family which it forms. Such, it strikes me, is the preper view in which to regard it, it is a great, many-chaptered work of authentic history, beginning with the consecutive creations, — dwelling at great length on the existing one, — taking up and pursuing through many sections the master production, Man, — exhibiting in the Egyptian section, not only what he did, but what he was, — illustrating in the Grecian and Roman sections the perfectibility of his conceptions in all that relates to external form, — indicating in the middle-age section a refolding of his previously-developed powers, as if they had shrunk under some chill and wintry influence, — exhibiting in the concluding section a broader and more general blow of sentiment and faculty than that of his earlier spring-time, — nay, demonstrating the fact of a more confirmed maturity, in the very existence and arrangement of such a many-volumed History of the Earth and its productions as this great collection constitutes. I found, in the geological department, — splendid, as an accumulation of noble specimens, beyond my utmost conception, — that much still remains to be done in the way of arrangement, — a very great deal even in the way of further addition. The work of imparting order to the whole, though in good hands, seems barely begun; and years must elapse ere it can be completed with reference to even the present stage of geologic knowledge. But how very wonderful will be the record which it will then form of those earlier periods of our planet, — its ages of infancy, childhood, and immature youth, — which elapsed ere its connection with the moral and the responsible began! From the Graptolite of the Grauwacke slate, to the fossil human skeleton of Guadaloupe, what a strange list of births and deaths — of the production and extinction of races — will it not exhibit! Even in its present half-arranged condition, I found the general progressive history of the animal kingdom strikingly indicated. In the most ancient section, — that of the Silurian system, — there are corals, molluscs, crustacea. In the Old Red, — for the fish of the Upper Ludlow rock are wanting, — the vertebræ begin. By the way, I found that almost all the older ichthyolites in this section of the Museum had been of my own gathering, — specimens I had laid open on the shores of the Cromarty Frith some ten or twelve years ago. Upwards through the Coal Measures I saw nothing higher than the reptile fish. With the Lias comes a splendid array of the extinct reptiles. The Museum contains perhaps the finest collection of these in the world. The earlier Tertiary introduces us to the strange mammals of the Paris Basin, — the same system, in its second stage, to the Dinotherium of Darmstadt and the Megatherium of Buenos Ayres. A still later period brings before us the great elephantine family, once so widely distributed over the globe : we arrive at a monstrous skeleton, entire from head to heel: 'tis that of the gigantic mastodon of North America, — a creature that may have been contemporary with the earlier hunter tribes of the New World ; and just beside it, last in the long series, we find the human skeleton of Guadaloupe. Mysterious frame-work of bone locked up in the solid marble, — unwonted prisoner of the rock ! — an irresistible voice shall yet call thee from out the stony matrix. The other organisms, thy partners in the show, are incarcerated in the lime forever, — thou but for a term. How strangely has the destiny of the race to which thou belongest re-stamped with new meanings the old phenomena of creation ! I marked, as I passed along, the prints of numerous rain-drops indented in a slab of sandstone. And the entire record, from the earliest to the latest times, is a record of death. When that rain-shower descended, myriads of ages ago, at the close of the Palæozoic period, the cloud, just where it fronted the sun, must have exhibited its bow of many colors ; and then, as now, nature, made vital in the inferior animals, would have clung to life with the instinct of self-preservation, and shrunk with dismay and terror from the approach of death. But the prismatic bow strided across the gloom, in blind obedience to a mere optical law, bearing inscribed on its gorgeous arch no occult meaning ; and death, whether by violence or decay, formed in the general economy but a clearing process, through which the fundamental law of increase found space to operate. But when thou wert living prisoner of the marble, haply as an Indian wife and mother, ages ere the keel of Columbus had disturbed the waves of the Atlantic, the high standing of thy species had imparted new meanings to death and the rainbow. The prismatic arch had become the bow of the covenant, and death a great sign of the unbending justice and purity of the Creator, and of the aberration and fall of the living soul, formed in the Creator's own image, — reasoning, responsible man.

Of those portions of the Museum which illustrate the history of the human mind in that of the arts, I was most impressed by the Egyptian section. The utensils which it exhibits that associate with the old domesticities of the Egyptians — the little household implements which had ministered to the lesser comforts of the subjects of the Pharaohs — seem really more curious, — at any rate, more strange in their familiarity, — than those exquisite productions of genius, the Laocoons, and Apollo Belvideres, and Venus de Medicis, and Phidian Jupiters, and Elgin marbles, which the Greek and Roman sections exhibit. We have served ourselves heir to what the genius of the ancient nations has produced, — to their architecture, their sculpture, their literature; our conceptions piece on to theirs with so visible a dependency, that we can scarce imagine what they would have been without them. We have been running new metal into our castings, artistic and intellectual; but it is the ancients who, in most cases, have furnished the moulds. And so, though the human mind walks in an often-returning circle of thought and invention, and we might very possibly have struck out for ourselves not a few of the Grecian ideas, even had they all perished during the middle ages, — just as Shakspeare struck out for himself not a little of the classical thinking and imagery, — we are at least in doubt regarding the extent to which this would have taken place. We know not whether our chance reproduction of Grecian idea wou d have been such a one as the reproduction of Egyptian statuary exhibited in the aboriginal Mexican sculptures, or the reproduction of Runic tracery palpable in the Polynesian carvings, — or whether our inventions might not have expatiated, without obvious reproduction at all, in types indigenously Gothic. As heirs of the intellectual wealth of the ancients, and inheritors of the treasures which their efforts accumulated, we know not what sort of fortunes we would have carved out for ourselves, had we been left to our own unassisted exertions. But we surely did not fall heir to the domestic inventions of the Egyptians. Their cooks did not teach ours how to truss fowls; nor did their bakers show ours how to ferment their dough or mould their loaves; nor could we have learned from them a hundred other household arts, of which we find both the existence and the mode of existence indicated by the antiquities of this section; and yet, the same faculty of invention which they possessed, tied down in our as in their case by the wants of a common nature to expatiate in the same narrow circle of necessity, has reproduced them all. Invention in this case has been but restoration; and we find that, in the broad sense of the Preacher, it has given us nothing new. What most impressed me, however, were the Egyptians themselves, — the men of three thousand years ago, still existing entire in their framework of bone, muscle, and sinew. It struck me as a very wonderful truth, in the way in which truths great in themselves, but commonplaced by their familiarity, do sometimes strike, that the living souls should still exist which had once animated these withered and desiccated bodies; and that in their separate state they had an interest in the bodies still. This much, amid all their darkness, even the old Egyptians knew; and this we — save where the vitalities of revela tion influence — seem to be fast unlearning. It does appear strange, that men ingenious enough to philosophize on the phenomena of the parental relation, on the mysterious connection of parent and child, its palpable adaptation to the feelings of the human heart, and its vast influence on the destinies of the species, should yet find in the doctrine of the resurrection but a mere target against which to shoot their puny materialisms. It does not seem unworthy of the All Wise, by whom the human heart was moulded and the parental relation designed, that the immature "boy" of the present state of existence should be "father to the man" in the next; and that, as spirit shall be identical with spirit, — the responsible agent with the panel at the bar, — so body shall be derived from body, and the old oneness of the individual be thus rendered complete,

"Bound each to each by natural piety."

CHAPTER XIX.

Harrow-on-the-Hill. — Descent through the Formations from the Tertiary to the Coal Measures. — Journey of a Hundred and Twenty Miles *Northwards* identical, geologically, with a journey of a Mile and a Quarter *Downwards*. — English very unlike Scottish Landscape in its Geologic Framework. — Birmingham Fair. — Credulity of the Rural English; striking Contrast which they furnish, in this Respect, to their Countrymen of the Knowing Type. — The English Grades of Intellectual Character of Immense Range; more in Extremes than those of the Scotch. — Front Rank of British Intellect in which there stands no Scotchman; probable Cause. — A Class of English, on the other Hand, greatly lower than the Scotch; naturally less Curious; acquire, in Consequence, less of the Developing Pabulum. — The main Cause of the Difference to be found, however, in the very dissimilar Religious Character of the two Countries. — The Scot naturally less independent than the Englishman; strengthened, however, where his Character most needs Strength, by his Religion. — The Independence of the Englishman subjected at the present Time to two distinct Adverse Influences, — the Modern Poor Law and the Tenant-at-will System. — Walsall. — Liverpool. — Sort of Lodging-houses in which one is sure to meet many Dissenters.

On the fifth morning I quitted London on my way north, without having once seen the sun shine on the city or its environs. But the weather at length cleared up; and as the train passed Harrow-on-the-Hill, the picturesque buildings on the acclivity, as they looked out in the sunshine, nest-like, from amid their woods just touched with yellow, made a picture not unworthy of those classic recollections with which the place is so peculiarly associated.

The railway, though its sides are getting fast covered over with grass and debris, still furnishes a tolerably adequate section of the geology of this part of England. We pass, at an early stage of our journey, through the London Clay, and then see rising from under it the Chalk,— the first representative of an entirely different state of things from that which obtained in the Tertiary, and the latest written record of that Secondary dynasty at whose terminal line, if we except one or two doubtful shells, on which it is scarce safe to decide, all that had previously existed ceased to exist forever. The lower members of the Cretaceous group are formed of materials of too yielding a nature to be indicated in the section; but the Oolite, on which they rest, is well marked; and we see its strata rising from beneath, as we pass on to lower and yet lower depths, till at length we reach the Lias, its base, and then enter on the Upper New Red Sandstone. Deeper and yet deeper strata emerge; and at the commencement of the Lower New Red we reach another great terminal line, where the Secondary dynasty ends, and the Palæozoic begins. We still pass downwards; encounter at Walsall a misplaced patch of Silurian,— a page transferred from the earlier leaves of the volume, and stuck into a middle chapter; and then enter on the Coal Measures,— the extremest depth to which we penetrate, in regular sequence, on this line. Our journey northwards from London to Wolverhampton has been also a journey downwards along the geologic scale; but while we have travelled *northwards* along the surface about a hundred and twenty miles, we have travelled *downwards* into the earth's crust not more than a mile and a quarter. Our descent has been exceedingly slow, for the strata have lain at very low angles. And hence the flat character of the country, so essentially different from that of Scotland. The few hills which we pass,— if hills they may be termed,— mere flat ridges, that stretch, rib-like, athwart the landscape,— are, in most cases, but harder beds of rock, intercalated with the softer ones, and that, relieved by the denuding agencies, stand up in bolder prominence over the general level. Not an eruptive rock appears in the entire line on to Walsall. How very different the framework of Scottish landscape, as exhibited in the section laid bare by the Edinburgh and Glasgow Railway! There, almost every few hundred yards in the line brings the traveller to a trap-rock, against which he finds the strata tilted at every possible angle of elevation. Here the beds go up, there they go down; in this eminence they are elevated, saddle-like, on the back of some vast eruptive mass; in yonder hill, overflown by it. The country around exists as a tumultuous sea, raised into tempest of old by the fiery ground-swell from below; while on the skirts of the prospect there stand up eminences of loftier altitude, characteristically marked in profile by their terrace-like precipices, that rise over each other step by step, — their *trap-stairs** of trappean rock, — for to this scenic peculiarity the volcanic rocks owe their generic name.

I found Birmingham amid the bustle of its annual fair, and much bent on gayety and sight-seeing. There were double rows of booths along the streets, a full half-mile in length, — gingerbread booths, and carraway and barley-sugar booths, and nut and apple booths, and booths rich in halfpenny dolls and penny trumpets, and booths not particularly rich in anything that seemed to have been run up on speculation. There were shows, too, of every possible variety of attraction, — shows of fat boys, and large ladies, and little men, and great serpents and wise ponies; and shows of British disaster in India, and of British successes in China; madcap-minded merry-andrews, who lived on their wits, nor wished for more; agile tumblers, glittering in tinsel; swings, revolvers, and roundabouts; and old original Punch, in all his glory. But what formed by far

* *Trap-stairs*: Scotice, a stair of one flight.

the best part of the exhibition were the round, ruddy, unthinking faces of the country-bred English, that had poured into town, to stare, wonder, purchase, and be happy. It was worth while paying one's penny for a sight of the fat boys and the little men, just to see the eager avidity with which they were seen, and the total want of suspicion with which all that was told regarding them was received. The countrywoman who, on seeing a negro for the first time, deemed him the painted monster of a show, and remarked that "mony was the way tried to wyle awa' the penny," betrayed her country not less by her suspicion than by her tongue. An Englishwoman of the true rural type would have fallen into the opposite mistake, of deeming some painted monster a reality. Judging, however, from what the Birmingham fair exhibited, I am inclined to hold that the preponderance of enjoyment lies on the more credulous side. I never yet encountered a better-pleased people: the very spirit of the fair seemed embodied in the exclamation of a pretty little girl from the country, whom I saw clap her hands as she turned the corner of a street where the prospect first burst upon her, and shriek out, in a paroxysm of delight, "O, what lots of — lots of shows!" And yet, certainly, the English character does lie very much in extremes. Among the unthinking, unsuspicious, blue-eyed, fair-complexioned, honest Saxons that crowded the streets, I could here and there detect, in gangs and pairs, some of the most disagreeably smart-looking men I almost ever saw, — men light of finger and sharp of wit, — full of all manner of contrivance, and devoid of all sort of moral principle.

Nothing in the English character so strikingly impressed me as its immense extent of range across the intellectual scale. It resembles those musical instruments of great compass, such as the pianoforte and the harpsichord, that sweep over the entire gamut, from the lowest note to the highest; whereas the intellectual character of the Scotch, like instruments of a narrower range, such as the harp and the violin, lies more in the middle of the scale. By at least one degree it does not rise so high; by several degrees it does not sink so low. There is an order of English mind to which Scotland has not attained: our first men stand in the second rank, not a foot-breadth behind the foremost of England's second-rank men; but there is a front rank of British intellect in which there stands no Scotchman Like that class of the mighty men of David, to which Abishai and Benaiah belonged, — great captains, who went down into pits in the time of snow and slew lions, or "who lifted up the spear against three hundred men at once, and prevailed," — they attain not, with all their greatness, to the might of the first class. Scotland has produced no Shakspeare; — Burns and Sir Walter Scott united would fall short of the stature of the giant of Avon. Of Milton we have not even a representative. A Scotch poet has been injudiciously named as not greatly inferior; but I shall not do wrong to the memory of an ingenious young man, cut off just as he had mastered his powers, by naming him again in a connection so perilous. *He* at least was guiltless of the comparison; and it would be cruel to involve him in the ridicule which it is suited to excite. Bacon is as exclusively unique as Milton, and as exclusively English; and though the grandfather of Newton was a Scotchman, we have certainly no Scotch Sir Isaac. I question, indeed, whether any Scotchman attains to the powers of Locke: there is as much solid thinking in the "Essay on the Human Understanding," greatly as it has become the fashion of the age to depreciate it, and notwithstanding its fundamental error, as in the works of all our Scotch metaphysicians put together. It is however, a curious fact, and worthy, certainly, of careful examination, as bearing on the question of development purely through the force of circumstances, that all the very great men of England — all its first-class men — belong to ages during which the grinding persecutions of the Stuarts repressed Scottish energy, and crushed the opening mind of the country; and that no sooner was the weight removed, like a pavement-slab from over a flower-bed, than straightway Scottish intellect sprung up, and attained to the utmost height to which English intellect was rising at the time. The English philosophers and literati of the eighteenth century were of a greatly lower stature than the Miltons and Shakspeares, Bacons and Newtons, of the two previous centuries: they were second-class men, — the tallest, however, of their age anywhere; and among these the men of Scotland take no subordinate place. Though absent from the competition in the previous century, through the operation of causes palpable in the history of the time, we find them quite up to the mark of the age in which they appear. No English philosopher for the last hundred and fifty years produced a greater revolution in human affairs than Adam Smith, or exerted a more powerful influence on opinion than David Hume, or did more to change the face of the mechanical world than James Watt. The "History of England" produced by a Scotchman is still emphatically *the* "English History;" nor, with all its defects, is it likely to be soon superseded. Robertson, if inferior in the untaught felicities of narration to his illustrious countryman, is at least inferior to none of his English contemporaries. The prose fictions of Smollett have kept their ground quite as well as those of Fielding, and better than those of Richardson. Nor does England during the century exhibit higher manifestations of the poetic spirit than those exhibited by Thomson and by Burns. To use a homely but expressive Scoticism, Scotland seems to have lost her *bairn-time* of the giants; but in the after *bairn-time* of merely tall men, her children were quite as tall as any of their contemporaries.

Be this as it may, however, it is unquestionable that England has produced an order of intellect to which Scotland has not attained; and it does strike as at least curious, in connection with the fact that the English, notwithstanding, should as a people stand on a lower intellectual level than the Scotch. I have had better opportunities of knowing the common people of Scotland than most men; I have lived among them for the greater part of my life, and I belong to them; and when in England, I made it my business to see as much as possible of the common English people. I conversed with them south and north, and found them extremely ready — for, as I have already had occasion to remark, they are much franker than the Scotch — to exhibit themselves unbidden. And I have no hesitation in affirming, that their minds lie much more profoundly asleep than those of the common people of Scotland. We have no class north of the Tweed that corresponds with the class of ruddy, round-faced, vacant English, so abundant in the rural districts, and whose very physiognomy, derived during the course of centuries from untaught ancestors, indicates intellect yet unawakened. The reflective habits of the Scottish people have set their stamp on the national countenance. What strikes the Scotch traveller in this unawakened class of the English, is their want of curiosity regarding the unexciting and the unexaggerated, — things so much on the ordinary level as to be neither prodigies nor shows. Let him travel into the rural districts of the Scotch Highlands, and he will find the inquisitive element all in a state of ferment regarding himself. He finds every Highlander he meets adroit of fence, in planting upon him as many queries as can possibly be thrust in, and in warding off every query directed against himself. The wayside colloquy resolves itself into a sort of sword-and-buckler match: and he must be tolerably cunning in thrusting and warding who proves an overmatch for the Highlander.* And in the Lowlands of Scotland, though in perhaps

* One of the most amusing sketches of this sort of sword-and-buckler play which I have anywhere seen may be found in Macculloch's "Travels in the Western and Northern Highlands." Were I desirous to get up a counter sketch equally characteristic of the incurious communicative turn of the English, I would choose as my subject a conversation — if conversation that could be called in which the speaking was all on the one side — into which I entered with an Englishman near Stourbridge. He gave me first his own history, and then his father and mother's history, with occasional episodes illustrative of the condition and prospects of his three aunts and his two uncles, and wound up the whole by a detail of certain love passages in the biography of his brother, who was pledged to a solid Scotchwoman, but who had resolved not to get married until his sweetheart and himself, who were both in service, should have saved a little more money. And all that the narrator knew of me, in turn, or wished to know, was simply that I was a Scot, and a good listener. Macculloch's sketch, however, of the inquisitive Highlander, would have decidedly the advantage over any sketch of mine of the incurious Englishman: his dialogue is smart, compact, and amusing, though perhaps a little dashed with caricature; whereas the Englishman's narratives were long, prosy, and dull. The scene of the dialogue furnished by the traveller is laid in Glen Ledmack, where he meets a snuffy-looking native cutting grass with a pocket-knife, and asks, — "How far is it to Killin?" — "It 's a fine day." — "Ay, it 's a fine day for your hay." — "Ah! there 's no muckle hay; this is an unco cauld glen." — "I suppose this is the road to Killin?" (trying him on another tack.) — "That 's an unco fat beast o' yours." — "Yes; she is much too fat; she is just from grass." — "Ah! it 's a mere, I see; it 's a gude beast to gang, I'se warran' you." — "Yes, yes; it 's a very good pony." — "I selled just sic another at Doune fair, five years by-past: I warran' ye she 's a Highland-bred beast?" — "I don't know, I bought her in Edinburgh." — "A-weel, a-weel, mony sic like gangs to the Edinburgh market frae the Highlands." — "Very likely; she seems to have Highland blood in her." — "Ay, ay: would you be selling her?" — "No, I don't want to sell

a less marked degree, we find the same characteristic caution and curiosity. In the sort of commerce of mutual information carried on, the stranger, unless he exercise very great caution

her; do you want to buy her?" — "Na! I was nae thinking o' that: has she had na a foal?" — "Not that I know of." — "I had a gude colt out of ours when I selled her. Ye 're na ganging to Doune the year?" — "No, I am going to Killin, and want to know how far it is." — "Ay, ye 'll be gaing to the sacraments there the morn?" — "No, I don't belong to your kirk." — "Ye 'll be an Episcopalian, then?" — "Or a Roman Catholic." — "Na, na; ye 're nae Roman." — "And so it is twelve miles to Killin?" (putting a leading question.) — "Na; it 's nae just that." — "It 's ten, then, I suppose?" — "Ye 'll be for cattle, then, for the Falkirk tryst?" — "No; I know nothing about cattle." — "I thocht ye 'd ha'e been just ane o' thae English drovers. Ye have nae siccan hills as this in your country?" — "No, not so high." — "But ye 'll ha'e bonny farms?" — "Yes, yes; very good lands." — "Ye 'll nae ha'e better farms than my Lord's at Dunira?" — "No, no; Lord Melville has very fine farms." — "Now, there 's a bonny bit land; there 's nae three days in the year there 's nae meat for beasts on it; and it 's to let. Ye 'll be for a farm hereawa?" — "No; I am just looking at the country." — "And ye have nae business?" — "No." — "Weel, that 's the easiest way." — "And this is the road to Killin?" — "Will ye tak' some nuts?" (producing a handful he had just gathered.) — "No; I cannot crack them." — "I suppose your teeth failing. Ha'e ye ony snuff?" — "Yes, yes; here is a pinch for you." — "Na, na; I 'm unco heavy on the pipe, ye see; but I like a hair o' snuff; just a hair," (touching the snuff with the end of his little finger, apparently to prolong time, and save the answer about the road a little longer, as he seemed to fear there were no more questions to ask. The snuff, however, came just in time to allow him to recall his ideas, which the nuts were near dispersing.) "And ye 'll be from the low country?" — "Yes; you may know I am an Englishman by my tongue." — "Na; our ain gentry speaks high English the now." — "Well, well, I am an Englishman, at any rate." — "And ye 'll be staying in London?" — "Yes, yes." — "I was ance at Smithfield mysel' wi' some beasts: it 's an unco place, London. And what 's your name? asking your pardon." The name was given. "There 's a hantel o' that name i' the north. Yere father 'll maybe be a Highlander?" — "Yes; that is the reason why I like the Highlanders. — "Well (nearly thrown out), it 's a bonny country now.

indeed, is in danger of being the loser. For it is the character of the common Scotch people, in this kind of barter, to take as much and give as little as they can. Not such, however, the character of the common English. I found I could get from them as much information of a personal nature as I pleased, and on the cheapest possible terms. The Englishman seems rather gratified than otherwise to have an opportunity of speaking about himself. He tells you what he is, and what he is doing, and what he intends doing, — gives a full account of his prospects in general, — and adds short notices of the condition and character of his relatives. As for you, the inquirer, you may, if you please, be communicative about yourself and your concerns, and the Englishman will listen for a little; but the information is not particularly wanted, — he has no curiosity to know anything about you. And this striking difference which obtains between the two peoples seem a fundamental one. The common Scot is naturally a more inquisitive, more curious being, than the common Englishman: he asks many more questions, and accumulates much larger hoards of fact. In circumstances equally unfavorable, he acquires, in consequence, more of the developing pabulum; just as it is the nature of some seeds

but it 's sair cauld here in the winter." — "And so it is six miles to Killin?" — "Ay, they ca' it sax." — "Scotch miles, I suppose?" — "Ay, ay; auld miles." — "That is about twelve English?" — "Na, it 'll no be abune ten short miles" — (here we got on so fast, that I began to think I should be dismissed at last), — "but I never seed them measured. And ye 'll ha'e left your family at Comrie?" — "No; I am alone." — "They 'll be in the south, maybe?" — "No; I have no family." — "And are ye no married?" — "No." — "I'm thinking it 's time?" — "So am I." — "Weel, weel, ye 'll ha'e the less fash." — "Yes, much less than in finding the way to Killin." — "O, ay, ye 'll excuse me; but we countra folk speers muckle questions." — "Pretty well, I think." — "Weel, weel, ye 'll find it saft a bit in the hill; but ye maun had wast, and it 's nae abune ten mile. A gude day."

to attract a larger amount of moisture than others, and to shoot out their lobes and downward fibres, while huskier germs lie undeveloped amid the aridity of their enveloping matrices.

But the broader foundations of the existing difference seem to lie rather in moral than in natural causes. They are to be found, I am strongly of opinion, in the very dissimilar religious history of the two countries. Religion, in its character as a serious intellectual exercise, was never brought down to the common English mind, in the way in which it once pervaded, and to a certain extent still saturates, the common mind of Scotland. Nor is the peculiar form of religion best known in England so well suited as that of the Scotch to awaken the popular intellect. Liturgies and ceremonies may constitute the vehicles of a sincere devotion; but they have no tendency to exercise the thinking faculties; their tendency bears rather the other way, — they constitute the ready-made channels, through which abstract, unideal sentiment flows without effort. The Arminianism, too, so common in the English Church, and so largely developed in at least one of the more influential and numerous bodies of English Dissenters, is a greatly less awakening system of doctrine than the Calvinism of Scotland. It does not lead the earnest mind into those abstruse recesses of thought to which the peculiar Calvinistic doctrines form so inevitable a vestibule. The man who deems himself free is content simply to believe that he is so; while he who regards himself as bound is sure to institute a narrow scrutiny into the nature of the chain that binds him; and hence it is that Calvinism proves the best possible of all schoolmasters for teaching a religious people to think. I found no such peasant metaphysicians in England as those I have so often met in my own country, — men who, under the influence of earnest belief, had wrought their way, all unassisted by the philosopher, into some of the abstrusest questions of the schools. And yet, were I asked to illustrate by example the grand principle of the intellectual development of Scotland, it would be to the history of one of the self-taught geniuses of England, — John Bunyan, the inimitable Shakspeare of theological literature, — that I would refer. Had the tinker of Elstow continued to be throughout life what he was in his early youth, — a profane, irreligious man, — he would have lived and died an obscure and illiterate one. It was the wild turmoil of his religious convictions that awakened his mental faculties. Had his convictions slept, the whole mind would have slept with them, and he would have remained intellectually what the great bulk of the common English still are; but, as the case happened, the tremendous blows dealt by revealed truth at the door of his conscience aroused the whole inner man; and the deep slumber of the faculties, reasoning and imaginative, was broken forever.

In at least one respect, however, religion — if we view it in a purely secular aspect, and with exclusive reference to its effects on the present scene of things — was more essentially necessary to the Scotch as a nation than to their English neighbors. The Scottish character seems by no means so favorably constituted for working out the problem of civil liberty as that of the English. It possesses in a much less degree that innate spirit of independence which, in asserting a proper position for itself, sets consequences of a civil and economic cast at defiance. In the courage that meets an enemy face to face in the field, — that triumphs over the sense of danger and the fear of death, — that, when the worst comes to the worst, never estimates the antagonist strength, but stands firm and collected, however great the odds mustered against it, — no people in the world excel the Scotch. But in the political courage manifested in the subordinate species of warfare that has to be maintained, not with enemies that assail from without but with class interests that encroach from within, they stand by no means so high: they are calculating, cautious, timid. The man ready in the one sort of quarrel to lay down his life, is not at all prepared in the other to sacrifice his means of living. And these striking traits of the national character are broadly written in the history of the country. In perhaps no other instance was so poor and so limited a district maintained intact against such formidable enemies for so many hundred years. The story so significantly told by the two Roman walls is that of all the after history of Scotland, down to the union of the two crowns. But, on the other hand, Scotland has produced no true patriots, who were patriots only, — none, at least, whose object it was to elevate the mass of the people, and give to them the standing, in relation to the privileged classes, which it is their right to occupy. Fletcher of Saltoun, though, from the Grecian cast of his political notions, an apparent exception, was, notwithstanding, but a mere enthusiastic Scot of the common national type, who, while he would have made good the claims of his country against the world, would, as shown by his scheme of domestic slavery, have subjected one half his countrymen to the unrestrained despotism of the other half. It was religion alone that strengthened the character of the Scotch where it most needed strength, and enabled them to struggle against their native monarchs and the aristocracy of the country, backed by all the power of the State, for more than a hundred years. Save for the influence over them of the Unseen and the Eternal, the Englishman, in his struggle with Charles the First, would have found them useless allies, Leslie would never have crossed the Borders at the head of a determined army; and the Parliament of England would have shared, in this century, the fate of the contemporary States-

General of France. The devout Knox is the true representative of those real patriots of Scotland who have toiled and suffered to elevate the cha:acter and standing of her common people; and in the late Disruption may be seen how much and how readily her better men can sacrifice for principle's sake, when they deem their religion concerned. But apart from religious considerations, the Scotch affect a cheap and frugal patriotism, that achieves little and costs nothing.

n the common English, on the contrary, there is much of that natural independence which the Scotchman wants; and village Hampdens — men quite as ready to do battle in behalf of their civil rights with the lord of the manor as the Scot with a foreign enemy — are comparatively common characters. Nor is it merely in the history, institutions and literature, of the country, — in its great Charter, — its Petition of Right, — its Habeas Corpus Act, — its trial by jury, — in the story of its Hampdens, Russells, and Sidneys, or in the political writings of its Miltons, Harringtons, and Lockes, — that we recognize the embodiment of this great national trait. One may see it scarce less significantly stamped, in the course of a brief morning's walk, on the face of the fields. There are in Scotland few of the pleasant styles and sequestered pathways open to the public, which form in England one of the most pleasing features of the agricultural provinces. The Scotch people, in those rural districts in which land is of most value, find themselves shut out of their country. Their patriotism may expatiate as it best can on the dusty public road, for to the road they have still a claim; but the pleasant hedgerows, the woods, and fields, and running streams, are all barred against them; and so generally is this the case, that if they could by and by tell that the Scotch had taken Scotland, just as their fathers used to te in joke, as a p'ece of intelligence. that "the Dutch nad taken Holland," it would be no joke at all, but, on the contrary, a piece of most significant news, almost too good to be true. From encroachments of this character the independent spirit of the English people has preserved them. The right of old pathways has been jealously maintained. An Englishman would peril his livelihood, any day, in behalf of a style that had existed in the times of his grandfather. And hence England, in its richest districts, with all its quiet pathways and pleasant green lanes, has been kept open to the English.

There are, however, at least two causes in operation at the present time, that are militating against this independent spirit. One of these is the Whig poor-law; the other, the tenant-at-will system, now become so general in England. Under the old poor-law, the English laborer in the rural districts indulged in a surly, and by no means either amiable or laudable, independence. The man who, when set aside from labor, or who, when employment could not be procured, could compel from his parish an allowance for his support, unclogged by the horrors of the modern workhouse, occupied essentially different ground from the man who, in similar circumstances, can but compel admission into a frightful prison. The exposures of journals such as the "Times" have been less successful in producing an influential reäction against the Union Bastiles, than in inspiring the poor with a thorough dread of them. A modern workhouse in the vista forms but a dreary prospect; and the independence of the English agricultural laborer is sinking under the frequent survey of it which his circumstances compel. Nor has the very general introduction of the tenant-at-will system been less influential in lowering the higher-toned and more manly independency of spirit of a better class of the English people. One of the provisions of the Reform Bill has had the effect of sinking the tenantry of England into a state of vassalage and political subserviency without precedent in the country since the people acquired standing-room within the pale of the constitution. It has been well remarked by Paley, that the more direct consequences of political innovation are often the least important, and that it is from the silent and unobserved operation of causes set at work for different purposes, that the greatest revolutions take their rise. In illustration of the remark, he adduces that provision in the Mutiny Act, introduced with but little perception of its vast importance, which, by making the standing army dependent on an annual grant of Parliament, has rendered the king's dissent to a law which has received the sanction of both houses too perilous a step to be advised, and has thus altered the whole framework and quality of the British constitution. He adduces, further, the arrangement, at first as inadequately estimated, which, by conferring on the crown the nomination to all employments in the public service, has well-nigh restored to the monarch, by the amount of patronage which it bestows, the power which the provision in the Mutiny Act had taken away. And thus the illustrations of the philosopher run on, — all of a kind suited to show that "in politics the most important and permanent effects have, for the most part, been incidental and unforeseen." It is questionable, however, whether there be any of the adduced instances more striking than that furnished by this indirect consequence of the Reform Bill on the tenantry of England. The provision which conferred a vote on the tenant-at-will abrogated leases, and made the tiller of the soil a vassal. The farmer who precariously holds his farm from year to year cannot, of course, be expected to sink so much capital in the soil, in the hope of a distant and uncertain return, as the lessee, certain of possession for a specified number of seasons but some capital he must sink in it. It is impossible, according to the modern system, or, indeed, any system of husbandry, that all the capital committed to the earth in winter and spring should be resumed in the following summer and autumn. A considerable overplus must inevitably remain to be gathered up in future seasons; and this overplus, in the case of the tenant-at-will, is virtually converted into a deposit lodged in the hands of the landlord, to secure the depositor's political subserviency and vassalage. Let him but once manifest a will and mind of his own, and vote in accordance with his convictions, contrary to the will of the landlord, and straightway the deposit, converted into a penalty, is forfeited for the offence.

I spent a few fine days in revisiting the Silurian deposits of Dudley, and in again walking over the grounds of Hagley and the Leasowes. I visited also the Silurian patch at Walsall, which, more than one-half surrounded by the New Red Sandstone, forms the advanced guard, or picket, of this system in England towards the east. It presents, however, over the entire tract of some six or eight square miles which it occupies, a flat, soil-covered surface, on which the geologist may walk for hours without catching a glimpse of the rock underneath; and it is only from the stone brought to the surface at sinkings made for lime, and wrought after the manner of coal-pits, that he arrives at a knowledge of the deposits below. I picked up beside the mouth of a pit near the town of Walsall at least two very characteristic fossils of the system, — the *Atrypa Affinis* and the *Catenipora Escharoides;* and saw that, notwithstanding the proximity of the Coal Measures, the rock, though mineralogically identical with the Carboniferous Limestone, cannot be regarded as belonging to that formation, which, with the Old Red Sandstone, is wholly wanting in the Dudley coal-field. The coal here rests on the Upper Silurian, just as the Lias of Cromartyshire rests on the Lower Old Red, or the Wealden of Moray on the Cornstone. On my way north, I quitted the train at Nantwich, to see the salt-works which have been carried on in that town for many years; but I found them merely editions in miniature of the works at Droitwich. I would fain also have visited the salt-mines of Cheshire, so famous for their beauty. They lay off my road, however; and, somewhat in haste to get home, I did what I afterwards regretted — quitted England without seeing them. Before nightfall, after leaving Nantwich, I got on to Liverpool, and passed the night in a respectable temperance coffee-house, — one of the lodging-houses of that middle grade in which, in England, the traveller is sure to meet with a great many Dissenters, and the Dissenter with a great many of his brethren; and in which both, in consequence, are apt to regard the cause of Dissent as rather stronger in the country than it actually is. But the consideration of this somewhat curious subject I shall defer till the next, — my concluding chapter.

CHAPTER XX.

Dissent a Mid-formation Organism in England. — Church of Englandism strong among the Upper and Lower Classes: its Peculiar Principle of Strength among the Lower; among the Upper. — The Church of England one of the strongest Institutions of the Country. — Puseyism, however, a Canker-worm at its Root; Partial Success of the Principle. — The Type of English Dissent essentially different from that of Scotland; the Causes of the Difference deep in the Diverse Character of the two Peoples. — Insulated Character of the Englishman productive of Independency. — Adhesive Character of the Scotch productive of Presbyterianism. — Attempts to legislate for the Scotch in Church Matters on an English Principle always unfortunate. — Erastianism; essentially a different thing to the English Churchman from what it is to the Scot. — Reason why. — Independent Scotch Congregation in a Rural District. — Rarely well based; and why. — Conclusion.

When I first came among the English, I was impressed by the apparent strength of Dissent in the country. At least two out of every three Englishmen I met in the lodging-houses, and no inconsiderable proportion of the passengers by the railways, so far as I could ascertain their denominations, were, I found, Dissenters. I had lodged in respectable second-class coffee-houses and inns: I had travelled on the rails by the second-class carriages: I had thus got fairly into a middle stratum of English society, and was not aware at the time that, like some of the geologic formations, it has its own peculiar organisms, essentially different, in the group, from those of either the stratum above or the stratum below. Dissent is a mid-formation organism in England; whereas Church of Englandism more peculiarly belongs to the upper and lower strata. Church of Englandism puts up at the first-class inns, travels by the first-class carriages, possesses the titles, the large estates and the manor-houses, and enjoys, in short, the lion's share of the vested interests. And in the lower stratum it is also strong after a sort: there exists in its favor a powerful prejudice, capable of being directed to the accomplishment of purposes of either good or evil.

Among the mid-stratum Dissent of England I found a marked preponderance of Independency, which, indeed, seems the true type of English Dissent in the middle walks; and shrewd, intelligent, thoroughly respectable men the English Independents are. But when I descended to a humbler order of lodging-houses, and got by this means among the lower English people, I lost sight of Independency altogether. The only form of Dissent I then encountered was Wesleyism, — in the New Connection, political, speculative, and not over sound in its theology, — in the Old, apparently much more quiet, more earnest, and more under the influence of religious feeling. The type of Dissent seems as decidedly Wesleyan among the humbler English, as it is Independent among the middle classes; nay, judging from what I saw, — and my observations, if necessarily not very numerous, were at least made at points widely apart, — I am inclined to believe that a preponderating share of the vital religion of the laborers and handicraftsmen of the English people is to be found comprised among the membership of this excellent body. And yet, after all, it takes up but comparatively a small portion of the lower population of the country. Among the great bulk of the humbler people, religion exists, not as a vitality, — not even as a speculative system, — but simply as an undefined hereditary prejudice, that looms large and uncertain in the gloom of darkened intellects. And, to the extent to which this prejudice is influential, it favors the stability of the Established Church. The class who entertain it evince a marked neglect of the Church's services, — give no heed to her teachings, — rarely enter her places of worship even, — nay, her right has been challenged to reckon on them as adherents at all. They have been described as a neutral party, that should be included neither in the census of Dissent nor of the Establishment. But to the Establishment they decidedly belong. They regard the National Church as theirs, — as a Church of which an Englishman may well be proud, and in which each one of them, some short time before he dies, is to become decent and devout. And there may be much political strength, be it remarked, in prejudices of this character. Protestantism in the Lord George Gordon mobs was but a prejudice, not a religion. These mobs, scarce less truly in history than as drawn by Dickens, were religious mobs without religion; but the prejudice was, notwithstanding, a strong political element, which, until a full half-century had worn it out of the English mind, rendered concession to the Papists unsafe. We see nearly the same phenomenon exhibited by the Orangemen of Ireland of the present day, — a class with whom Protestantism is a vigorous, influential principle, though it bears scarce any reference to a world to come; and find, in like manner, the Episcopalian prejudice strong among the English masses broken loose from religion.

Church of Englandism is peculiarly strong in the upper walks of English society. Like the old brazen statue, huge enough to hold a lighthouse in its hand, it strides across the busy current of middle English life, and plants its one colossal foot among the lower orders, and the other among the aristocracy. It undoubtedly possesses among the higher classes a double element of strength. It is strong, on the principle eulogized by Burke, from the union which it exhibits of high rank and the sacerdotal character. Religion developed in the Puritanic type, and existing as an energetic reforming spirit, is quite as independent of riches and exalted station in its ministers now as in the days of the apostles; but to religion existing simply as a conservative influence, — and such is its character in the upper walks of English society, — wealth and title are powerful adjuncts. When the mere conservative clergyman has earls and dukes to address, he is considerably more influential as a rector than as a curate, and as an archbishop than as a dean. The English hierarchy is fitted to the English aristocracy. And, further, the Church of England, as an Establishment, derives no little strength through an element from which the Establishment of Scotland, owing in part to its inferior wealth, but much more to the very different genius of the Scotch people, derives only weakness, — it is strong in its secular and Erastian character. There is scarce an aristocratic interest in the country, Whig or Tory, with which it is not intertwined, nor a great family that has not a large money stake involved in its support. Like a stately tree that has sent its roots deep into the joints and crannies of a rock, and that cannot be uprooted without first tearing open with levers and wedges the enclosing granite, it would seem as if the aristocracy would require to be shaken and displaced by revolution, ere, in the natural course of things, the English Establishment could come down. The Church of England is, at the present moment, one of the strongest institutions of the country.

There is, however, a canker-worm at its root. The revival of the High Church element, in even its more modified form, bodes it no good; while in the extreme Puseyite type it is fraught with danger. In the conversions to Popery to which the revival has led, the amount of damage done to the Establishment is obvious. We see it robbed of some of its more earnest, energetic men. These, however, form merely a few chips and fragments struck off the edifice. But the eating canker, introduced by the principle into its very heart, threatens results of a greatly more perilous cast, — results none the less formidable from the circumstance that the mischief inflicted is of too covert a nature to be exactly estimated. If the axe of an enemy has assailed the supporting posts of the hut of the Indian, he can at once calculate on the extent of the damage received; but the ravages of the white ants, that scoop out the body of the wood, leaving merely a thin outside film, elude calculation, and he trembles lest the first hurricane that arises should bury him in the ruins of the weakened structure. This much, at least, is obvious, — the position in which the revived influence has placed the English Church is one of antagonism to the tendencies of the age; and equally certain it is that institutions waste away, like ice-flows stranded in thaw-swollen rivers, when the general current of the time has set in against them. The present admiration of the mediæval cannot be other than a mere transitory freak of fashion. The shadow on the great dial of human destiny will not move backward: vassalage and serfship will not return. There is too wide a diffusion of the morning light for bat-eyed superstition; and the light *is* that of the morning, — not of the close of day. Science will continue to extend the limits of her empire, and to increase the numbers of her adherents, unscared by any spectre of the defunct scholastic philosophy which Oxford may evoke from the abyss. Nay, the goblin, like those spirits that used to carry away with them, in their retreat, whole sides of houses, will be formidable, in the end, to but the ecclesiastical institution in which it has been raised. It is worthy of notice, too, that though Popery and Puritanism — the grand antagonistic principles of church history for at least the last four centuries — are both possessed of great inherent power, the true analogue of modern Puseyism proved but a weakling, even when at its best: it was found *not* to possess inherent power. The Canterburianism of the times of Charles the First did that hapless monarch much harm. But while many a gallant principle fought for him in the subsequent struggle, from the old chivalrous honor and devoted loyalty of the English gentleman, down to even the poetry of the playhouse and the *esprit du corps* of the green-room, we find in the thick of the conflict scarce any trace of the religion of Laud. It resembled the mere scarlet rag that at the Spanish festival irritates the bull, but is of no after use in the combat. It is further deserving of remark, that an English Church reformed in its legislative and judicial framework to the very heart's wish of the Puseyite, would not be greatly more suited to the genius of the English people than in that existing state of the institution over which the Puseyite sighs. To no one circumstance is the Church more indebted for its preservation than to the suppression of that Court of Convocation which Puseyism is so anxious to restore. The General Assemblies and Synods of Presbyterian Scotland form, from their great admixture of the lay element, ecclesiastical parliaments that represent the people; and their meetings add immensely to the popular interest in the Churches to which they belong; but the Convocation was a purely sacerdotal court. It formed a mere clerical erection, as little representative in its character as the Star Chamber of Charles. It was suppressed just as it was becoming thoroughly alien to the English spirit; and its restoration at the present time would be one of the greatest calamities that could befall the English Establishment.

Of the partial successes of Puseyism I cannot speak from direct observation. There are cases, however, in which it seems to have served to some extent the ends which it was resuscitated to accomplish; — in one class of instances, through the support lent it by a favoring aristocracy, — in another class, through the appliance of means more exclusively its own. And, at the risk of being somewhat tedious, I shall present the reader with a specimen of each.

It has been told me by an intelligent friend, who resided for some time in a rich district in one of the midland counties, in which the land for many miles round is parcelled out among some three or four titled proprietors, that he found Protestant Dissent wholly crushed in the locality, — its sturdier adherents cast out, — its weaker ones detached from their old communions, and brought within the pale of the Establishment, — and a showy if not very earnest Puseyism reigning absolute. The change had been mainly brought about, he ascertained, by the female members of the great landholding families. The *ladies* of the manors had been vastly more active than their lords, with whose Conservative leanings, however, the servile politics of Puseyism agreed well. Charities to the poor of the district had been extensively doled out on the old non-compulsory scheme; but regular attendance at the parish church, or the chapel attached to the mansion-house, was rendered all-essential in constituting a claim: the pauper who absented himself might, if he pleased, fall back on the workhouse and crush bones. Schools had been erected in which the rising generation might be at once shown the excellence and taught the trick of implicit submission to authority; and the pupils who attended school had to attend church also, as a matter of course. Even their parents had been successfully hounded out. Lords of the manor have no little power in England where their tenants are tenants-at-will, and where almost every cottage of the villages on their lands is their own property. Obstinate Dissenters found the controversy speedily settled by their removal from the scene of it; while the less stubborn learned in time to grope their way to the parish church. Even the itinerant preacher now finds himself barred out of districts in which he could draw around him considerable audiences only a few years ago. There are eyes on his old hearers, and they keep out of ear-shot of his doctrine. And this state of things obtains in localities in which the clergy, though essentially Puseyite, are by no means so overburdened by earnestness as to be in danger of precipitating themselves on Rome. I have heard of a whole parish brought out by such means to listen to a zealous sprig of High Churchism who preached to them with a broken face, — the result of an accident which he had met at a fox-hunt a few days before.

This, however, is not a safe, nor can it be an enduring triumph. To use Cowper's figure, the bow forced into too violent a curve will scarce fail to leap into its "first position with a spring." The reäction in English society on the restraint of the times of Cromwell, which so marked the reign of Charles the Second, will be but faintly typical of the reäction destined to take place in these districts. It is according to the unvarying principles of human nature, that the bitterest enemies of High Churchism and a High Church aristocracy England ever produced should be reared at the Puseyite schools and churches, which mere tyrant compulsion has thus served to fill. In the other class of cases in which the revived religion has triumphed, its successes have been of a more solid and less perilous character. I have been informed by a friend resident in one of the busier English towns, that by far the most influential and flourishing congregation of the place is a Puseyite one. Some eight or ten years ago it had been genteelly Evangelistic; but, without becoming less earnest, it had got fairly afloat on the rising tide of revived Anglo-Catholicism, and had adopted both the doctrines and the policy of the Puseyite party. It has its energetic, active staff of visiting ladies, who recommend themselves to the poor of the district by their gratuitous labors and their charities. Its clergyman, too, is a laborious, devoted man, frequent in his visits to families saddened by bereavement or afflicted by disease; and the congregation have their missionary besides,—a person of similar character,—to second and multiply in the same walk the endeavors of his superior. Whatever Moderatism and its congeners may think of the aggressive system of Dr. Chalmers, Puseyism at least does not deem it either unimportant or impracticable. The revived principle is, besides, found supplementing the system with expedients of its own. The Whig poor-law adds, as has been shown, to Puseyite influence; and Puseyism adds to that influence still more, by denouncing the Whig poor-law. Is a pauper in the locality aggrieved through the neglect or cruelty of some insolent official?—Puseyism in this congregation takes up his cause and fights his battle; and hence great popularity among the poorer classes, and pews crowded with them to the doors; while Evangelistic clergymen of the Establishment, in the same town, have to preach to nearly empty galleries, and the Dissenters of the place are fain to content themselves with retaining unshortened, and hardly that, their old rolls of membership. The only aggressive, increscent power in the locality is Puseyism. Nor is it found, as in the case of the Popish converts, precipitating itself on Rome. Much must depend, in matters of this kind, on the peculiar character of the leading minds of a congregation. Mr. Newman has become a zealous Papist; but Dr. Pusey, on the other hand, is still a member of the Church of England; and it is a well-known historical fact, that Laud, with all his Popish leanings, refused a cardinal's hat, and died an English bishop. There are minds that, like Mahomet's coffin, can rest in a middle region, surrounded by balancing attractions, — that can dwell on premises without passing to conclusions, — and thus resist the gravitating influence; and in the English Establishment the balancing attractions are many and powerful. Hence the midway position occupied by the great bulk of the English Puseyites, and the bad metaphysics with which they bemuse themselves, in justifying their sudden halt at what should be so palpable a point of progress. As has been quaintly remarked by an English clergyman on the opposite side of the Church, "they set out for Rome, but stopped short on reaching Appii Forum, and got drunk at the Three Taverns."

But enough, and, I am afraid, more than enough, of Puseyism. It forms, however, one of the most remarkable features of the domestic history of England in the present day; and seems destined powerfully to affect, in the future, the condition and standing of the great ecclesiastical institution of the country. And it is worth while bestowing a little attention on a phenomenon which the future chronicler may have to record as by far the most influential among various causes which led to the downfall of the English Establishment. It may yet come to be written as history, that this great and powerful institution, when casting about for an element of strength, instead of availing herself of the Evangelism of her first Reformers, — the only form of religion fitted to keep ahead of the human mind in its forward movement, — attached herself to that old stationary religion of resuscitated tradition, idle ceremony, and false science, which her reformers had repudiated; and that, unable, in consequence, to prosecute the onward voyage, the great tidal wave of advancing civilization bore her down, and she foundered at anchor.

I was a good deal impressed by the marked difference which obtains between the types of English and Scotch Dissent. They indicate, I am of opinion, the very opposite characters of the two countries. No form of Dissent ever flourished in Scotland that was not of the Presbyterian type. The Relief body, — the various branches of the Secession, — the Free Church, — the followers of Richard Cameron, — are all Presbyterian. Wesleyism thrives but indifferently; — Independency, save where sustained by the superior talents of its preachers in large towns, where the character of the people has become more cosmopolitan and less peculiarly Scotch than in the smaller towns and the country, gets on at least no better; — Episcopacy, with fashion, title and great wealth, on its side, scarce numbers in its ranks the one-sixtieth part of the Scotch people. Presbyterianism, and that alone, is the true national type of the religion of Scotland. In England, on the other hand, there are two distinct national types, — the Episcopalian and the Independent; and both flourish to the exclusion of almost every other. Wesleyism also flourishes; but Wesleyism may be properly regarded as an off-shoot of Episcopacy. In the New Connection there is a palpable development of the Independent spirit; but in that genuine Wesleyism established by Wesley, which gives its preachers at will to its people, and removes them at pleasure, and which possesses authority, order, and union, without popular representation, the spirit and principle is decidedly Episcopalian. It may be worth while examining into a few of the more prominent causes in which these ecclesiastical peculiarities of the two countries have in a great measure originated, altogether independently of the *jus divinum* arguments of the theologian, or of the influences which these exercise.

There obtains a marked difference in one important respect between English and Scotch character. The Englishman stands out more separate and apart as an individual; the Scotchman is more mixed up, through the force of his sympathies, with the community to which he belongs. The Englishman's house is his castle, and he glories in its being such. England is a country studded over with innumerable detached fortalices, each one furnished with its own sturdy independent castellan, ready, no doubt, to join, for purposes of mutual defence, with his brother castellans, but not greatly drawn towards them by the operation of any internal sympathy. Englishmen somewhat resemble, in this respect, particles of matter lying outside the sphere of the attractive influences, and included within that of the repulsive ones. The population exists as separate parts, like loose grains of sand in a heap, — not in one solid mass, like agglutinated grains of the same sand consolidated into a piece of freestone. Nothing struck my Scotch eyes, in the rural districts, as more unwonted and peculiar than the state of separatism which neighbors of a class that in Scotland would be on the most intimate terms maintain with respect to each other. I have seen, in instances not a few, the whole farmers of a Scotch rural parish forming, with their families, one unbroken circle of acquaintance, all on visiting terms, and holding their not unfrequent tea-parties together, and all knowing much of one another's history and prospects. And no Scotchman resident in the parish, however humble, — whether hind or laborer, — but knew, I have found, who lived in each farm-house, and was acquainted in some degree with at least the more palpable concerns of its inmates. Now, no such sociableness appears to exist in the rural parishes of England; and neighbor seems to know scarce anything of neighbor.

In the "Essay on National Character," we find Hume remarking a different phase of the same phenomenon, and assigning a reason for it. "We may often observe," he says, a wonderful mixture of manners and characters in the same nation, speaking the same language, and subject to the same government; and in this particular the English are the most remarkable of any people that perhaps ever were in the world. Nor is this to be ascribed to the mutability and uncertainty of their climate, or to any other physical causes, since all these causes take place in the neighboring country of Scotland, without having the same effect. Where the government of a nation is altogether republican, it is apt to beget a peculiar set of manners. Where it is altogether monarchical, it is more apt to have the same effect, — the imitation of superiors spreading the national manners faster among the people. If the governing part of a state consists altogether of merchants, as in Holland, their uniform way of life will fix the character. If it consists chiefly of nobles and landed gentry, like Germany, France, and Spain, the same effect follows. The genius of a particular sect or religion is also apt to mould the manners of a people. But the English government is a mixture of monarchy, aristocracy, and democracy. The people in authority are composed of gentry and merchants. All sorts of religion are to be found among them; and the great liberty and independency which every man enjoys allows him to display the manners peculiar to him. Hence the English, of any people in the universe, have the least of a national character, unless this very singularity may pass for such." Such is the estimate of the philosopher; and it seems but natural that, in a country in which the people are so very various in character, the extreme diversity of their tastes, feelings, and opinions, should fix them rather within the sphere of the repulsive than of the attractive influences.

Certain it is that the multitudinous sources of character in England do not merge into one great stream: the runnels keep apart, each pursuing its own separate course; and hence, apparently, one grand cause of the strange state of separatism which appears among the people. It seems scarce possible to imagine a fitter soil, than that furnished by a characteristic so peculiar, for the growth of an Independent form of Christianity. The influences of Evangelism are attractive in their nature: they form the social prayer-meeting, the congregation, the national Church, and, spreading outwards and onwards, embrace next the Church catholic and universal, and then the whole human family. And unquestionably in the Evangelism of Independency, as in Evangelism in every other form, there is much of this attractive influence. But it is the distinctive peculiarity of its structure that it insulates every congregation, as forming of itself a complete Christian Church, independent in its laws, and not accountable to any ecclesiastical body for its beliefs; and this peculiarity finds in the English mind the most suitable soil possible for its growth. The country of insulated men is the best fitted to be also the country of insulated Churches. Even the Episcopacy of the national Church has assumed in many districts a decidedly Independent type. The congregations exist as separate, detached communities, — here Puseyite, there Evangelical, — High Church in one parish, Rationalistic in another; and, practically at least, no general scheme of government or of discipline binds them into one.

But while the Englishman is thus detached and solitary, the Scotchman is mixed up, by the force of his sympathies, with the community to which he belongs. He is a minute portion of a great aggregate, which he always realizes to himself in its aggregate character. And this peculiarity we find embodied in our proverbs and songs, and curiously portrayed, in its more blamable or more ludicrous manifestations, in the works of the English satirists. "Most Scotchmen," said Johnson, in allusion to the Ossianic controversy, "love Scotland bett than truth, and almost all of them love it better than inquiry." "You are almost the only instance of a Scotchman that I have known," we find him saying, on another occasion, to Boswell, "who did not at every other sentence bring in some other Scotchman."—"One grand element in the success of Scotchmen in London," he yet again remarks, "is their nationality. Whatever any one Scotchman does, there are five hundred more prepared to applaud. I have been asked by a Scotchman to recommend to a place of trust a man in whom he had no other interest than simply that he was a countryman."—"'Your Grace kens we Scotch are clannish bodies,'" says Mrs. Glass, in the "Heart of Mid Lothian," to the Duke of Argyll. "'So much the better for us,'" replies the Duke, "'and the worse for those who meddle with us.'"—"Perhaps," remarks Sir Walter, in his own person, in the same work, "one ought to be actually a Scotchman, to conceive how ardently, under all distinctions of rank and situation, the Scotch feel the mutual connection with each other, as natives of the same country." But it may seem needless to multiply illustrations of a peculiarity so generally recognized. The gregariousness of the Scotch,—"Highlanders! shoulder to shoulder,"—the abstract coherency of the people as a nation,—their peculiar pride in the history of their country,—their strong exhilarating associations with battle-fields on which the conflict terminated more than six hundred years ago,—their enthusiastic regard for the memory of heroes many centuries departed, who fought and bled in the national behalf,—are all well-known manifestations of a prominent national trait. Unlike the English, the Scotch form, as a people, not a heap of detached particles, but a mass of aggregated ones; and hence, since at least the days of Knox, Scotland has formed one of the most favorable soils for the growth of Protestantism, in a Presbyterian type, which the world has yet seen. The insulating bias of the English character leads to the formation of insulated Churches; while this aggregate peculiarity of the Scottish character has a tendency at least equally direct to bind its congregations together into one grand Church, with the area, not of a single building, but of the whole kingdom, for its platform. It is not uninstructive to mark, in the national history, how thoroughly and soon the idea of Presbyterianism recommended itself to the popular mind in Scotland. Presbyterianism found a soil ready prepared for it in the national predilection; and its paramount idea as a form of ecclesiastical government seemed the one natural idea in the circumstances. An Englishman might have thought of gathering together a few neighbors, and making a Church of *them;* the Scotchman at once determined on making a Church of all Scotland.

It seems necessary to the right understanding of the leading ecclesiastical questions of Scotch and English history, that these fundamental peculiarities of the two countries should be correctly appreciated. The attempt to establish a Scottish Church on an English principle filled an entire country with persecution and suffering, and proved but an abortive attempt, after all. And a nearly similar transaction in our own times has dealt to the cause of ecclesiastical Establishments in Britain by far the severest blow it has ever yet sustained. What was perhaps the strongest of the three great religious Establishments of the empire, has become, in at least an equal degree, the weakest; and a weak State Church placed in the midst of a polemical people, is weakness very perilously posted.

In no respect did the national Churches of England and Scotland differ more, as originally established, — the one at the

Reformation and Restoration, the other at the Reformation and Revolution,—than in the place and the degree of power which they assigned to the civil magistrate. The Scottish Church gave up to his control all her goods and chattels, and the persons of her members, but allowed him no voice in ecclesiastical matters; fully recognizing, however, as an obvious principle of adjustment, that when their decisions chanced to clash in any case, the civil magistrate should preserve his powers as intact over the temporalities involved, as the Church over the spiritualities. The magistrate maintained his paramount place in his own province, and disposed at will, in every case of collision, of whatever the State had given to the Church,—lands, houses, or money; while the Church, on the other hand, maintained in her own peculiar field her independence entire, and exercised uncontrolled those inherent powers which the State had not conferred upon her. She wielded in the purely ecclesiastical field a sovereign authority; but, like that of the British monarch, it was authority subject to a stringent check: the civil magistrate could, when he willed, stop the supplies. In England, on the contrary, it was deemed unnecessary to preserve any such nice balance of civil and ecclesiastical power. The monarch, in his magisterial capacity, assumed absolute supremacy in all cases, spiritual as well as temporal; and the English Church, satisfied that it should be so, embodied the principle in the Articles, which all her clergy are necessitated to subscribe. So essentially different was the genius of the two countries, that the claim on the part of the civil magistrate which convulsed Scotland for more than a hundred years, to be ultimately rejected at the Revolution, was recognized and admitted in England at once and without struggle.

The necessary effects of this ecclesiastical supremacy on the part of the sovereign are of a kind easily estimated. One has but to observe its workings, and then try it by its fruits. That there exists no discipline in the Anglican Church, is an inevitable consequence of the paramount place which her standards assign to the civil magistrate. For it is of the nature of civil law that it will not bear — let men frame its requirements and penalties as they may — against what happen for the time to be the gentlemanly vices. If hard drinking chance to be fashionable, as fashionable it has been, no one is ever punished for hard drinking. A gentleman may get drunk with impunity at a chief magistrate's table, and have the chief magistrate's companionship in the debauch, to set him all the more at his ease. In like manner, if swearing chance to be fashionable, as fashionable it has been, even grave magistrates learn to swear, and no one is ever fined for dropping an oath. Exactly the same principle applies to the licentious vices: there are stringent laws in the statute-book against bastardy; but who ever saw them enforced to the detriment of a magistrate or a man of fortune? And it is by no means in exclusively a corrupt state of the courts of law that this principle prevails: it obtains also in their ordinary efficient condition, in which they protect society against the swindler and the felon, and do justice between man and man. It is of their nature as civil courts, — not a consequence of any extraordinary corruption, — that they will not bear against the gentlemanly vices; and it is equally of their nature, too, in a country such as Britain, in which the influence of the toleration laws has been directing for ages the course of public opinion, that they should be thoroughly indifferent to the varieties of religious belief. Unless the heresiarch be an indecent atheist, who insults society and blasphemes God, he is quite as good a subject, in the eye of the law, as the orthodox assertor of the national creed.

Now, the magistrate does not relinquish this indifferency to mere matters of doctrine, and this leniency with regard to the genteeler offences, by being made supreme in ecclesiastical matters. On the contrary, he brings them with him into the ecclesiastical court, where he decides in the name of the sovereign; and the clergyman, whom he tries in his character as such, is quite as safe, if his vices be but of the gentlemanly cast, or his offences merely offences of creed, as if he were simply a layman. Hence the unvarying character of decisions by the English judges in Church cases. Is an appeal carried to the civil magistrate by a clergyman deprived for drunkenness? — the civil magistrate finds, as in a late instance, that the appellant is, in the main, a person of kindly dispositions and a good heart, and so restores him to his office. Is an appeal carried by a clergyman deprived for licentiousness and common swearing? — the magistrate concludes that there would be no justice in robbing a person of his bread for mere peccadilloes of so harmless a character, and so restores him to his office. Is an appeal carried by a clergyman deposed for simony? — the civil magistrate finds that a man is not to be cut off from his own living for having sold some two or three others, and so restores him to his office. Is a clergyman a frequenter, on his own confession in open court, of houses of bad fame? — What of that? What civil magistrate could be so recklessly severe as to divest a highly connected young man for so slight an offence, of thirteen hundred a-year? As for mere affairs of doctrine, they are, of course, slighter matters still! Let the Socinian teach undisturbed in this parish church, and the Puseyite in that, — let the Arminian discourse yonder, and the Calvinist here, — the civil magistrate in the British empire is toleration personified, and casts his shield over them all. And such, in its workings, is that flagrant dread and abhorrence of the Evangelistic Scotch, Erastianism.

It is impossible, in the nature of things, that it can coëxist with discipline; for it is inherent and constitutional to it to substitute for the law of the New Testament the indifferency of the civil magistrate to mere theological distinctions, and his sympathy with the gentlemanly vices.

But while such seems to be the real character of this Erastian principle, the Scotch Presbyterian who judges the devout English Episcopalian in reference to it by his own moral standard, and the devout English Episcopalian who decides respecting the Presbyterian Scot with regard to it by his own peculiar feelings, may be both a good deal in error. In order to arrive at a just conclusion in either case, it is necessary to take into account the very opposite position and character of the parties, not only as the members of dissimilar Churches, but also as the inhabitants of different countries. That adhesive coherency of character in the Presbyterian Scot, which so thoroughly identifies him with his country, and makes the entire of his Church emphatically his, gives to the Erastian principle a degree of atrocity, in his estimate, which, to the insulated English Episcopalian, practically an Independent in his feelings, and deeply interested in only his own congregation, it cannot possess. A John Newton at Olney may feel grieved as a Christian that Mr. Scott, the neighboring clergyman of Weston-Underwood, should be a rank Socinian, just in the way a devout Independent minister in one of the chapels of London may feel grieved as a Christian that there should be a Unitarian minister teaching what he deems deadly error in another of the city chapels half a street away. But neither John Newton nor the Independent feel aggrieved in conscience by the fact: enough for them that they are permitted to walk, undisturbed, their round of ministerial duty, each in his own narrow sphere. The one as an insulated Englishman and an Independent, is the leading member of a little congregational state, and all congregations besides are mere foreign states, with whose internal government he has nothing to do. The other, as an insulated Englishman, and as holding in an unrepresentative slumbrous despotism a subordinate command, which resolves itself practically, as certainly as in the case of the Independent, into a sort of leading membership in a detached congregational state, feels himself as entirely cut off from the right or duty of interference with his neighbors. And so long as the Erastian decision, unequivocally legalized by statute, fails to press upon him individually, or to operate injuriously on his charge, he deems it a comparatively light grievance: it affects a foreign state, — not the state that is emphatically his. But not such the estimate or the feelings of the Presbyterian Scot. He is not merely the member of a congregation, but also that of a united, coherent Church, coëxtensive with his country, and whose government is representative. There is not a congregation within the pale of the general body in which he has not a direct interest, and with regard to which he may not have an imperative duty to perform. He has an extended line to defend from encroachment and aggression; and he feels that at whatever point the civil magistrate threatens to carry in the contamination which, when he assumes the ecclesiastical, it is his nature to scatter around him, he must be determinedly resisted, at whatever expense. Erastianism to the Scot and the Presbyterian is thus an essentially different thing from what it is to the Episcopalian and the Englishman. It is a sort of iron boot to both; but, so far at least as feeling is concerned, it is around the vital limb of the Scotchman that it is made to tighten, while in the case of the Englishman it is wedged round merely a wooden leg.

The errors committed by the government of the country, in

legislating for Scotland in matters of religion as if it were not a separate nation, possessed of a distinct and strongly-marked character of its own, but a mere province of England, have led invariably to disaster and suffering. Exactly the same kind of mistakes, however, when dissociated from the power of the State, have terminated in results of rather an amusing than serious character. In a country district or small town in Scotland, in which the Presbyterian clergy were of the unpopular Moderate type, I have seen an Independent meeting-house get into a flourishing condition; its list of members would greatly lengthen, and its pews fill; and, judging from appearances on which in England it would be quite safe to calculate, one might deem it fairly established. The Independent preacher in such cases would be found to be a good energetic man of the Evangelistic school; and his earnest evangelism would thus succeed in carrying it over the mere Presbyterian predilection of the people. The true Scotch feeling, however, would be lying latent at bottom all the while, and constituting a most precarious foundation for the welfare of the Independent meeting-house. And when in some neighboring Presbyterian church an earnest Evangelistic minister came to be settled, the predilection would at once begin to tell: the Independent congregation would commence gradually to break up and dissipate, until at length but a mere skeleton would remain. The Independent minister would have but one point of attraction to present to the people, — his Evangelism; whereas the Presbyterian would be found to have two, — his Evangelism and his Presbyterianism also; and the double power, like that of a double magnet, would carry it over the single one. Some of my readers must remember the unlucky dispute into which the editor of a London periodical, representative of English Independency, entered about a twelvemonth after the Disruption, with the Free Church. It hinged entirely, though I dare say the English editor did not know it, on the one *versus* the two attractive points. An Independent chapel had been erected in the north of Scotland in a Moderate district; and Evangelism, its one attractive point, had acquired for it a congregation. But through that strange revolution in the course of affairs which terminated in the Disruption, the place got a church that was at once Evangelistic and Presbyterian; and the church with the two points of attraction mightily thinned the congregation of the church that had but one. The deserted minister naturally enough got angry and unreasonable; and the Congregationalist editor, through the force of sympathy, got angry and somewhat unreasonable too. But had the latter seen the matter as it really stood, he would have kept his temper. The cause lay deep in the long-derived character of the Scotch; and it was a cause as independent of either Congregationalism or the Free Church, as that peculiarity in the soil and climate of an African island which makes exactly the same kind of grapes produce Madeira in its vineyards, that in the vineyards of Portugal produce Sherry.

After a stay of rather more than two months in England, I took my passage in one of the Liverpool steamers for Glasgow, and in somewhat less than twenty-four hours after, was seated at my own fireside, within half a mile of the ancient Palace of Holyrood. I had seen much less of the English and their country than I had hoped and proposed to see. I had left the Chalk, the Wealden, and the London Clay unexplored, and many an interesting locality associated with the literature of the country unvisited. But I had had much bad weather, and much indifferent health; I had, besides, newspaper article-writing to the extent of at least a volume, to engage me in dull solitary rooms, when the pitiless rain was dropping heavily from the eaves outside. And so, if my journey, like that of Obidah, the son of Abensina, has in its discrepancies between expectation and realization, promise and performance, resembled the great journey of life, I trust to be not very severely dealt with by the reader who has accompanied me this far, and to whom I have striven to communicate, as fairly as I have been able, and as fully as circumstances have permitted, my First Impressions of England and its Peop e.

Gould and Lincoln's Publications.

(SCIENTIFIC.)

ANNUAL OF SCIENTIFIC DISCOVERY. 11 vols., from 1850—1860. By D. A. WELLS, A. M. With Portraits of distinguished men. 12mo. $1.25 each.

THE PLURALITY OF WORLDS; a new edition, with the author's reviews of his reviewers. 12mo. $1.00.

COMPARATIVE ANATOMY OF THE ANIMAL KINGDOM. By Profs. SIEBOLD and STANNIUS. Translated by W. I. BURNETT, M. D. 8vo. $3.00

HUGH MILLER'S WORKS. *TESTIMONY OF THE ROCKS.* With Illustrations. 12mo, cloth. $1.25.

——— *FOOTPRINTS OF THE CREATOR.* With Illustrations. Memoir by LOUIS AGASSIZ. 12mo, cloth. $1.00.

——— *THE OLD RED SANDSTONE.* With Illustrations, etc. 12mo, cloth. $1.25.

——— *MY SCHOOLS AND SCHOOLMASTERS.* An Autobiography. Full-length Portrait of Author. 12mo, cloth. $1.25.

——— *FIRST IMPRESSIONS OF ENGLAND AND ITS PEOPLE.* With fine Portrait. 12mo, cloth. $1.00.

——— *CRUISE OF THE BETSEY.* A Ramble among the Fossiliferous Deposits of the Hebrides. 12mo, cloth. $1.25.

——— *POPULAR GEOLOGY.* 12mo, cloth. $1.25.

HUGH MILLER'S WORKS, 7 vols., embossed cloth, with box, $8.25.

UNITED STATES EXPLORING EXPEDITION, under CHARLES WILKES. Vol. XII., Mollusca and Shells. By A. A. GOULD, M. D. 4to. $10.00.

LAKE SUPERIOR. Its Physical Character, Vegetation, and Animals. By L. AGASSIZ. 8vo. $3.50.

THE NATURAL HISTORY OF THE HUMAN SPECIES. By C. HAMILTON SMITH. With Elegant Illustrations. With Introduction, containing an abstract of the views of eminent writers on the subject, by S. KNEELAND, M. D. 12mo. $1.25.

THE CAMEL. His organization, habits, and uses, with reference to his introduction into the United States. By GEORGE P. MARSH. 12mo. 63 cents.

INFLUENCE OF THE HISTORY OF SCIENCE UPON INTELLECTUAL EDUCATION. By W. WHEWELL, D. D. 12mo. 25 cents.

SPIRITUALISM TESTED; or, the Facts of its History Classified, and their causes in Nature verified from Ancient and Modern Testimonies. By GEO. W. SAMSON, D. D. 16mo, cloth. 38 cents.

Gould and Lincoln's Publications.

(LITERARY.)

THE PURITANS; or, the Court, Church, and Parliament of England. By SAMUEL HOPKINS. 3 vols., 8vo, cloth. $2.00 per volume.

HISTORICAL EVIDENCES OF THE TRUTH OF THE SCRIPTURE RECORDS, STATED ANEW, with Special Reference to the Doubts and Discoveries of Modern Times. Bampton Lecture for 1859. By GEORGE RAWLINSON. 12mo, cloth. $1.00.

CHRIST IN HISTORY. By ROBERT TURNBULL, D. D. A New and Enlarged Edition. 12mo, cloth. $1.25.

THE CHRISTIAN LIFE; Social and Individual. By PETER BAYNE. 12mo, cloth. $1.25.

ESSAYS IN BIOGRAPHY AND CRITICISM. By PETER BAYNE. Arranged in two series, or parts. 2 vols., 12mo, cloth. $1.25 each.

THE GREYSON LETTERS. By HENRY ROGERS, Author of the "Eclipse of Faith." 12mo, cloth. $1.25.

CHAMBERS' WORKS. CYCLOPÆDIA OF ENGLISH LITERATURE. Selections from English Authors, from the earliest to the present time. 2 vols., 8vo, cloth. $5.00.

———— *MISCELLANY OF USEFUL AND ENTERTAINING KNOWLEDGE.* 10 vols., 16mo, cloth. $7.50.

———— *HOME BOOK;* or, Pocket Miscellany. 6 vols., 16mo, cloth. $3.00

THE PREACHER AND THE KING; or, Bourdaloue in the Court of Louis XIV. By L. F. BUNGENER. 12mo, cloth. $1.25.

THE PRIEST AND THE HUGUENOT; or, Persecution in the age of Louis XV. By L. F. BUNGENER. 2 vols, 12mo, cloth. $2.25.

MISCELLANIES. By WILLIAM R. WILLIAMS, D. D. 12mo, cloth. $1.25.

ANCIENT LITERATURE AND ART. Essays and Letters from Eminent Philologists. By Profs. SEARS, EDWARDS, and FELTON. 12mo, cloth. $1.25.

MODERN FRENCH LITERATURE. By L. RAYMOND DE VERICOUR. Revised, with Notes by W. S. CHASE. 12mo, cloth. $1.25.

BRITISH NOVELISTS AND THEIR STYLES. By DAVID MASSON, M. A., Author of Life of Milton. 16mo, cloth. 75 cents.

REPUBLICAN CHRISTIANITY; or, True Liberty, exhibited in the Life, Precepts, and early Disciples of the Redeemer. By E. L. MAGOON. 12mo, cloth. $1.25.

THE HALLIG; or, the Sheepfold in the Waters. Translated from the German of BIERNATSKI, by Mrs. GEORGE P. MARSH. 12mo, cloth. $1.00.

MANSEL'S MISCELLANIES; including "Prolegomina Logica," "Metaphysics," "Limits of Demonstrative Evidence," "Philosophy of Kant," etc. 12mo. *In press.*

www.ingramcontent.com/pod-product-compliance
Lightning Source LLC
LaVergne TN
LVHW021143110826
845150LV00005B/1109
* 9 7 8 1 4 2 5 5 4 7 9 8 1 *